Mission Improbable:
How the Gospel Set the World on Fire

Mission Improbable:
How the Gospel Set the World on Fire

Kevin Dodge

©2017 by Incarnation Classics Publishing
All Rights Reserved.
ISBN-13: 9780692911518
ISBN-10: 0692911510
Library of Congress Control Number: 2017910340
Incarnation Classics Publishing, Dallas, TX

Cover Design: Courtney Burrow

For the Incarnation Prayer Posse
In gratitude for their faithful ministry of intercession

The Acts of the Apostles were to convey that name of Christ Jesus and to propagate his gospel throughout the whole world. Beloved, you too are actors on this same stage. The end of the earth is your scene. Act out the Acts of the Apostles!
JOHN DONNE (1572-1631)

The believer of tomorrow will be a mystic, one who has experienced something, or he will not be.
KARL RAHNER (1966)

PREFACE

Warning: The Bible May be Hazardous to Your Current Way of Life

In 1975, John Kavanaugh was a young Jesuit priest, undergoing the multi-year formation process the Society of Jesus offers its recruits. During their last year of training, most Jesuits are usually sent to work with the poor for a period of time and Kavanaugh elected to spend this season in India. During part of his time in India, he had occasion to work with Mother Teresa and her Missionaries of Charity organization.

Towards the end of his work there, Kavanaugh was wrestling with what to do next. Should he go back to the United States, leaving the abject poverty around him for a life of (comparatively) greater comfort? Mother Teresa was unequivocal in counseling Kavanaugh that he should return, arguing that there was far greater poverty in the US than in India because of its "absence of love."

But far more puzzling was an exchange Kavanaugh had with Mother Teresa right before he left Calcutta to return to the US. Kavanaugh went to Mother Teresa and asked her to pray for him. She asked, "For what?" "For clarity," Kavanaugh retorted. Mother Teresa immediately responded, "No, I will not pray for that."

Now, this was awkward. The greatest living Saint at the time was refusing to grant his perfectly pious and reasonable prayer request? So, Kavanaugh, asked, "Well, why not? You always seem to have clarity and certitude." Mother Teresa responded, "I've never had clarity and certitude. I only have trust. I'll pray that you trust."[1]

Wow. Mother Teresa, a great Saint, never had clarity, only trust. I suspect that this is what we need to learn as well. We need to learn how to trust

God, in good times and bad, in prosperity and in poverty, in sickness and in health. Trust is central to what the Christian life is about.

But this is not usually how we approach the Christian life. We drill arcane doctrines into you. We stress the importance of the Eucharist and the Creed. We explain that you would do well to adopt our Anglican approach to spirituality. We encourage (but never obligate) you to start bowing at the right time. We sign you up for volunteer activities, tell you that you need to be in a small group and exhort you to start giving. Does any of this really involve learning how to trust God? To be clear, none of these things is bad. I really want you to be conversant in Christian theology, to use the Book of Common Prayer, and to be involved in the church. Yet we pretty much allow life to be the great teacher of trust. Isn't there a more systematic way to approach this?

Perhaps a better place to start would be with the Bible. After all, the Bible is a collection of texts written over a fifteen-hundred year period, many of which describe how different people in different times learned how to trust God. Some did well and some didn't, but trust is a big deal in the Bible.

Yet isn't the Bible boring and hard to understand? How can the average person without access to ancient history, philosophy, languages, and theology ever hope to really understand a book written so long ago within a very different set of cultural norms? How can the Bible teach us to trust if we can't figure out what it means?

The Acts of the Apostles

This book is an interactive guide to the Acts of the Apostles ("Acts"), perhaps the greatest collection of stories in the Bible about ordinary people who learned how to trust God. The story revolves around two central characters — Peter and Paul — one of whom was a simple uneducated fisherman and, the other, a highly-educated, up-and-coming religious leader. Neither had sophisticated plans for changing the world, but both had encounters with Jesus that changed their lives and ended up setting the world on fire.

The Acts of the Apostles is the second volume of Luke's chronicle about Jesus' life and ministry. Writing for a patron named Theophilus, Luke pretty much picks up the story where he finished his gospel.

In his last meeting with the disciples, Jesus tells them that they are about to receive "power" when the Holy Spirit comes upon them and that they would be his witnesses "in Jerusalem, in Judea, and Samaria, even "to the ends of the earth." (Acts 1.7-8). Jesus then ascends into heaven while the disciples stand around, looking into the sky and wondering what to do next. Right from the beginning, the disciples had to learn to trust God without a detailed blueprint. All they had was the OT and their religious traditions, but no idea what to do next.

This Guide

We too have our traditions (Anglicanism) and the scriptures (both the OT and NT),[1] but need help integrating them. Thus, in this guide, I am attempting to do something strangely atypical when writing about the Bible – I am consciously trying to integrate both tradition and the scriptures in a straight-forward, non-technical way, because I think they are both essential for deeper understanding.

What do I mean by tradition? I mean primarily the universal church's tradition of interpretation that goes all the way back to the church fathers, but has continued into modern times. In short, I want us to read Acts with sensitivity to what others have observed in the text and passed down to us. But I do not want to be so slavishly beholden to ancient interpretation that we miss the very real advances in understanding that have continued into our day. Thus you will find both ancient and modern viewpoints standing side-by-side in this guide.

But I also want us to read Acts within a particular context, in this case, within the Anglican tradition. Anglicanism is by no means a perfect guide to the scriptures. But it does claim to stretch all the way back to the early church, and it does have a rich set of resources that can help us. As we go along, I am trying to explain, using the story of Acts, how our unique tradition might approach understanding this text. I am also trying to explain

---

1 Throughout this guide, I will abbreviate Old Testament with "OT" and New Testament with "NT."

why we do some of the things we do, many of which derive from the text of Acts. Because Acts tells the story of how the church got going and Anglicans claim to be in continuity with the teaching of the apostles, we should be able to recognize ourselves (at least faintly) in this story.

This is quite a different approach than most studies about Acts take. In our day, most think that a far better approach is to rid the text of any theological or traditional baggage, attempting to get back to the "original meaning" of the author, in this case, Luke. Yet, if Acts is about the growth and development of the early church, it seems just plain foolish to me to ignore the insights of the church as we're reading it. We'll pay a lot of attention to why Luke writes the things that he does in the ways that he does, but I am less interested in probing what was in Luke's mind than in fleshing out how Acts might be meaningful to us in our day and within our Anglican tradition. What others might see as bias, I call common sense.

One of the real strengths of the Anglican tradition, in my opinion, is its diversity. We have racial, cultural and national diversity well represented within the Anglican Communion, of course. But there is also lots of theological and political diversity as well. As a result, we don't claim to have all the right answers, just a few distinctive features that mark us off from other traditions.

As a result, I will not at all be shy about drawing from the insights of other traditions as well as we go along, especially when they help to clarify the text. One of the best parts of Anglicanism is that we are Catholic enough to recognize our need to be connected to others and to be fed spiritually by the sacraments, but Protestant enough to think the Bible ought to be central to everything we do. Moreover, we live in a very unique time in history when some parts of the global church are listening to each other and talking together again. I want to encourage this process to continue by drawing on others' insights.

Finally, I am consciously trying to mirror the way Acts itself teaches us how to approach the Bible. In Acts 17 (Chapter 34 of this guide), we will meet the Bereans, a group of Jews, who received Paul kindly and searched "the scriptures daily" to see if the things that Paul was teaching them were true (Acts 17.11). By the way, when this text tells us that they "searched the scriptures," this must mean the OT because this was the only part of the Bible that was available to them. If this is what the text of Acts itself considers to be a good approach to the Bible, perhaps we should consciously emulate it.

Thus, in addition to providing a reading from Acts in every Chapter, this guide will also provide two other short readings to help us "search the scriptures." In the beginning, these readings will typically be from the OT, but as we go along, I will start introducing more NT passages as well. What I am trying to do is to bring out some of the allusions (sometimes explicit and sometimes more subtle or thematic) that Luke is making to other parts of the Bible.

Each of the readings from the Bible will come with a very short explanation (usually just a few sentences) that will introduce what we are about to read. Then, a longer comment section will draw out certain theological or practical implications from the text or provide some helpful background information to aid our understanding. Finally, each day will conclude with a series of interactive reflection questions that you might use on your own, with your family, or with a group that might help start a conversation about what you have read.

In all, there are fifty-five lessons in this guide that should not take very long to read. I encourage you to tackle one lesson per day. That way, if you read five lessons per week (giving you the weekends off), this means you will have read the whole Book of Acts with understanding in just eleven weeks.

Some Caveats

This is a guide, not an answer book. It is very important to me that you do not see this work as a set of "right" answers about the text of Acts. Rather, I hope that you approach this guide as a set of meditations that will hopefully lead to greater understanding and appreciation not only for your faith, but for our Anglican tradition as well. However, please do not think that this guide even comes close to answering all the questions Acts raises.

In fact, I hope that you will feel free to disagree with me along the way. That's really ok with me. I certainly have points of view on how certain sections of Acts should be read. However, please do not think that you have to agree with all my conclusions. At the very least, please realize that there is no way, in a few short pages, that I can ever be exhaustive or even thorough in my explanations. On every topic I cover in this guide, there is much more that could (and probably should) be said.

I hope you will find this guide edifying. Writing it has been a great joy and I have learned much. If the Spirit of God can use it to help you trust God a little bit more, it will have all been worth it.

ACKNOWLEDGEMENTS

Writing a book about Acts is a daunting task, and I could never have done it alone. In particular, I could not have written this book without drawing on the insights and erudition of the scholarly community, both present and past. My debts here are too many to mention, but include Loveday Alexander, C. K. Barrett, F.F. Bruce, Joe Fitzmyer, Luke Timothy Johnson, David Bentley Hart, Richard Hays, Craig Keener, Matthew Levering, Howard Marshall, Jaroslav Pelikan, Kavin Rowe, John Stott, Ben Witherington and N.T. Wright. If this work has any insight at all, it is because I am standing on the shoulders of giants who have taught me much.

I am also indebted to the leadership team at Church of the Incarnation who were generous with their time and enthusiastically embraced this project from the start. Rector Tony Burton was always encouraging and wise. Father Thomas Kincaid provided helpful input along the way. This project simply would not have happened without the enormous trust Father Kincaid has extended to me. I'm deeply grateful for it.

My editing team spent hours puzzling over awkward phrases and attempting to figure out just what I was trying to say, often without much help from me. Deacon John Sundara was especially helpful with his counsel on how to present the various texts so that it would make sense to readers. The shape of the current book is better thanks to him. Kate Smith read the whole manuscript and made very insightful comments along the way with remarkable speed. This guide is certainly better because of her contributions. As always, Ellora Hermerding was extraordinarily detailed in her feedback and has saved me from countless embarrassing blunders. Ellora kept editing right until we submitted the manuscript.

Special thanks goes to Courtney Barrow who once again did a terrific job on the design work for the cover. Courtney also created the remarkably-detailed maps contained within the book. Her patience at dealing with my many nit-picky, last-minute changes might qualify Courtney for sainthood.

Jen LeBlanc was my partner and sounding board for this project. In fact, the whole idea for this guide came up as a result of a lunch we had together. Jen was always available to me, even at odd hours, and was an unflagging supporter. She even let me whine when I needed to, which is a truly welcome skill when one is writing. Jen also did the hard work of shepherding this book through production with the publisher, probably saving me several ulcers. I simply could not have completed this work without Jen's unwavering enthusiasm and support.

There is also a group of parishioners at Church of the Incarnation who took a special interest in this project early on and agreed to pray for me while I was writing. I suspect their prayers were instrumental in enabling the project's completion. This same group, whose members wish to remain anonymous, has been quietly praying for decades. I would be surprised if their perseverance in prayer over a long period of time hasn't contributed greatly to the growth, dynamism, and energy at Church of the Incarnation. Thus I dedicate this guide to the Incarnation Prayer Posse in special thanks for their often unheralded, but vital, service to our parish.

Despite the terrific assistance I have received, any errors, omissions, or other mistakes are mine alone.

June 29, 2017, Feast Day of St. Peter and St. Paul

TABLE OF CONTENTS

INTRODUCTION

In many ways, the book of Acts is exciting. There are riots and shipwrecks, dramatic courtroom scenes and perilous journeys, traitors, and miracles. Yet because we, as readers, are so far removed from the first-century culture that produced this great work, the story can be very easy to misunderstand.

I have written this guide to help readers get more out of their reading. However, our task will be immeasurably improved if we can set the stage with some critical background information. For example, understanding why Luke bothered to write Acts might be important for uncovering the major themes we will explore. We might also want to review the evidence for and against Luke as the author and try to determine when Acts was written. All of these issues will come up as we try to interpret this story.

Further, theological issues surrounding church governance, the Holy Spirit, and relations with the Jews will emerge again and again. A basic introduction to these central theological topics might prove helpful for us as well.

Finally, the book of Acts has more pesky textual issues than almost any other book in the NT. In fact, we have evidence that three different versions of the book of Acts were making their rounds in the ancient world. I won't spend a lot of time reviewing these textual issues in this guide, but knowing that they are there might prove helpful as well. After all, how can we be sure that the text we are reading is actually what Luke wanted us to read? I'll lay out my assumptions for this issue in this Introduction.

If you are pressed for time, you can profitably skip this Introduction and just head for the first chapter. But, if at all possible, please try to digest some of the information in this Introduction. It will likely help you as you go along.

Occasion/Purpose

Why did Luke write Acts? Luke-Acts was written as a two-volume work, recounting the life and ministry of Jesus. If this is the case, then Acts was written specifically to showcase how Jesus' work continues even after his resurrection and ascension.[2] Since the Holy Spirit is the key player in this story (more on that, below), Acts demonstrates how God is spiritually present in the church as it grows and expands in its earliest days.

Specifically, Luke tells us that he is writing to Theophilus. However, we know almost nothing about Theophilus, except to observe that he has a Greek name and was probably Luke's patron. He seems to have already heard about some of the things that had taken place, but was in need of "an orderly account" (Luke 1.1-4) to put it all together.

Scholars have proposed a whole host of theories for why Acts was written. For example, perhaps Luke wanted to provide teaching about the Holy Spirit who is the power at work in the church. Perhaps he wanted to provide a defense (an apologetic) for Christians who were on trial before the Roman government. Perhaps he wanted to demonstrate the diversity of early Christian thought. Perhaps he wanted to explore the relationship between Judaism and Christianity. Perhaps he wanted to underscore the triumph of Pauline Christianity. Perhaps he wanted to depict what life was like in the early church. Perhaps he wanted to show how Christians might figure out what God was up to in the world. I could go on. These are just a small sampling of proposed theories. The lack of consensus in the scholarship is fairly remarkable.

Yet there are two purposes for writing that I want to describe briefly here. I think Luke writes Acts primarily (1) to show the remarkable spread of the gospel throughout the whole known world and (2) to defend Christians against claims of sedition.

First, let's explore the spread of the gospel. Right in the first episode of Acts, we hear that Jesus intends his message to spread throughout the whole

known world to "the ends of the earth" (Acts 1.8). As we'll learn by the conclusion of Acts, the "ends of the earth" is specifically about Paul's eventual
journey to Rome. The gospel has to be preached in the heart of the Roman
Empire.

But this brings up the question about what the gospel really is. I will
usually refer to the "gospel" in this volume as the "good news" because this
is what the word "gospel" actually means. The word "gospel" comes from
two Greek words, "eu" which means "good" and "angellion" which means
"proclamation" or declaration." Thus the "*Eu-Angellion*" is a "good report"
or "good news."

The background for this phrase is that when Caesar would win a military victory or was newly ascended to the throne, he would send messengers
around to tell everyone the "good news." N.T. Wright, who has done more
than anyone to promote the understanding of the gospel employed in this
guide, describes it well:

Caesar's birth, his accession, and his rule itself were spoken of as
'good news' – as indeed they were, in a fairly limited sense, for
those who had suffered the chaos of civil war and all that went with
it....But when Paul spoke of 'gospel' he thereby denoted a message
which, in fulfillment of the scriptural prophecies and in implicit
confrontation with the newer imperial realities, declares the 'good
news' of God's kingdom in and through the life, messianic achieve-
ment and supremely the death and resurrection of Jesus.[3]

N.T. Wright then continues:

The 'good news' is that [through] the covenant, God has fulfilled
his ancient promises and is now rescuing his people from the slavery
caused by their own sin, defeating the pagan empire that has held
them captive and sending them home to their promised land – and,
in so doing, is *revealing himself*, his sovereign kingship, his righteousness, his salvation, and above all his glory.[4]

We toss around the word "gospel" rather loosely in the church these days. Gospel can mean almost anything depending on who is talking about it. However, because it is so central to Acts, I want to try to be clear from the start about what I think Luke (and through him, Paul) means in Acts.

To be clear, the "gospel" has little to do with "being saved" or "going to heaven when you die."[5] I know that many of us might have grown up having heard this, but I am not at all convinced that this is what Luke means.

Of course, I'm also not trying to deny that heaven exists. After all, for centuries, Christians have understood the fulfillment of our longings as the "beatific vision," in which we are united to God in perfect communion with him.[6] My central problem is the stark separation between heaven and earth that many assume today.

Put simply, most in the history of the church would have found such a separation difficult to understand since the church on earth is united with the church in heaven by the sacraments and by prayer. This disjointed understanding of the spiritual life results from an unfortunate, but widespread, tendency among modern Christians to separate the natural and supernatural realms into starkly disconnected categories.[7] As such, "going to heaven" cannot not be the promise of the gospel.

Rather, the gospel for Luke is simply the proclamation of the resurrection and ascension of Jesus. Thus, to speak of the gospel without proclaiming that Jesus has been resurrected and ascended to the right hand of the Father is to have spoken of the good news in seriously deficient terms.

As plainly as I can state it, the good news in Acts is as follows: since Jesus has been resurrected and has ascended to the right of the Father, he is now King over God's creation. This is really good news! As a result, the world has to change, as there is a new King on the throne, and his kingdom rule has been inaugurated. The great sign of this inaugurated rule is the sending of the Spirit of God to take up residence in the church and, by extension, in the lives of believers. This fulfills the expectations of the OT prophets that God's glory would return to the temple.[8]

But this proclamation of "good news" sets up a huge problem which is what we will spend most of the pages of this guide untangling. If there is a new King on the throne – Jesus – what does that mean for Caesar? Everywhere the Christians go, the charge against them is sedition and treason. In particular, the Jews in our story will often depict the Christians as undermining the good order of the Roman Empire and threatening the lordship of Caesar. The Christians are saying there's a new King who is Lord, and it is not Caesar.

Thus the central problem in Acts is not how to recount the growth of the early church. It is primarily about a clash of cultures. Luke's purpose in writing (and it's a very difficult one) is to demonstrate that Christians are good, loyal Roman citizens, who pose no threat to Caesar, while at the same time proclaiming that Jesus is King and Lord. Duke's Kavin Rowe, to whom I am indebted for this clash of cultures insight, wrote the following:

> On the one hand, Luke narrates the movement of the Christian mission into the gentile world as a collision with the culture-constructing aspects of that world…On the other hand, Luke narrates the threat of the Christian mission in such a way as to eliminate the possibility of conceiving it as in direct competition with the Roman government. Of all forms of sedition and treason, Luke tells us, Christianity is innocent…The question then becomes what to make of this tension. If both aspects of Luke's portrayal are essential to his conception of the Christian mission, what is Christianity according to Acts?[9]

Luke's purpose in Acts is to show that Christians are not guilty of sedition, yet, at the same time, to demonstrate that the gospel, with its proclamation that Jesus is King and Lord, needs to spread throughout the whole known world under the agency of the Holy Spirit. This clash of cultures is why there is unrest, even riots, almost everywhere the Christian missionaries go. The Christian response is always to claim that what they are proclaiming is broadly in line with the OT prophets and what faithful Jews everywhere were confessing.

This means that a huge chasm is developing between Jews and Christians about what the OT means. The Christians are claiming that Jesus is the long-awaited Messiah and that the entire OT must be read with that in mind. The Jews claim that Christians are just making up novelties.

The message of good news then is primarily a re-reading of the OT in light of the death, burial, resurrection, and ascension of Jesus. The Christian understanding of the OT is different than the Jewish understanding primarily because Christians are not reading the OT at the literal sense of the text, but spiritually, in light of Jesus.

Thus Acts will employ key texts from the OT – Psalms 2, 16, 82, 91, 110 and 118, 146; Isa 6, 35, 40, 42, 49, 52-53, 57, 58, 65-66; Ezekiel 1, 2, 34, 44; Amos 9, Joel 2, Hosea 6 and Daniel 12 — in fundamentally new ways. Much of what we will do in this guide is to explore these "new" Christian readings of some very ancient texts.

How will we do this? Every day we will explore the various allusions to the scriptures the Christians are making. Only by unpacking these texts in Acts with its allusions and thematic links will we be able to see how the gospel message really unfolds.

Date

Dating the composition of Acts is no easy task, but is important to consider because it determines what information Luke could have accessed as he wrote. Most are in agreement that Acts could not have been written before AD 62 because of the discussion of Paul's imprisonment in Rome at the end of the story.[10] However, there are basically three schools of thought on how to date Acts – Early, Middle, and Late.

The early school places the date of composition sometime in the early 60s, probably just before Paul's arrest in Rome. The key piece of evidence for an early date is that Luke says little about how Paul dies. The simplest way to explain this is that Paul had not yet been executed when Luke composed Acts. Further, Luke does not seem to be aware of the details of some of Paul's letters, in particular, Galatians, which would be odd if it had been written late enough for Paul's letters to have been collected.[11] Thus the most straightforward explanation is that Paul's letters had not yet been collected.

Externally, Luke also makes no mention of Nero's persecution of the Christians in AD 64, which, by tradition, is when Paul lost his life. Given the interest that Luke shows throughout Acts in the politics of the Roman Empire, this would have been a hard-to-explain omission if he had known about it.

However, none of these details are compelling on their own. As we'll see at the end of this guide, I think Luke had a literary reason for not telling us about Paul's death. Perhaps there are other ways to explain the discrepancies between Paul's letters and what Luke writes in Acts (as we will see, there are). Further, arguments from silence (for example, with Nero) are inherently weak. Therefore, I am not convinced by the arguments of the early school.

The late-date school proposes that Acts was composed sometime in the second century by someone who did not know Paul. This school tends to note how similar Luke's details are to what Josephus writes.[12] Further, the lack of external evidence for the details in the story of Acts until the late second century is also a point in favor of a later date. Yet the similarities between Acts and Josephus are probably because Luke was a careful historian. Thus I also find the late-date theory unconvincing.

A middle date, probably sometime in the 70s or 80s, is the position I will adopt in this book. The main reason for this dating is that Luke's gospel needed to be written first, and there is some fairly strong evidence that the author of Luke was aware of the destruction of the temple in AD 70.[13] This would seem to preclude a date in the 60s for Acts.

Further, at the beginning of Luke's gospel, Luke writes that "many" accounts of Jesus' life and ministry had already been undertaken (Luke 1.1). For many accounts to have been circulating, this would have required enough time for that to happen, further casting doubt on a date in the 60s. At the very least, we have almost no evidence that there were any such accounts in the 50s or 60s.[14]

Luke's gospel is also heavily dependent on Mark's gospel. If we are to believe that Acts was written in the 60s, this would require an extremely early date for the composition of Mark, something the vast majority of scholars do not support. In fact, most scholars date Mark to the late 60s at the earliest, since Mark would have needed to have been written after the death of Peter and after the onset of the persecutions in Rome.[15]

Lastly, the author of Acts seems to know nothing about the persecution of Christians during the reign of the Emperor Domitian (81-96).[16] Although this is once again an argument from silence, it does suggest pushing the date back somewhat. As a result, I think Acts was probably written sometime between late 70s or early 80s.

Authorship

With some notable exceptions, there is a general consensus that Luke is the author of Acts. But, as in most things in the field of Biblical Studies, this is not a straightforward or even an easy conclusion to reach. Some hold strong opinions that the author of Acts is unknown to us or was anonymous.

The big problem is that Luke's name is nowhere specifically mentioned in the book. So, scholars wonder, how can we ever really be sure that Luke was the author? Further, if Luke was the author, how can we be sure that it is the same Luke who was Paul's traveling companion (Col 4.14, Phil 24, 2 Tim 4.11)?

The external evidence for Lukan authorship is reasonably strong, since most of the church fathers recognized Luke as the author. This would include Irenaeus, Eusebius, Origen, Tertullian, Athanasius, and Jerome. For example, the 2nd-century church Father Irenaeus, employing Acts to argue against Gnostic teachings, quotes from Acts extensively, and appears to understand Luke as the author.[17] Irenaeus writes the following:

> But that this Luke was inseparable from Paul, and his fellow laborer in the gospel, he himself clearly evinces, not as a matter of boasting, but [as he] was bound to do so by the truth itself...All the remaining details of his course with Paul he recounts [in Acts], indicating with all diligence both places and cities, and number of days, until they went up to Jerusalem; what befell Paul there, [and] how he was sent to Rome in bonds.[18]

Thus, at least by the end of the second century, there is good evidence that Luke was understood by the church to be the author of Acts. Moreover, the earliest manuscript fragment that we possess (dating somewhere between AD 175-225) ends with the title "The Gospel according to Luke."[19] The external evidence therefore is pretty solid for Lukan authorship.

However, the internal evidence is even more compelling. Following the typical practice of the time for a multi-volume work, the author specifically ties Acts to his gospel textually. Acts is dedicated to the same person (Theophilus), and employs similar language, content, vocabulary, and expressions.[20] Thus almost all agree that Acts is the second volume of the work that is known today as Luke-Acts.[21]

Finally, there is the issue of the so-called "we passages" in Acts. Starting in Acts 16, some of Acts is written in the first person plural instead of in the third person. It is startling when the author begins writing as "we." This causes some (I count myself among them) who take this as evidence that the author of Acts was an eye-witness to some of the events recounted into the book. Buttressing this claim is the heightened level of detail we find in these "we" sections (Acts 16.10-17, 20.5-15, 21.1-18, 27.1-28.16).

Thus, because of the quality of the external evidence and what I consider to be the compelling internal evidence, I will assume that Luke is the author of Acts throughout this volume.

Church Governance

Acts tells us the story of how the church got started and grew. Ever since the universal church began breaking apart into its Roman Catholic, Eastern Orthodox, and Protestant wings, Christians have been reading Acts to try to locate their preferred church governance structure in the Text.

For example, some leaders in the Reformation found clear evidence for a Presbyterian form of church governance in Acts, arguing that the early church was run by an elder board of "presbyters." When Paul appoints presbyters "in every church," they seem to have a point (Acts 14.23). Although it is very difficult to find elsewhere, there is even some (not very convincing) evidence for a Congregational form of church governance that elects its officers because of some of the language Luke employs when Paul appoints leaders on his first missionary journey (Acts 14.23)

By contrast, Roman Catholics, Eastern Orthodox, and Anglicans find clear evidence for a bishop-run church because in Acts, at least in the early sections, Peter seems to be clearly in charge. Peter, as he travels around, certainly seems to be doing the visitation work that a bishop would perform around his diocese even today. Later, James is clearly in charge of the Jerusalem church and makes authoritative pronouncements on behalf of the whole church (Acts 15.13-19). This sounds like something the Archbishop of Canterbury or a presiding bishop might do.

However, exceptions abound. Because the evidence is ambiguous enough, most traditions can usually find what they want to see in Acts by emphasizing certain texts and ignoring others. I am going to try to refrain from doing this. There is a great temptation to declare that a church without a bishop is no church at all since one could make that argument from the early chapters of Acts and from many of the church fathers, but frankly the evidence is just too ambiguous in Acts to be convincing. Moreover, explaining to other Christian traditions why only we read the Bible correctly is tiresome and not terribly productive, in my opinion.

Although part of my aim in writing this guide is to stake out a distinctly Anglican reading of Acts, I want to be careful not to overstate this. It will become readily apparent that I am borrowing as much from other traditions as my own in this guide. One of the great advantages to Anglicanism is that we are not afraid to look for insight wherever we can find it. As a result, my plan is to be deliberately ambiguous about how I translate certain words, usually with regard to ordained offices in the church.

For example, it is certainly tempting to translate the Greek word "presbyter" with "priest" since this is how Anglicans usually understand it. At times, Acts will depict a church governance structure very much akin to ours (bishops, priests, and deacons) while at other times it will seem completely different than anything in effect today in any tradition. For example, the church at Antioch (Acts 13.1) was being run by "prophets and teachers." How do we figure out what that means?

Here's my basic point – Luke is not trying to tell us that there is one God-given way to govern the church. He is giving us descriptive language, not offering us "the" single inspired model for governing a church. As an Episcopalian, I am mostly convinced that bishops ran the church from the beginning of the second century, but it seems needlessly polemical to press this point.

Thus I plan to leave the word "presbyter" untranslated when it is being used in a Christian context. This retains the proper sense of ambiguity that exists throughout Acts. However, when the word "presbyter" is used in a Jewish context, particularly with regard to the synagogue, there I will translate it as "elder" since this seems clearly to be what Luke intended, and we have good evidence that "elders" played a very important role in Jewish governance.

The Holy Spirit

The real star of our story is not really Peter or Paul at all, but the Holy Spirit. The Spirit descends on the church at Pentecost (Acts 2) and plays a very significant role in our story. In fact, there are sixty-six references to the Spirit in Acts, representing about 10% of all the references to the Spirit in the whole Bible. As a result, it might be worth saying something briefly about the theological discipline that studies the Holy Spirit, called Pneumatology. This derives from the Greek word, *Pneuma*, which means "wind," "breath," or "spirit". We get our English words "pneumonia" and "pneumatic" from *Pneuma*.

Westerners are usually charged with having a truncated Pneumatology. Put plainly, we don't quite know what to do with the Holy Spirit. There are many possible reasons for this, the most likely one being the West's fixation with Jesus. It seems like everything in the western church revolves around the Person of Jesus, which many would say is not a bad thing. Yet this admirable focus on Jesus means that some western churches have had comparatively little to say about the Father and the Holy Spirit. This creates a lack of appropriate balance when we think about God.

This lack of focus on the Spirit seems to be changing, most visibly with the development and spread of the Charismatic and Pentecostal movements over the past century or so. Pentecostalism, with its intense focus on the "signs" of the Spirit such as speaking in tongues, baptism in the Spirit, healing, prophecy, and visions, has worked hard to bring a greater appreciation of the work of the Spirit back to the West. Given that Pentecostals went from having almost no members at the turn of the twentieth century to almost 280 million adherents as of 2011, this has forced western Christians to take note.[22] The rise of Pentecostalism might just be one of the great visible works of the Spirit in our age.

As Christians, we believe that there is one God and that God eternally exists in the three persons, Father, Son, and Holy Spirit. Therefore, to elevate Jesus above the Father and the Spirit in importance is, in a very real sense, to have an unbalanced view of God. Since the Doctrine of God is a traditional starting point for theology, this lack of balance at the source of our theology creates problems elsewhere in western practice and belief.

For example, we see a lack of balance most tangibly appearing in the lack of respect that some western Christians give to charismatic movements. Admittedly, some of the claims that charismatics make can be a bit outlandish. Moreover, the teaching that every "real" Christian must have had an experience of speaking in tongues is difficult to sustain and, worse, denigrates the efficacy of the sacraments. Yet the distrust and vitriol that is sometimes extended to charismatics, who can be found in most traditions of the church, including our own, is a sign that westerners have allowed rationalism to infect their theology.

By contrast, eastern churches have typically had a more balanced view of God and thus have had greater room for the work of the Spirit in their tradition. We see this most starkly in how differently the West and East approach salvation. Whereas the West has tended to see salvation in legal and forensic terms (election, justification by faith, etc.), the East is almost mystical in its teachings about salvation, arguing that the goal of the spiritual life is "union with God," or *theosis,* [23] an understanding many Anglicans have adopted.

Fairly or not, many blame the West's relatively unbalanced approach to the Holy Spirit on St. Augustine, who figures so prominently in the development of western theology. Yet what many critics fail to understand about Augustine is just how committed to the Holy Spirit he really was.

In his great work, *On the Trinity*, Augustine makes a decision to start with the unity or oneness of God. In attempting to demonstrate how the Father and the Son are co-equal and co-eternal, Augustine begins his exploration by noting that they share various attributes in common.[24]

This starting point seems innocent enough, but it comes to define the different paths taken by some in the West and the East. In eastern traditions, ancient theologians tended to start with the three Persons of the Trinity because easterners reasoned, quite understandably, that we cannot really know much about the one essence of God, shrouded as it is in incomprehensible mystery. By starting with the Persons of the Trinity, rather than the one-ness of God, easterners had an easier time finding balance between the three Persons when they thought about God.

Yet Augustine's great contribution to Pneumatology, and to Christian theology in general, is his marvelous insight that the Holy Spirit is the "bond" of love between the Father and the Son, something he derives from 1 John 4. The Spirit, by providing the bond of love, is what brings unity to the Trinity. Thus all three Persons of the Trinity are in an eternal and perfectly-reciprocated love relationship with each other in the Godhead. To Augustine, it is the Holy Spirit that ultimately makes this possible by providing the bond of love.

But, here's where the problem emerges. Augustine's analysis, while profound and beautiful, was not only a bit speculative, but some say had the effect of subordinating the Person of the Spirit to the Father and the Son. The description of the Father was clear – he is the source of all divinity and is the maker of heaven and earth. The description of the Son was also clear – he is eternally begotten of the Father and all things were made "through" him. But The Spirit just becomes, in a sense, the "glue" in the Trinity, making the third Person of the Trinity at times appear to be subordinate as a Person to the Father and the Son. To some, this sounds like the Spirit has no real distinctive existence. To be clear, this was certainly not Augustine's intension. But the charge against westerners is that we don't have much room for the Spirit in our theology because we get lost in speculations about the oneness of God and in our intense focus on Jesus. Practical experience sometimes bears out this criticism.

All this is important because the work of the Spirit in Acts might at times seem bizarre and almost make-believe. So I simply want to encourage you to keep an open mind as you're reading. The Spirit does some remarkable things – people speak in tongues rather frequently in Acts. They frequently prophesy, so much so, in fact, that there seem to be prophets running around all over the place in Palestine and beyond, a phenomenon confirmed by early extra-biblical sources. People are healed, sometimes in very remarkable ways, most notably, when Peter's mere shadow (Acts 5.15) or Paul's handkerchiefs (Acts 19.12) started making people well. Both Peter and Paul will resurrect people. Our western, rationalistic mindsets might cause us to think these things as just made up. I would encourage you – perhaps implore you— not to do that. These were very real events for the early apostles, and we should read them as such.

But this brings up the important question about whether these Charismatic gifts and signs are valid in our day and age. The Reformed tradition has tended to say that they were valid in apostolic times, but quickly died out and thus are not valid today. I find myself suspect of this position.

I am not going to tell you what to believe on this, nor develop an affirmative case for charismatic spirituality, but my encouragement is always to be open to the work of the Spirit, even if it takes forms that might make you a uncomfortable or do not make rational sense. Some westerners really need to learn that they cannot control the Spirit, but they sure can quench it through unbelief and cynicism (1 Thes 5.19).

No matter what position you end up taking on charismatic gifts, my hope is that you will simply be willing to read Acts with an attentive and open mind. Like Christians have done through the centuries, you should probably assume that what Luke is writing really happened (as we'll see, Luke is a careful historian).

But you should also feel free to interact with the story critically. As we'll see at times, Luke may be telling us a true story, but the real meaning of the story often lies below the surface level of the text. As your guide through this marvelous and endlessly fascinating book of the Bible, it's my job to at least point you in the right direction, even if you might have more questions at the end than when you started. Learning to be open to the work of the Spirit, however, might just change your life. It certainly will improve your relationship with God and with others.

The Jews

Luke's constant foil for the Christians in this story is the Jews. Although we find many admirable, faithful, and open-minded Jews, their leaders were a constant source of misinformation and resistance to the spread of the gospel.

We are going to have to guard against an overly literalistic reading, however. Unfortunately, Acts has been a key source for justifying some of the worst periods of anti-Semitism in Christian history. The theory goes something like this: the Jews rejected the gospel, sent Jesus to the cross, and therefore deserve our enmity for doing so. If the Jews have suffered through history, this is simply evidence of God's judgment against them. They will either convert or continue to suffer.

I want to state as clearly as I can that this is not my view nor is it what I think Luke is trying to tell us. Yet if all we do is read the text of Acts in a literal and simplistic fashion, we might very well end up with that as a conclusion. I think it would be a grave mistake to do so.

However, we also need to realize that in the Jews' own writings that come down to us in the centuries before Christ, the rabbis bemoaned the fact that God did not seem to be in their midst in the same way he had with their forefathers. Almost all the literature we have in the post-exilic period looks forward to the return of God's Shekinah glory in their midst, suggesting that it had vanished after the Exile. Even though a remnant had returned to the Promised Land and the temple had been rebuilt, God's Shekinah glory did not seem to reside in the temple anymore. Among many examples I could cite, the book of Jubilees, probably written 100 BC says it well:

> I shall descend and dwell with them in all the ages of eternity. And
> he said to the angel of the presence, 'Write for Moses from the first

creation until my sanctuary is built in their midst for ever and ever. And the Lord will appear in the sight of all. And everyone will know that I am the God of Israel and the Father of all the children of Jacob and King upon Mt. Zion for ever and ever. And Zion and Jerusalem will be holy' (Jubilees 1.26-28).[25]

Why was God's glory missing from the temple? The most popular explanation in Jesus' day was because of the occupation of the Roman government. This is why the Jewish expectation of the Messiah was for a political transformation. The Messiah was to come as a great conquering Davidic king and throw off the yoke of the occupying Roman forces. Once the Messiah did this, thus re-establishing justice and righteousness in the land, God's glory would once again come to reside in their midst.

Because this comes directly from the Jewish sources, I am going to make use of this perspective in this guide. It has been one of N.T. Wright's great contributions to NT scholarship to convince interpreters that this understanding is correct. My debt to Wright for this insight (and others) will be obvious in this guide.

The risk in following this perspective is that some readers might get the wrong idea that I think God simply doesn't care about the Jewish people anymore. In this view, God's presence leaves the temple at the Exile and never returns. I do not believe this at all.

In fact, Acts is all about how God's glory is taken up in his people again through the coming of the Spirit. The hope of the prophets that the Messiah would come back and set things right is partially fulfilled at Pentecost when the Spirit falls upon everyone present.

But this does not preclude God's being at work in faithful Jews as well. Here, I agree with the Christian theologian Robert Jenson who argues that it was always God's intension for the synagogue and the church to operate on parallel, if separate, tracks. As Jenson writes,

The embodiment of the risen Christ is whole only in the form of the church *and* an identifiable community of Abraham and Sarah's descendants. The church and the synagogue are together, and only together [do they make present the] availability to the world of the risen Jesus Christ.[26]

Thus we must be careful to realize that although there are polemics flying back and forth between the Jews and Christians in Acts, this does not mean that the early Christians thought of themselves as something other than Jewish. The Christians will consistently argue that their claims are nothing different than what the OT prophets, or even the Pharisees, taught.

As a result, neither Peter nor Paul ever stops being Jewish in orientation. The seeds of the split between the synagogue and the church have been sown, but at this point in history, the Christian movement saw itself as a "sect" within Judaism. My plan is simply to present Paul and his relationship with his fellow Jews in this light. Paul himself describes it very well in the book of Romans:

I ask, then, has God rejected his people? By no means! I myself am an Israelite, a descendant of Abraham, a member of the tribe of Benjamin. God has not rejected his people whom he foreknew (Rom 11.1-2, RSV).

If Paul did not think God had rejected Israel, neither should we.

The Text of Acts

There are more tricky textual discrepancies between manuscripts in Acts than almost any other NT book.[27] The text of Acts comes down to us in thirteen papyrus fragments that date from the third to the eighth centuries.[28] I am going to spare you any involved discussion of these difficult textual issues as we go through this guide, but it is probably worth commenting on them, at least a big picture sense, here.

The textual issues arise primarily because there were very clearly three different versions of Acts making their way around the ancient world.[29] These versions arise from three different textual families — the first source,

I'll refer to as the "Western Text," the other as the "Alexandrian Text," and the third as the "Byzantine Text." These names simply refer to the places of origin of the textual families that produced the papyrus fragments or manuscripts.

The Western Text is about ten percent longer than its Alexandrian counterpart.[30] Usually, the Western Text adds to what we find in the Alexandrian Text by trying to smooth out rough language or by offering slightly fuller explanations to events that are not clear. It has certain tendencies – the Western Text tries to downplay the role of women in the church, highlights the Jewish rejection of the gospel, and shines a particular spotlight on the work of the Holy Spirit.[31]

The Byzantine text is the basis for the majority of the manuscripts that have come down to us after the fifth century. As such, it serves as the textual foundation for the King James Bible, which only had a few manuscripts to work from in the seventeenth century when it was made, and put particular weight on what the majority reading was. The Byzantine text type has a tendency to improve the grammar and style of the Western Text. Since there are no extant manuscripts of Acts from the Byzantine family before the fifth century, most scholars think that its changes to the Western Text are later additions.[32] I agree with this conclusion and thus will almost completely ignore the Byzantine variations.

Since ancient scribes rarely subtracted from the text of the Bible, but would sometimes add to it (to clarify things), we usually prefer the shorter reading when there are discrepancies in manuscripts. As a result, most (but by no means all) scholars think that the Western Text represents a set of later additions to the Alexandrian Text because of its greater length. I also concur with this view.

However, the additions that the Western Text makes are often very interesting and tell us something about how Acts was being read by its earliest Christian interpreters. Thus, in this guide, I will, for the most part, ignore the Byzantine readings, but will pay some attention to the discrepancies between the Western and the Alexandrian Texts. Given the space constraints of this guide, however, I will almost never comment on them, even if they are at times fascinating.

A Note on Translations

Unless otherwise noted, all the translations in this guide are my own. I am offering my own translations in this guide not because I think commercial translations are in some way deficient (they decidedly are not), but primarily to avoid issues of copyright infringement. Most of this guide consists of long passages from the Bible so to use someone else's work seemed to violate at least the spirit, if not the letter, of commercial copyright agreements. To not run afoul of this, I did my own.

However, a second reason for doing my own translations is I am especially eager to point out how the main characters in Acts, in almost every chapter, are simply re-reading or re-incorporating texts from elsewhere in the Bible into the story. This is a story about how Christians, reading the OT in light of Jesus, came to some very different conclusions than their Jewish brethren about what the Bible was saying. Doing my own translations will make it much easier to make these nuances explicit.

My translations from the OT all come from the Septuagint ("LXX"), the Greek translation that was the Bible for the early church. The LXX was Luke's Bible and thus will be ours as well for this guide. You will probably not notice too many differences. But, in a few cases, slight textual ambiguities lead to big differences in interpretation. I will point these out as we go along.

My NT translations come from the Nestle-Aland Greek text (28th edition) while my OT translations come from Alfred Rahlfs revised 2006 Edition of the LXX. As I was translating, I evaluated the decisions of many standard translations, including the RSV, NASB, NIV, ESV, NRSV, JPS and NET. I found the translation notes in Luke Johnson and Joe Fitzmyer's commentaries to be especially helpful as was the United Bible Society's Translator's Handbook.[33] I also regularly consulted Brenton's older (1870) translation of the Septuagint[34] and paid particular attention to the translation notes in the Net Bible.

In translating, I have tried to err more on the side of clarity than literal fidelity to the text and thus have followed a dynamic equivalence approach to the translations. All translations of the Bible have to make hard decisions on how to render the text into a different language with its different grammatical structure and idioms. Mine freely clarifies pronouns or references and smooths out rough grammar in an effort to help us understand the text better. I have also employed colloquial language, where appropriate, as I freely make use of contractions and the syntax of every-day speech. My hope is that this makes the text a bit easier to read.

As always, all translation errors or misjudgments in this guide are mine alone.

PART I: PETER AND THE SPREAD OF THE GOSPEL

PETER AND THE SPREAD OF THE GOSPEL

Our story begins in Jerusalem after Jesus ascends into heaven. The disciples head into town and start praying. Days later, the Holy Spirit descends upon those present, and the church is born. As we will observe again and again in Acts, various "signs and wonders" accompany the outpouring of the Spirit, thus authenticating the experience for those present.

The gospel (which means "good news") starts with the resurrection and ascension of Jesus. The good news that will be proclaimed throughout Acts is that since Jesus has been raised and ascended to sit at the right hand of the Father, he is now King. Jesus' kingdom rule has been inaugurated and the world is about to change. The apostles then go forth to proclaim this message.

Thus, for the most part, this first part of our story explains how the good news gets its start and then spreads throughout Jerusalem. After the descent of the Spirit at Pentecost, Peter starts preaching and the response is simply remarkable. By the end of this section, as much as ten to twenty percent of the city of Jerusalem will have been baptized and come into the church. It is a remarkable beginning.

Yet, as we take a closer look at Peter's early sermons in Acts, we will discover that what he is really doing is offering a fresh reading of the OT, a reading in light of the resurrection and ascension of Jesus. Peter is taking several key OT texts and claiming that they always pointed forward to Jesus, an interpretive move that might have been downright bewildering to first-century Jews.

As a result, Peter's claims do not go unchallenged. The Jewish leadership becomes very disturbed at the reaction of the crowds to the good news and the various signs and wonders that accompany its proclamation. This resistance builds in intensity throughout this first section of our story. At first, Peter and John are just held overnight, but are released with a warning. At a little later, they are again hauled before the council which results in physical abuse. The only reason the persecution isn't worse is the intervention of a wise Jewish Elder, Gamaliel, who warns them not to act on their hostility.

Our story in this section then climaxes when Stephen, a leader set apart for providing assistance to the widows in Jerusalem, is challenged by certain Jewish groups. Stephen responds with a lengthy recitation of the history of Israel, arguing that their forefathers had resisted the work of God at every turn. Enraged, the Jewish leadership erupts, drags Stephen outside Jerusalem and stones him to death. A young man named Saul watches the whole thing take place and approves of their actions.

One of the things that becomes clear from this first section is that Peter is in charge. He makes all the big decisions, delivers the important sermons and accepts suffering on behalf of Christ. He is a changed man. Peter is no longer the flighty and inconsistent person we encountered in Luke's gospel.

What is different? The presence of the Holy Spirit in his life transforms him into a powerful preacher and leader. Despite threats that develop both from outside the church and from within, the early church becomes an unstoppable force in this first section of Acts because the Spirit of God is propelling it forward.

CHAPTER 1

THE ASCENSION
Acts 1.1-11

Acts 1.1-11

> *In this introduction to the book of Acts, Luke revisits several important themes from the end of his gospel, clearly demonstrating that Acts is a continuation of the first volume. Whereas Luke's gospel focused on the life and teachings of Jesus, the book of Acts, the sequel to the story, focuses on how Jesus' teachings came to be spread throughout the Roman Empire under the direction of the Holy Spirit.*

O Theophilus, in the prior account I produced about everything that Jesus began to do and to teach, until the day he was taken up, Jesus gave orders through the Holy Spirit to the apostles that he had chosen. To the apostles, Jesus presented himself alive after his passion with many convincing proofs. He appeared to them over a period of forty days, speaking about the kingdom of God. After Jesus shared a meal with the apostles, he commanded them, "Don't leave Jerusalem, but wait for the promise of the Father which you heard from me, since John baptized with water, but you will be baptized with the Holy Spirit not many days from now."

Now when they had gathered together, they were asking him, "Lord, is now the time that you're going to restore the kingdom to Israel?" Jesus said to them, "It's not for you to know the times or seasons which the Father has set by his own authority. But you will receive power when the Holy Spirit has come upon you and you will be my witnesses in Jerusalem, and in all Judea and Samaria, and to the end of the earth."

Then, after Jesus had said this, right before their eyes, he was lifted up, and the cloud took him away ["hupolambano"] from their sight. Now, while they were still staring into space, as he was going, two men suddenly appeared beside them in white garments. They said, "Men of Galilee, why are you standing there, staring into space? This same Jesus who was taken up from you into heaven, he will come back the same way you saw him going into the sky."

2 Kings 2.9-12

Some early Christians read this story of Elijah's rapture as a foreshadowing of Jesus' ascension. Both Elijah and Jesus were taken up suddenly — Elijah with a whirlwind while Jesus disappeared into a cloud. Since Jesus himself claimed that his appearance was connected with Elijah (Mark 9.13) and since Elijah appeared at Jesus' Transfiguration to discuss Jesus' "exodus" from the earth (Luke 9.30), the church has usually linked these stories. In both, the protagonists must physically leave to enable the next stage of God's plan to unfold.

So when they had crossed over, Elijah said to Elisha, "Ask what I should do for you before I am taken up ["analambano"] from you." And Elisha responded, "Please let me have a double portion of your spirit upon me." Then Elijah said, "You have asked for a hard thing. If you see me being taken up from you, then it shall be so, but if not, then it won't." And it happened as they were going along and conversing that there was a chariot of fire and horses of fire which separated the two of them. Then Elijah was taken up in a whirlwind as if into heaven. And Elisha looked on and cried out, "Father, Father, the chariot of Israel and its charioteer!" But Elisha did not see him anymore.

Luke 24.44-53

This passage completes Luke's gospel, the first volume of the two-volume work known as Luke-Acts. In it, Luke demonstrates how Jesus has fulfilled the OT scriptures. Luke depicts Jesus as the interpretive key for understanding the Bible, which, in his day, would have meant the OT. When Jesus mentions the Law of Moses, the Prophets and the Psalms, these represent the three major divisions of the OT scriptures. Luke's terse, but suggestive, description of Jesus' "being taken up" suggests that the account of the ascension serves as the hinge between Luke's gospel and the book of Acts. Thus the beginning verses of Acts are a reworking of the ending of Luke's gospel.

Then Jesus said to them, "These are my words that I spoke to you while I was still with you, that everything written in the Law of Moses and the Prophets and the Psalms concerning me has to be fulfilled." Then he opened their minds to understand the Old Testament. And he said to them, "Thus is it written that the Christ will suffer and be raised from the dead on the third day and repentance for the forgiveness of sins will be proclaimed to all the nations in his name, beginning from Jerusalem. You are witnesses of these things. Now, look, I am sending the promise of my Father upon you. So stay in the city until you have been clothed with power from on high."

Then Jesus led them out as far as Bethany and he lifted up his hands and blessed them. And as he was blessing them, he was taken away from them and was taken up ["anaphero"] into heaven. And they worshipped him and returned to Jerusalem with great joy. And they were all in the temple blessing God. Amen.

Comment

Luke is introducing us to the second part of his story, and is subtly laying out how it is going to unfold. The good news is that Jesus is King and has been faithful to his covenant promises, which are now going to go out from Jerusalem to the whole known world. As Luke puts it, the disciples will be witnesses to the resurrected Jesus "in Jerusalem, in all Judea and Samaria, and to the end of the earth."

This is pretty much how the story in Acts unfolds. The first part of the story takes place in Jerusalem as the early church is formed after the anointing of the Holy Spirit at Pentecost. Peter preaches several remarkable sermons and thousands come into the church. Then, despite great resistance, the good news spreads into the Judean and Samarian countryside, through the work of great Evangelists. Since many of the Jews considered the Samaritans to be a detestable half-breed (the indigenous people had intermarried with their Assyrian conquerors and other foreign groups), their inclusion in the family of God would likely have been very surprising.[1]

Then the good news spreads even farther afield, spreading to the Gentiles through Peter and moving to far off places like Asia Minor and modern-day Europe during Paul's three missionary journeys. By the last part of the story, the gospel travels to Jerusalem during Paul's trials before representatives of the Roman Government before ending up in Rome. Despite corruption in the church, despite resistance from adversaries, despite beatings, riots, arrests, and a persistent lack of resources, Luke presents the gospel as an unstoppable force because the Holy Spirit is behind its advance.

A second focus in this passage is the ascension of Jesus. Of all the things Luke could have chosen, he decided to make the ascension the key hinge between the two volumes of his story. This must have some significance.

In fact, the ascension is every bit as important as the resurrection of Jesus. Why? Well, for one thing, the ascension represents the enthronement of Jesus as King at the right hand of God.[2] The ascension is also central to the sending of the Holy Spirit.[3] Jesus said that he had to go away so the Holy Spirit could come. This is exactly what happens in the early chapters of Acts.

It's unfortunate, but one could sit in church for a lifetime and never hear about how the ascension is really the key to the gospel. If Jesus has ascended to the right hand of God and has been enthroned, this means that Jesus is King.[4] This is the good news that ought to be proclaimed!

Thus the gospel is not primarily about how you were a terrible sinner, but how Jesus has saved you from all that so that you can go to heaven when you die. As we see from the OT story of Jacob's ladder and from the appearance of angels throughout the Bible, there was no stark separation between heaven and earth in the scriptures.

Yet the good news suggests that since Jesus is now reigning as King, new life becomes possible on the earth.[5] This is why the confession of the early church was that "Jesus is Lord" is so important. Because Jesus is now reigning as King, he is Lord.[6] Everything is different, and life is going to change.

As a result, the ascension is essential for the propagation of the good news, which is a major focus of the book of Acts. Whereas the focus in the first part of the story (Luke's gospel) was on Jesus and his mighty works, the focus of the second part (the book of Acts) is on the Holy Spirit and the remarkable spread of the good news that Jesus is King.

Lastly, the disciples' question is interesting: "Lord, is now the time that you're going to restore the kingdom to Israel?" The word "restoration" in Greek brings with it the sense of "re-establishment" or "renewal."[7] We shouldn't miss the subtle point Luke is making: the disciples seem to have very little understanding of what the gospel was all about. They had been with Jesus for three years, and had heard him preach about the kingdom of God over and over again.[8] They had even experienced the power of being sent out on mission for him. But they were still defaulting to the popular ideas of what the Messiah was supposed to do.

In Jewish expectation, the Messiah was supposed to come back and bring justice and righteousness to Israel (Ps 72.1, Isa 9.7, Jer 23.5), ushering in a great reversal that would cause Israel's oppressors to "lick the dust" (Ps 72.9) under the reign of a truly righteous king. In other words, many were conceiving of Jesus in political terms, as a revolutionary who would throw off the yoke of the occupying Roman forces.

Although the Jews had rebuilt the temple after coming back from their exile, the common consensus among the people was that the glory of God had never really returned and taken up residence in their midst.[9] God's Shekinah glory simply wouldn't return, or so it seemed, while the Romans were in charge. The Messiah was supposed to fix all that. He was supposed to get rid of their Roman oppressors and restore Jewish independence.

But this was not God's plan. More fundamental than a political solution in Palestine was the restoration of God's creation. If God's ultimate plan is to remake his creation, the book of Acts describes how this plan starts to unfold. The ultimate goal – salvation, as it were – is about embodied participation in God's new heaven and new earth, which is the culminating vision of both the OT prophets (Isa 66.17-22) and the NT apostles (Rev 21.1-2).

Notice that Jesus doesn't rebuke the disciples for asking a bad question here. He simply says the timing of this restoration is a mystery. Jesus never spiritualizes this promise of restoration, but insists that "what [had] been accomplished in Christ must yet be accomplished in us and in the world."[10] In other words, Jesus redirects the disciples' attention from apocalyptic speculation to the proclamation of the gospel, the good news that Jesus is King.[11]

Luke's story is exceedingly surprising. The Book of Acts is Luke's shocking tale of how love and lowliness triumphed over might and money. It's about how God's kingdom starts to spread on the earth. It should never have happened…but it did. God's work is in continuity with what had come before, but unfolds in surprising ways.

Questions for Reflection:

1. Does the description of the "good news" in this chapter surprise you? If the gospel is really about Jesus' resurrection and ascension, how might this change how you think about your life on earth? How might you explain this "good news" to someone outside the church in every-day terms?

2. Hope is a key Christian virtue. If God's glory has already been restored in part through the Holy Spirit, yet we still await a full restoration at Christ's return, how would you describe what your

hope for the future looks like? Is it to escape this world? Is it to observe changes in this world? *yes*

3. If God is enthroned and ruling over the earth, why does suffering and injustice seem so insurmountable? How do you square a sovereign God with the obvious injustice and evil that exists in the world?

CHAPTER 2

THE APOSTLES
Acts 1.12-26

Acts 1.12-26

In this passage, we encounter the first significant challenge for the apostles: how should they deal with apostasy in their midst? Judas, having betrayed Jesus for a pittance and having killed himself, must be replaced. In Luke's account of the Last Supper, Jesus made clear that it was significant that there were twelve disciples, since they would eventually judge "the twelve tribes of Israel" (Luke 22.30).[12] But, in yesterday's reading, it became clear the restoration of Israel was something that would ultimately take place in the future — the apostles didn't need to know the times or seasons when it would happen. Thus this passage was pivotal in forming the emerging theology of the church because it clearly demonstrated it was God who chooses its leaders. Yet, as we will see over and over again in the book of Acts, treachery cannot derail this movement. The good news can advance even when its key leaders fail.

Then the disciples turned back to Jerusalem from the Mount of Olives which is near Jerusalem, about a Sabbath day's journey away. When they entered into Jerusalem, they went up to where they were staying. Peter and John, James and Andrew, Philip and Thomas, Bartholomew and Matthew, James, son of Alpheus, and Simon the Zealot and Judas, son of James were there. All these persisted in prayer with one mind along with the women and Mary, the mother of Jesus, as well as Jesus' brothers.

Now, in those days, Peter stood up in the midst of the brethren (there was a crowd of about 120 people there) and said, "Brethren, it was necessary for the scriptures to be fulfilled which the Holy Spirit spoke beforehand through the mouth of David concerning Judas who acted as a guide to those who arrested Jesus." (Judas was counted among us and received a share in this ministry. So Judas acquired a field from the proceeds of his wickedness and falling headlong, his innards burst open and all his entrails gushed out. And this became known to all the inhabitants of Jerusalem, so that this field came to be called (in Aramaic) "Akeldamax," which means (in Greek) "field of blood"). "For, it stands written in the book of Psalms: 'Let his place ["epaulis"] become deserted and let there be no one to dwell in it' (Ps 69.25). And, 'Let another take his office'" ["episkopen"] (Ps 109.8).

"Therefore it is necessary for one of the men who has traveled together with us the whole time the Lord Jesus went in and out among us, beginning from the baptism of John until the day Jesus was taken up from us, to be a witness to his resurrection along with us." So they nominated two: Joseph, called Barsabbas (surnamed Justus) and Matthias. Then they prayed, saying, "You, Lord, know the hearts of all, show us which one of these two you have chosen to take up the place of this ministry and apostleship from which Judas turned aside to go to his own place." Then they cast lots for them, and the lot fell on Matthias and he was counted with the eleven apostles.

Psalm 69.1-9, 22-26

Psalm 69 is a lament that had enormous significance for early Christians because they associated it with Jesus' passion. The imagery is particularly vivid, as the frequent employment of water depicts a drowning victim, a metaphor associated with Christ's descent

into the realm of the dead, known as Sheol.[13] *For our purposes,
the Psalmist's complaint of being given "gall to eat" and "vinegar
to drink" look forward to what Jesus experienced on the cross. In
Acts, Luke applies this Psalm to Judas who deserted his place with
the apostles to betray Jesus. Luke plays on the ambiguity of the
Greek word "epaulis"* (dwelling, residence, place) *to suggest the
Psalmist foresaw Judas' desertion of his place with the apostles.*[14]

For the End, for those who will be changed, a Psalm of David

Save me, O God since the waters have come into my soul. I am caught in
the deep mire, and there is no firm ground for my feet; I have come into
the depths of the sea, and the squall has thrown me down; I am tired
from my weeping, my larynx is sore; my eyes have given out from looking for my God. Those who hate me without cause are more than the
hairs of my head; my foes who persecute me unjustly are strong; must I
then repay what I never plundered?

O God, you know my foolishness, and my sins are not hidden from
you; let not those who wait for you be put to shame, O Lord, God of
Might; let not those who seek you be put to shame, O God of Israel;
since, for your sake, I have suffered reproach and humiliation has covered my face. I have become a stranger to my own brethren and a foreigner to my mother's children, since zeal for your house has devoured
me, and the reproaches with which they reproached you have fallen on
me.

For you have known my reproach, my shame and my humiliation,
and all those who afflict me are before you; my soul has waited for
reproach and misery; I waited for someone to grieve with me, but none,
for comforters, but found no one; they gave me gall to eat and vinegar
to drink.

Let their table be a trap before them, a recompense and a stumbling
block; let their eyes be darkened so they cannot see, and bend down their
back always; pour out your wrath upon them, and let your fierce anger

seize upon them. Let their dwelling ["epaulis"] be desolate, and let there be no one to dwell in their tents, since they hunt for those whom you have smitten, and add to the pain of those whom you have pierced, add transgression to their transgression, and let them not come into your righteousness; let them be blotted out of the Book of the Living; let them not be registered with the righteous.

Psalm 41.9-13

Jesus taught the disciples to read the OT, in light of him. As a result, early Christians had no problem interpreting Psalm 41 in light of Jesus' conflict with Judas, especially since the text rendered "enemy" in the singular. God vindicated Jesus for his innocence by raising him from the dead, thus winning a great victory over the forces of sin and death, which held his people in bondage.

For even the man of my acquaintance who I trusted, who ate my bread, has magnified his treachery against me. But you, O Lord, have mercy on me. Raise me up that I may repay them. This I know that you have delighted in me and that you will not let my enemy rejoice over me. But you came to my aid because of my innocence and you established me before you forever. Blessed be the Lord, God of Israel from age to age. Let it be! Let it be!

Comment

The instructions the apostles received from Jesus were to wait in Jerusalem, so they made good use of the time by praying together. It's striking that women were included in in this scene. First-century Judaism was a culture that usually promoted separate spheres for women and men to occupy. When it came to the core functions of ministry, of which prayer must be accounted a significant role, women were as welcome as men in the early church. Thus there exists an egalitarian spirit in these early days of the church. Both women and men were to play essential roles in the church, something that would have been noteworthy in a society in which women and men were regularly separated.[15]

However, when the apostles chose a replacement for Judas, the text implies that this was a role reserved for men.[16] When Peter lists the criteria for choosing Judas' replacement, he specifically uses the word "*aner*," a Greek word almost always restricted to the male gender.

Thus, at the beginning of the movement called "The Way," women were expected to play key roles, which was counter-cultural; yet some roles, namely that of apostle were reserved for men. This is, in part, why some traditions still reserve the role of bishop and presbyter for men. Yet, since other traditions, including our own, have shown more openness to women in senior roles of late, we should see this passage as more descriptive than foundational in determining the roles women can play in the church. In Acts, women perform all kinds of roles, including one mention of a woman (Tabitha) as a disciple (9.36). No matter one's position on gender roles in the church, almost everyone will find things both to like and dislike in this passage and in Acts in general.

We should also pay attention to the remarkable statements Peter makes about the interpretation of Scripture in this passage. When Peter says, "It was necessary for the scriptures to be fulfilled which the Holy Spirit spoke beforehand through the mouth of David," this underlines why most Christians through the ages have insisted that the Bible really is the Word of God. Peter believes that he can relate texts from the OT to his day because the Holy Spirit enabled David, the purported author of these Psalms, to write better than he knew. If the scriptures have God as their ultimate author, this is why taking the time to study, learn, and ponder them is something every Christian should do. After all, through the scriptures, God speaks to his people.

Finally, we should notice the significant role that Peter plays in this episode. So often in the Gospels Peter was depicted as unreliable. But here Peter plays a primary role. Peter is the one interpreting the scriptures and setting the agenda. It appears a governance structure within the church took shape very early that had one person clearly in charge, interpreting the scriptures in an authoritative way.

However, as our story progresses, we will see how this picture gets muddied. There is no doubt that Peter is in charge here, but by the middle of the book when James takes over as head of the Jerusalem church (Acts 12.17, 15.13, 21.18), it won't seem so clear. We will consistently discover in Acts that Luke is not particularly interested in giving us precise information about how authority structures should work. He will even use words like bishop and presbyter interchangeably at times (Cf. Acts 20.17, 28), indicating that Luke was employing them without precision. Yet the general subject of authority is very important to Luke and will emerge quite often throughout the book of Acts.

Even when the language gets muddied, however, Acts, particularly in the early chapters, still supports the later emergence of bishops for the governance of the church. For example, when Peter quotes from Psalm 109.8 in today's Acts reading, the text says, "Let another take his *office.*" The word "office" in Greek is the word "*episkopen,*" the word from which we get "Episcopal."

In one of the earliest descriptions we have, Peter thought the term apostle was not just a nice name, but actually designated a real office. As a result, bishops ["*episkopoi*"] would come to be seen as the successors of the apostles. As always, we shouldn't press the evidence too hard, but the Episcopal structure at work in our tradition seems well supported, at least from today's passage.

As Episcopalians, one of our distinguishing beliefs is that one finds a true church where there is a duly-constituted bishop ["*episcopos*"] exercising authority. This, of course, does not mean that we should thumb our noses at other traditions who read the scriptures differently. At the very least, however, it does suggest our distinctive approach to governance has ample support in the Bible.

Questions for Reflection:

1. If the scriptures really are the inspired Word of God, what does that say about the authority of the Bible? What do you do when you encounter parts of the Bible you don't like?

2. The depictions of Judas' death are meant to be disturbing. Why did Judas think he couldn't be forgiven for his betrayal? Do you think anything you've done is unforgivable?

3. Should the ordained offices of the church be open to both men and women? How, if at all, does this passage challenge your opinion?

CHAPTER 3

PENTECOST
Acts 2.1-13

Acts 2.1-13

> *At the Feast of Pentecost, Jews from all over were required to gather together to celebrate the harvest and to pay their tithes and offerings to the Lord. But this would turn out to be no ordinary Feast because a group of Jews from diverse nations would be baptized with the Holy Spirit. Thus the church gets its start, as the Holy Spirit descends on this first group of believers. For Christians, Pentecost marks the promised ingathering of the people of God.*

Now, on the day of Pentecost, they were all together in the same place. And suddenly there was a noise ["ekos"] from heaven, a rushing violent wind ["pnoes"], and it filled the whole house where they were sitting. And tongues as of fire appeared, distributed and resting on each of them. And they were all filled with the Holy Spirit and they began to speak in other tongues, as the Spirit gave utterance to them.

Now there were devout Jewish men dwelling in Jerusalem from all the nations under heaven. And, at this sound, a large crowd gathered together and was bewildered, since each one heard the others speaking in his own tongue. Being astonished and amazed, they said, "Look, are not all who are speaking Galileans? So how can we hear, each one of us, in our own native tongue?" There were Parthians, Medes, Elamites and inhabitants of Mesopotamia, Judea and Cappadocia, Pontus and the region of Asia, Phrygia and Pamphylia, Egypt and regions of Libya, near Cyrene, as well as visitors from Rome, Jews and proselytes, Cretans and Arabs. We heard them speaking in various languages the great things of God." So we were all astonished and perplexed, asking, "What does this mean?" But others were jeering at us, saying, "They have been filled with too much sweet wine."

Genesis 11.1-9

The story of the Tower of Babel is justifiably famous, yet often misread. Many follow medieval interpreters, thinking the tower was a prideful attempt to climb up to God. Yet the protagonists were likely building a Ziggurat, a Babylonian religious structure, which functioned as an enticement for God to come down and bless the people, generally with a favorable harvest. Sure enough, God does come down, but is dismayed at what he finds. God confuses their language, scattering them across the earth. In Hebrew, the city in question is called "Babel." So this passage might very well serve as a polemic against the pride of Babylon, thought to be a place irredeemably hostile to God.

Now the whole earth had one language and one tongue was for all. Then it happened, while they were moving from the east, they found a plain in the land of Shinar, and they dwelt there. And every man said to his neighbor, "Come, let us make bricks, and let us bake them with fire." (They used brick instead of stone and bitumen instead of clay). Then they said, "Come, let us build for ourselves a city and a tower whose top will reach to the sky, that we might make a name for ourselves, so that we might not be scattered across the face of the whole earth."

So the Lord came down to see the city and the tower, which the sons of men were building. And the Lord said, "Look, there is one tribe and one tongue for everyone, and they have begun to do this thing and now nothing will be impossible for them, whatever they set out to do. Come, let us go down and confuse their language so that no one will understand the voice of his neighbor."

So the Lord scattered them from that place across the face of the earth and they ceased building the city and the tower. As a result, its name is called "Confusion" [in Hebrew, "Babel"], since there the Lord confused the language of the whole earth and the Lord God scattered them across the face of the whole earth.

Leviticus 23.15-21

In the OT law, the Feast of Pentecost was one of the obligatory religious events of the year. All males in Israel were required to attend (Deut 16.16). Taking place fifty days after Passover, the Feast of Pentecost celebrated the spring harvest. It required Israelites to recognize God as the source of all their material blessings by bringing a choice portion of their harvest and laying it before God. Early Christians read this figuratively. The required sin offerings prefigured the necessity of Jesus' sacrifice for sins, while the two loaves, held together by oil, represented unity in the community.[17]

And you shall number from the day after the Sabbath, from the day on which you offer the sheaf of the wave-offering, seven full weeks, until the day after the last week, you shall number fifty days and you shall bring a first-fruits offering to the Lord. You shall bring loaves from your dwellings as a contribution — two loaves, and a double tithe of wheat flour, leavened and baked, you shall offer to the Lord. And you shall offer with the loaves seven spotless lambs, each one-year old, and a single ox from the herd and two spotless rams, as a sweet savor offering to the Lord. You shall also offer one male goat as a sin offering and two lambs, each one year old, as a peace offering along with the loaves of the first-fruits. And the priest shall lay them out with the loaves of the first fruits, laying them before the Lord with the two lambs; they shall be holy to the Lord. **They shall belong to the priest who brings them. And, on this day, you shall call an assembly; it shall be holy to you; you must not do any serious work on it. This is a statute forever for your generations in all your dwellings.**

Comment

The baptism of the Spirit at Pentecost is one of the essential stories in Acts. Strangely, even though Matthew and John were both participants at Pentecost, only Luke, who was evidently not an eyewitness, records it so extensively.[18] In John, Jesus simply breathes on the disciples to give them the Spirit (John 20.22). Luke and John are probably describing the same event, but Luke is describing it in a much more extensive way.[19] John wanted to emphasize that it was Jesus who sent the Spirit; Luke simply provides more details on how it all took place.

Luke tells us a surprising story. It's surprising because the Spirit seemed to act differently in the OT. The Spirit would rush on selected individuals, often political leaders, to enable them to carry out specific tasks. The presence of the Spirit was almost always temporary, so much so that David pleaded with God after his affair with Bathsheba to "take not your Holy Spirit from me" (Ps 51.11).

Jesus' earlier prediction, "You will be baptized with the Holy Spirit not many days from now" (Acts 1.5), is fulfilled here. Moreover, this is also the fulfillment of John the Baptist's prophecy just before Jesus' baptism that the disciples would be baptized "with the Holy Spirit and with fire" (Luke 3.16).

In the Old Testament and in the Gospels, the image of "fire" was typically employed to depict the eschatological judgment that was to come. In this scene, however, the image of fire prepares the disciples for ministry. The fire from heaven, prominent at the original giving of the Law to Moses on Mt. Sinai (Ex 19.18), takes up residence in a new way in the lives of God's anointed by means of the Spirit.

This becomes a significant theme throughout Acts. God's Shekinah glory, which had been reserved for the Most Holy Place in the temple, now takes up residence in believers instead. As we will see subsequently, the special anointing of the Spirit enables the disciples' teaching and preaching ministries, a forerunner to ordination in our day (2 Tim 1.6). [20]

We shouldn't miss the subtle textual link to the creation account in Genesis 2. Luke chooses a rare word to describe the rushing wind that comes ["*pnoes*"], its only NT appearance. This is the same word used when God breathed the "breath ["*pnoen*"] of life" into Adam (Gen 2.7). [21] Thus, in a sense, God is breathing new life into his people.

There is significant disagreement about the meaning of "speaking in tongues." The text tells us "they began to speak in other tongues," and they understood "in their own native tongue." Is this an example of "ecstatic speech" or an example of people simply speaking in other languages they had not previously known? Frankly, one could build a good case for either option.

It seems more likely that those at Pentecost were hearing and understanding foreign languages ["*xenolalia*"] rather than engaging in ecstatic speech ["*glossolalia*"]. [22] The real miracle is that despite the many different languages and dialects spoken, they could all understand one another in their mother tongues. This is a signal that as the gospel spreads, language will not necessarily be a barrier to its propagation. The laundry list of people groups represented at Pentecost indicates that Pentecost is the beginning of the ingathering of the people of God promised by the prophets. [23]

The result of all this is remarkable unity. Not only did they pray with "one mind," they all understood each other despite speaking different languages. Cultural differences would enhance the gospel, not prevent its spread. As a result, it's common to read the story of Pentecost as reversing the effects of God's confusion of language at Babel. United by God's Spirit, each person who has been filled by the Spirit understands the other, making the spread of the good news possible. This really is a remarkable reversal and a sign of what God intended for the church.

Luke is depicting the church as united in a way that seems almost unthinkable today. When, in the Creed we confess "One holy, catholic, and apostolic church," we are affirming the importance of this unity. The hopelessly divided state of the church in our day is clearly not what God intended.

Questions for Reflection:

1. In our Leviticus reading today, the whole point of the Pentecost Festival was to remind Israel that everything, including their produce and their land, ultimately belonged to God. Have you ever considered that God is the real owner of your wealth, your house, your car, even your own soul? How might it change how you think about the material things in your life?

2. God wants unity in the church. Yet there seems to be nothing but division. What, if anything, are you doing to promote the unity rather than the disunity within the church?

3. How do you feel about speaking in tongues? The early church seems to have thought it was an important practice that authenticated the presence of God. Is this something we should expect today? Why or why not?

CHAPTER 4

A TRULY GREAT SERMON
Acts 2.14-36

Acts 2.14-36

> *This is Peter's first sermon in Acts and is undoubtedly one of the greatest sermons ever preached. In it, Peter demonstrates that Jesus had to be the Messiah from the OT. He begins by refuting scoffers who thought that the strange speech of those filled with the Spirit was evidence of drunkenness. Then, employing Joel and the Psalms, Peter shows how Jesus fulfilled OT prophecy. How did an uneducated fisherman see things the greatest scribes had never even contemplated? Luke thinks this is the power of the Holy Spirit at work.*

Then Peter, standing with the other eleven disciples, lifted up his voice and declared to them: "Men of Judea and all inhabitants of Jerusalem, know this, pay attention to my words. Don't think we're drunk, since it's only about 9:00 AM, but this coming of the Spirit was what was written through the prophet Joel:

And it will come to pass in those days, says the Lord that I will pour out my spirit upon all flesh. Your sons and your daughters will prophecy; your young men will see visions, and your old men will dream dreams. Even on your male and female slaves in those days will I pour out my Spirit and they will prophecy.

And I will give signs in the sky above: blood and fire and clouds of smoke. The sun will be turned to darkness and the moon to blood before the great and terrible Day of the Lord comes. And it will happen that everyone who calls on the name of the Lord will be saved (Joel 2.28-32).

Fellow Israelites, hear these words. Jesus, the Nazarene, is a man attested to you by God with powerful deeds, wonders and signs that God did through him in your midst, as you well know. This Jesus, appointed by the sure intention and plan of God, you killed by nailing him to a cross at the hands of lawless men. This is the one God raised up, having freed him from the pangs of death, since it was impossible for him to be held by it. For David says this about him:

I keep foreseeing the Lord before me through everything, since he is at my right hand, I won't be shaken. Therefore my heart is gladdened and my tongue is overjoyed. Even my flesh will rest in hope, since you will not abandon my soul to Hades nor will you give your Holy One over to see corruption. You have made me know the ways of life; you will fill me with joy at your presence (Ps 16.8-11).

My brothers, it is possible to say with confidence to you concerning our patriarch David that he both died and was buried. In fact, his tomb is with us to this day! So, because David was a prophet and saw that God had sworn with an oath to seat one of his descendants on his throne, having foreseen it, David spoke concerning the resurrection of the Christ that he would not be abandoned to Hades nor would his flesh see corruption. God has raised this Jesus, an event to which you all are witnesses. Therefore, having been exalted to the right hand of God, and having received the promise of the Holy Spirit from the Father, he poured out what you both see and hear. For David did not ascend to heaven. But David himself said:

The Lord said to my Lord, sit at my right hand
Until I make your enemies a footstool for your feet (Ps 110.1).

Therefore let all the house of Israel know beyond a doubt that God made Jesus both Lord and Christ, this Jesus who you crucified.

Psalm 16.1-2, 7-11

Psalm 16 figures prominently in Peter's Pentecost sermon. His interpretation of the Psalm is strikingly original, as nothing in the history of interpretation to that point indicated it was about resurrection. Peter plays on the ambiguity of the word "corruption." In Hebrew, the word was "shakat," which was translated "pit," a typical image for the grave. The Septuagint, the OT translation employed by Luke, translated the word "shakat" into Greek with "diaphroan" meaning "corruption." This emphasized the effect of going down into the grave. Peter's main point was that Jesus never saw corruption to his body. Peter describes the effects of the resurrection as on-going, eventually culminating in the resurrection of all believers.

A Psalm of David

Protect me, O Lord, since I have hoped in you. I said to the Lord, you are my God; you have no need of my good things...I will bless the Lord who has instructed me; even during the night my mind tutors me. I kept foreseeing the Lord before me through everything, since he is at my right hand, I wouldn't be shaken. Therefore, my heart is gladdened and my tongue is overjoyed. Even my flesh will rest in hope, since you will not abandon my soul to Hades nor will you hand your Holy One over to see corruption ["diaphroan"]. You have made me know the ways of life; you will fill me with joy at your presence, pleasures at your right hand forevermore.

Psalm 110.1-5

> *Psalm 110 is quoted fourteen times in the NT, more than any other.*[24] *Early Christians saw the language of this Psalm as pointing forward to Jesus' resurrection and ascension. The text repeats that the Lord is seated at the "right hand" twice, a reference to Jesus' enthronement at the right hand of the Father. Whereas an earthly king would often have a favorite subject sit at his right hand, the Christian reading of Psalm 110 insisted it was Jesus, given "all authority in heaven and earth" (Matt 28.18), who sat down at God's right hand.*[25] *For Peter, this Psalm had to be about Jesus, since David never ascended to heaven.*

A Psalm of David

The Lord said to my Lord, sit at my right hand until I make your enemies a footstool for your feet. The Lord will send forth your rod of power out of Zion: rule in the midst of your enemies. With you is authority in the day of your power, in the splendors of your Saints. I have begotten you from the womb before the morning star. The Lord has sworn and he will not change his mind: You are a priest forever according the order of Melchizedek. The Lord is at your right hand; he has crushed kings on the day of his wrath. He will judge the nations.

Comment

Imagine, if you would, the task before Peter. He, together with one-hundred-twenty people, had just had one of the seminal religious experiences in history. A new age had dawned with the outpouring of the Spirit of God on his people. God's covenant promises, and his faithfulness had been vindicated both in the resurrection and ascension of Jesus as well as in the outpouring of the Holy Spirit.

These events occurred together with all kinds of supernatural activity. People started speaking in foreign tongues. Everyone in the room could somehow understand each other. But, for some reason, outsiders to the community couldn't understand. This led them to scoff that the believers were drunk at 9:00 AM because their speech sounded like gibberish. How could Peter explain what had just happened?

Through Peter's sermon, Luke is trying to explain, in theological terms, the remarkable beginnings of the church. Luke's way of shaping the narrative reveals his literary objective. He's trying to make the Christian movement understandable to a Gentile audience, and, in particular, to his patron Theophilus.

Luke is also trying to explain the good news. We will see this again and again in the book of Acts. The gospel is not about dying and going to heaven. The gospel is not that Jesus has a wonderful plan to make his followers rich and comfortable. The gospel is not that God, if you're good, will solve all your problems. The gospel is primarily about the resurrection and ascension of Jesus.

All throughout Acts, in many different ways, we will see the bodily resurrection of Jesus front and center.[26] Their strategy for proclaiming the good news was not to make their hearers feel good or to titillate their emotions. The apostles' strategy is to tell their hearers what has really happened because the reality of their message is life changing. If Jesus really is King, the world is about to change.

What Luke reveals in this passage is the earliest short-hand confession of the early church, namely, the belief that Jesus was Lord. Paul famously puts it this way in Philippians: "that every knee should bow in heaven and on earth and under the earth, and every tongue confess that Jesus Christ is Lord, to the glory of the Father" (Phil 2.8-9). To confess that Jesus was "Lord and Christ" was to believe he was really the Anointed One, the Messiah, and that God had vindicated him by raising him from the dead.

It's also interesting to observe how Luke works with the first extended quote in this passage from the prophet Joel. Joel was writing at a time of great distress when a plague of locusts had devoured the produce and livelihoods of just about everyone in the southern country of Judah.[27] This had been followed by bands of marauding armies that had trampled everything in sight.[28]

Into this chaos, Joel wrote of a great reversal that was to come – the great and terrible Day of the Lord. God would come and stop the devastation brought by the invading armies and set things right. The signs of this were certain omens that would occur: visions, dreams, and darkness. The promise was that God's Spirit would be poured out on all in Judah – men and women, rich and poor, Jews, and Gentiles.

Peter is interpreting the tongues of fire, rushing wind and supernatural speech at Pentecost in light of Joel's prophecy of the Day of the Lord. Note, for example, how Peter subtly changes the quote right at the beginning of the passage. Originally, the first line of the text read, "and it shall come to pass *afterward*" (Joel 2.28, LXX). But Peter changed it ever so subtly: "It shall come about *in the last days*." He's saying, in effect, these are the last days about which Joel spoke.

Peter is claiming the long-promised ingathering of God's people was starting to take place.[29] All the prophets had looked forward to the day when believers would come to Jerusalem from all nations to worship God. According to Peter this great hope starts to be fulfilled in the church.

It probably would have surprised both Luke and Peter that 2,000 years later we are still in the last days, and still awaiting the return of Christ. Yet our task is broadly similar to theirs. We are to proclaim Jesus' resurrection and ascension, the good news, until he returns (1 Cor 11.26).

Reflection Questions:

1. **If the gospel is such good news, what signs of Jesus' Kingship do you see on earth? How different is the world from two-thousand years ago? From fifty years ago? From five?**

2. **The great and terrible "Day of the Lord" was all about judgment. Is it possible to conceive of a God who is both perfectly loving,**

yet ready to judge the world for its injustice and wrongdoing? Can someone really be loving without making judgments about right and wrong?

3. What do you think about Peter's way of reading the Bible? He assumes we can relate texts across the books of the Bible (paying little attention to context or authorship). This is a typical pre-modern approach to reading, but is it legitimate? Why?

CHAPTER 5

MARKERS OF THE EARLY CHURCH
Acts 2.37-47

Acts 2.37-47

> *The reaction to Peter's sermon was dramatic as three-thousand
> people were baptized and many "wonders and signs" ensue. Peter
> exhorts his hearers to "repent" and "be baptized." To Peter, repen-
> tance was not primarily about feeling sorry for sins. It involved
> a whole re-orientation of life. In this passage, we find emerg-
> ing several distinctive marks of the early church, including com-
> mitments to (1) radical generosity, (2) apostolic teaching, (3)
> the sacraments, (4) prayer, and (5) community fellowship.*

Now, when they heard this, they were pierced to the heart. They said to Peter and to the rest of the apostles, "Brothers, what should we do?" Then Peter said to them, "Repent and be baptized, each one of you, in the name of the Lord Jesus for the forgiveness of your sins, and you will receive the gift of the Holy Spirit. For this promise is yours and your children's and to all who are far off, as many as the Lord our God might call to himself." And with many other words, Peter exhorted and encouraged them saying, "Save yourselves from this crooked gen-eration." Then all who favorably welcomed his message were baptized. And in that day they added about 3,000 souls.

They were devoting themselves to the teaching of the apostles and to the fellowship, to the breaking of bread and the prayers. And fear came upon every soul because of the many wonders and signs that came through the apostles. And all who believed were together and held all things in common. And the apostles began selling their possessions and property and distributing the proceeds to all, as anyone had need. And day after day they were of one mind, meeting together in the temple, breaking bread from house to house, sharing food with glad and simple hearts, praising God and enjoying the favor of all the people. And the Lord was increasing the numbers of those being saved day after day.

Deuteronomy 15.1-4, 7-11

As Moses leads the Israelites into the Promised Land, he pays attention to economic issues. His assumption is that the basic needs of each person in the community are the ultimate responsibility of the community itself. While these regulations will not completely end poverty (as Moses himself implies at the end), they make it difficult for a permanent underclass to develop. The unheralded key to this system is the right of the community to determine for itself what a "need" actually entails. If there is a genuine need, the community must provide it. The way that the early church set itself up was partially a reflection of Moses' model.

Every seven years, you shall make a release from debts. This is the statute of the release. You shall forgive every debt that your neighbor owes you and you shall not demand repayment from your brother since the release has been proclaimed by the Lord your God. You may ask a foreigner for repayment of whatever belongs to you, but regarding your brother, you shall release him from his debts. As a result, there will be no poverty among you, since the Lord your God will undoubtedly bless you in the land which the Lord your God is giving you to inherit.

However, if someone is impoverished among you from your brethren in one of your cities in the land that the Lord your God is giving you, you shall not harden your heart nor shall you close your hand against your brother who is in need, but you must open your hands to him; you must lend him as much as he wants, according to his need. Keep watch over yourself that there is no hidden transgression in your heart, saying "the seventh year, the year of release, is near" and your eye transgresses your brother in want and you do not give to him and you do not help him and he cries out concerning you to the Lord. In that case, great sin shall be upon you. You must give to him and you must lend to him as much as he needs. In giving to him, your heart must not be vexed since for this very reason, the Lord your God will bless you in all your works and in everything that you set out to do. For the poor will not cease from the land. Therefore I am commanding you to do this thing, saying, "You must open your hands to your brother who is poor and in want who is on your land."

Isaiah 57.15-19

> *This passage likely takes place after the fall of Babylon when King Cyrus, the sixth century BC ruler of the Medo-Persian Empire, had turned out to be a disappointment.[30] The oracle implies sin was a major reason for this disappointment. But the oracle also promises a great reversal, as God would vindicate the people both "those who are far off and those who are near."[31] This was a favorite trope for NT writers, employed by Peter to great effect in Acts.*

Thus says the Lord, the Most High, who dwells on high forever, Most Holy is his name. The Lord Most High rests in the holy places, and gives perseverance to the faint of heart and gives life to the brokenhearted. I will not punish you forever nor will I always be angry with you, for my Spirit shall go forth from me, for I have created all breath. On account of sin, for a time, I distressed him and struck him and turned my face away from him. He was distressed and became sullen in his ways. I have seen his ways and I healed him and comforted him, giving him genuine comfort, peace upon peace to those who are far off and to those who are near. The Lord has said, "I will heal them."

Comment

In 1534, about fifteen years after the start of the Reformation, Melchior Hoffman, enthralled by the teachings of Martin Luther, became convinced he was the reincarnated prophet Elijah who had come to announce Christ's return. His followers, the Melchiorites, decided, on the basis of Scripture alone, that the German town of Münster would be the place of Christ's return and declared it to be the New Jerusalem.

Melchiorite followers flocked to Münster and took over the economic and political structures of the town. They set up this "New Jerusalem" using just the Bible. Abolishing private property, they abrogated legal contracts and forbade the use of currency. All property was declared to be the common possession of the community.

The new government burned all books outside the Bible, and all churches in town were stripped of any artwork to remove idolatry from their interiors. Even baptisms were suspended until Christ's return. Later, polygamy was introduced into the city, once again based on its use in the OT. It took a joint military operation from Catholics and Protestants to quell this rebellion, perhaps the only thing Catholics and Protestants could agree on during this period.[32]

We might scoff at such apocalyptic fervor, but it is a useful reminder that the Bible always needs to be read in light of the historical understanding of the church, in light of reason, and with lots of prayer to guide us. Not a few have taken today's passage to mean that capitalism is inherently immoral, that private property is the source of all evil, and that we could get rid of poverty just by abolishing its use. This, of course, is nonsense, even if capitalism and the enlightenment-era liberalism that underlies it also come with deep flaws.

Rather, radical generosity is one of the marks of a true Christian life.[33] It should shame us that the general view in the culture is that the church cares more about politics, personal financial gain, and culture-war issues than the common good.

As noted above, the early church in Acts got many of its economic ideas from the OT itself. One of the bedrock economic principles in the OT is that God is the owner of everything. Thus if God never ceded his ownership of the material goods he created, this implies we are merely caretakers on God's behalf, not actual owners.

The early church was also committed to apostolic teaching. It helped that all the apostles were in the same room together — one hopes the teaching was apostolic! Our goal as we are reading the Bible is to have as our starting point what the apostles taught. This is because the Holy Spirit is still at work in the church, guiding our understanding of the scriptures. Thus reading the Bible with the Great Tradition, not against it, should be our common starting point.

Third, the early church was committed to the Eucharist. Some might find it fanciful that a simple phrase "the breaking of bread" gets interpreted as the Eucharist and, admittedly, there is an endless debate in about what Peter means here. However, not only later in Acts (cf. Acts 20.7), but also elsewhere in the NT (Luke 24.35; 1 Cor 10.16), "the breaking of bread" often implied something distinct from a normal meal.

To be clear, there is ample early evidence that the Eucharist was frequently celebrated right after a common meal in the early church. At the Last Supper, for example, the text describes the institution of the Eucharist as taking place "after supper" (Luke22.20). Further, as today's text implies, the disciples went from house to house and "broke bread together." It is clear that the Eucharist was central to the Christian community from the start and took place frequently.

The early church not only emphasized the Eucharist, but also baptism as well. The church has always considered the Sacrament of Holy Baptism as the usual way one enters the Christian community. A formal confession of faith typically goes together with the baptism.

Fourth, the church was committed to prayer. Prayer appears in one form or another over thirty times in Acts. But note that Luke renders this as a plural noun here, as the "prayers," which seems to suggest the beginnings of some kind of formal liturgical practice.

Lastly the early church was committed to fellowship. The Greek word here is "*koinonia*." They knew each other. The most remarkable thing about this fellowship was its unity, a theme that keeps appearing. They were in the same place, taking care of one another, praying together, worshipping together, and learning. This may be an idealized vision, but it's still a powerful one. The remarkable results that come from this small community in Jerusalem invite us to take each of these markers seriously.

Questions for Reflection:

1. Are you a generous person? How important is it to give of your time, talent, and treasure?
2. How important is fellowship with other Christians to you? Do you feel isolated and alone or are you tapped in to the various resources the church offers for connection?
3. If you have been baptized, was it an important event in your life? Do you see your Christian life as an outgrowth of the vows you took at your baptism? How so?

CHAPTER 6

WALKING, LEAPING, AND PRAISING GOD
Acts 3.1-10

Acts 3.1-10

> *This is the first of fourteen miracle stories in the book of Acts.[34]*
> *Luke portrays Peter and John as pious Jews, who go to evening*
> *prayer and give alms.[35] But Peter's miraculous healing of the*
> *lame man demonstrates that the healing ministry of Jesus will*
> *continue on in the apostles through the Holy Spirit. The age of*
> *the Spirit does not come quietly — it comes with signs and won-*
> *ders, confirming God's plan to renew his entire creation.*

Now Peter and John were going up to the temple at 3:00 PM, the hour of prayer. And a man, lame from birth, was being carried. Now this man was laid day after day at the door of the temple, which is called "beautiful," in order to beg alms from those going into the temple. When Peter and John were about to enter the temple, the lame man saw them and asked to receive alms from them. Peter, together with John, stared intently at him and said, "Look at us." Then the lame man fixed his gaze on them, thinking he was about to receive something from them.

But Peter said, "I own no silver and gold, but what I do have, this I give to you. In the name of Jesus Christ, the Nazorean, rise up and walk!" Then, taking hold of his right hand, Peter raised him up ["egeiren"]. And immediately his feet and his ankles became steady. After leaping up, he stood and started walking around. He entered into the temple with Peter and John, walking and leaping and praising God. And when all the people saw him walking around and praising God, they recognized him as the one who was sitting at the beautiful gate begging alms. So they were filled with wonder and amazement at what had happened to him.

Isaiah 35.4-10

In this passage, Isaiah foresees the destruction of Edom, a nation that had plundered the Promised Land.[36] Isaiah is probably using Edom as a representative figure for all the nations that had harmed Israel.[37] Although Judah had been harassed by these nations, God would not allow this situation to persist. In fact, God would make a "clean way," a kind of highway, which would enable all those scattered to return. Of particular interest is the reversal promised to the Lame, who would leap like a deer. This bears a striking similarity to the crippled man in today's Acts reading, not only in the literal sense of the healing, but also in the spiritual sense of the restoration of the people of God.

Comfort each other, O faint hearted; be strong, do not be afraid. Behold, our God will render judgment; he will repay. He will come, and he will save us. Then the eyes of the blind will be opened and the ears of the deaf will hear. Then the lame will leap like a deer and the tongue of the dumb will become articulate, since water has gushed out in the desert and in ravines in a thirsty land. Then the waterless place will become a marsh and a fountain of water will be in the thirsty land. There birds will be merry and the homestead will have reeds and marshes.

There will be a clean way and the way will be called holy. No one unclean will ever pass by there, nor will there be an unclean way. But those scattered will walk on it and they will by no means go astray. No lions or fierce beasts will go up on it, nor will any be found there, but the redeemed will go on it and the gathered will return because of the

Lord, and they will come to Zion with joy. Everlasting joy will be on their heads, for on their head, will be praise and rejoicing. Joy will seize upon them; distress, sorrow, and mourning will run away.

Luke 7.18-23

John the Baptist seems confused. Although John had previously expressed great hopes for Jesus ("whose sandal strap I am not worthy to untie"), it's not turning out like he thought. Jesus was supposed to be a "fiery reformer," but there is no winnowing fork, no threats of apocalyptic judgment, just love and compassion for the poor, sick, and suffering.[38] The Messiah was supposed to come back for judgment and for the restoration of Israel. What was Jesus doing healing Gentiles? Jesus not only reaffirms his role as a healer, but the Proverb he utters at the end warns those with misconceived notions of him. Most importantly, the healings are a sign that the restoration of God's people is at hand.[39]

John summoned two of his disciples and sent them to the Lord, saying, "Are you the one who is to come or should we await another?" When the men came to Jesus, they said, "John the Baptist sent us to you to ask if you are the one who is to come or should we await another?" In that hour, Jesus was healing many from their sicknesses, infirmities and wicked spirits. He also enabled many blind people to see. Jesus answered and said to them, "Go tell John what you have seen and heard: The blind see, the lame walk; lepers are cleansed, and the deaf hear; the dead are raised, and the poor are preached the gospel. And blessed is the one who is not offended by me."

Comment

According to Jewish law, someone lame or crippled was automatically ostracized from the priestly service (Lev 27.17-20).[40] But later rabbinic interpretation went even further, concluding that any physically deformed person would have to be ostracized from the temple since things like "knee-pads," an "artificial arm" or the "wooden stump of a cripple" would all be susceptible to uncleanness and thus not appropriate for the sanctuary.[41] To have a physical deformity was essentially to be put outside the community.

Don't miss the poignant symbolism of the lame man. He's outside the temple begging because he's not allowed to go inside. Luke is subtly pointing out the absurdity of this. Notice as well that the man is not looking to be healed. He's looking for money. What happens to him is a shock both to the man himself and to those who recognized him at the temple.

Luke is not being arbitrary with the choice of this story. After all, Jesus had memorably healed a lame man in Luke's gospel (Luke 5.17-26). In that story, Luke showed the "power of the Lord" was with Jesus. By choosing a vignette that mirrors the essential features of Jesus' healing ministry, especially in the restoration of the lame man to full inclusion in the community, Luke is demonstrating the power that was at work in Jesus is also at work in the apostles.[42]

We live in an age of skepticism more than an age of faith. All of us, for better or for worse, are children of the Enlightenment, the movement starting in the eighteenth century that sought to embrace reason as its guiding principle. Many positive advances in medicine, technology, and economics can be traced to this era.

Yet one of the unfortunate legacies of the Enlightenment is its pervasive skepticism concerning the supernatural. We can tie this skepticism, in part, to the work of David Hume who lived in Scotland in the eighteenth century.

By all accounts Hume was a good man, generous to friends, patient with adversaries, and kindly disposed to everyone.[43] This drove people in the Church of England crazy because atheists were not supposed to be good people. Reports that Hume died peacefully in his sleep, assuming he would just sink back into the earth after his death, simply infuriated pious Christians who couldn't imagine that his conscience could be clear.

In his famous work, *An Enquiry Concerning Human Understanding*, Hume advanced an argument against miracles that still holds sway today.[44]

Hume thought that miracles, especially healing miracles, were highly unlikely. His basic argument was that since we have to believe the testimony of others with reports of miracles (most of which have proved to be untrustworthy) and because miracles involve abrogating fixed natural laws, which we can't empirically observe, we should distrust any miraculous activity.

It didn't take long for biblical scholars, particularly in the nineteenth and early twentieth centuries, to embrace Hume's ideas and cast serious doubt on whether things like healings or other miracles could ever occur. Just because the Bible claimed miracles happened did not mean they did. After a while, elaborate theories emerged to explain how the apostles, embarrassed by Jesus' death at the hands of the Roman government, simply made up most of the supernatural parts of Jesus' story, miracles and all.

Protestants at the Reformation didn't help matters by also being skeptical about miracles. Since Roman Catholics believed strongly in miracles, elements of the Reformed tradition simply denied their possibility in this age, arguing (on flimsy evidence) that some church fathers had claimed the cessation of miracles. This is how Martin Luther put it:

> Those visible works are simply signs for the ignorant, unbelieving crowd, and for their sakes that are yet to be attracted; but as for us who already know all we do know, and believe the gospel, what do we want them for?...Wherefore it is no wonder that they have now ceased since the gospel has sounded abroad everywhere and has been preached to those who had not known of God before, whom he had to attract with outward miracles, just as we throw apples and pears to children.[45]

Yale's Carlos Eire describes the Protestant rejection of miracles this way:

> One of the most distinctive traits of Protestantism was its rejection of miracles, and all of those practically-oriented supernatural events...God could work miracles, certainly, but as Protestants saw it, the age of miracles had passed, and God's supernatural

interventions were a thing of the past, strictly limited to biblical times...Protestantism might have desacralized and disenchanted the world much more through this take on miracles than through any other of its principles.[46]

Thus skepticism toward the supernatural can be traced directly back to Protestantism itself and its effort to desacralize the world. By all means we should evaluate claims of miracles critically, but denying that people can be healed in this age by supernatural means is a collapse into rationalism and skepticism. Genuine miracles are admittedly rare. But they undoubtedly occur. Let's never become too skeptical to notice. Moreover, let's have enough faith to believe early Christians had enough integrity not to make up the supernatural portions of the NT. After all, they went to their deaths defending it.

Questions for Reflection

1. **Does God still work through miracles today? What do you think about the Reformed Protestant denial of miracles in this age?**

2. **Luke really emphasizes the mercy of Peter and John toward the lame man. In what ways do you extend mercy to people who are suffering as you pass by them in every-day life?**

3. **How do the exclusionary tactics of the first-century rabbis make you feel, especially with regard to disabled people? In what ways can the church extend "welcome" instead of building barriers for people?**

CHAPTER 7

UNIVERSAL SALVATION?

Acts 3.11-26

Acts 3.11-26

> *Peter and John have just healed a crippled beggar. The people were*
> *astounded and rushed out to see the beggar "walking and leap-*
> *ing and praising God." Taking the lead as usual, Peter is quick to*
> *deny any credit for the miracle. Peter then lays out the case against*
> *his fellow Jews, showing how they had betrayed their Messiah.*
> *He implores them to repent and to turn (literally, to convert).*
> *Peter proclaims the risen Christ from the OT, arguing convinc-*
> *ingly that the prophets were looking forward to this day.*

While the formerly crippled man was clinging to Peter and John, all the people ran to them at the covered walkway, called Solomon's Colonnade, and were utterly astonished. When Peter saw them, he called out to the people, "Fellow Israelites, Why are you amazed at this? Why are you staring at us as if by our own power or piety we made this man walk? The God of Abraham, the God of Isaac, and the God of Jacob, the God of our Fathers, he glorified his servant Jesus whom you betrayed and disowned before Pilate after he had decided to release him. But you disowned the Holy and Just One, demanding instead a convicted murder to be released to you. You killed the Author of Life whom God raised from the dead — to this we are witnesses! On the basis of faith in his name, this man who you see and know, this very name has strengthened him. The faith, which is through Jesus, gave him perfect health before all of you.

And, now, brethren, I know you acted in ignorance just as your rulers did. But God announced beforehand through the mouth of all the prophets that his Christ would suffer, and this has taken place! Repent therefore and convert so that your sins may be blotted out, so the times of renewal might come from the Lord, and so he might send the Christ appointed for you, that is, Jesus. It was necessary for heaven to receive him until the time of the restoration ["apokatastasis"] of all things which God spoke through the mouth of his holy prophets ages ago.

"Look," Moses said, "The Lord your God will raise up for you a prophet out of your brethren like me. You must listen to him in everything he says to you (Deut 18.15). Now, anyone who does not listen to that prophet will be utterly cut off from the people (Lev 23.20; cf. Deut 18.19). You see, all the prophets from Samuel on down, as many as who spoke, they announced this day. You are sons of the prophets and of the covenant which God decreed to your fathers, saying to Abraham, 'And in your seed, all the families of the earth will be blessed' (Gen 22.18). After God raised up his Servant, he sent him first to you to bless you by turning each one of you from your wickedness."

Deuteronomy 18.13-22

Israel was supposed to be visibly different than other nations. They were to live a life defined by holiness. In this passage, God is promising his people that after Moses dies (which would take place shortly), God would raise up another to take Moses' place. Peter employs this text to show that Jesus was the intended referent of this promise all along, making this one of the more important Messianic prophecies of the OT.

You must be perfect before the Lord your God, for these nations whose land you will dispossess, they listen to omens and oracles, but the Lord has not given such to you.

The Lord your God will raise up for you a prophet out of your brethren. You must listen to him concerning everything you yourselves demanded from the Lord your God in Horeb on the day of the assembly, when you said, "We won't hear the voice of the Lord our God anymore, nor will we see this great fire anymore, so we won't die." But the Lord said to me, "In everything they've said, they've spoken rightly. I will raise up a prophet for them out of their brethren, one like you, and I will put my words into his mouth and he will speak to them as I order him. Now if anyone should not to listen to whatever the prophet speaks in my name, I will exact vengeance from him."

"However the prophet who improperly speaks a word in my name that I have not appointed him to speak, and whoever should speak a different word in the name of God, that prophet will be put to death. Now if you should say in your mind, 'How can we tell if the Lord has not spoken a word?' If the prophet should speak in the name of the Lord and that word does not come to pass and does not happen, this word, which the Lord has not spoken, the prophet spoke without authorization. You shall not spare him."

Genesis 22.15-19

Isaac had been born to Abraham when he was well over one-hundred years old. But shockingly, God commanded Abraham to sacrifice his beloved son (at almost exactly the same place that Jesus was later crucified). In unfathomable faith, Abraham was about to do so when an angel stopped him. In response to Abraham's faith, God declared an oath, saying that through Abraham's offspring, all nations of the earth would be blessed. In Acts, Luke shows that God's intention was even broader. It was to renew and restore the entire cosmos, leading to the question of just how universal God's saving plan really is.

Then the angel of the Lord called Moses a second time from heaven, saying, "By myself I have sworn," says the Lord, "because you have done this thing and you have not spared your beloved son for my sake, I will certainly bless you, and I will certainly multiply your offspring like the stars of the sky and like the sand of the seashore. Your offspring will inherit the cities of their enemies. And in your seed shall all the nations of the earth be blessed, because you have obeyed my voice." Then Abraham returned to his servants, and they arose and went together to the Well of the Oath. And Abraham stayed at the Well of the Oath.

Comment

In our readings about Pentecost a few chapters ago, we encountered a group of Jews who were experiencing remarkable "wonders and signs." Filled with the Holy Spirit, they were speaking in different languages, yet somehow being understood. This led to the beginning of a mission to spread the good news to the whole known world. This continues throughout the book of Acts.

Today, we observe another "filling," but with a very different response. The crowds in the temple, when they saw the remarkable restoration of the crippled beggar, were "filled" with wonder and astonishment.[47]

Why do so many in the temple not repent and turn? Despite what popular preaching sometimes suggests, conversion is not just a "change of mind." It's more like a total change in orientation — mind, body, soul, and spirit. It entails a complete refocusing of one's life. Conversion starts with some content, namely believing that Jesus is Lord. But genuine conversion ultimately involves incorporation into the new community called the church.

Peter tells his listeners that he knows that they "acted in ignorance" when they delivered up their Messiah to Pilate and refused Jesus' release. Peter is not trying to say that their crime wasn't grave. He's just trying to demonstrate how powerful the offer of forgiveness is.

Peter is highlighting a little-known feature in the OT law. One's attitude toward sin really mattered. So-called high-handed sin, done with the express intention of violating the law of God, was essentially unforgiveable. There were no sacrifices allotted for it. By contrast, unintentional sin was what the sacrificial system was about. All unintentional sin was forgivable.

By claiming that they acted in ignorance, Peter was saying their sin was forgivable if they would just humble themselves and turn to the Lord.[48] The language that Peter employs here is interesting. He tells them that God would "blot out ["*exeleipho*"] their sin" (Acts 3.19). As William Barclay explains, this metaphor derives from ancient writing practices. Because ancient papyrus did not allow ink to soak in as paper does, the ink would sit on the surface. Thus it was easy to erase, to blot out, or simply to wipe off the writing with a wet sponge.[49]

But what about those who didn't turn? Should we assume that they're lost forever? On the one hand, Peter suggests that those who do not turn "will be cut off" (Lev 23.29). Yet Peter also uses a loaded word, "*apokatastisis*" or "the restoration of all things," to highlight God's intention to remake his whole creation. This is what the idea of "new creation" is all about. Peter's use of "*apokatastisis*" in today's Acts reading is the only time it appears in the NT.[50]

Peter's employment of "*apokatastisis*" forms the basis for the church father Origen's hope that God would restore all created things, even the devil, to its pre-fall condition. In other words, all would eventually be saved through the mercy of God. This has led to centuries of suspicion about Origen's teaching since no one could fathom why God would restore Satan.

Should we believe that all will be saved in the end? This idea has become more popular in our day. But Origen himself wasn't sure it was right. Origen's point was that it was the express desire of God for all people to be saved (1 Tim 2.3-4). Moreover, if there is going to be a remaking of the entire cosmos with a "new heavens and new earth," as Isaiah envisions (Isa 65.17), this might require universal restoration.[51]

The problem is that there is so much in the Bible about eternal condemnation. Consider just one example: "If any one's name was not found in the Book of Life, he was thrown into the Lake of Fire (Rev 20.15). In the Bible, those separated from God seem to suffer eternal punishment.

Origen does not deny the reality of punishment for those who die separated from Christ. He simply sees it as a process of purification to help sinners come to a knowledge of the truth. Origen thinks, based on today's passage, that this process of purification requires the restoration of the whole creation.

It was Hans Urs von Balthasar, one of the greatest theologians of the twentieth century, who tried to resolve this dilemma. He observed that there are some passages in Scripture that hint at universal salvation while others speak of eternal punishment for those who do not turn toward God.[52] While fully recognizing the possibility of damnation, von Balthasar argued that if God is loving and merciful, we have to at least accept the possibility that all might eventually receive the salvation God offers.[53] Yet von Balthasar further observed that while we can never really know in advance whether all will be saved, we should nevertheless hope and pray that it happens. After all, a God of love often acts in surprising ways.

As von Balthasar puts it:

> The more that grace wins ground from the things that had filled the soul before it, the more it repels the effects of the acts directed against it. And to this process of displacement there are, in principle, no limits. If all the impulses opposed to the spirit of light have been expelled from the soul, then any free decision against this has become infinitely improbable. Then faith in the unboundedness of divine love and grace also justifies *hope for the universality of redemption*, although, through the possibility of resistance to grace that remains open in principle, *the possibility* of eternal damnation also persists.[54]

So will all be saved in the end? No one except God really knows. Nevertheless, with von Balthasar, we should pray that it might be so. Perhaps a loose rendering of a nineteenth-century Russian proverb says it best, "Anyone who does not believe in the universal restoration is an uncaring ox, but anyone who teaches it is a dumb ass."[55]

Questions for Reflection:

1. **We observed today how radical God's offer of forgiveness is. In what areas of your life do you feel that you can't be forgiven or can't forgive others? What holds you back from a fuller relationship with God?**

2. If our attitudes toward sin matter, are you deliberately doing anything against God's expressed will in your life? What effect has this had on your life?

3. If we spend our whole lives ardently working at our spiritual lives, is it fair that someone who rejected God would be offered post-mortem forgiveness? Where's the justice in that?

CHAPTER 8

NO OTHER NAME
Acts 4.1-22

Acts 4.1-22

> *Troubles abound for the religious leaders in this passage. The leadership is trying to deny Peter and John the right to speak about Jesus and about resurrection, yet can find no evidence to refute their claims. They prohibit teaching in Jesus' name, yet cannot deny the crippled man who was just healed. They cannot figure out how a couple of uneducated fisherman could speak with such power. Despite all the religious leaders' authority, they release Peter and John with a warning, a typical response for a first-time offense. The name of Jesus carries with it undeniable power, in contrast to the feckless response of the religious leaders.*

Now while Peter and John were speaking to the people, the priests, the captain of the temple guard, and the Sadducees were annoyed that they were teaching the people and that they were proclaiming the resurrection from the dead in Jesus. So they seized them with their hands and put them in prison until the next day, since it was already evening. But many who heard the message believed and the total number of men was about five thousand.

The next day, they assembled — the leaders, the elders and the scribes — in Jerusalem, along with Annas, the former high priest and Caiaphas, John, Alexander, and as many as were from the line of the high priesthood. They stood Peter and John in their midst and inquired by what authority or by what name ["onoma"] they had done these things.

Then Peter, filled with the Holy Spirit, said to them, "Leaders of the people and elders, if we today are being interrogated for a good work done for a sick man by which this man was restored to health ["sotzo"], let it be known to all of you and to all the people of Israel that by the name ["onoma"] of Jesus Christ, the Nazarene, whom you crucified, whom God raised from the dead, by this name, the sick man stands before you in perfect health. This Jesus is the stone rejected by you builders that has become the chief cornerstone (Ps 118.22). So there is salvation ["soteria"] in no other, for there is no other name ["onoma"] under heaven given by men by which one must be saved" ["sotzo"].

Now seeing the boldness of Peter and John and realizing that they were unlettered men and amateurs, they were amazed, and they realized that they had been with Jesus. But since they saw the man who had been healed standing with them, they had no way to contradict ["anteipon"] them. So they ordered them to go out from the council, while they conferred with one another.

They said, "What shall we do to these men, since it is obvious to all the inhabitants of Jerusalem that a remarkable sign has taken place through them? We can't deny it. But, so it doesn't spread much further to the people, let's warn them not to speak to anyone in this name ["onoma"] any longer." So after summoning them, they warned them not to speak or to teach in the name ["onoma"] of Jesus ever again.

But Peter and John responded to them, "Whether it is right before God to obey you rather than God, you be the judge, but it is impossible for us not to speak of what we have seen and heard." Then threatening Peter and John more severely, the council tossed them out, not finding anything for which to punish them. This was done on account of the people since everyone was praising God for what had happened. Now the man on whom this sign of healing had taken place was forty years old.

Psalm 118.19-29

The importance of Psalm 118 comes mainly from its liturgical use in Israel. The end of the Psalm, cited here, formed the backbone for the liturgy at the Feast of Tabernacles, the fall harvest festival.[56] According to the Mishnah, congregants would shake "lulabs" or palm branches, while chanting the Hallel Psalms (Psalms 113-118).[57] Christian interpretation of Psalm 118 played on the idea that "builders" could metaphorically be understood as "teachers." Thus Christians interpreted the Psalm as the Jewish leaders' rejection of Jesus.[58] Peter directly quotes from this Psalm in today's Acts passage.

Open for me the gates of righteousness. Entering into them, I will give praise to the Lord. This is the gate of the Lord – the righteous will enter through it. I will give praise to you since you were responsive to me and have become my salvation.

The stone, which the builders rejected, this has become the chief cornerstone. This is from the Lord and it is marvelous in our sight. This is the day that the Lord has made; let us rejoice and be glad in it! O Lord, save ["sotzo"] us now; O Lord, grant us prosperity. Blessed is the one who comes in the name ["onoma"] of the Lord. We have blessed you from the house of the Lord.

God is the Lord, and he has illumined us. Commence the Feast with thick branches up to the horns of the altar. You are my God; I will give thanks to you, since you were responsive to me and have become my salvation ["soteria"]. Give thanks to the Lord for he is good; his mercy endures forever.

Luke 21.5-19

Jesus was standing in the temple predicting the demise of the impressive temple complex.[59] This destruction took place in AD 70 under the Roman general Titus.[60] But the second part of the discourse, the prediction that the apostles would be handed over "to the synagogues and prisons," clearly finds its analogue in today's passage. Of particular interest is the textual link between the two stories. The rare Greek word "anteipon" is only found twice in the NT, here in Luke's gospel and in today's Acts passage. Just as Jesus predicted, the temple leadership was not able to contradict Peter and John's testimony despite their lack of training in the arts of classical rhetoric.

Now some of the disciples were speaking about the temple, that it was decorated with precious stones and votive offerings. Jesus responded, "These things which you see: the days are coming when not one stone will be left on another that will not have been thrown down."

Then they asked him, saying, "Teacher when will these things take place and what will be the sign that these things are about to happen?" Jesus said, "Be careful that you are not led astray. For many will come in my name ["onoma"], saying, 'I am the one'! This means the season is near. Do not go after them. But when you hear of wars and rumors of wars do not be frightened. For these things must happen first, but the end will not come immediately."

Then he said to them, "Nation will rise up against nation and kingdom against kingdom, and there will be great earthquakes in various places; there will be famine and plagues, fearful sights, and great signs from the sky.

But before all these things, they will seize you with their hands and persecute you, handing you over to the synagogues and prisons, hauling you before kings and governors for my name's sake. This will lead to your testimony. But settle in your hearts not to prepare your defense. For I will give you such speech and wisdom that your adversaries will not be able to resist or to contradict ["anteipon"] anything. But you will be betrayed by parents and brothers and relatives and friends; some of you, they will even put to death. In fact, you will be hated by everyone because of my name ["onoma"]. But not one hair of your head will perish. By your perseverance, you will gain your souls."

Comment

The church is continuing its growth. About five-thousand men were now in the church. Given that there were only about seventy to eighty-thousand people in Jerusalem at the time (and women and children weren't included in the church's census), those who converted probably represented a significant chunk of the population, perhaps as much as ten or twenty percent.[61]

One of the more notable parts of this passage is Peter's unequivocal statement that salvation is found in no other name but Jesus. To understand this, we should focus (1) on the power of the name of Jesus, (2) on what salvation really means in this context, and (3) how the name of Jesus is connected to salvation.

Jesus' name means "savior," as it derives from the Hebrew equivalent for "Joshua," which translates "Yahweh saves."[62] When combined with the title "Christ," the Greek word that translates the Hebrew "*meshiach*" or "Anointed One," we observe that Jesus' name describes what he had come to do – to save his people from their sins.[63] Jesus, as the true Messiah, is the only one who can bring about salvation, according to Peter.

Christians throughout the history of the church have found great power in the invocation of Jesus' name. Often in the NT, Jesus' name denotes his character and authority.[64] For example, the disciples are able to heal and cast out demons in his name in the Gospels (Matt 10.8). In fact, his opponents often misunderstand the power of Jesus' name, claiming that he must have had some demonic power (Beelzebub) that enables him to do his miracles (Luke 11.18-20).

In the liturgical calendar, there is even a Feast of the Holy Name of Jesus. We observe this on January 1st. This Feast remembers Jesus' circumcision which took place eight days after his birth in accordance with the OT law (Luke 2.21) and has been celebrated from at least the time of St. Bernard of Clairvaux who found great profit in the veneration of Jesus' name.[65]

Next, what does salvation mean here? Not infrequently, readers of this passage tend to neglect the context of the passage when explaining it. When Peter claims that salvation is "in no other name," this has little to do with going to heaven. In fact, the typical use of the Greek word for salvation ["*sotzo*"] in Acts comes with the sense of "healing" or deliverance."

For example, when Peter says (Acts 4.9) that he is "being interrogated for a good work *done* for a sick man by which this man was restored to health ["*sotzo*"]," this is a good example of the typical use of "sotzo" for healing. So the key to understanding this passage is asking, "What are we being saved from?"

I suspect Charles Barrett, one of the best NT scholars of the twentieth century, is correct when he writes the following:

> The theological sense of ["*sotzo*"] can thus be understood only by asking from what theological distress or disability or danger...man needs to be delivered. The basic meaning is provided by Acts 2.40: those who are saved are saved from belonging to this perverse generation and from sharing its fate; they are no longer perverse, and they will not experience the punishment of perversity...Thus the primary meaning of salvation is detachment from the world of the unbelieving and disobedient and attachment to the true people of God of the last days, the church.[66]

Thus salvation, the church, and the name of Jesus are connected in an important way. But how? The connection between salvation and the name of Jesus seems to come from baptism which is how one typically enters the church and receives the Spirit in Acts.

When Peter claims that there is "no other name under heaven given by men by which one must be saved," he is simply saying that Jesus is the one who brings salvation. He's not specifically trying to explain *how* salvation happens. Luke is telling his readers how Christians appropriate that salvation which is by coming into the church by being baptized.[67] There is no other name that brings salvation because, in Acts at least, it is into the name of the Lord Jesus that one is baptized.[68]

One of the things that is difficult for moderns to see, but is nevertheless critically important for reading Acts well is realizing that there is no concept of privatized and individualistic salvation in Acts. Salvation is always about joining a community (the church) and living a different kind of life in the context of that community. Duke's Kavin Rowe describes this very well:

> Against all spiritualizing tendencies, Luke narrates the salvation that attends the Christian mission as something that entails necessarily

the formation of a community, a public pattern of life that witnesses to the present dominion of the resurrected Lord of all. If, after the unavoidable impact of the Reformation, the Enlightenment and our contemporary consumerist culture, we have trouble grasping this point, we would do well to remember that the ancient pagans did not: the community of Jews and Gentiles gathered around a new pattern of life is the [basic] sociological presupposition.[69]

Notice that this does not at all negate the necessity of individual repentance and a genuine confession of faith, both of which would have been included as an integral part of any baptismal service when one came into the church. But it's the invocation of Jesus' name over the one being baptized that usually brings the Spirit upon a person and that enables that person to start leading the Christian life.

Unfortunately, in our day, the name of Jesus has become a swear word. This is an exceedingly odd appropriation of it. Jesus, who came to save his people from their sins, is now invoked as curse.

Like those who have come before us, we should resist the culture and reverence the name of Jesus. This does not mean adopting a holier-than-thou moralism. But if Jesus loved us enough to give up his unending bliss in the Godhead, took on human flesh in the Incarnation and shared our infirmities, the least we can do is to show his name some respect.

Questions for Reflection

1. How do you show respect for the name of Jesus? How do you deal with others who use Jesus' name in blasphemous ways?
2. Other religious traditions find the Christian claim that salvation is only in Christ to be very offensive. How should we interact with people who might think differently?
3. How do you make of the boldness of Peter in this passage? Are you comfortable speaking out about Jesus or is this too embarrassing to do? Why?

CHAPTER 9

GOD'S PROVIDENCE
Acts 4.23-31

Acts 4.23-31

> *Having been released from prison, Peter and John recount what happened with the healing of the beggar, and with their arrest and interrogation before the council. The community then turns to prayer, making use of Psalm 2 and Psalm 146. Of particular importance is the unity of the community, their commitment to prayer, and their belief that everything was unfolding according to God's plan. Instead of praying for their health and well-being, the community prays for boldness to proclaim the good news and to withstand the persecution that is sure to come. At the end, the ground starts shaking beneath them, an outward sign of the Holy Spirit's presence in their midst and a confirmation that their prayers have been heard.*

After Peter and John were released, they came to their own community and told them everything that the high priests and the elders had said to them. Now those who heard were of one mind, and they lifted up their voice to God and said, "O Sovereign Ruler ["despota"], you are the one who made heaven and earth, the sea and everything in them" (Ps 146.6). Our Father spoke through the Holy Spirit by the mouth of David, your servant, saying, "Why were the nations arrogant, and why did the peoples imagine vain things? The kings of the earth took their stand, and the rulers gathered together against the Lord and against his Anointed" (Ps 2.1-2).

For truly Herod and Pontius Pilate, together with the nations and the peoples of Israel, gathered together against your holy servant Jesus, whom you anointed, to do whatever your hand and your will foreordained ["proorizo"] to take place.

And now, Lord, pay attention to their threats and give to your servants all boldness to speak your word, while you stretch out your hand to heal and while signs and wonders come through the name of your holy servant Jesus." Having prayed, the place where they were gathered shook and they were all filled with the Holy Spirit and they were speaking the word of God with boldness.

Psalm 2.1-12

Psalm 2 was originally used for the coronation of Israel's kings. The king was "begotten" from God and thus became God's anointed.[70] However, Christian interpretation was different since it read the "anointed" as God's Messiah. The justification for this was that the Greek word for "anointed" was "Christos," found in the text of the Psalm itself in its Greek translation. Moreover, God himself alluded to elements of this Psalm at Jesus' baptism when he referred to Jesus as "my Son." Peter reads Psalm 2 as if it had been written all along to describe resistance to the work of the true King, Jesus.

Why were the nations arrogant, and why did the peoples imagine vain things? The kings of the earth took their stand and the rulers gathered together against the Lord and against his Anointed ["christou"], saying, "Let us break their bonds and let us cast off their yoke from us."

He who dwells in the heavens will laugh at them and the Lord will mock them. Then he will speak to them in his wrath and, in his fury, he will stir up trouble for them.

But I have been appointed king by him over Zion, his holy mountain, declaring the decree of the Lord. The Lord said to me, "You are my son, today I have begotten you." Ask of me and I will give the nations as your inheritance and the ends of the earth as your possession. You will shepherd them with an iron rod and like a potter's vessel you will dash them in pieces. And now, O kings, understand. Be instructed, all you Judges of the earth. Serve the Lord with fear and rejoice in him with trembling. Receive correction lest the Lord become angry and you depart from the righteous way, for his wrath is quickly kindled. Blessed are all who trust in him.

Psalm 146.1-7

Psalm 146 is the beginning of a cluster of hymns at the end of the Psalter that all start with the word "Halleluiah." It is a Psalm of praise that emphasizes God's "universal royal rule."[71] Peter alludes to this Psalm in today's Acts passage when he calls on God as "the one who made heaven and earth, the sea and everything in them." He's hinting that we should be aware of the whole Psalm in today's Acts reading because, at its conclusion, the psalmist praises God as the one who "sets prisoners free." This is precisely what happened to Peter and John. The Psalm also exhorts its hearers not to put trust in "rulers" or "sons of men" who "cannot save," reflective of their experience with the leaders of the council.[72]

Halleluiah, by Aggaeus and Zacharias

Praise the Lord, O my soul. I will praise the Lord with my life. I will sing to my God while I have being. Do not put your trust in rulers or in the sons of men who cannot save. His spirit will go forth and will return to his land; on that day, all their thoughts will perish.

Blessed is the one whose helper is the God of Jacob, whose hope is in the Lord his God, the one who made heaven and earth, the sea and everything in them, who guards truth forever, who executes judgment on wrongdoers, who gives food to the hungry; the Lord sets prisoners free.

Comment

Peter and John return from their ordeal, recount what happened and then the community turns to prayer. The prayer begins by referring to God as "*despota*," the Greek word from which we get our English term "despot." In first-century Greek, this word carried none of the negative connotations it would later take on.[73] It is usually employed in Greek literature in connection with God's being the Creator of the universe.

This connection to the creative activity of God is important because there is a consistent theme concerning God's providence in this passage. We see this most clearly in Peter's employment of the term "*proorizo*," which I have translated as "foreordained." This, in part, is where "predestination" comes from. Peter is saying God has determined beforehand what is taking place in this story.

Do we really have to believe that God determines history ahead of time, including our salvation? Does this leave any room for human free choice? Did God predetermine something like the Holocaust?

One of the hardest things to keep straight in Christian theology is the paradox between God's sovereignty and human free choice. Both concepts are clearly taught in the pages of the Bible. To us, however, they seem like contradictory ideas. Yet it certainly seems like we make free choices. Are we just deluded?

Even if they seem contradictory, both free choice and God's sovereignty have to be true. The question is how. One of the more ingenious responses to this dilemma came from the Spanish Jesuit Luis de Molina in the seventeenth century. Molina came up with the idea of "middle knowledge" as a way of finding a solution between these seemingly contradictory concepts.

Molina's idea was that God not only has knowledge of how things will turn out in the end, but also how things could have turned out. This is called middle knowledge. According to Molina, God perfectly orders the universe to get the end results he wants. Since God foresees all things, he knows all the choices, good or bad, that we will make in our lifetimes. He then orders all these foreseen choices to get a desired end. This has the effect of protecting our ability to make free choices, but preserving God's sovereignty as well.

Molinism has many critics. It is certainly not the last word on what is inherently a mystery, but it does suggest that free choice and predestination are not necessarily at odds.

This is important to keep in mind because one of the major themes of the book of Acts is that the spread of the gospel is unstoppable because God is behind it. We are starting to see resistance come from the temple leadership. But God is still getting the result he wants. Theologian Jaroslav Pelikan puts it as follows:

> Here in Acts and in the rest of Scripture, the mysterious relation between such 'persuading' and the converting initiative of the Holy Spirit is neither psychologized nor resolved by recourse to a deterministic or fatalistic theory that would negate the role of free will, but left to stand as a mystery.[74]

Peter underscores this message with his use of Psalm 2. Peter is doing something pretty unique here. His reading of the Psalm employs a classic rabbinic technique called "Pesher." The word Pesher means "interpretation" or "solution."[75] In a Pesher interpretation, a rabbi would take a text and read it theologically in light of the community he was teaching.

Peter does not read Psalm 2 in its original, historical context. Rather, he interprets it in light of the situation he has just experienced. The arrogant "nations" represented the Romans, particularly the Roman soldiers at the cross, and the Praetorian Guard that tortured Jesus.

Peter also implicates the "peoples," who imagine vain things. In part, these are the Jewish people who had encouraged Jesus' crucifixion and refused his release. Peter reads the "rulers" as those who had just detained him. The "kings" are Herod and Pontius Pilate under whose authority Jesus was crucified. They put to death the Christ, the Anointed One, the Messiah. Peter reads Psalm 2 not only in light of his own situation, but also in light of what happened at Calvary.

Further, Peter invokes Psalm 146, not only because God is the "one who made heaven and the earth," but also because the psalmist proclaims "release for the prisoners" (Ps 146.7).[76] The Psalm even admonishes its listeners not to put their trust in "rulers" or "sons of men" who can't save (Ps 146.3).

This is a very important aspect of our story to understand. Christians do not read the OT the same way as others do. We read it the way Jesus taught us to read it – as a text fulfilled in Christ. This is one reason why I have you reading OT texts alongside the book of Acts in this guide. I'm consciously trying to get you to read the Bible in a thoroughly Christian way, the way it's been done for centuries.

At the conclusion of the passage in Acts, God shakes the earth.[77] In the Hebrew text of Psalm 2, it describes the "nations" as being in "tumult" or in "commotion." Thus, once again, Peter finds in the Psalms the language to describe what is happening.

Perhaps it's John Chrysostom, the greatest preacher of the fourth century, who said it best in a homily on this passage: "The place was shaken and that made [the apostles] all the more unshaken."[78] In the power of the Spirit, nothing can hold back the good news.

Questions for Reflection

1. **Does God pre-determine history? If so, to what extent? If not, what is God's role in the world?**
2. **Do you employ the Psalms in your prayer life? How do you do it? If you don't, how could you make this a regular practice?**
3. **What do you make of the prayer in this passage when the apostles pray not for their own health or safety or prosperity, but for boldness to proclaim the gospel? Do you pray this way?**

CHAPTER 10

FINANCIAL FRAUD
Acts 4.32-5.11

Acts 4.32-5.11

> *The idyllic unity of the early church is shattered because*
> *of financial fraud. Luke sets up a contrast between pious*
> *Barnabas who willingly submits to the authority of the apos-*
> *tles, and greedy Ananias and Sapphira who do so only out-*
> *wardly, being more concerned with appearances. When their*
> *fraud is discovered, the result of their betrayal is death.*

Now the group of those who believed was of one heart and one soul. No one considered his possessions to be his own, but everything was held in common. With great power, the apostles were bearing witness to the resurrection of the Lord Jesus, and great grace was on all of them. For there was no one needy among them, since as many as were the owners of fields or houses were selling them, bringing the proceeds from what was sold, and laying them at the feet of the apostles. And the proceeds were distributed to each, to the degree that each one had need.

Then Joseph, who was nicknamed Barnabas by the apostles (which when translated means "son of encouragement"), a Levite, a native of Cyprus, owned a field. After selling it, he brought the proceeds and laid them at the feet of the apostles.

But there was a man named Ananias, with his wife Sapphira, who sold a piece of property. And he held back ["nosphitzo"] for himself part of the proceeds with his wife's knowledge. Bringing the proceeds he laid some at the feet of the apostles. Then Peter said, "Ananias, why has Satan filled your heart, to lie against the Holy Spirit by holding back ["nosphitzo"] some of the proceeds from the land? Before it was sold was it not under your authority, and doesn't it continue to be? Why have you contrived this matter in your heart? You have not lied to men, but to God." As soon as Ananias heard these words, he fell down and breathed his last. And great fear came on all who heard about it. Then the young men wrapped Ananias up in a shroud, brought him out, and buried him.

Then, after an interval of three hours, his wife entered, not knowing what had happened. And Peter said to her, "Tell me, whether you and Ananias sold the property for such and such a price." And she said, "Yes, such and such." And Peter said to her, "Why have you agreed together ["symphoneo"] to test the Spirit of the Lord? Look, the feet of those who buried your husband are at the door and they will carry you out." Just then, she fell at Peter's feet and breathed her last. And great fear came over the whole church ["ekklesia"] as well as everyone who heard about these things.

Joshua 7.1-11, 19-26

After entering the Promised Land and winning a resounding victory against the hardened military fortification at Jericho, Joshua and his army lose a battle against the weakly-defended town of Ai. The problem is not Israel's military might but avarice. God had commanded the spoil from Jericho to be put under the ban, or set aside for God. Yet, Achan took some of the sacred spoils and hid them in his tent. This financial fraud is a direct affront to the holiness of the community and must be ruthlessly stamped out. Despite Achan's straightforward confession, the community puts him to death for embezzling from the things of God.

But the sons of Israel trespassed ["nosphitzo"] with a grave sin, as they embezzled some of the things under the ban. Achan...son of Zara, from the tribe of Judah, took from the things under the ban, and the anger of Lord was provoked against the sons of Israel.

Now Joshua sent men to Ai, which is across from Bethel, saying, "Spy out Ai." So the men went up and spied out Ai. Then they reported to Joshua and said to him, "Don't make all the people go up, but just two-thousand to three-thousand men will do; let them put the city under siege. But don't bring up all the people since they are few in number." So about three-thousand men went up. But after they did, the men fled from the presence of the men of Ai. And the men of Ai slew about thirty-six men and pursued the rest out of the gate and crushed them at the steep hill. So the heart of the people was terrified and became like water.

Then Joshua tore his garment and fell to the ground on his face before the Lord until evening; both Joshua and the elders of Israel heaped dust on their heads. So Joshua said, "I pray, O Lord, why have you made your servant bring this people across the Jordan? To hand them over to the Amorites in order to destroy us? If we had stayed behind, we could have settled beside the Jordan. What shall I say since Israel has become vulnerable to the enemy? So when the Canaanites and all the inhabitants of the land surrounding us hear about it, they'll wipe us off the land. And what will your great name do?" Then the Lord said to Joshua, "Arise, why have you fallen on your face? The people have sinned and have broken the covenant I established with them, having stolen from the things under the ban, and have taken them into their possession."

Then Joshua said to Achan, "Give glory to the God of Israel today and make your confession, and tell me what you have done. Do not hide it from me." Achan answered Joshua and said, "Truly I have sinned before the God of Israel, this is what I did: I saw among the plunder from Jericho a beautiful embroidered mantle, 200 drachma of silver and a bar of gold, fifty drachma in weight. After planning, I took them and then hid them in my tent; the silver was hidden beneath them." Then Joshua sent messengers and they ran to the tent in the camp and found these things hidden in the tent; the silver was underneath them.

So Joshua took Achan, son of Zara, and led him to the valley of Achor with his sons and his daughters, his cattle, his donkeys, and his sheep, along with his tent and all his possessions...Then Joshua said to Achan, "Why have you destroyed us? Now today may the Lord destroy you"! So all Israel stoned him and set up a giant heap of stones over him. Then the Lord ceased from his fierce anger.

1 Corinthians 5.9-13

Paul founded the church in Corinth, a wealthy economic center because of its seaport.[79] Yet, not long after Paul departed, problems developed in the community. They divided into doctrinal factions, were showing disregard for the poor, were abusing the sacraments, were acting immorally, and were suing each other. It is interesting to note that for Paul, greed, drunkenness, and dishonesty were as important as sexual sin.

I wrote to you in my previous letter not to associate with immoral people. I didn't at all mean the wicked of this world or the greedy or swindlers or idolaters, since then you would have to go out of the world. But now I write to you not to associate with one calling himself a brother who is immoral or greedy or an idolater or verbally abusive or a drunkard or a swindler – don't even eat together with someone like that. For what do I know about judging an outsider? Judge those who are inside the church. God will judge those outside. "Drive out the immoral person from among you" (Deut 17.7).

Comment

Difficulties abound in this passage from Acts. Let's focus on the most obvious one. Does God's punishment really fit the crime here? By our standards, few would last very long if God struck dead everyone who spoke a half-truth. So how should we make sense of this?

This is probably a good time to remind ourselves of Augustine's instructions on how to interpret the Bible. Augustine wrote the following in his handbook on interpretation called *On Christian Teaching:*

> So first of all we must point out the method for discovering if an expression is proper or figurative. And here, quite simply, is the one and only method: anything in the divine writings that cannot be referred either to good, honest morals or to the truth of the faith, you must know is said figuratively...So then anything we read of in the scriptures as coming from the person of God or his saints that sounds harsh and almost savage in deed and word is...to be treated as metaphorical.'[80]

Augustine's point is that all valid interpretation of the Bible should lead one toward greater love of God and neighbor. So Augustine would probably advise us to look for a figurative meaning underlying this story because of the justice issues it surfaces. This doesn't mean the literal story is untrue; it simply means its main importance for us is beneath the surface level of the text.

Joseph Fitzmyer, one of the most respected interpreters of the book of Acts, lists at least six different figurative directions we could take when interpreting this story:

1. The story is explaining why there is death in the early church when Jesus's resurrection was supposed to have destroyed death;
2. Luke is recounting the Essenes, authors of the Dead Sea Scrolls, who required all goods to be held in common;
3. This is a story about obstacles to the gospel which the Spirit will break through;
4. This is a story about Original Sin which would always plague the Christian community;
5. This is a story about excommunication;
6. This is a story framed in terms of Achan found in Joshua 7.[81]

Because of space constraints, we only have room to develop one of these avenues of interpretation. So, briefly, let's focus on the relationship between Achan and our story in Acts.

There are many similarities between the story of Achan and this one. They both employ the rare Greek word "*nosphitzo*," usually employed in the context of financial fraud. Both involve a member of the community acting dishonestly in something dedicated to God. Both stories take place at the start of communities (in Joshua's case, the community has just come into the Promised Land). Both see sin as potentially threatening the purity of the community. The penalty in both stories is death, which seems a bit draconian.

But there are differences as well. Achan was put to death because he violated a vow he had taken. Ananias and Sapphira took no such vow. It's easy to see the effect on the community in Joshua's case because they lost a battle, but where was the direct harm to the community in Luke's rendering? Finally, God kills Ananias and Sapphira, while the community kills Achan. Thus the stories don't perfectly match up. Yet Luke probably has Achan in mind as he's writing.

This will not be the last time in Acts that we will encounter Luke's unique vantage point on money and possessions. For Luke, how we handle money directly correlates to the health of our spiritual lives. Thus figuring out whether we are supposed to understand this story "literally" or not, probably shouldn't be our main concern.

Yet Luke really wants us to see is that fraud and a lack of generosity are key threats to the unity of the young Christian community. For Luke, only those who freely share their possessions and genuinely care about the needs of those around them are fit for life in God's kingdom.

Reflection Questions

1. **Luke seems to highlight the importance of generosity and transparency in the church. Do you see generosity and transparency as a key components of your spiritual life?**

2. How do you respond to the justice issues raised in this story? Was God wrong to take Ananias and Sapphira's lives? How about Achan?

3. The penalties for violating a sworn duty in our society are harsh (at least on paper). For example, lawyers have a duty to maintain confidentiality. Money managers and corporate executives have a fiduciary duty. Doctors have a duty to "do no harm." What should the penalties be like for violating a religious duty?

CHAPTER 11

RELICS AND CIVIL DISOBEDIENCE
Acts 5.12-42

Acts 5.12-42

The good news continues to be an unstoppable force in Jerusalem, as more miraculous events take place through the disciples. Peter is so filled with the power of the Spirit, his mere shadow heals — an important illustration of the power of relics. An angel breaks the apostles out of prison, enabling them to keep preaching. Even the council, under the wise guidance of the elder-statesman Gamaliel, decides not to hold them. Despite being beaten, the apostles express joy at bearing shame, an unthinkable turn of events in a society where shame was to be avoided at all costs.

Through the hands of the apostles, many signs and wonders took place among the people. The apostles were all gathered together in the covered walkway at Solomon's Portico. None of the rest of the unbelievers dared to associate with them there, but the people held them in high regard. And the apostles were adding more and more to those who believed in the Lord, a large number of both men and women. The people were even carrying the sick into the street and putting them on cots and mattresses so that when Peter would pass by, his shadow might overshadow some of them. And a crowd of people from all the towns surrounding Jerusalem was gathered together, bringing the sick and those tormented by unclean spirits. They were all being healed.

Then the high priest arose and all those with him, who were of the party of the Sadducees, were filled with zeal. And they laid their hands on the apostles and put them into the public jail. But an angel of the Lord came at night and opened the doors of the prison and brought them out, saying, "Go, stand in the temple, and tell the people all the words of this life." Hearing it, they went into the temple at daybreak and started teaching.

But when the high priest and those with him came, they convened the council with all the elders of the sons of Israel and they sent to the prison to summon them. But when the officers went, they didn't find the apostles in the prison. So the officers returned and explained, "We found the prison securely locked and the prison guards standing at the door, but when we opened it, we found no one inside." Now when the captain of the temple guard and the high priests heard these words, they were flabbergasted, wondering what could have happened. But, just then, someone came in and reported to them that the men who were formerly in the prison were standing in the temple, teaching the people! So the captain went out with the officers, and brought the apostles without violence since they were afraid of being stoned by the people.

Having brought the apostles, the officers stood them in the midst of the council. Then the high priest said, "We sternly instructed you not to teach in this name and now look, you have filled Jerusalem with your teaching. You intend to bring this man's blood on us!" But Peter and the apostles answered and said, "We have to obey God rather than men. The God of our Fathers raised up Jesus whom you killed, hanging him on a tree (Deut 21.23). God has exalted him at his right hand as ruler and savior to give repentance to Israel and the forgiveness of sins. And we are witnesses to these things, and so is the Holy Spirit, whom God has given to those who obey him."

Now when they heard this, they were enraged and wanted to execute them. But a member of the council, a Pharisee named Gamaliel, a teacher of the law held in high esteem by the people, stood up and ordered the men to be taken outside for a short time. Then he said to the officers, "Fellow Israelites, be careful what you are about to do with these men. For, not that long ago, Theudas arose, claiming to be somebody, with whom a number of men — about four thousand — joined. He was killed and all those following him were scattered and it came to nothing. After this, Judas, the Galilean, arose in the days of the census and he drew people to him. He died and all who were following him were similarly scattered. So, now, I say to you, keep away from these men and let them go, since if this plan or this movement comes from men, it will amount to nothing. But if it comes from God, you won't be able to stop them, or even worse, you'll be found to be fighting against God."

So they summoned the apostles, and after flogging them, the officers released them, giving orders not to speak in the name of Jesus. Then the apostles left the council rejoicing that they were counted worthy to bear shame on behalf of the name. And day after day in the temple and from house to house, they did not cease teaching and proclaiming the good news that Jesus was the Messiah.

Deuteronomy 21.22-23

This text, cited frequently in the NT to describe Jesus' crucifixion, became an important crux for the Christian understanding of the atonement. The atonement is how the work of Jesus on the cross reconciles sinful humanity to God. [82] Peter alludes to this text in today's Acts passage using the metaphor of a tree to describe the crucifixion.

Now if there is sin in anyone, and the death sentence is pronounced, and he is put to death, then you shall hang him on a tree. His body shall not be left upon the tree, but you shall bury him that day, since everyone who hangs on a tree is cursed by God. So you must not defile the land which the Lord your God is giving to you as an inheritance.

Comment

For the past week or so, there has been a key underlying question to our story: "Who's in charge," the council or the apostles?[83] It's becoming ever clearer, as the people continue to hold the apostles in high regard and as the number of those who trust in Jesus continues to grow, there is a tectonic shift going on within the leadership. The temple authorities are helpless to stem its tide. The promised ingathering of the people of God is taking place right before us.

In a sense, our story today is fairly straight-forward. The persistent theme that the good news cannot be stopped because the Spirit is behind it is plain to see. But how do we explain the healing power of Peter's shadow?

Let's start by realizing that how we think about the human body is quite a bit different than the ancients. As Princeton's Peter Brown puts it, the body "was embedded in a cosmic matrix in ways that made its perception of itself profoundly unlike our own…[energy] was seen as pulsing, through the body, of the same energies as kept the stars alive."[84] To those in the first century, the body was not a machine, it was part of a great chain of being, kept "alive" by spiritual forces. Being embodied was a critical part of experiencing God.

Ephraim Radner describes this well:

> It is also the case that only as creatures do we know God. Every other aspect of our knowing and every other aspect of our peculiar *religious* knowing, derives from and is shaped by this one fact – that we are creatures. Creaturely knowing means that God stands to us as the one who gives the very possibility of knowing anything… to say that we are creatures is, therefore, a quintessentially *religious* claim…we cannot claim to be creatures apart from some fundamentally religious understanding of reality.[85]

In other words, embodiment is a key part of our ability to relate to God.

This is one reason why relics became such a big deal for early Christians. Examples of the healing power of relics can be found throughout the history of the church. For example, when St. Ambrose found the bones of the martyrs Gervasius and Protasius (today recognized as the Patron Saints of Milan) during a particularly contentious fight with the Arian Empress Justina, a blind man received his sight when he touched the bones.[86] This is similar to what happened with the bones of Elisha: "As a man was being buried, a marauding band was seen, and the man was cast into the grave of Elisha; and as soon as the man touched the bones of Elisha, he revived and stood on his feet" (2 Ki 13.21).

Relics tell us something important about our spiritual lives. In a limited sense, all Christians are saints, since Christians are indwelt with the Spirit of God. Yet the Saints officially recognized by the church are those who are so fully united with Christ that the power of the Spirit flows through them. Peter is a perfect example of this. His mere shadow can heal, and this fact attracts quite a bit of attention. If the goal of our spiritual lives is union with Christ, then imitating the Saints is an important part of how we should live.

But really, aren't these just apocryphal stories from long ago? Believe it or not well-documented healings are still taking place not far from us. For example, in his 2016 book *History and Presence* (published by Harvard Press), Richard Orsi recounts many instances of how God has made himself present in ordinary things with extraordinary results. For years, Orsi has been trying to get his colleagues in the field of Religious Studies to take the supernatural seriously, arguing that it's a legitimate avenue for serious research.

In the book, Orsi describes the shrine at Chimayo in New Mexico.[87] Scores of healings have occurred at the Shrine when people take some of the dirt, which is blessed daily by a group of priests, and ingest it. There is nothing special about the dirt (the priests and monks who maintain it readily admit that they periodically dump regular dirt into the shrine), but somehow this sacred place mediates the power of God for some. To the uninitiated, this is just silly. How can ingesting dirt help anything? Yet the scores of pictures on the walls of people who have been healed after visiting the Shrine tell a powerful story of the reality of God's healing presence there.

Luke also raises the issue of civil disobedience in today's reading. Was it wrong for Peter to defy the religious authorities in this scene? If not, when can we properly exercise disobedience to authority?

Peter sums up his view well: "We have to obey God rather than men." Yet this is only marginally helpful. We can probably all cite examples of those who thought they were doing God's will but who ended up causing great pain for others. The wars of religion after the Reformation are a great example.

How do we know when resistance to authority is required? In his famous *Letter from a Birmingham Jail*, written primarily as a call to action for moderate white clergy sitting on the sidelines, Martin Luther King invoked Thomas Aquinas and natural law as his standard. As King put it:

> How does one determine whether a law is just or unjust? A just law is a man-made code that squares with the moral law or the law of God. An unjust law is a code that is out of harmony with the moral law. To put it in terms of St. Thomas Aquinas: An unjust law is a human law that is not rooted in eternal law and natural law. Any law that uplifts human personality is just. Any law that degrades human personality is unjust. [88]

Of course, it would be anachronistic to judge Peter's actions by Thomas Aquinas, much less Martin Luther King. But the timeless principle embedded in Dr. King's letter is that we know our laws are just when they help us to be better people and to leave others in peace. King is also drawing on a long theological tradition, stretching back to the church father Irenaeus that says there is real harm done to the perpetrator of an evil act, not just the victim. [89]

Surely, the treatment of Peter and the apostles did not accord with this ideal. If Jesus really was risen from the dead, then they had a responsibility to proclaim it. Predictably, violence and hatred fell on the apostles from the religious leaders whose power and status were threatened by the good news.

But notice their response. Peter and the apostles didn't return violence with more violence. They rejoiced for the opportunity to suffer on behalf of the Christ who had suffered for them. May we be found similarly faithful.

Questions for Reflection:

1. How do you sense God's "real" presence in your life? Has it ever felt like Gamaliel did in today's reading when the things you have to deal with in life come out of the blue and can't be stopped?

2. To you, what does it mean to obey God rather than men? What are the things we must not do in order to call ourselves Christian? What are the things we must do?

3. What do you make of the healing power of relics? Are these just pious legends or is there something "real" about a Saint's on-going participation with God?

CHAPTER 12

CHURCH GOVERNANCE
Acts 6.1-7.1

Acts 6.1-7.1

> *More difficulties come to the formerly idyllic community. Now
> there are administrative problems. With the growth of the church,
> the twelve apostles cannot do all of the work. So more leaders are
> commissioned with the specific charge to administrate the distribu-
> tion of food and other supplies to widows. Even though the word
> "deacon" is not specifically used as an office in this text, this story
> is usually understood to be instituting the three-fold structure of
> ordained ministry found in bishops, presbyters, and deacons.*

Now, in those days, when the disciples were growing in number, the
Greek-speaking Jews ["the Hellenists"] were grumbling against the
Aramaic-speaking Jews ["the Hebrews"] since their widows were being
slighted in the daily service ["diakonia"]. And the twelve summoned the
whole group of disciples and said, "It's not good for us to neglect the
word of God in order to do table service. Brethren, examine and select
["episkeptomai"] seven men from among you, of good repute, full of
the Spirit and wisdom, whom we will appoint for this necessary work.
And we will devote ourselves to prayer and to the ministry ["diakonia"]
of the word."

Now this idea pleased the whole group. They chose Stephen, a man
full of faith and the Holy Spirit, as well as Philip, Prochorus, Nicanor,

Timon, Parmenas, and Nicolas, a Gentile convert from Antioch. They stood them before the apostles, and having prayed, they laid hands on them. Now the word of God kept spreading, and the number of the disciples in Jerusalem greatly increased. Even a large group of priests became obedient to the faith.

Now Stephen, full of grace and power, was doing great wonders and signs among the people. But some from the assembly called "the Freedmen," in particular the Cyrenians, the Alexandrians, and some from Cilicia and Asia, stood and argued with Stephen. They weren't skilled enough to resist his wisdom and the Spirit with which he was speaking, so they underhandedly instigated men to testify that he had spoken blasphemous words against Moses and against God. They also incited the people, the elders, and the scribes.

Approaching him, they seized Stephen and brought him to the council. They called false witnesses who said, "This man does not cease speaking words against the holy temple and the law, for we have heard him say, 'Jesus the Nazarene will destroy this place and he will change the customs Moses handed down to us.'" All sitting in the council looked intently at Stephen and saw his face become like the face of an angel. And the high priest said, "Are these things true?"

Exodus 34.29-35

As Moses comes down the mountain with the law, his face shines with the glory of God. This glory is so disturbing for the people that Moses is forced to wear a veil over his face — otherwise the people can't stand to be near him. Moses' shining face is emblematic of the transformation not only of Moses, but of all Israel that would occur if they lived by Torah.[90] When, in today's Acts passage, Stephen's face "shines like an angel" after properly interpreting the law, we should see him as a prophet, like Moses, imbued with the glory of God — something the sinners in the council can't stand to be around.

Later, Moses went down from the mountain (the two tablets were in Moses' hands). As he went down from the mountain, Moses did not know that the appearance of his facial skin shone when he spoke with God. Then when Aaron and all the elders of Israel saw Moses that the appearance of his facial skin shone, they were afraid to approach him. But Moses summoned them. So Aaron, with all the leaders of the Assembly, turned toward him, and Moses started speaking with them.

After these things, all the sons of Israel came to him and he instructed them in all things, as much as the Lord had spoken to him on Mt. Sinai. Now, when he ceased speaking to them, he put a veil over his face. So whenever Moses would go before the Lord to speak to him, he would take off the veil until he left. Then he went to speak to all the sons of Israel, whatever the Lord had commanded him. And the sons of Israel saw the face of Moses shining, and he placed a veil over his face, until he would go in to speak with God.

Numbers 27.18-20, 22-23

When Moses dies, there is a need to transfer leadership to Joshua. Central to this transfer is the laying on of hands, by which Moses passes on not only his authority, but his "glory" as well, signifying the unique filling of the Spirit that would enable Joshua to accomplish his new leadership role. The laying on of hands, plus the confirming charge from the high priest, establishes the continuity of leadership.[91] Thus when the apostles appoint other ministers in Acts, they are following an OT practice by laying hands on the person to equip him for ministry.

And the Lord spoke to Moses, saying, "Take for yourself Joshua, son of Nun, a man who has the Spirit within him. Lay your hands on him and stand him before Eleazar the priest and command him before the whole congregation, and give him a charge before them. You shall place your glory on him so that the sons of Israel might listen to him."

And Moses did just as the Lord commanded him. He took Joshua, stood him before Eleazar, the priest and before the whole assembly. He laid his hands on him, and Moses appointed Joshua, just as the Lord had commanded him.

Comment

In addition to the biblical testimony in the early chapters of Acts, we have very early evidence from the church fathers that the early church was organizing itself using the distinct offices of bishop, priest, and deacon. As just one example: Irenaeus, Bishop of Lyon in the second century, writes the following:

> Wherefore it is incumbent to obey the presbyters who are in the church, those who, as I have shown, possess the succession from the apostles; those who, together with the succession of the Episcopate [bishops], have received the certain gift of truth, according to the good pleasure of the Father.[92]

The reason the church needed an administrative structure was because of its success. It had grown by leaps and bounds. With thousands of baptisms needing to be performed, twelve apostles could no longer take care of everything that needed to be done. So, quite sensibly, the church started to delegate its tasks. Some were set apart to serve the poor and to ensure that administrative snafus didn't occur.

In today's story, the Greek-speaking Jews became upset because their widows were being slighted. This doesn't appear to have been intentional; it reflected instead mediocre administrative practices. Collectors would go around and gather money and goods from the people at their houses every Friday morning.[93] Later in the day, they would distribute the goods to those who had need.

Thus many read today's passage as the place where this three-fold ministry structure gets started. Peter and the apostles "ordained" successors to ensure that essential needs were met. Notice that the apostles did not impose their will on the people. They essentially asked the community to nominate people of good repute who were filled with the Spirit. The apostles then "anointed" these nominees by laying hands on them, just as Moses had done with his successor Joshua.

But there's a problem. It's not wrong to see the basic outline of an administrative structure forming in this passage, but one is hard pressed to see how this is Luke's primary concern. All throughout Acts we will encounter slightly different leadership models. There was probably no single way to do things so early in the church's history.

As a result we should be careful not to press the evidence too hard. Luke doesn't seem to care as much about the details of how the church administrates itself, as he does that these people, set apart for the work of ministry, were given an anointing to spread Jesus' teachings. Luke is trying to say that there needs to be a means of appointing leaders *as successors to* the apostles.

This helps to explain one of the problems in this passage. Stephen and Philip, the only ones of the seven who we're told anything about it, spent no time (as far as we can tell) serving widows. They spend all their time preaching and doing signs and wonders.[94]

Luke's main focus is on how apostolic authority is handed down. Thus the Christian movement is not completely dependent upon the apostles as it grows. The apostles' successors are called to reflect the apostolic witness to Jesus' teaching.

And this is one of the essential things to notice. When Stephen is hauled before the council, we should pay particular attention to how they accuse him. Notice what they say:

- Stephen has blasphemed against Moses and God.
- He's created unrest among the people.
- He's threatened to tear down the temple.
- He's saying the Mosaic Law is no longer valid (presumably since Jesus came and fulfilled it).
- He's changed the customs handed down from the patriarchs and prophets.

These should all sound familiar because they are all things Jesus did that infuriated the same council. This is Luke's way of saying that these new leaders were continuing in the teaching of Jesus and the apostles. They've been given a share of a special charism to carry out prophetic tasks in imitation of Christ.

While not the main thrust of today's Acts reading, as Episcopalians, we nevertheless think that this three-fold structure of bishop, priest, and deacon is essential. Our administrative structure is in our name, after all. The name Episcopal comes from the Greek word *"Episcopos,"* which means "bishop." In our polity, one finds a church where there is a bishop. Thus our administrative structure defines how we do church.

We have good evidence that this structure goes all the way back to apostolic times. But we must not get so enamored with an administrative structure that we lose sight of the most important thing: We are all called to reflect Jesus' teaching in our lives.

Where do we find this teaching? Primarily in the Bible, through the writings of the apostles, prophets and Patriarchs who bore witness to God. But we also get it from the oral tradition, handed down through the church Fathers, who gives us the earliest evidence of how the scriptures were understood. In the early Fathers there is an unmistakable testimony to the use of bishop, priests, and deacons in the church.

In fact, after Stephen is hauled before the council, notice that they treat him like Jesus, directing false testimony at him. But Stephen's face starts shining like an angel. Stephen was so united with Jesus through the Spirit, that he was reflecting God's glory on his face, just as Moses did when he came down the mountain.

The glory on Stephen's face is the glory that had been absent from the temple ever since Jews were sent into Exile. And Jesus is the one who restored it after his ascension, when he sent the Spirit to enable the early church's mission. As the Spirit comes upon the apostles and subsequently on other believers, God's glory is again in the temple — that is, in the hearts of his people.

God's glory is in us as well if we'll just reflect it. But this all starts with taking seriously the apostolic witness to Jesus' teaching and the spreading of the good news to a country and culture that so desperately needs to hear it.

Questions for Reflection

1. To what extent do you consider yourself in full-time ministry, serving God wherever you are?
2. Have you ever been falsely accused of something (as Stephen was in today's Acts reading)? What did this feel like? Would you be willing to be falsely accused or publicly ridiculed to uphold the teachings of Jesus and the apostles?
3. What difference do ordained clergy make in your life? How have they helped you or hurt you in the past? Have you ever thanked them for their service?

CHAPTER 13

REVISIONIST HISTORY
Acts 7.2-8.1a

This is, by far, the longest passage we will read in the study. Because
of its importance, this speech deserves to be read in one sitting.
Stephen reviews the history of Israel and shows how significant
resistance came to the work of God at every turn. The temple lead-
ers were taking their place in a long line of resisters, acting like the
brothers who sold Joseph into slavery, like Pharaoh, who persecuted
Israel, and like the Jews who troubled Moses. By killing Jesus, trou-
bling the disciples, and now Stephen, the temple leaders were resist-
ing the work of God. What had been a somewhat muted response
to the apostles now breaks out into violence as the temple leader-
ship puts Stephen to death. In dying, Stephen perfectly models Jesus
in both word and deed, becoming the first Christian martyr.

Acts 7.2-8.1a
Abraham

Then Stephen responded, "Men, brothers, and fathers, listen. The God of glory appeared to our father Abraham while he was in Mesopotamia, before he moved to Haran. Then God said to him, 'Go forth from your land and from your relatives, and come to the land that I will show you' (Gen 12.1).

Then going forth from the land of the Chaldeans, he dwelt in Haran. Further, after his father died, God resettled him in this land that you now inhabit. But God did not give Abraham an inheritance in it, not even a foot's length, but he promised to give it to him as a possession and to his offspring after him, even though he had no child. Thus God was saying that 'his offspring were to be resident aliens in a foreign land' and that 'they would enslave and mistreat them for four-hundred years' (Gen 15.13). God also said, 'I will judge the nation they will serve as slaves,' and after these things, they will come out (Gen 15.14) and 'worship me in this place' (Ex 3.12). So God gave Abraham the covenant of circumcision and later he bore Isaac. He circumcised him on the eighth day. Later Isaac also bore Jacob and Jacob bore the twelve Patriarchs.

Joseph

Then the Patriarchs, being jealous against Joseph, sold him as a slave to the Egyptians. But God was with him. And he rescued him from all his afflictions and gave him favor and wisdom before Pharaoh, king of Egypt. Pharaoh appointed Joseph governor over Egypt and over his whole household. But a famine came over the whole land of Egypt and Canaan, causing great affliction, and our forefathers could not find food. But, when Jacob heard that there was grain in Egypt, he sent our forefathers the first time. And during the second time, Joseph became reacquainted with his brothers and Joseph's family became known before Pharaoh. And Joseph sent them to summon Jacob, his father, and all his relatives, seventy-five souls in all. So Jacob came down to Egypt and he expired there, so too, our forefathers. And their remains were moved to Shechem where they were laid in the tomb that Abraham bought for a certain amount of silver from the sons of Hamor in Shechem (Gen 49.29-32).

Moses

But as the time drew near for the promises that God had assured Abraham, the people grew and filled Egypt until a different king who had not known Joseph arose over Egypt (Ex 1.8). Acting deceitfully toward our race, he mistreated our forefathers, ordering their infants to be exposed so they were not kept alive. In that time Moses was born and he was beautiful before God. For three months he was brought up in the house of his father. Then, being exposed, the daughter of Pharaoh raised him as her own son. So Moses was educated in all the wisdom of the Egyptians and became mighty in word and deed.

Reaching the age of forty, it came into his heart to visit his brothers, the sons of Israel. When he saw someone being mistreated, he defended him, executing vengeance on the oppressor and slaying the Egyptian. He figured his brethren would understand since God had given deliverance to them through his hands. But they did not understand. The next day he saw them fighting and he tried to reconcile them to peace, saying, 'Men, you're brothers, why are you mistreating each other?' And the one mistreating his neighbor pushed him aside, saying, 'Who appointed you ruler and judge over us? You don't want to slay me the way you slew the Egyptian yesterday, do you' (Ex 2.14)? So Moses fled at this word and was a resident alien in the land of Midian, where he bore two sons.

Now, after forty years, an angel appeared to Moses in the desert at Mt. Sinai in the flame of the burning bush (Ex 3.2). When Moses saw it, he was amazed at the sight. As he was contemplating it, the voice of the Lord came: 'I am the God of your Forefathers, the God of Abraham and Isaac and Jacob' (Ex 3.6). So Moses began trembling and did not dare to peer at it. Then the Lord said to him, 'Take off the sandals from your feet, since the place on which you're standing is holy ground (Ex 3.5). I have certainly seen the oppression of my people by the Egyptians and I have heard their groaning and I have come down to rescue them (Ex 3.7-8). Now, come, I am sending you to Egypt' (Ex 3.10).

This very Moses they had disowned, saying, 'Who appointed you ruler and judge' (Ex 2.14)? Therefore, by the hand of the angel, God sent a ruler and redeemer, who appeared to him at the Burning Bush. Thus, having done wonders and signs in the land of Egypt and at the Red Sea and in the wilderness for forty years, Moses brought the Israelites out from Egypt. This same Moses is the one who said to the sons of Israel, 'God will raise up for you a prophet out of your brethren like me' (Deut 18.15). This is the one who was in the assembly in the desert with the angel, who spoke to him at Mt. Sinai and with our forefathers. He's the one who received the living oracles to give to you.

Our forefathers were not willing to obey him, but they rejected him and turned their hearts toward Egypt, saying to Aaron, 'Make for us gods that will go on before us (Ex 32.1), for this Moses who led us out from the land of Egypt, we don't know what's happened to him' (Ex 32.23). So they manufactured a calf in those days and brought a sacrifice to the idol and they began celebrating at the works of their hands. But God turned away from them and handed them over to worship the stars of the sky just as it was written in the Book of the Prophets:

> You didn't bring me sacrifices and offerings
> During the 40 years in the desert, did you, O house of Israel?
> But you adopted the tent of Moloch,
> And the star of the god Saturn (Raphan),
> The images you made to worship;
> But I will resettle you beyond Babylon (Amos 5.25-27).

David/Solomon

Our forefathers had the Tent of Testimony in the desert since God commanded Moses to construct it according to the model that he had seen. Our forefathers went into the Promised Land with Joshua and in turn took possession of the nations that God drove out from before our forefathers until the days of David. David found favor before God and he inquired about finding a dwelling place for the God of Jacob. So Solomon constructed a house for him, but the Most High does not dwell in a man-made house, just as the prophet says:

Heaven is my throne,
And the earth is my footstool,
What sort of house will you construct for me, says the Lord?
Or what is the place where I might find rest?
Did not my hand make all things (Isa 66.1-2)?

Conclusion

You stiff-necked and stubborn of hearts and ears, you are always resisting the Holy Spirit just as your forefathers did! Which of the prophets did your Forefathers not persecute? They killed those who announced beforehand the coming of the Righteous One, whose traitors and murderers you have now become! You received the law from the decrees of angels, but you did not keep them."

After hearing these things, they were cut to the heart and gnashed their teeth at him. But Stephen was filled with the Holy Spirit, and staring intently into heaven, he saw the glory of God and saw Jesus standing at the right hand of God. And he said, "Look, I see the heavens opening and the Son of Man standing at the right hand of God'! Then, crying out with a loud voice, they stopped their hearts and rushed together right at him. They took him outside the city and started stoning him.

The disciples of the Jews laid their garments at the feet of a young man named Saul. While they were stoning Stephen, he cried out and said, "Lord, Jesus, receive my spirit!" And taking a knee, Stephen cried out with a loud voice, "Lord, do not hold this sin against them!" Having said these things, he fell asleep. Now, Saul was in complete agreement with Stephen's killing.

Comment

This is the climactic scene in the first part of Acts.[95] We will revisit Jerusalem, but it will never again be the focus in Acts. The good news must go forward. It won't stay behind in Jerusalem.

Stephen, with a great rhetorical flourish, shows how the people of Israel had always resisted the work of the patriarchs and prophets. Stephen's interpretive move is to place the current religious leadership directly in this line of resistance. By killing Jesus and by persecuting the apostles, they were in the way of the work of God.[96] At the end, Stephen was proved correct when, in a fit of mob violence, the Jewish leaders stoned him to death — something the Jews were expressly forbidden from doing under Roman law (John 18.31).[97]

The point that Luke keeps making in this passage is that God is not confined to a building. Abraham was called before the temple even existed. Joseph experienced God while in Egypt. Moses met God at the Burning Bush in the Arabian Desert. Christians can separate from the temple where God's glory no longer resides. Thus Judaism and Christianity start their slow process of breaking apart right here.

In fact, Luke reads the OT Patriarchs as if they were just like Jesus. Joseph is rejected by his kinsmen, is arrested, but winds up as the savior of his people because God is with him (sound familiar?). Moreover, Moses finds God in the desert, demonstrating that the Holy Land is wherever God's presence makes itself manifest.[98] Moses is then sent to his people with a message of salvation ("let my people go!"). He does signs and wonders, and leads the people out of slavery. Yet the people turn from him to worship idols. Moses ministered like Jesus, yet the people resisted him, too.

But notice what Stephen does at the end. He looks up and gazes at the risen Christ enthroned in the heavens. Stephen sees the glory of God and will do almost anything, even allowing himself to be stoned to death, to join with him. I like how the eighth-century church father John of Damascus puts it:

> Now, we say that Christ sat in His body at the right hand of the Father, yet we do not mean a physical right hand of the Father... What we call the right hand of the Father is the glory and honor of the Godhead in which the Son of God existed as God...He sits

corporeally with His flesh glorified together with Him, for He and His flesh are adored together with one adoration by all creation.[99]

In Stephen's martyrdom, he adores (literally, worships) the risen Christ. This is a very useful metaphor for what we should be doing in our own way. We shouldn't court martyrdom, but we must court the presence of God in our lives. Quiet adoration is often the great missing piece in our spiritual lives.

We are living through a time of ideologically-driven strife that seems to have no solution and no end in sight. How then shall we live? Perhaps we should start by looking up instead of down. Instead of taking our cues from the mob, let's take our cues from the glorified Christ in heaven. Instead of reacting to the latest news event, let's divert our attention to what is wholesome and leads to unity.

If what you're pursuing doesn't result in greater love of God or neighbor, if it doesn't feed your soul, if it doesn't engender peace in your heart, then *fugeddaboudit*! We're supposed to be like Jesus, not everyone else. What do you need to do to rid yourself of the anxiety, the anger or just the plain drudgery of daily life? Looking up before you look down sure helps.

Yes, we need our activists. Yes, we need to stand against injustice when we see it. But those who have done so most effectively as Christians have usually started with quietness and prayer. If we start with simple, quiet adoration and then go about our work, we just might find ourselves able to live in peace while everyone around us is at war.

Questions for Reflection

1. **When was the last time you turned off your phone, radio, or TV and fasted from the relentless news cycle? Doing so is usually a help to your spiritual life because it might demonstrate how reliant you have become on filling your life with noise.**

2. **How can you cultivate a greater sense of adoration in your life? How might more regular participation in the Eucharist play a role in this?**

3. Many Christians around the world are being persecuted and martyred for their faith right now. How might you learn about their struggles and take time to pray for them? Could you find a way to make this a more regular part of your spiritual life?

PART II: INTERMEZZO: PETER AND SAUL

INTERMEZZO: PETER AND SAUL

I have titled this second part of our story an "Intermezzo." In music, an "intermezzo" is a piece which connects major sections of a longer composition. I think something similar is going on here in Acts. We are starting the transition from focusing almost exclusively on Peter to a greater focus on Paul.

This does not mean, however, that this section is somehow unimportant. Some of the best-known stories in all of Acts are included in this second section, including Paul's conversion along the Damascus road, the story of Philip and the Ethiopian Eunuch, who is converted after being taught how to read Isaiah in light of Christ, the story of Simon the Magician, who tries to purchase the power of the Holy Spirit, thus inventing the sin of "Simony," and the spread of the good news to the Gentiles through Peter and the Roman centurion, Cornelius.

Yet this section is defined by the various transitions that we will encounter. Besides the transition from Peter to Paul, there is a transition from an almost exclusive focus on the Jews to a focus on the Gentiles. There is a geographic transition from a focus on Jerusalem alone to a focus on the surrounding regions of Judea and Samaria. There is also a transition from the initial task of preaching the good news to the longer-term task of building churches and implementing an administrative structure to govern them.

One thing becomes clear as we go through this section — God seems to have special care for those who have been excluded or marginalized. As we will see, the Ethiopian Eunuch was cut off from the temple, and the Roman Cornelius was an outsider to Jewish life as a Gentile, as were the Samaritans, one of the most detested people-groups in the whole region because of their lack of ethnic purity. In fact, one of the most important themes to emerge will be in the centrality of table fellowship between Jews and Gentiles, as the custom of separation over food regulations is abrogated. In the church, there will be no division between Jew and Gentile —all are to be welcomed.

The turn to the Gentiles is one of the most important events in all of Acts. In the beginning, the church was in danger of just becoming a small, localized, ethnically-focused sect within Judaism. Yet God had something else in mind. The status of Christianity as a universal religion that encompasses all peoples and nations gets its start here and is confirmed later in our story. As we will see, it was always God's intention to include both Jews and Gentiles in his redemptive plan as partakers of the covenant promises that he originally made with Abraham.

We will also observe many things in this section that will resonate with our Anglican tradition. For example, we will observe the importance of "catholicity" in this section. The parishes that start popping up everywhere think of themselves not as autonomous local bodies, but as being part of something bigger. We will observe the earliest evidence for the work of bishops, as Peter plays a key role in bringing the Spirit not only to the Samaritans, but to the Gentiles as well.

Finally, we will observe how important baptism is as a sacrament in this section. In Acts, baptism is not just a simple ritual done to mark one's conversion; it carries power with it, the power to bring the Spirit into someone's life, the power to wipe away sins, and the power to incorporate someone into the church. This leads to some of the earliest evidence for why Episcopalians separate baptism and confirmation, a practice initially born out of necessity, but that finds its warrant here. Above all, we will see God's promise continues to unfold that the good news must spread to all peoples and nations.

JERUSALEM AND THE SPREAD OF THE GOSPEL
INTO JUDEA AND SAMARIA (ACTS 1–11)

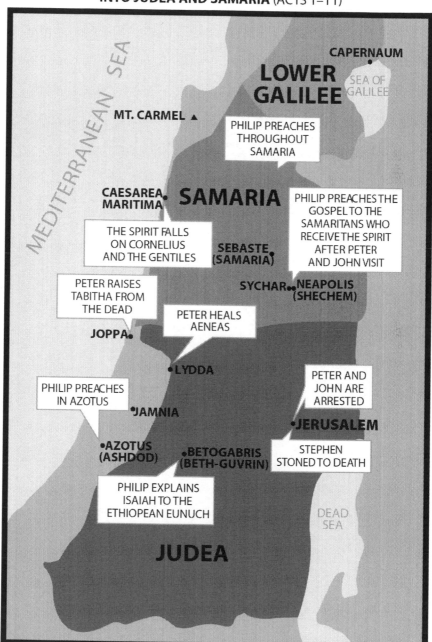

CHAPTER 14

SIMONY
Acts 8.1b-25

Acts 8.1b-25

> *We now transition to the second part of our story as the good news spreads outside Jerusalem. When persecution arises against the church from the authorities, most are forced to leave town. The spread of the good news comes not through any prescient plan of the apostles, but in response to suffering. Philip, one of those set apart for service in Acts 6, went to Samaria. At the time, Samaria was a detested region. Its inhabitants were of mixed-race and of lower social status. These were the "untouchables" of their day and yet, in sharp contrast to the temple leadership, they embraced the good news enthusiastically and many were baptized. However, Simon, a magician, tried to commercialize the gift of the Holy Spirit, a request that draws a sharp rebuke from Peter.*

Now on [the day of Stephen's death], there arose a great persecution against the church in Jerusalem, and everyone except the apostles was scattered to the districts of Judea and Samaria. Some God-fearing men buried Stephen, and they mourned for him greatly. But Saul was ravaging the church, going from house to house, dragging away men and women and delivering them to the prison.

So those who were scattered went about proclaiming the good news. Now Philip went down to a city of Samaria and preached Christ to them. And the crowds were paying attention with one mind to what was said by Philip when they heard and saw the signs that he performed. For many who had unclean spirits were shrieking with a loud voice, and many who were disabled and crippled were being healed. And there was much joy in that city.

But there was a man named Simon who, for some time, had been practicing magic in the city and amazing the people of Samaria, claiming to be someone great. Everyone, from the least to the great, was paying attention to him, saying, "This is the divine force that is called 'the Great Power.'" They stayed devoted to him for a long time because his magic had astounded them. So when they believed in the good news that Philip was proclaiming about the kingdom of God and the name of Jesus Christ, both men and women were being baptized. In fact, Simon himself believed and after he was baptized, he attached himself to Philip. When Simon saw the great signs and wonders, he was astounded.

When the apostles in Jerusalem heard that the Samaritans had been given the word of God, they sent Peter and John to them. They came down and prayed for them to receive the Holy Spirit (for the Spirit had not yet come on any of them who had believed, as they had only been baptized in the name of the Lord Jesus). But when Peter and John laid their hands on them, they received the Holy Spirit.

Then, when Simon saw that the Spirit was given through the laying on of the apostles' hands, he offered money to them, saying "Give me this authority too so if I should lay my hands on anyone, he might receive the Holy Spirit." But Peter said to him, "May your silver perish with you, since you thought that you could procure the gift of God with money. You have no portion or share in this ministry since your heart is not right before God. Therefore repent of this wickedness of yours and pray to the Lord that perhaps the intent of your heart might be forgiven. For I see the gall of bitterness and unjust bonds ["susdesmon"] are with you." Simon responded, "Pray for me to the Lord so that none of what you have said may come upon me."

Then after they had borne witness and had spoken the word of the Lord, Peter and John started back for Jerusalem and they kept proclaiming the good news in the many towns of Samaria.

Exodus 7.8-12

> *This text begins the so-called plague narratives in Exodus where God turns Egypt's rivers into blood, sickens their livestock, and sends frogs, lice, flies, locusts, boils, hail and darkness, all to get Pharaoh to relent and to let God's people go. Many have seen these plagues as a kind of anti-creation event.[1] God reverses the good things of creation to punish the Egyptians for their recalcitrance. This text is related to Acts primarily through the magicians. In both stories, signs and wonders play a prominent role, as does magic. Yet, in both, the power of God is far greater than the magicians' capacities.*

Then the Lord spoke to Moses and Aaron, saying "Now if Pharaoh should speak to you, saying, 'Give us a sign or a wonder,' then you shall tell Aaron your brother, 'Take the staff and throw it upon the ground before Pharaoh and before his attendants, and it will become a serpent.'" So Moses went in together with Aaron before Pharaoh and his attendants, and they did so, just as the Lord had commanded them. So Aaron cast down the staff before Pharaoh and before his attendants and it became a serpent.

Then Pharaoh summoned the wise men of Egypt and also the magicians, and they did likewise, so too did the enchanters of Egypt with their magic. They threw down their staffs and they became serpents, but Aaron's staff swallowed up their staffs. And Pharaoh's heart was hardened. He did not listen to them, just as the Lord had said.

Isaiah 58.5-9

> *This passage envisions what a redeemed community looks like. If Israel has been restored back to the land, and their enemies have been thrown down, they will be truly free when they extend that freedom to others by pursuing justice and righteousness.[2] Peter alludes to this passage in Acts when he accuses Simon the Magician of being under an*

"unjust bond." Simon must not pursue his own notoriety and finan-
cial gain, but must use the gift of the Spirit for the benefit of others.

I have not chosen this day as a fast, nor such a day for a person to humble his soul, nor should you bend your neck as a ring, nor should you
lay sackcloth or ashes under you. Do not call such a fast acceptable. This
isn't the kind of fast I have chosen, is it, says the Lord? Instead, release
every unjust bond ["susdesmon"]; untie the knots of hard bargains; proclaim forgiveness to the oppressed, and tear up every unjust contract.
Break bread with the hungry; bring the homeless poor into your house.
If you see someone naked, clothe him; and do not neglect your own family. Then your light will break through as the morning and your healing
will quickly come forth; your righteousness will advance before you,
and the glory of God will cover you. Then you will cry out and God will
listen to you. While you're still speaking God will say, "Look, I'm here."

Comment

Today's Acts passage has been very important in Christian theology, and
its details have been endlessly debated. The first issue this passage raises is
about baptism. As Episcopalians, we usually separate baptism and confirmation. The practice of confirmation developed early in the church's history
because bishops simply could not be at every baptism. Not wanting to delay
baptism for those who had come to faith, the church developed the practice
of baptizing new believers regularly, but reserving confirmation for when
the bishop was present. Thus confirmation was born out of necessity.

The primary biblical justification for separating baptism and confirmation, however, comes from this passage. Notice that those who Philip
baptized in Samaria did not receive the Spirit until Peter, the leader of the
apostles had laid his hands on them. Thus confirmation came to be seen as a
kind of baptism of the Spirit. One problem with this is that it ignores what
happens at Saul's baptism which is coming up in Acts 9. There, Ananias,
who was not an apostle, lays hands on Paul, and he receives the Spirit. This

inconvenient deviation in the pattern is rarely discussed. This reminds us that we should be wary of building a whole sacramental theology based on a single passage in Acts. Luke is rarely thinking systematically as he writes this story. Pressing the details too hard often leads to headaches.

Another way of looking at this passage comes from Pentecostals who insist that water baptism is more about conversion (which may or may not be genuine, like we observe with Simon). By contrast, a second baptism of the Spirit involves an anointing of the Holy Spirit during which one speaks in tongues, as a visible confirmation that one's conversion is genuine. According to many Pentecostals, without speaking in tongues, one cannot ever be really sure one is in the family of God. There are some major problems with this understanding, most obviously, because it appears to exclude anyone who has not had this experience.

Yet the Samaritans likely didn't receive the Spirit right away, not because anything Philip did was somehow deficient, but because the leader of the church, Peter, was needed to confirm the spread of the good news into a different people group.[3] We will see this pattern hold with some consistency throughout Acts. When the gospel goes to a completely new place or people group, speaking in tongues as well as signs and wonders often accompany it. The presence of an apostle then brings and confirms the presence of the Spirit. It doesn't always happen like this, but it is the usual pattern in Acts.

Thus it's not wrong to have confirmations (the same problem of the bishop's availability still holds in our day), but we should probably see the reception of the Spirit as normatively flowing directly from conversion and baptism, which is the pattern we observed after Peter's first sermon in Acts 2. The usual pattern is that one makes a confession of faith, is baptized, and receives the Spirit along with the forgiveness of sins.

A second issue in this passage surrounds Simon the Magician. Simon gives us the term for the sin called "Simony." Simony is the buying and selling of clerical offices. In the Late Middle Ages, the practice of buying ecclesiastical office was so widespread that it rightly became a major complaint of the early Reformers, most memorably in Martin Luther's Ninety-Five Theses.

What is especially interesting about Simon is that he appears to convert and is baptized. So how is that Simon, following the normative pattern discussed above, misses out on the Spirit? I tend to agree with ancient interpreters who were quite sure that Simon was not redeemed.

It appears that Simon does not receive the Spirit because his faith was not genuine. This causes a problem for those who see God's grace as a kind of "irresistible" force that overwhelms us. What we observe with Simon is something quite different. Simon's conversion is not real because his confession of faith is not genuine. God's grace always has to be received with genuine faith. Or, as Thomas Aquinas memorably puts it, "Grace does not destroy nature but perfects it."[4]

In other words, we can resist God's gracious invitations because of our ability to make free choices. Although some Christians deny this idea, many in the early church would have had no problem with it. For example, Irenaeus, the greatest theologian of the second century, wrote the following:

> God made man a free agent from the beginning, possessing his own power, even as he does his own soul, to obey the behests of God voluntarily and not by compulsion of God. There is no coercion with God, but a good will [towards us] is present with Him continually."[5]

In short, grace is there to help us, not compel us. God is more like a lover who woos us than like a tyrant who coerces us.

The practical implication is that we can deny our baptismal vows and, sadly, some do. It simply will not do to claim that we've been "saved" and yet have our lives consistently contradict this testimony. God's offer of grace may be universal and free, but Simon shows that it is also possible to resist it.

Questions for Reflection:

1. **In what ways have you seen God's grace at work in your life? Have there been times when you resisted God? What was that like?**

2. What do you make of the presence of signs and wonders in Acts? In our story, they seem to come as a way of confirming a new outpouring of the Spirit. Do you know anyone who has experienced such things in our day?

3. Clerical offices aren't sold so much in our day, but media exposure is. What do you make of people who make religion into a marketable product to be sold? What are the pros and cons of doing so?

CHAPTER 15

THE ETHIOPIAN EUNUCH
Acts 8.26-40

Acts 8.26-40

> *Philip proclaims the good news from the OT. The key question in this text — "Is he speaking about himself or another?" — is central to a Christian understanding of the OT. Luke demonstrates that early apostolic teaching was centered on Jesus as the interpretative key for the whole Bible. Once again, we see our normative framework for conversion play out: the Ethiopian Eunuch believes, is baptized for the remission of sins, and receives the Spirit. He then goes on his way rejoicing.*

Then an angel of the Lord spoke to Philip, saying, "Arise and go south on the road going down from Jerusalem to Gaza" (this is a desert road). So Philip arose and went. Now there was an Ethiopian man, a eunuch, an official of Candice, Queen of Ethiopia, in charge of her treasury, who had come to worship in Jerusalem. As he was returning home, he was sitting on his chariot and reading Isaiah the prophet.

Then the Spirit said to Philip, "Go and join this chariot." So, running over, Philip overheard him reading the prophet Isaiah and said, "Do you understand what you're reading?" The man responded, "How can I unless someone guides me?" He then invited Philip to come up and sit with him. Now the section of Scripture that he was reading was this:

Like a sheep led to slaughter,
And like a lamb mute before its shearers,
He did not open his mouth.
In humiliation, justice was taken from him.
Who will tell his generation?
Since his life was taken up from the earth (Isa 53.7-8).

Answering, the Eunuch said to Philip, "Please tell me, is the prophet speaking about himself or about someone else?" So Philip opened his mouth and began to tell him the good news about Jesus from this passage.

Now, as they were going along the road, they came upon some water and the Eunuch said, "Look, water! What prevents me from being baptized?" So he ordered the chariot to stop and both got down into the water and Philip baptized him.

Then, when they came up from the water, the Holy Spirit snatched Philip away and the Eunuch did not see him anymore and he went on his way rejoicing. But Philip was found in Azotus. He went about, proclaiming the good news to all the cities until he came to Caesarea.

Isa 52.13–53.12

Many consider this text, quoted in Acts, to be the most important prophetic section of the Hebrew Bible because its imagery remarkably anticipates Jesus' passion, resurrection, and ascension. However, there is on-going disagreement between Christians and Jews about its interpretation. Early Jewish interpretation read it in light of a coming Messiah, but by the Middle Ages, the rabbis interpreted it as a prophecy for the nation of Israel as a whole.[6] Christians have read this passage as telling the essential story of the gospel because its details only seem to make sense in light of Jesus' resurrection and ascension. If the syntax of the text seems rough, this is because the underlying Hebrew is very difficult to decipher at points. The Septuagint translators were clearly struggling as they rendered it.

Look, my servant will gain understanding. He will be exalted and will be greatly glorified. As many as were astonished at you, so shall your appearance and your glory be held in no esteem by men. Many nations will be amazed at him, and kings will shut up their mouths since those to whom no report was given will see; and those who have not heard will understand.

Lord, who has believed our report? And to whom has the arm of the Lord been revealed? We brought a report of him as a child, as a root in a thirsty land. He had neither form nor glory. We saw him, and he had no lovely appearance, but his appearance was ignoble and inferior to all men. He was a man of suffering and acquainted with sickness since he was rejected, dishonored, and held in no esteem.

He bears our sins and undergoes torment for us, and we didn't regard him. We saw him in distress, in misfortune, and in suffering. And yet he was wounded because of our iniquities and was made sick because of our sins, the chastisement of our peace is upon him, and by his wounds we are healed.

All we like sheep have wandered off, everyone has wandered his own way, but the Lord handed him over for our sins. And he, despite his affliction, did not open his mouth. In humiliation, justice was taken from him, and who will tell his generation since his life was taken up from the earth. Because of the iniquities of my people, he was led to death.

So what shall I give the wicked in exchange for his grave and the rich in exchange for his death, since he did no wrong, nor was any deceit found in his mouth? The Lord also wants to cleanse his wounds. If you make an offering for sins, your soul will see a long-lived seed, since the Lord wants to take away the travail of his soul to show him light and to form understanding, to vindicate the one who serves many well, and to bear their sins. Therefore, he will inherit the many and will divide the spoils of the strong because his soul was handed over to death, and he was accounted with the transgressors. But he bore the sins of many and was handed over for their sins.

Zephaniah 2.4; 3.9-13

> *Given the references to Gaza, Ethiopia, Azotus, the midday hour, and the restoration of God's people, some think Luke frames Philip's encounter with the Ethiopian Eunuch as the fulfillment of the promise in this passage.[7] In particular, Zephaniah looks forward to the ingathering of his people where the confusion of languages at Babel would be reversed, and the scattered peoples from as far away as Ethiopia would be restored.[8]*

Therefore, Gaza will be plundered and Ascalon will be destroyed, and Azotus will be driven out at noon day and Accaron will be rooted out... for I will change the language for her generation that they all may call on the name of the Lord to serve him under a single yoke. From the borders of the rivers of Ethiopia, I will receive my sacrifices. In that day, you will by no means be disgraced because of all your pursuits, wherein you transgressed against me, for I will remove from you your contemptable hubris and you will no longer magnify yourselves on my holy mountain. I will leave behind a meek and humble people, and they will fear the name of the Lord. The remnant of Israel will do no iniquity nor speak vanities, neither shall a deceitful tongue be found in their mouths, since they shall graze and come to rest, and there will be none to frighten them.

Comment

Philip has just come from a great ministry success, as the good news was introduced into Samaria and scores of people were baptized. But God instructs him to leave the crowds and seek out a single person, an Ethiopian

Eunuch. A Eunuch was typically a castrated male who had responsibility for the king's harem.[9] In this case, he's in charge of the Ethiopian treasury and works for the Queen.[10]

His castrated state would have prevented this man from entering the temple. As the OT law put it, "No one who has been emasculated by crushing or cutting may enter the assembly of the Lord" (Deut 23.1, NIV). Thus, once again, we encounter someone who was formerly excluded, but who is now sought out. This is becoming a familiar pattern, as it happened to the apostles themselves, to the crippled man Peter healed, and to the people of Samaria. Jesus' mission to preach the good news to those who are marginalized continues unabated through the early church (Isa 61.1).

Another interesting detail is that Philip is told to depart at noontime. Very few would have traveled at this hour because it was so hot. Yet we have no record of protest or complaint. Philip was simply available to be called into action. Philip travels down to Gaza, which is the last place to get water before the desert begins on the road down to Egypt.[11]

The Eunuch is on his way to Ethiopia, which is probably not the modern-day Ethiopia, but was a region just south of Egypt, known as Cush.[12] The original hearers of this story might have heard this as like being from "Timbuktu." It was the end of the world as far as they were concerned. And this is the point – the good news has to go to the "ends of the earth."

When Philip encounters the Eunuch, he finds him reading Isaiah out loud, which was the typical way of reading in the ancient world. But the Eunuch has his own Isaiah scroll, which tells us he's very wealthy. It was exceedingly rare for anyone to have a private copy of the scriptures because it had to be reproduced by hand and was very expensive. Yet economic status does not preclude one from the good news. One's willingness to embrace the message is what matters. The Eunuch had "ears to hear."

Of particular interest in the quoted Isaiah passage is the last line: the suffering servant was "taken up" from the earth. There had to be meaning beyond just the original, historical context of the passage. What suffering servant was ever "taken up" from the earth? Although this was almost certainly read originally as someone's death, early Christians saw this as inarguable evidence that Isaiah foresaw the resurrection and ascension of Jesus. Thus, within the text of Isa 53 was the contents of the good news itself.

This passage demonstrates once again that Christians read the OT in a unique way. Those who argue for a reading of the Bible limited to the "original historical context" may be suggesting something not particularly Christian. This difference is a major reason why some academic readings of the Bible and the church's interpretations diverge. We are sometimes following different interpretive methods.

However, the injustice that fell on Jesus, the suffering servant par excellence, and his ultimate vindication were all right there in the OT for those who would read with the eyes of faith in light of Christ. Either this was a remarkable set of coincidences or it was there by divine design. Christians have always argued for the latter.

The Eunuch may have been rich, but he was still on the outside looking in. Excluded from the temple, he was humiliated. But through Philip, he's baptized. Let's never get too enamored with big crowds, slick marketing campaigns or ministry "success." Listening for the leading of the Spirit and seeking out a single lost soul rejected by others is what Philip does. It should be what we're doing as well.

Questions for Reflection

1. **What prevents you from being more active in Evangelism? Sharing the good news is as simple as telling the story of how God has been at work in your life. In what ways can you do this in your own life with your friends and neighbors?**
2. **What does it mean that God cared enough to take Philip away from the crowds to focus on one person? Who is that one person in your life who is marginalized and rejected that you should be focusing on?**
3. **How available are you to be used by God? What could make you freer for ministry? What specific changes would you have to make?**

CHAPTER 16

BETTER CALL SAUL

Acts 9.1-19a

Acts 9.1-19a

> *The calling of Saul is one of the central stories in Acts; so impor-*
> *tant, in fact, that Luke narrates it three different times.[13] Although*
> *some just emphasize the conversion aspect of this story, Luke*
> *seems more focused on Saul's new calling. God's selects the person*
> *whom was most zealous in persecuting the early Christian church*
> *to carry the good news to the Gentiles. Jesus' appearance to Saul*
> *settles the reality of Christ's resurrection for him. As an eyewit-*
> *ness to the risen Christ, Saul becomes an apostle.[14] If Christ really*
> *is risen and ascended, the basic Christian story must be true.*

Then Saul, still breathing out threats and murder against the followers of the Lord, went to the high priest and asked for letters of introduction to the synagogues in Damascus so that if he found any of The
Way, either men or women, after binding them, he might bring them to
Jerusalem.

But while he was going along, as he approached Damascus, suddenly a light from heaven flashed brightly around him. He fell to the
earth and heard a voice saying, "Saul, Saul, why are you persecuting
me?" He responded, "Who are you, Lord?" And he said, "I am Jesus who
you are persecuting. But rise up and enter into the city. You will be told
what you must do."

Now the men who were accompanying him had been standing there, speechless, having heard the voice, but not seeing anyone. Then Saul arose from the ground, and though his eyes were open, he could see nothing. So leading him by the hand, they brought him to Damascus. And he was unable to see for three days. He ate and drank nothing.

Now there was a certain disciple in Damascus named Ananias. The Lord said to him in a vision, "Ananias!" And he said, "I'm here, Lord." The Lord said to him, "Rise up, go to the street called Straight and seek out at the house of Judas a man of Tarsus named Saul. Look, he's praying and in a vision, he has seen a man named Ananias come in and lay hands on him to restore his sight." Ananias responded, "Lord I have heard from many about this man, about all the terrible things he did to the saints in Jerusalem. And in Damascus he has authority from the high priest to arrest everyone who calls on your name." And the Lord said to him, "Go, since he is my chosen vessel to carry my name before the Gentiles as well as before the kings of the sons of Israel. For I will show him all the things that he must suffer for my name."

So Ananias went out and entered the house. After he had laid hands on him, he said, "Brother Saul, the Lord Jesus, who appeared to you on the way as you were coming here, sent me so that you might receive your sight and be filled with the Holy Spirit." And, just then, something like scales fell from his eyes, and he received his sight. And rising up, he was baptized. Then he took food and regained his strength.

Exodus 19.16-24

This is a classic example of a theophany, a visible manifestation of God. God appears on Mt. Sinai with great fireworks and summons Moses up the mountain before giving him the Ten Commandments.[15] Note that the holy place at the top of the mountain where God's presence resides is separated from the people. Approaching God is an awesome thing, reserved only for a few. Episcopalians symbolically

*represent this separation between the holy place and the people
through the altar rail, at which we kneel to receive the Eucharist.*

Then, on the third day, just before daybreak, there was thunder and lightning and a dark cloud on Mt. Sinai as well as the sound of a very loud trumpet. All the people in the camp trembled. Then Moses brought all the people out of the camp to meet with God, and they stood at the foot of the mountain. Now the whole mountain was wrapped in smoke because God had descended upon it in fire. The smoke arose like the smoke of a furnace, and all the people were exceedingly astonished. As the sound of the trumpet grew ever louder, Moses started speaking and God answered him with an audible voice. Then the Lord came down onto Mt. Sinai, at the peak of the mountain, and summoned Moses up to the summit of the mountain. And Moses went up.

Then God said to Moses, "Go down and warn the people not to approach God to gaze on him, lest many of them fall. Let the priests who draw near to the Lord sanctify themselves, lest the Lord depart from them." Moses said to God, "The people will not be able to ascend up Mt. Sinai because you solemnly charged us to set off boundaries for Mt. Sinai and to make it holy." Then the Lord said to him, "Go, descend and then come back up — you and Aaron with you. But let not the priests and the people force their way up to God, lest the Lord destroy some of them." So Moses went down to the people and told them these things.

Ezekiel 1.25-2.3

With its barely describable phenomena and flashing lights, Ezekiel's call to be a prophet is similar to Saul's. In particular, note its audible character. This is nothing less than a revelation of the glory of God.[16] Like Saul, Ezekiel is called to take an important message to a people cut off from God.

Then there was a voice from above the sky, over their heads, in appearance like a sapphire, with a throne upon it. And upon the likeness of the throne was something like the appearance of a man. And I saw something like the outward appearance of amber from the waist upward. And from the waist downward, I saw something like fire and light flickering about. The appearance of brightness all around was like a rainbow in a raincloud. This was the appearance of the likeness of the glory of the Lord.

Then I heard a loud voice and fell on my face. I heard a voice, saying, "Son of man, stand on your feet and I will speak with you." And the Spirit came to me and took me, lifted me up, and raised me on my feet. Then I heard him saying to me, "Son of man, I am sending you to the house of Israel to those embittered against me who have provoked me, both they and their fathers, until this day."

Comment

Many read Saul as having a "crisis" conversion experience in this passage. In this view, Saul simply cannot live with the inner contradictions in his life as a persecutor of innocent people, and thus he undergoes a powerful conversion understood in religious terms. Some, trying to explain away the supernatural parts of the story, have even suggested Saul had an epileptic seizure that might account for the lights and the temporary blindness.[17] These readings largely miss the mark because they refuse to take Saul's spiritual experience seriously.

Moreover, this story is less about conversion (as we will see throughout Acts, Saul never really stops being culturally Jewish), but is more about a new vocation and a new understanding of what it was to be right with God. [18] Vocation comes from the Latin word "*vocare*," which means "to call."[19] God calls Saul to a new relationship and ministry. Of course, this implies that an important change takes place. But those who make this episode all about conversion are sometimes reading their own experience back into the text.

We must also resist the urge to explain away the details of this story as some artifact of pre-modern times. Instead, we ought to take these details seriously and consider them as eyewitness testimony. Jesus really did appear to Paul and his life was never the same. In fact, we would also do well to consider conversion as something that happens daily, rather than as a one-time crisis event.

There were many stories of calling in the OT, especially among the prophets. But what is unique with Saul's is its demand for a complete change of life.[20] This is what Luke really seems to care about. Saul's turn directly impacts his vocation to take the good news to the Gentiles. A new and important section of our story is unfolding as we start to transition away from focusing on Peter.

Saul's story also stands in stark contrast to the history of American Protestantism. In the eighteenth century, during the so-called Second Great Awakening, evangelists fanned out across America preaching the gospel with great fervency. Since America had no official religion, anyone with a horse, a Bible, and some wherewithal could go and preach.

Since there were few doctrinal standards, what mattered was the size of the crowd one could draw. If an evangelist could "convert" large groups of people, this would bring credibility. The size of the crowd became the chief measure of the work of the Spirit.

Thus American popular religion was born. Emotionalism and crisis conversion became more important than catechesis, sacraments, or growth in godliness. The church itself played little to no role – one simply "made a decision" for Christ. Baptism was important, but not essential, as the church itself was simply the holding pen for those on their way to an incorporeal heaven. What one did on earth mattered little to nothing for salvation. It was important to be good and moral, of course, but one's works simply played no role in one's salvation.

One of the favorite tactics of these frontier evangelists was the "anxious seat." For those not so sure of the evangelists' apocalyptic message, they were invited to sit on the "anxious seat" until they made their decision. Peer pressure was thus harnessed for religious purposes and religion was reduced to emotion.

These tactics are still with us and in some ways continue to define American Protestantism. Many mistakenly look for the Spirit where the largest crowd gathers. Yet, for Saul, conversion led to a vocation of suffering and service to small fledgling groups of believers. His focus was on building the church, not relegating it to some irrelevant position. Moreover, he made no "decision for Christ;" rather, Christ seems to have chosen him.[21] Presumably, Saul could have resisted this call (he could have refused baptism or sent Ananias away). But, a lifetime of faithful piety made him receptive to the Spirit.

I want to be clear that in saying these things I am criticizing some characteristically American religious practices, but not the traditions themselves. Most American Protestant traditions have venerable histories and have done enormous good for their communities. This was never truer than in the nineteenth century when evangelicals were at the forefront of starting hospitals, giving service to the downtrodden, and starting missionary movements. The problem comes when we begin seeing the church as another consumerist commodity to be sold.

The fruit of true conversion — greater humility, a commitment to contemplative prayer, more radical generosity, and a desire for Christian service — appears over a lifetime of living and cooperating with the Spirit. This is not to say that conversion doesn't matter. Of course it does – the Christian life has to start before it grows.

But, traditionally, the church has understood this starting point to occur when one enters the church and receives the Spirit at baptism. The church is an essential part of conversion because the community must welcome and acknowledge those who have genuine faith.[22] We don't get to do this ourselves.

We should never forget that Jesus often distrusted crowds, but instead longed to be alone and pray. Worshipping together is essential, but truly knowing Christ also develops in solitude and quietness. The typical approach of American popular religion matches up quite uneasily with the call of Saul.

Questions for Reflection:

1. When do you remember taking responsibility for your faith? How would you describe the growth in your spiritual life over time? Are you different as a person than you were five years ago?

2. Saul has to be led into Damascus by the hand because he has been blinded, which carries great symbolism. How would you explain the meaning of that symbolism? Who are those in your life that are helping you with your struggles and in your walk with God?

3. How would you describe the vocation (the "calling") to which God has called you. Has this ever involved suffering? Does it bring you joy? If so, in what ways?

CHAPTER 17

SAUL'S NARROW ESCAPE

Acts 9.19b-31

Acts 9.19b-31

> *After regaining his strength, Saul wastes no time and starts boldly proclaiming Jesus, the very name he had come to Damascus to stamp out. No one quite knows what to do with this sudden turnabout. But, when the synagogue tries to kill him, Saul makes a narrow escape.[23]*
>
> *Saul is next found in Jerusalem where he submits to the church's leadership. After proclaiming Christ, the Greek-speaking Jews try to kill him, forcing Saul to make another narrow escape. Eventually Saul winds up in his hometown of Tarsus, which is in modern-day Turkey.*

Then it happened, after being in Damascus several days, Saul suddenly started proclaiming Jesus in the synagogues that he was the Son of God. Now those who heard him were all amazed and were saying, "Isn't this the one who ravaged those who called on this name in Jerusalem? Hadn't he come here to arrest them and to bring them to the high priests?" But more and more Saul was strengthened. He kept confounding the Jews who dwelt in Damascus, proving convincingly that Jesus was the Christ.

Now, after many days had passed, the Jews started plotting together to kill him. But their plot against Saul became known. The Jews were keeping watch at the gates day and night to destroy him. But Saul's disciples took him by night, lowering him down through an opening in the wall in a basket.

Then, coming to Jerusalem, Saul attempted to join the disciples, but they were all afraid of him, not believing that he was a disciple. But Barnabas took Saul and brought him to the apostles, and related to them, how on the road, Saul saw the Lord who had spoken to him, and how in Damascus, he had boldly proclaimed the name of Jesus. So Saul was openly associating with the apostles in Jerusalem, boldly proclaiming the name of the Lord. Saul was also speaking and debating with the Greek-speaking Jews (the Hellenists), but they started trying to kill him. So when the brethren recognized this, they brought Saul to Caesarea and sent him on to Tarsus. Now the church throughout the whole of Judea, Galilee, and Samaria had peace, and was being built up, walking in fear of the Lord, and being filled with the consolation of the Holy Spirit.

Joshua 2.1-15

Although the OT law expressly forbade any agreements with the indigenous people of the Promised Land (Deut 7.2-5), the spies in this passage draw on a central Jewish principle that the preservation of life is always the highest goal of the law.[24] Since dwellings were typically built into the city walls, Rahab lowers the spies down to safety from her home. The thematic analogue with Acts is plain — both characters find safety in unlikely places, and both stories emphasize the role that the marginalized play in carrying out God's will.

Then Joshua, son of Nun, sent two young men from Shittim to spy out the land, saying, "Go up and observe the land and Jericho." So the two young men went and entered into Jericho and into the house of a female prostitute whose name was Rahab. They lodged here.

Then the king of Jericho sent messengers who said to Rahab, "Bring out the men who have entered into your house tonight, since they have come to spy out the land." But Rahab had taken the men and hidden them. And she said to the messengers, "The men did come in to me, but while the gate was shut they left in darkness. I don't know where they've gone. Hunt for them over there and perhaps you'll find them." But Rahab had brought the spies onto the roof and had hidden them in the flax she had spread out on the roof. So the messengers pursued them on the road to the crossing of the Jordan, and the gate was shut.

Now, once their pursuers had left, but before the spies had gone to sleep, she went up to them on the roof and said, "I know the Lord has given the land to you, since fear of you has fallen on us. For we have heard that the Lord God dried up the Red Sea before you when you came out from the land of Egypt as well as all the things he did to the two kings of the Amorites, Sihon and Og, whom you destroyed on the other side of the Jordan. When we heard about it, our hearts were stunned and there was no longer any spirit left in us because of you, since your God is Lord over heaven above and earth below.

Now swear to me by the Lord God that since I have shown you mercy, that you also will show mercy to the house of my father. You must spare the house of my father and my mother, my brothers and all my household, everyone as many as belong to them. You must rescue my life from death." And the spies said, "Our lives for yours unto death." Then she said, "When the Lord has delivered the city to you, you must deal mercifully and truthfully with me." Then she lowered them down through an opening in the wall.

2 Corinthians 11.30-33

St. Paul is clearly referencing today's Acts story in this passage. Aretas IV, king of Damascus, was a Nabatean, a quasi-independent kingdom bordering Judah but under Roman jurisdiction.[25] Aretas had a stormy relationship with the Herods, since Herod Antipas had divorced Aretas' daughter to marry Herodias, who, in turn, had John the Baptist beheaded. In today's Acts passage, we discover that Aretas had a common interest with the Romans in quelling unrest.[26] *Thus Aretas, whose rule extended to Damascus, tried to put Saul to death, but failed.*

If I must boast, I will boast in the things that demonstrate my weaknesses. The God and Father of Jesus Christ, who is blessed forever, knows that I am not lying. In Damascus, the governor under King Aretas, guarded the city of Damascus to arrest me. But I was lowered down through an opening in the wall in a basket and fled from his hands.

Comment

One of the challenges in today's Acts passage is making sense of the different chronologies various authors record when recounting the events in our story. For example, when Paul describes this story in Galatians, he seems to employ a different chronology. There, Paul says he stayed in the Arabian Desert for three years before going up to Jerusalem (Gal 1.18). Paul also claims he only met with Peter in Jerusalem. In Luke's account in Acts, however, Paul goes straight to Jerusalem, without any mention of Arabia, and seems to meet with all the disciples after Barnabas intervenes, not just Peter. Who's right?

There are many elaborate attempts to harmonize these accounts. Most of them involve turning the phrase "after many days" (Acts 9.23) into three years and seeing Damascus as Saul's home base, not the Arabian Desert.[27] But these attempts at harmonization aren't very convincing. The problem is that it's hard to believe that the apostles in Jerusalem had not heard that Saul had turned to Christ three years after the fact. Were they really not aware that Saul had been baptized and was proclaiming the good news? If they had heard about it, why were the apostles still afraid of Saul when he showed up in Jerusalem three years later? Many scholars, rightly I think, prefer Paul's chronology in Galatians from his own hand rather than Luke's second-hand account in Acts. But we simply don't have enough information to resolve the apparent discrepancies. Put simply, the chronologies in Acts and Galatians simply don't fit together well.

I highlight these difficulties to emphasize an important point. It should be evident to us that some textual discrepancies exist in the Bible. Frankly, they're what one would expect from a story recounted decades after-the-fact by different authors for various purposes. But this need not overly concern us, even if we can't resolve all the problems with the evidence we have. One of the keys to reading the scriptures well is to take the Bible as it is, and approach it with faith.

Where did Saul get the understanding so that he could preach Christ boldly within days of his conversion? Some might argue he was "zapped" with revelation. This could be. After all, Saul had just met the risen Christ. But it seems more likely that Saul already had a pretty good idea of what the early Christians were teaching. After all, he had been present when Stephen walked through the OT and showed how Israel continuously resisted the work of God. It also doesn't stretch the imagination to think that Saul might have been present at the deliberations of the council in Jerusalem (Acts 4.13-22) when they discussed what to do with the disciples. Paul had undoubtedly heard what Peter and the other apostles were claiming. He just hadn't believed it until now.

Why the sudden change? Well, he had encountered Jesus. I really think it's that simple. If Jesus was raised from the dead, this at least makes the chief claims of Christianity probable. Of course, if Jesus wasn't raised from the dead, none of the Christian story can be true (1 Cor 15.14). But, if Saul really did see the risen Christ, the content of his proclamation would have fallen quickly into place for him.

But, what exactly fell into place? Saul, in an instant, would have come to realize that the OT had to be interpreted in light of the risen Christ. This is why he turned on a dime and suddenly started proclaiming Jesus as the Messiah. Given what he had seen, his turn was quite natural.

One of the great unsung heroes in the book of Acts is Barnabas. Barnabas is a nickname which means something like "Son of Encouragement." He certainly lives up to that moniker here. When the apostles are understandably afraid to meet with Saul, Barnabas sees clearly what is happening and intervenes. Almost everyone lauds Saul for his great preaching, but none of it would have happened without Barnabas. Notice here the subtle tie to today's Joshua reading. The apostles thought Saul was a spy. In both stories, it took someone outside the leadership structure to help the alleged spies escape to safety.

Few will ever be intellectually powerful enough and bold enough to preach the gospel like Saul does. Few will want to put their lives on the line like Saul does in almost every chapter of Acts. Yet the church needs more people like Barnabas, those who quietly work behind the scenes to make sure things get done. Servants like Barnabas don't care about getting the credit, but do care quite a bit that the good news is proclaimed. If you would rather die than give a public speech, perhaps consider being a Barnabas. To do so takes character and credibility, something built up over long periods of time. It also requires seeing the best, not the worst in people.[28] But, without people like Barnabas, the mission of the church never runs as smoothly.

Questions for Reflection:

1. **Saul ends up back in his hometown of Tarsus. What was your hometown like? Would you be eager to return there or have you been content to leave for good? What are the pros and cons of a society where mobility is so easy and where families are usually so spread out?**

2. **Would you identify more as a Barnabas or a Saul? Do you like to work behind the scenes or be out in front? Can you appreciate the necessity of both sets of gifts in the church?**

3. **The claim that there are contradictions "all over the Bible" is undoubtedly overblown. But what do you do when you come across something in the Bible that doesn't make sense? What is the role of the church (as opposed to something like the History Chanel) in helping you?**

CHAPTER 18

THE CHURCH CATHOLIC
Acts 9.31-43

Acts 9.31-43

> *We last encountered Peter as he was preaching throughout
> Samaria. Peter now makes his way north to Galilee, first to
> Lydda and then to the seacoast town of Joppa.[29] Acting a lot like
> Jesus, Peter continues his apostolic ministry by healing and rais-
> ing the dead. Thus the ministry of Jesus carries on in the apostles
> under the agency of the Holy Spirit. Of particular interest is
> the favorable descriptions of Tabitha, highlighting the leader-
> ship roles that women were taking in the early church.*

Now the church throughout the whole of Judea, Galilee, and Samaria
had peace, and was being built up, walking in fear of the Lord and
being filled with the consolation of the Holy Spirit. Then it happened
while Peter was traveling through various places, he also came down to
the saints dwelling in Lydda. And he found there a certain man named
Aeneas, who had been lying on a mat ["krabattos"] for eight years
because he was paralyzed. And Peter said to him, "Aeneas, Jesus Christ
heals you! Rise up and roll up your mat." And right away, Aeneas arose.
So all the inhabitants of Lydda and the Coastal Plain of Sharon saw him
and turned to the Lord.

Then, in Joppa, there was a certain female disciple named Tabitha,
which when translated means Dorcas. She was full or good works and

acts of charity. Now, it happened in those days that she became sick and died. Having washed her body, they placed her in the upper room. Now Lydda was near Joppa.

So when the disciples heard that Peter was there, they sent two men to him, exhorting him, "Don't delay to come to us." Then Peter arose and went together with them. When they arrived, they brought him to the upper room ["huperoon"]. Now all the widows were beside him weeping ["klaio"] and showing Peter the garments and other items Dorcas had made while she was with them.

After sending them all outside, Peter knelt down and prayed. Turning toward the body, he said, "Tabitha, arise!" And she opened her eyes. When she saw Peter, she sat up. Giving her a hand, Peter helped her up. Then, calling the saints and widows, Peter presented her alive. This became known throughout all of Joppa and many believed in the Lord. And Peter remained in Joppa for many days with a man named Simon, a tanner.

1 Kings 17.17-24

Luke appears to have recounted the story of Tabitha's healing with Elijah in mind. Note the similar language and themes: both stories take place in an upper room, both involve women with leadership roles (the text here refers to the woman as "kurias," the feminine form of "lord or master"), both lie on mats, both are raised from the dead, and both serve to authenticate the status of prophets. The location of the "upper room" seems to be particularly important since this is often the place in the Bible where prophets (and apostles) encounter God.[30]

Now it happened after these things that the son of a woman, the mistress ["kurias"] of her household, became ill. And the son's illness was very severe, to the point that there was no breath remaining in him. So she said to Elijah, "O man of God, why have you come to me, to remind of my wickedness and to kill my son?" Then Elijah said to the woman, "Give me your son." So he took him from her bosom and brought him to the upper room ["huperoon"], the room where he was staying, and he laid him on his mat ["klines"].

Then Elijah cried out and said, "O Lord, the one who testifies to the widow with whom I'm staying, you have brought calamity upon her by killing her son." Then Elijah breathed on the child three times and called on the Lord, saying, "O Lord, my God, please let the life of this child return to him." And it was so, and the child cried out. So he brought him down from the upper room to the house and he gave him to his mother. And Elijah said, "Look, your son lives." And the woman said to Elijah, "Indeed, now I know you are a man of God, and the word of the Lord in your mouth is true."

Mark 5.35-43

There are obvious parallels between this story in Mark and Peter's miracle with Tabitha. Although Tabitha (the woman resurrected in today's Acts passage) means "Gazelle" in Aramaic,[31] it is one letter removed from "Talitha," the Aramaic word Jesus employs here for "little girl."[32] Both stories involve resurrections and both situations amaze everyone around them. Luke seems to have deliberately framed the language in Acts to match this one. He does this to show how Peter is carrying out Jesus' ministry even after his resurrection and ascension.

Now it happened while Jesus was speaking, some from the house of the head of the synagogue came and said, "Your daughter has died. Why trouble the teacher anymore?" But when Jesus overheard what they had said, he replied to the head of the synagogue, "Don't be afraid, just believe." Jesus did not let anyone follow him except Peter, James, and John, the brother of James. And when he came to the house of the head of the synagogue, he saw a commotion with much weeping ["klaio"] and wailing. Now, when he came in, he said to them, "Why are you in a commotion and weeping ["klaio"]? The child isn't dead, but sleeping." At this, they laughed at him.

So, putting them all outside, he took along the father of the child and the mother as well as the disciples who were with him and came to where the child was. And taking the hand of the child, he said to her in Aramaic, "Talitha cumi," which when translated means, "little girl, I say to you, arise!" And just then, the little girl rose up and was walking around. Now she was about 12 years old. And they were completely astonished. Then he strictly ordered them not to make this known and he told them to give her something to eat.

Comment

It may seem a bit strange that, having focused on Saul for the past several days, we suddenly switch back to Peter. This move is probably intentional on Luke's part. We'll see why more clearly in the coming chapters. Luke is trying to authenticate Saul's broader ministry to the Gentiles.[33] And the way he's going to do this is to demonstrate that Peter independently comes to the same conclusion about the Gentiles as Paul does.

However, today's Acts passage begins with an important statement, highlighting the continued spread of the church into various regions of Palestine. Of particular interest is Luke's rendering of "church" ["*ekklesia*"] in the singular. Although we should be careful not to read too much into a single word, it appears the early church saw itself as "one." This anticipates what St. Paul would write in Ephesians, a text that we repeat at every baptism: "There is one body and one Spirit…one Lord, one faith, one baptism, one God and Father of us all" (Eph 4.4-5). We are baptized into the universal church, not simply a local body.

When we confess in the Creed that the church is "one, holy, catholic and apostolic," we observe the importance of catholicity. This is also true in our story in Acts. There were small parishes all over the place, but they saw themselves as part of a single, united church. This is a good description of what it means to be catholic (literally, "of the whole"). These weren't autonomous parishes making it up as they went along, but instead were knit together by their common baptisms, by the presence of an authority structure, by the scriptures, and, most importantly, by the presence of the Spirit in their lives.

We see this confirmed in Peter who continues to travel around to various regions, including Galilee, to visit Christian communities already in existence. How they were founded we simply don't know. Since Peter's visitations look very much like what a bishop would do even in our day, many, not implausibly, see Peter functioning as a bishop here. I would also hasten to point out that Luke doesn't explicitly say so.

As Episcopalians, we make a big deal out of being "catholic." In this view, our tradition was not founded at the Reformation, but has its roots going all the way back to the first centuries after Christ. For example, the church father, Tertullian, in AD 208, writes, "The haunts of the Britons — inaccessible to the Romans [have been] subjugated to Christ."[34] Evidence for English bishops emerges in AD 314 when three attended the Council of Arles.[35] Moreover, the bishop of York was present at the first Ecumenical Council at Nicaea in 325.[36] Our tradition was catholic long before it was "Anglican."

To be sure, being catholic is different from being Roman Catholic. For example, when we receive someone from certain traditions into our fold (Roman Catholic, Eastern Orthodox, Lutheran, etc.), the bishop acknowledges it with these words: "We recognize you as a member of the one, holy, catholic and apostolic church and we receive you into the fellowship of this Communion" (BCP, P. 418). This language recognizes the obvious: the Episcopal Church is not the only true church, but simply subsists within the universal church.[37] The Spirit is at work in many traditions, not just in ours.

What is also fascinating about this passage is the depictions of women in the early church. Although some have seen Luke's descriptions as simply carrying on the patriarchal structures of Roman society, others (I think, rightly) have observed the very counter-cultural roles women were playing in the early church. The text even calls Tabitha a female "disciple." This is probably not an official title, but it probably suggests that women were seen as equal in status before God. This might not seem very revolutionary to us, but, if true, it would have been truly radical for its time.

Ben Witherington, who has written extensively on the role of women in the early church expresses this view well:

Luke and Paul, like other early Christians, believed that their faith committed them to the reforming of some of the existing patriarchal structures so that women could play more vital and varied roles in the community of faith...In the story of Tabitha (Acts 9), a notable female disciple with an ongoing ministry, we find someone providing material aid to a particularly needy group of early Christians – widows... [Thus Luke] shows how the gospel liberates and creates new possibilities for women.[38]

In particular, Tabitha finds favor from God in today's Acts reading. However, too many ignore the role that Tabitha's generosity plays in finding that favor. Tabitha's good works and her acts of charity are not incidental details in this story. Notice, in fact, that when Peter comes beside her, he deliberately surrounds her with the recipients of her good works and charity.[39] As we will observe repeatedly over the next several chapters, Luke seems to think that alms and acts of charity have great power in living out the Christian life.[40] Tabitha, an extremely generous person, receives divine favor by being raised from the dead in imitation of Jesus.

Questions for Reflection:

1. What does the word "catholic" conjure up for you? Is it a good or a bad thing that Episcopalians are part of the catholic (universal) church?
2. The great criticism of a catholic structure is that it can lead to institutional rigidity and slow decision making. How does our system (in which authority is centered in a bishop, but parishes are run by Clergy with some autonomy) either contribute to or mitigate against institutional rigidity and slow decision making? What is the role of the Vestry in all this?
3. Should all the leadership roles in the church be open to women? Who decides this?

CHAPTER 19

PIETY AND RECEPTIVITY
Acts 10.1-23a

Acts 10.1-23a

> *Luke narrates how the good news comes to the Gentiles. In this passage, there are two interrelated visions. Both serve to break down the barriers between Jews and Gentiles that developed, in part, because of Israel's food laws. Cornelius, a Roman centurion, who found favor with God because of his piety, summons Peter at the behest of an angel. Yet three times Peter resists the instructions from heaven to eat unclean foods, thus reminding us of Peter's three-fold denial of Christ during the Passion.[41] At the behest of the angel, Peter welcomes Cornelius' messengers and prepares to travel with them.*

Now there was a certain man in Caesarea named Cornelius, a centurion of what was called the Italian Cohort. He, together with his whole household, was devout and feared God, giving generously to the needy and praying to God often. In a vision ["horama"] at around 3:00 PM, he clearly saw an angel of the Lord coming to him and saying, "Cornelius." He stared at him and was afraid, saying, "What is it, Lord?" And he said to him, "Your prayers and your alms have arisen as a memorial offering before God. So now, send men to Joppa and summon a certain Simon who is known as Peter. This Peter is staying with a certain Simon, the tanner, who has a house along the sea."

When the angel who was speaking with him departed, Cornelius summoned two men from his household and a devout soldier, one of his orderlies. Having explained everything to them, he sent them to Joppa.

Then the next day around noon, they were on their way and drawing near to the city, when Peter went up to the roof to pray. Peter became hungry and wanted to eat. As they were preparing a meal, a trance ["exstasis"] came upon him, and he saw heaven open and an object coming down like a large, sheet being let down by its four corners upon the earth. On it were all manner of four-footed creatures and reptiles of the earth as well as birds of the sky. And a voice said to him, "Arise, Peter, slaughter and eat." And Peter said, "By no means, Lord, since I have never eaten anything common or unclean." And the voice said to him a second time, "That which God has made clean, you must not call common." Now this happened three times, and then suddenly the sheet was taken up into heaven.

While Peter was puzzling over the vision that he had seen, the men sent by Cornelius, found out where Simon's house was, and were standing at the gate. They called out and asked if Simon, who is called Peter, was a guest there. While Peter was reflecting on the vision, the Spirit said to him, "Look, three men are seeking you. Arise, go down and accompany them without wavering since I have sent them." Then Peter went down to the men and said, "Look, I'm the one you're seeking. Why are you here"? They responded, "Cornelius, the centurion, a just and God-fearing man, well-regarded by the whole nation of Jews, was instructed by a holy angel to summon you to his house to receive a message from you." Then Peter invited them in and received them as guests.

Genesis 15.1; 5-15, 17-18

God makes a covenant with Abram through a vision, promising that he would receive land and offspring as an inheritance. While neither promise seemed possible at the time, Abram became the Patriarch of the Jewish nation and at the conquest of Canaan, his many descendants received the land of Palestine as an inheritance. The original promise to Abram (Gen 12.3), that he would be a vehicle of blessing to all nations, suggests that it was always God's intention to include the Gentiles in his redemptive plan. The use of the vision, the trance and the unclean animals all parallel today's Acts reading.

Then, after these things, the word of the Lord came to Abram in a vision ["horama"], saying, "Do not be afraid, Abram, I am your shield, your reward shall be very great." God brought him outside and said to him, "Look up toward the sky and count the stars if you're able to count them." And he said, "So shall your descendants be." And Abram believed God and it was accounted to him as righteousness." Then God said to him, "I am the God who brought you from the land of the Chaldeans to give you this land as an inheritance." But Abram said, "Almighty Lord, how will I know that I am to inherit it?"

And God said, "Take a three-year-old heifer, a three-year-old goat, a three-year-old ram as well as a turtledove and a pigeon. So Abram brought all these things to God and divided them in two and laid them opposite one another, but the birds he did not divide. And the birds came down upon the carcasses of the cut up animals, but Abram drove them away.

Around sunset, a trance ["exstasis"] fell upon Abram and a great dark fear fell upon him. And it was said to Abram, "You will surely know that your offspring will be resident aliens in a land not their own and that they will enslave them and mistreat them and humiliate them for 400 years. And the nation that enslaves them, I will judge, but afterwards they will come out here with much prosperity. But you will depart to your fathers with peace. You will be buried at a ripe old age."

Then, as the sun was setting, there was a flame, a smoking oven and a fiery torch, which passed in the midst of the divided carcasses. In that day, the Lord made a covenant with Abram, saying, "To your offspring, I will give this land from the river of Egypt to the great river, the Euphrates."

Leviticus 11.39-47

*If Israel was to live in the presence of God, they had to take elabo-
rate steps to ensure holiness in the community. This need for holiness
leads to the law of clean and unclean animals. Holiness implies a
separation from what is defiling or impure, thus ensuring that Israel
would be distinct from other nations.[42] However, when Jesus declared
all foods to be clean (Mark 7.19), reflecting the broken-down barriers between Jews and Gentiles, these regulations in their literal
sense become obsolete, something Peter has a hard time understanding. In the spiritual sense, however, these regulations live on in the
need for the people of God to separate from what is impure. The
goal becomes for all nations to live in relationship with God.[43]*

Now if a head of cattle should die, which is unclean for you to eat, he
who touches its carcass shall be unclean until evening. And he who eats
any of these carcasses must wash his clothes and will be unclean until
evening. He who picks up any of these carcasses must wash his clothes
and bathe himself in water and will be unclean until evening.

Now every reptile which creeps upon the earth, this will be a loathsome thing for you; it must not be eaten. And everything that goes on
its belly and everything that walks on all fours, anything that abounds
with feet among all the creeping things that go upon the earth, you must
not eat it, since it is a loathsome thing for you. And you absolutely must
not defile your souls with any of the creeping things that creep upon the
earth and you must not be defiled by them and you must not become
unclean by them. For I am the Lord your God and you must not defile
your souls with any of the creeping things that move upon the earth,
since I am the Lord who brought you out of the land of Egypt to be your
God. You must be holy, since I the Lord am holy.

This is the law concerning the beasts and the birds and all the living
creatures that move in the water and all the living things that creep upon

the earth, to make a distinction between clean and unclean, between living creatures that are edible for you, and living creatures that are not edible.

Comment

In the last chapter, we left Peter at the house of Simon the tanner. Since a tanner handled the carcasses of dead animals all day, this is a curious place for a pious Jew like Peter to be staying since, as our Leviticus passage makes clear, contact with dead animal bodies would automatically render someone unclean. For some reason, this doesn't particularly bother Peter.

Yet, when God instructs Peter to satisfy his hunger by eating unclean food, this was simply too much for him. Peter strongly objected. Note how strange this is. Although the text tells us that it was an "angel" that visited Peter, he consistently responds with "Lord." Peter probably recognizes the voice in the vision as divine, but cannot bring himself to do something that deviates from his religion. He's willing to disobey a command of God rather than do something that offends his piety.

God responded with a vision of a sheet let down by its four corners with the carcasses of animals on it. Many early Christians saw the sheet as symbolic of the four corners of the earth.[44] All the nations of the earth were to be brought together in Christ, who had made them clean by his death on the cross.[45]

The law of clean and unclean was never meant to evoke a superior moral status.[46] Rather, as we saw in our Genesis reading today, Abram was supposed to have descendants greater than the stars of the sky, suggesting that he was to be a blessing for all nations, not just Israel.

If this is the case, then it was always God's intention to include Gentiles in his redemptive plan. It's the spiritual significance of the law that lives on in our day, in particular, in the need for God's people to be set apart. Thus, by declaring all foods clean, God has made it possible for Jews and Gentiles to worship God together and to eat together. This is an essential development in our story because it's a key reason why Christianity becomes a universal, and not a localized religion.[47]

It falls to Cornelius, a Roman centurion, to be God's vehicle for this development. A centurion was a non-commissioned officer in the Army in charge of about 80-100 men.[48] As was typical, Cornelius was probably a freed slave who had risen to a position of responsibility.

But Luke depicts Cornelius as someone who had *already* found favor with God. He hadn't been circumcised or baptized, but nevertheless his prayers had been heard and his alms had been accepted. He was *already* in a relationship with God even though no one had yet explained the good news to him.

Cornelius was probably a so-called "God fearer," one who was attracted to the moral vision of Judaism but who didn't want to be circumcised, the essential last step in fully converting. People like Cornelius would have formed the backbone of the early church.

Why was Cornelius accepted? The text says that his alms had "ascended as a memorial before God (Acts 10.4). In ancient Judaism, there was a wide-spread belief that alms could actually intercede one's behalf.[49] We'll have more to say about this in the next chapter, but it's a very important point. Giving alms actually had spiritual power.

Among Protestants, such piety is often looked upon as something superfluous, since the assumption is that good works do not matter for our spiritual lives. Many say that what matters is your heart toward God, not external manifestations of religion. In fact, with Peter, we can see the dangers of getting too hung up on pious practices, making us unable to respond to God's call.

Yet Cornelius is a great example of how pious practices can be really helpful because, done with the right motivations, it makes us receptive to the leading of the Spirit. Piety alone may not save us, but it does form us, and makes us more receptive to the leading of God. This seems to be the case with Cornelius.

Cornelius immediately obeyed God's call, thus demonstrating his receptivity. Let's never forget that almsgiving and formal prayer are key inputs to the spiritual life, not simply optional extras.

Questions for Reflection:

1. Describe your "spiritual practice" or "Rule of Life." Do you have one? What does it entail?

2. In Protestantism, spiritual disciplines and piety are labeled by some as "legalism". However, Cornelius' piety was accepted by God in a remarkable way. In what ways can pious practices become legalistic? In what ways are pious practices a path to become more receptive to God?

3. Are there things that you abstain from for reasons other than health or diet (alcohol, meat, caffeine, etc.)? How does this help you in your spiritual life? Are there things in your life that you should give up but have a hard time doing so?

CHAPTER 20

ACCEPTABLE ALMS?
Acts 10.17-35

Acts 10.17-35

> *Peter arrives the next day at Cornelius' house in Caesarea. Cornelius recounts his vision to Peter. Luke's deliberate decision to repeat the details of the vision demonstrates its importance. In the vision, an angel tells Cornelius that his alms had been accepted before the Lord. The angel tells Cornelius to invite Peter to his house. Given that rabbinic interpretation of the law in Peter's day forbade any fellowship with Gentiles, this passage represents a remarkable meeting of Jews and Gentiles, two separated groups. Peter recognizes that not only does food not defile a person, neither does fellowship with Gentiles, a huge advance for the cause of unity.[50]*

While Peter was puzzling over the vision that he had seen, the men sent by Cornelius, found out where Simon's house was, and were standing at the gate. They called out and asked if Simon, who is called Peter, was a guest there. While Peter was reflecting on the vision, the Spirit said to him, "Look, three men are seeking you. Arise, go down and accompany them without wavering since I have sent them." Then Peter went down to the men and said, "Look, I'm the one you're seeking. Why are you here"? They responded, "Cornelius, the centurion, a just and God-fearing man, well-regarded by the whole nation of Jews, was instructed by a holy angel to summon you to his house to receive a message from you." Then Peter invited them in and received them as guests.

So the next day, Peter arose and went out with them. He took along with him some of the brothers from Joppa. One day later he arrived at Caesarea. Now Cornelius was waiting anxiously for him and had gathered together his relatives and intimate friends. When Peter arrived, Cornelius met him, fell at his feet and started worshipping him. But Peter raised him up, saying, "Please get up. I'm a mere mortal like you." Conversing with Cornelius as he came in, Peter found a large group assembled.

Peter said to them, "You must know that it's not customary for a Jewish man to fellowship with or to approach a non-Jew. But God has also shown me that speaking with another person is neither defiling nor unclean. So, without any objection, I came when you invited me. So might I ask why you sent for me?"

Cornelius responded, "Four days ago, at 3:00 PM, I was praying in my house when a man stood before me in a glowing garment and said, 'Cornelius, your prayer has been heard and your alms have been remembered before God. Therefore, send someone to Joppa and invite Simon, who is called Peter. He is a guest at the house of Simon, the tanner, next to the Sea.' So right away, I sent for you and you were nice enough to come. And now we all have come before God to listen to everything decreed to you by the Lord." Then Peter opened his mouth and said, "Now I see – God truly shows no partiality. But in every nation, the one who fears God and works righteousness is acceptable to him."

Psalm 82.1-6

The psalmist pictures God as Ruler of the divine assembly, and is critical of human judges for "showing partiality" to sinners. This is the OT basis for Peter's realization that God shows no partiality between Jews and Gentiles.

A Psalm of Asaph

God stands in the Assembly of the gods, in the midst of the gods, judging. How long will you judge unjustly and show partiality toward sinners? Give justice to the orphan and the poor; vindicate the lowly and needy. Deliver the needy and the poor; rescue them from the hand of the sinner. Do you not know or understand; do you go about in darkness? All the foundations of the earth shall be shaken. I have said, "You are gods and sons of the Most High, all of you." But you will die like humans and you will fall as one of the rulers. Arise, O God, and judge the earth since you will take possession of all the nations.

Sirach 29.8-13

> *The Book of Sirach was probably written in the second-century BC by Jesus ben Sira. The book has come down to us in the Septuagint, the Greek translation of the OT used by the early church. It records the wise sayings of Ben Sira's grandfather and is one of the best witnesses we have to the Jewish culture of biblical times. This passage shows the centrality of almsgiving in ancient Judaism and the belief that giving to the poor funded a "treasury in heaven," a concept that Jesus would invoke approvingly in the Sermon on the Mount. When the angel tells Cornelius his "alms have been accepted before God," he finds approval from God in the same way that a pious Jew would.*

Nevertheless, show patience to one in humble circumstances, and do not keep him waiting for your alms. On account of the commandment, help a poor man and according to his need, do not turn him away empty. Lose your silver for the sake of a brother or a friend, and do not let it rust away under a stone and be lost. Lay up treasure for yourself according to the commandments of the Most High, and it will work to your advantage more than gold. Store up alms in your heavenly treasury and

it will deliver you from all calamity; more than a strong shield or a heavy spear, it will fight on your side against your enemy.

Comment

When Peter arrives at Cornelius' house, this represents a momentous turn in our story. The good news is now spreading to the Gentiles. But there are barriers to overcome, in particular the custom that Jews and Gentiles were to have nothing to do with each other. Keep in mind that this is nowhere to be found in the OT law, but had nevertheless become an accepted practice in Peter's day.

For example, the book of *Jubilees*, likely written around the same time as *Sirach*, says the following:

> Separate yourself from the Gentiles and do not eat with them. Do not do according to their works and do not fellowship with them, for their works are unclean and all their ways are a pollution and an abomination and uncleanness (Jubilees 22.16).[51]

Thus it was only by custom, and not by statute, that Jews and Gentiles were separated. I can't resist pointing out the parallels to our current times when Christians are told over and over again to separate from the culture out of fear that they'll be defiled. Yet Jesus said, "There is nothing outside a man which by going into him can defile him; but the things which come out of a man are what defile him" (Mark 7.15).

Jesus was speaking specifically about the food laws in Mark, but we need to remind ourselves that artificial barriers that separate people are not what God wants. True, our lives ought to be visibly different than the culture, but hermetically sealing ourselves off from it helps no one.

In fact, Christians should be the best citizens, active, energetic members of our communities, promoting the common good and working to garner harmony among estranged groups. We are called to be the salt of the earth. We should engage with those different from us out of sheer love for our neighbors.

One puzzling thing we need to answer in this passage is what Cornelius is doing bowing down to Peter. Some become very uncomfortable at this point and suggest that Cornelius is just showing Peter great deference.[52] This reading is possible, but seems to disregard first-century norms.

Roman culture was steeped in mythology. What the movie *Star Wars* is for us, Homer and Ovid would have been for them. Anyone who has read Homer's *Iliad* or *Odyssey* knows that the gods frequently show up looking like normal human beings with extraordinary powers. In that culture, a hero (like Achilles) had a status somewhere between the gods and mortals.[53]

Well, isn't this how Peter appears? His very shadow heals people in Jerusalem. His touch can cause the Holy Spirit to rush upon a person. Angels break him out of prison. Was it not reasonable for Cornelius to think that Peter was a kind of demi-god — perhaps a manifestation of Zeus or Apollo or a lesser god from the Divine Assembly?

Part of the problem is a tension that exists in the OT about how to understand God. It's long been noted that two interpretations of monotheism sit side by side in the OT. An example of the first comes from today's Psalm 82 reading. In this view, there is one God "far above other gods" (Ps 97.9). Other gods exist, but Yahweh is the greatest in the Divine Assembly.

Contrast that with Isaiah: "I am the Lord and there is no other, besides me there is no God" (Isa 45.5, RSV). The idea that there is one God, and only one God, is the concept of monotheism that eventually wins out in most Christian circles. Yet this tension exists in the Bible.

Thus Luke is not making a statement about monotheism or criticizing an inappropriate practice. He's threatening the entire edifice of the pantheistic Roman religious system in this passage.[54] This is subtle, but important to see. Peter's insistence that one God, and only one God, is worthy of worship will ultimately spell the demise of the entire Roman pantheon, an idea we'll return to frequently in the coming chapters.

One other thing to note is how uncomfortable parts of this passage are for standard Reformation theology. How can Cornelius' prayers and alms be remembered before God if he's outside the church? Moreover, why is Cornelius accepted for "*working* righteousness" (or, as the RSV translates it, by *doing* "what is right")? Aren't works supposed to have no bearing on our salvation?

In the *Thirty-Nine Articles*, the Reformation-era confessional statement for Anglicans, it says the following about works before justification:

> Works done before the grace of Christ and the Inspiration of his Spirit, are not pleasant to God, forasmuch as they spring not of faith in Jesus Christ; neither do they make men meet to receive grace… rather, for that they are not done as God hath willed and commanded them to be done, we doubt not but they have the nature of sin.[55]

Yet Cornelius' works were explicitly accepted by God even though he had not yet heard the gospel, had not yet been baptized and had not yet received the Spirit. Today's passage seems to sit very uneasily with the theology espoused in the *Thirty-Nine Articles*.

Yet, perhaps Cornelius has exercised "implicit" faith, even if he was missing the details. This appears to be John Calvin's perspective. In his masterwork, *The Institutes of the Christian Religion*, Calvin explains that Cornelius was acting in faith and thus his faith was accepted, not his works.[56] But surely this is a stretch since the text specifically says that Cornelius' "alms" were "remembered" before God. Calvin might have been uncomfortable with the implications of this verse since he simply skips over it in his commentary on Acts, something he did fairly infrequently.[57]

Maybe there's a better solution that takes more seriously what first-century Jewish culture was like. This is why I included the reading from *Sirach* today. First-century Jews (and almost all early Christians) believed that giving to the needy funded a heavenly treasury. We should really have no problem with this concept since Jesus himself taught it in the Sermon on the Mount, when he said, "Do not lay up treasure for yourself on earth…but lay up treasure for yourself in heaven" (Matt 6.7). Jesus' language is drawn straight from *Sirach*, suggesting that this belief was a well-accepted part of Jewish culture.

As Notre Dame's Gary Anderson has written, early Christians saw almsgiving as akin to "making a loan to God."[58] This is why Cornelius' alms are remembered. It didn't at all negate the need for God's grace in salvation. Grace is at work in the astounding return God gives to our paltry gifts that fund the heavenly treasury. But Cornelius' generosity really seems to matter here.

Thus we should realize that our works and God's grace are not really at odds. To be sure, we don't "earn" our salvation through almsgiving. On this the Reformers were certainly right. God is the one who does the saving. But how we live our lives seems to matter greatly to God, especially in our generosity to others; for it is in generosity that we most visibly show that our faith and our love for others are real.

Thus Cornelius is accepted not because he's a nice guy. After all, as a centurion, his profession involved ruthlessly killing people. Undoubtedly he was a sinner. Rather, he's accepted by God because his actions matched his confession.

God is often surprising in his choices. Cornelius, a key figure in the Roman occupation, becomes the opening for the gospel among the Gentiles. A whole new phase in the spread of the gospel is underway.

Questions for Reflection:

1. How has generosity had an effect on your life, either by receiving it or providing it? How can a commitment to generosity develop your spiritual life?

2. How do you square Cornelius' job as a ruthless killer with God's seemingly warm reception of him? Why do you think God chose someone like Cornelius to be the person through whom the good news comes to the Gentiles?

3. Some have said that America is the most pantheistic nation ever known because so many Americans adore themselves. Can you see this at work in our culture through things like gym memberships, professional sports, celebrity adoration, and materialism? In what ways are we passionate about things that have little to do with the pursuit of God?

CHAPTER 21

THE GENTILE PENTECOST
Acts 10.34-48

Acts 10.34-48

> *Peter's sermon is stopped in mid-course as the Holy Spirit falls on the Gentiles. Like Pentecost, this arrival of the Spirit is accompanied by speaking in tongues, an outward confirmation of the presence of the Spirit. Cornelius and his household are then baptized and reconciled to God. There is no longer any obstacle to Gentile inclusion in the church. This is a true turning point in our story since, from here, the gospel's spread throughout Gentile lands and people groups will be a central focus of our story.*

Then Peter opened his mouth and said, "Now I see – God truly shows no partiality. But in every nation, the one who fears God and works righteousness is acceptable to him. You're aware of the message that he sent to the sons of Israel, heralding the gospel of peace through Jesus Christ — this one is Lord of all. You also know what happened throughout all Judea, beginning in Galilee with the baptism that John proclaimed, concerning Jesus of Nazareth — the one God anointed with the Holy Spirit and with power, who came through, doing good and healing all who were oppressed by the devil since God was with him.

And we are witnesses to everything he did both in Judea and in Jerusalem. They killed him, hanging him on a tree. But God raised him up on the third day and had him appear — not to all the people, but to us, witnesses chosen beforehand by God. We ate and drank with him after he had risen from the dead. And he gave us orders to proclaim and to solemnly testify to the people that Jesus is the one appointed by God as Judge of the living and the dead. All the prophets testify to these things, that everyone who believes in him receives forgiveness of sins through his name.

While Peter was still speaking these words, the Holy Spirit fell on all who heard the message. And the circumcised Jews who had come with Peter were astonished since God poured out the gift of the Holy Spirit on the Gentiles, also. For the Jews heard them speaking in tongues and glorifying God.

Then Peter said, "Who can withhold the water of baptism from anyone who has received the Holy Spirit just as we have?" So Peter commanded them in the name of Jesus Christ to be baptized. Then they asked him to stay for several days.

Ezekiel 34.22-31

> *Writing after the exile, Ezekiel looks forward to the restoration of the nation of Judah and the whole cosmos, under a "covenant of peace" when a righteous shepherd like David would rule. Here, peace is not just the cessation of war, but "shalom" — the state of well-being and prosperity found in God.[59] This shepherd would be a spirit-filled servant who would not be like the other rulers Judah had known.[60] Only Jesus who was both a descendant of David and fully God could make these promises come true.[61]*

Therefore, thus says the Lord God, "Look, I will judge between the strong and the weak sheep. You pushed away with your sides and with your shoulders, and you butted them with your horns and afflicted all the faint. But I will save my sheep and they will by no means be held captive anymore, but I will judge between one ram and another. And I will raise up a single shepherd over them and he will shepherd them; as my servant David, he will be a shepherd to them. And I, the Lord, will be God to them and David will be a ruler in their midst, I, the Lord, have spoken.

I will make a covenant of peace with David, and I will utterly destroy the wicked beasts from the land and they will dwell in an isolated place and they will sleep in a thicket. And I will give them a home around my mountain and I will give you rain, the rain of blessing. And the trees in the field will yield their fruit, and the land will yield its strength and they will dwell on their land in the hope of peace.

And they will know that I am the Lord who broke their yoke into pieces. And I will deliver them from the hand of those who enslaved them. And they will not be plundered by the nations anymore and the beasts of the earth will no longer eat them, but they will dwell in hope and none will make them afraid. And I will raise up for them a plant of peace and they will no longer perish from hunger on the land and they will by no means bear the reproach of the nations anymore. And they will know that I am God, the Lord to them, and they are my people." "O house of Israel," says the Lord, "you are my sheep and the sheep of my pasture and I am the Lord your God," thus says the Lord God.

Ephesians 2.11-18

St. Paul recounts the result of Jesus' work on the cross. Gentiles, who were once estranged from God have now been grafted into the people of God. Thus Jesus' work on the cross broke down the dividing wall that separated them, in particular the food and ceremonial laws that prevented table fellowship between Jews and Gentiles. The result was peace. If God is Lord of all, then the good news of Jesus' Kingship must go out to all nations and races. [62]

Therefore, remember that you Gentiles were once in the flesh called the "uncircumcision" by those called the "circumcision" made in the flesh by human hands. Now at that time we were without Christ, separated from the commonwealth of Israel and strangers to the covenant of the promises, without hope and without God in the world.

But now, in Christ Jesus, you who were once afar off, have been brought near by the blood of Christ. For he himself is our peace, who made the two groups one, breaking down the dividing wall of hostility, the law, when he nullified in his flesh its legal demands and decrees. He did this so that the two groups might become one new man in him, thus making peace and reconciling both groups in one body to God through the cross, thus destroying the enmity in him. And he came proclaiming the good news of peace to you who are far off and the good news of peace to you who are near since, through him, both have access by one Spirit to the Father. Therefore, you are no longer strangers and sojourners, but you are fellow citizens of the saints and of the household of God.

Comment

It doesn't get more important than this. The good news has come to the Gentiles and nothing will be the same. As a result, the church will not be a tiny sect within Judaism confined to the lands of Palestine. Rather, there is a universally saving orientation to the gospel. If Acts is, in part, about the spread of the good news to the ends of the earth, this only becomes possible because the Gentiles are included.

Yet there is also an easy-to-miss detail in the midst of Peter's dialogue. Peter repeats his earlier claim (from Acts 2.36) that Jesus is Lord, but renders it slightly differently this time, saying that Jesus is Lord *of all*. This is an explosive statement because it goes after what Caesar was claiming about himself. In the first century, the Caesars frequently called themselves "lord" (or "*dominus*" in Latin).[63] But Luke is subtly saying that Jesus is something more – he is Lord of all, and thus even Caesar is in a subordinate position to him. As we'll see in the coming chapters, this is one reason why the Christians start receiving more coordinated and intellectually-coherent resistance from the Jews. The Jews rightly see how potentially subversive Jesus' claim to lordship is, and they start using this against the early church. The burden of much of the book of Acts is to refute the charge that Christians are trying to overthrow the Roman government.[64] There is a profound tension between Christians' Christological claims and their loyalty to the state. This tension is on display throughout the second half of Acts.[65]

Just so we don't miss it, Luke gives us another easy-to-miss detail that wraps into this subversive claim. This is all taking place in Caesarea, a place named for the Roman Caesar.[66] Moreover, the gospel's turn to the Gentiles happens through Cornelius, a Roman military officer. These can't be incidental details. Peter is claiming that the name of Jesus is more powerful than the whole apparatus of the Roman state, a claim that seems (at least on the surface) to be seditious.[67]

Similarly, don't miss the other subordinate adversary in this passage, the devil. The devil plays a very important behind-the-scenes role in Acts resisting the spread of the good news. More generally, the devil was a serious problem because he had wrongly put God's people in bondage, meaning they were separated from God and from each other. This is why Peter says that Jesus came to set free "those who were oppressed by the devil" (Acts 10.38). Thus the devil is attempting to disrupt God's plan of salvation.

In the early church, there was surprisingly little discussion of how salvation works. We might find this odd. For example, have you ever noticed there is almost nothing said about salvation in the Creeds? This doesn't mean salvation wasn't important. It was simply left to later generations to argue about the details.

Yet two basic models for understanding the work of Christ developed early on. One model came from Athanasius, Bishop of Alexandria, in the fourth century, who argued that salvation came from Jesus' standing in our place on the cross. When we say, "Jesus died for our sins," this reflects Athanasius' understanding. We might call this the "substitutionary" model.

But another metaphor that developed alongside it suggested that Jesus won a great victory over the devil by his work on the cross. We might call this the "victory" model. We shouldn't see this as a competing model, but a complement to substitution. Some simply preferred to describe Jesus' work on the cross as a rescue operation to save humanity.

Peter seems to like this "rescue" motif. In this view, we were held down by the oppressive forces of sin, the devil, and death. Jesus came to release us from this bondage so that we might be renewed in a relationship with God. To do this, Jesus not only had to break down the barriers between Jews and Gentiles (as we read in Ephesians today), but also to break down the barriers that sin erected between God and his creatures.

This is probably why we pray in the Lord's Prayer at the end – "Deliver us from evil." It's likely this was originally meant to be understood as, "Deliver us from the evil one" — the devil — whose temptations draw us away from the things of God.[68]

Notice as well the language Luke employs when he describes the Gentile Pentecost. Luke records Peter as saying, "God poured out the *gift* of the Holy Spirit on the Gentiles, also." This is very easy to miss, but the word "gift" here is more important than it might first appear.

One of St. Augustine's greatest (and least read) works is his treatise, *On the Trinity*. Augustine comes to understand that "gift" in relation to the person of the Holy Spirit is a name, not a descriptive term. The problem Augustine was trying to solve was how the name "Holy Spirit" could uniquely apply to the 3rd Person of the Trinity. After all, the Father and the Son are both "holy" and "spirit" so how can the Holy Spirit be a distinct Person within the Trinity?[69]

What Augustine figured out was that the Holy Spirit could only be properly understood in the context of "gift," as the manifestation of the outpouring of the love between the Father and the Son. This is one reason why in the Creed, we confess a God who is "God from God." Admittedly, this language applies specifically to Christ, but we can also employ it to help understand the Spirit as well. The Holy Spirit is fully God, but also given by God as the gift of his love. Or, as Paul puts it, the gift of the Holy Spirit is "the love of God shed abroad in our hearts by the Holy Spirit that was given to us" (Rom 5.5).

The reason the gift of the Holy Spirit is so essential is that this is what really marks someone off as being a Christian. In particular, the gift of God is the Holy Spirit poured out not only on the Jews, but on the Gentiles, also. This gift manifests itself as love, the same self-giving love that the Father, Son, and Holy Spirit pour out towards each other in the Trinity.

Thus to be "spiritual" is not about being necessarily "deep" or "contemplative." Being spiritual is about being touched by the Spirit and marked off by love. We're most spiritual when we love one another. Or, as St. John puts it, "If we love one another, God abides in us and his love is perfected in us" (1 John 4.12, RSV).

Questions for Reflection:

1. Think about the people you consider uniquely "spiritual." What are they like? What would you like to emulate in them that would draw you closer to God?
2. Do you think the devil exists? If so, how does this belief inform your Christian life? If not, how do you explain the Bible's insistence that he does?
3. If the Spirit manifests itself as love, how is this any different from non-Christians who also show love to others? Is there anything distinct about being a Christian with regard to love?

CHAPTER 22

CHANGE IS HARD
Acts 11.1-18

Acts 11.1-18

> *When Peter returns to Jerusalem, he meets resistance from Jewish Christians who cannot fathom his cavalier attitude towards accepting Gentiles as full members of the community. After all, the OT law had said explicitly not to do this. Yet as Peter walks them through what happened "point by point," the community comes to accept the surprising turn – the good news has come to the Gentiles as well.*

Then the apostles and the brethren who were in Judea heard that the Gentiles had received the word of God. But when Peter went up to Jerusalem, the party of the Jewish Christians were criticizing him, saying, "You were a guest in the home of uncircumcised men and ate together with them"?

Then Peter began explaining it to them point by point, saying, "I was in the city of Joppa, praying and in an ecstatic vision, when I saw a vessel coming down like a large sheet, being let down by its four corners from heaven, and it came to me. While I stared intently and was contemplating it, I saw earth-bound quadrupeds and savage beasts as well as reptiles and birds of the sky. And I also heard a voice, saying to me, 'Arise, Peter, slaughter and eat!' And I responded, 'By no means, Lord since no common or unclean thing has ever come into my mouth.' And the voice spoke a second time from heaven, 'What God has made clean is by no means common.' This happened three times and then everything was taken up into heaven.

And then suddenly three men were standing outside the house where I was staying, sent by Cornelius to me. And the Spirit told me to go together with them without hesitation. So they went with me, along with six brothers who were also guests in the house of our host. He explained to us how he had seen an angel in his house, standing and saying, 'Send someone to Joppa and invite Simon, who is called Peter. He will speak words to you by which you and your whole household will be saved.'

After I had begun speaking, the Holy Spirit fell upon them just as on us at the beginning. Then I remembered the word of the Lord when he used to say, 'John baptized with water, but you will be baptized with the Holy Spirit' (Luke 3.16). Therefore, if God gave the same gift to them as he did to us who believed in the Lord Jesus Christ, who was I to get in the way of the power of God?" Now when they heard these things, they fell silent and glorified God, saying, "Wow! God has granted the repentance unto life to the Gentiles as well."

Exodus 12.43-49

The Passover was one of the central feasts of the year for pious Jews, where they remembered God's graciousness when he freed them from the bondage of slavery in Egypt. Israel was called to live in a covenant relationship with God, and the outward physical sign of that covenant was circumcision. Although circumcision is not yet the primary issue in our story, it becomes a key problem down the road. If the Spirit falls on the uncircumcised and they're baptized, this implicitly removes the requirement for circumcision in order to be in a covenant relationship with God.

Then the Lord spoke to Moses and Aaron, saying, "This is the law of the Passover. No foreigner shall eat of it. You must circumcise every slave bought with money, and then he may eat of it. No sojourner or wage-earning servant may eat of it. It must be eaten in one house. You shall not eat from house to house, nor carry flesh outside of your house. You must not break a bone of it. The whole assembly of the sons of Israel must observe it.

But if anyone comes to you as a sojourner to make the Passover of the Lord, you must circumcise all males before coming near to observe it. Then he shall be like one who is indigenous to the land. But no uncircumcised person shall eat of it. One law shall cover both the native and the sojourner who has come among you.

Leviticus 20.22-26

In order to live in close proximity to God, Israel must separate from other nations (the Gentiles). They must be set apart (holy) because God is holy. This holiness extends to how they eat. God has made distinctions between certain kinds of animals as clean and unclean. Israel must separate from unclean animals as they have separated from the surrounding nations and their "detestable" practices. Given this clear-cut prohibition, one can readily understand the Jewish Christians' criticism of Peter's embrace of table fellowship with Gentiles. Peter is acting directly against the plain language of the Bible.

Therefore, you must keep all my ordinances and my judgments. You must perform them so that the land to which I am bringing you to dwell does not become angry at you. And you must not walk by the laws of the nations that I am driving away from you since they have done all the things that I detested. And I told you, "You shall inherit their land, and I will give you it as a possession, a land flowing with milk and honey."

I am the Lord your God who separated you from all the nations. Therefore, you must make a distinction between clean and unclean cattle and between clean and unclean birds. You must not defile your souls with cattle or with birds or any quadruped of the earth from which I have separated you because of uncleanness. But you must be holy since I, the Lord your God, am holy. I am the one who separated you from all the nations so that you might be mine.

Comment

Imagine for a moment that you're one of the Jewish Christians hearing Peter recount what had just happened with Cornelius and his household at Caesarea. As a Jewish Christian, you might still be disturbed by the Roman occupation of Palestine. You probably really like Jesus and are convinced that he's the Messiah because of all he did. He was a great rabbi, who came and gave a different reading of the OT from what you had heard before.

But now, the leader of your band comes back and says that you should entirely ignore what the Bible says about separating from Gentiles and instead embrace a Roman centurion, a potent symbol of the occupation. What about all that language about holiness and being set apart? We might have had some tough questions for Peter just like the Jewish Christians did.

But, then, it gets worse. What is Peter's justification for ignoring the plain language of the OT law? God told him to do it! Where? In a vision! That's right — the unchangeable God has apparently changed his mind about what he had said previously. Didn't Jesus say that he came to fulfill the law, not abolish it (Matt 5.17)? All of a sudden, Jesus' re-reading of the OT becomes a little harder to swallow.

Yet, to their credit, the church comes around. The gospel has gone out to the Gentiles as well. This is surprising, but is undoubtedly good news.

It's hard for us to see just how shocking these events would have been to Jewish Christians. It's one thing to believe that Jesus is the Messiah, but do we have to fellowship with sinners like the Samaritans? Do we have to actually love a Roman centurion as a brother?

How easy it is to make a confession of faith. But how hard it is to change our ways! This is why I keep trying to point out that our lives must match our confessions. The criticism Peter faces here is simply racism backed up with Bible verses. It wouldn't be the last time the church would grapple with such issues.

In the late eighteenth century, William Wilberforce was a comfortable upper-class politician in England. But, after a powerful conversion experience, he became less enamored with his dissolute life and decided to use his influence to do some good.

Wilberforce settled on two aims – (1) the destruction of the slave trade and (2) the reformation of manners. He tirelessly pursued both, recognizing especially the dehumanizing effect the slave trade was having on the society at large. Civility toward others was manifested in both goals.

At the start, Wilberforce's crusade against the slave trade seemed like a hopeless task. The trade was fueling Britain's unquenchable demand for sugar, and thus had become essential to the growth of the economy. To ban the slave trade was to act directly contrary to the nation's economic interest.

Although slavery had largely died out in Europe by the thirteenth century, the age of exploration revived it. So a theology developed that said it was wrong to enslave Christians, but that everyone else was fair game.[70] It had become accepted that the Bible never really spoke out against slavery, and thus it was the natural order of things that Africans could be enslaved to enable England to consume what they wanted.

It was mainly Quakers, driven by the Enlightenment idea of equality, that pushed back early and often against this. The problem was that the Quakers had no power. So it fell to Wilberforce, an evangelical, to take up the charge, a task he only saw completed on his deathbed.

Slavery is an excellent example of how our understanding of the Bible develops. After all, slavery had been a common practice in Israel.[71] In the NT, St. Paul wrote, "Were you a slave when called? Never mind. But if you can gain your freedom, avail yourself of the opportunity" (1 Cor 7.21).

Freedom is better, but slavery is permissible. Paul would say roughly the same thing to Onesimus in the book of Philemon.

Yet it took the Enlightenment to bring the biblical notion of the inherent dignity of all people to the fore. In Christian terms, since we all bear the image and likeness of God, slavery is an abhorrent practice. Thus, what had been plainly permissible became plainly repulsive.

Doctrinal development is a really difficult issue to grapple with in the church. Put simply, can our practices and understandings change? Today, with Peter, we clearly observe that they can. Peter, having received a vision from God, goes against the plain language of the OT law. Thus both within the Bible itself and within history, we find strong evidence that not only can our understandings change, but, in some cases, they must change.

So how do we know when a development is legitimate or not? Most of the issues we fight about within the church have this as the key underlying question. While there is no perfect answer for it, it seems that legitimate doctrinal development deepens what was always there, rather than destroys it.

In the case of slavery, for example, Christians started emphasizing texts that necessitated the inherent dignity of each person and de-emphasizing texts that permitted slavery. Both of them were in the Bible, but one set of texts was emphasized over another. In a sense, we came to see that much of the OT law was like modern-day case laws. They were valid and helpful for a period of time, but were not timeless. What was timeless was the underlying spiritual sense — namely love of God and neighbor that Jesus emphasized. For the British, it was hard to understand how enslaving hundreds of thousands of people, many of whom died within a few years of being enslaved, was leading towards greater love.

Wouldn't it be nice if the skies would just part and God would tell us what he wants like he did with Peter? Perhaps some of our fights in the church would become less raw. But we must never forget that God, though the Holy Spirit, is still at work, deepening our understanding of the scriptures and what it means to walk faithfully with God.

Questions for Reflection

1. What practices in our church or in Christianity in general would you like to see change? What things should never change?
2. We might all agree that slavery is a bad idea, but in what ways do we tolerate "soft racism" in our communities? What groups of people do you not like just because they are different than you?
3. Can you think of any leaders who are like William Wilberforce in our culture today? Who is fighting for justice with a long-term perspective? How might you help them?

CHAPTER 23

APOSTOLIC TEACHING
Acts 11.19-30

Acts 11.19-30

> *The gospel now spreads into Asia Minor. This passage forms an important transition in our story away from the Jews of Palestine and toward the Gentiles. Additionally, the focus shifts from being primarily about the ministry of Peter to being about the ministry of Saul (soon to be called Paul). At the end, we find evidence for the emergence of itinerant prophets who could successfully predict the future. In this case, Agabus predicts an empire-wide famine, which would have appeared to the first readers as a sign of the end times.*

Now those who had been scattered because of the persecution ["thilpsis"] that happened in the aftermath of Stephen, went through as far as Phoenicia, Cyprus and Antioch, proclaiming the message to no one except Jews. But there were some of them, men from Cyprus and Cyrene, who came to Antioch, proclaiming the good news about the Lord Jesus to the Greeks as well. Now, the hand of the Lord ["keir kuriou"] was with them, and a large number believed and turned to the Lord.

Then, when the news was heard in the ears of the church, which was in Jerusalem concerning them, they sent Barnabas to Antioch. When he came and saw the grace of God, he rejoiced and encouraged everyone with resolute heart to remain true to the Lord. Barnabas was a good man, full of the Spirit and faith. And large numbers were being added to the Lord.

Then Barnabas went to Tarsus to seek out Saul. And when he found him, Barnabas brought him to Antioch. For an entire year Paul and Barnabas gathered together with the church to teach large crowds. And for the first time in Antioch the disciples were referred to as "Christians."

But in those days, prophets went down from Jerusalem to Antioch. And one of them, named Agabus, stood up and indicated through the Spirit, that a great famine was about to descend over the whole Roman Empire. This took place under the Emperor Claudius. So the disciples, as each had ability, resolved to send financial relief to the brethren living in Judea. They did so, sending it to the presbyters through the hands of Barnabas and Saul.

1 Samuel 5.2-7

In a scene deliberately written to be comedic, the "hand of the Lord" prevails against the Philistines and their god, Dagon.[72] The Israelites were treating the Ark of the Covenant as a kind of talisman, believing that as long as it went before their armies, they were invincible. Yet, because of the outrageous sins of the sons of the High Priest Eli, God allowed the armies of Israel to be defeated. God demonstrates his superior power by cutting off the god Dagon's head, and slitting his wrists, thus defiling the threshold which the Philistines took to be sacred.[73] In today's Acts reading, Luke draws on the phrase of the "hand of the Lord" to denote God's mighty power. Notice as well the ironic contrast between the true prophet, Agabus, who "stood up" to give a valid prophecy versus the false god, Dagon, who was "stood back up" only to topple over.

Then the Philistines captured the Ark of the Lord and brought it to the house of Dagon and they set it up before Dagon. And the people of Azotus awoke early and went into the house of Dagon, and they looked and said, "Look, Dagon has fallen on his face before the Ark of the God. So they drew near to Dagon and stood him back up in his place.

But the hand of the Lord ["keir kuriou"] was heavy upon them and he punished them and he struck them on their seats, from Azotus to their seacoasts. Now, it happened when they awoke early in the morning, that Dagon had fallen on his face before the Ark of the Covenant of the Lord and Dagon's head as well as both of his hands were lopped off, each before the threshold, not to mention his wrists had fallen into the doorway. Only the rump of Dagon was left. This is why, to this day, the priests of Dagon, and any who enter into the house of Dagon, do not step on the threshold of the house of Dagon at Azotus. Instead, they step over it.

So the hand of the Lord ["keir kuriou"] was heavy upon Azotus and the Lord brought great calamity upon them. It burst upon them in their ships and in the midst of their land mice sprang up. There was a great tumult of death in the city. Then the men saw what happened to Azotus and they said, "The Ark of the God of Israel must not stay with us since his hand is heavy upon us and upon Dagon our God."[74]

1 Peter 4.7-19

Peter thinks that the consummation of all things is at hand, much like Agabus does. Thus he exhorts his readers toward good works, love for neighbor and fervent prayer. This text represents the only place in the Bible (outside of Acts) where the word "Christian" is used. Notice that Peter implies that the term "Christian" was a nickname given by outsiders. Thus it's likely the name "Christian" was originally a term of derision coined by opponents of the faith.

Now the end of all things is near. Therefore, be serious and sober for the sake of prayer. Above all, have fervent love for each other, since love covers a whole multitude of sins (Prov 10.12). Show hospitality to one another without grumbling. Each one has received a gift — employ it in the service of others as good stewards, according to the manifold grace of God. Whoever teaches, let it be as oracles of God. If anyone serves, let it be with strength as God supplies, so that in everything God might be glorified through Jesus Christ to whom be glory and power forever and ever, amen.

Beloved, do not be surprised at the fiery ordeal occurring among you, as if it were some strange event. But to the degree that you participate in the sufferings of Christ, rejoice, so that, at the revelation of his glory, you might rejoice and be glad. If you are reviled for the name of Christ, blessed are you, since the spirit of glory and the Spirit of God rest on you. But let none of you suffer as a murderer or thief or evil-doer or as a troublemaker. But if, as a Christian you suffer, don't be ashamed but glorify God in this name, since it is time for judgment to begin, starting with the household of God. And if it begins with us, what is the end for those who are disobedient to the good news of God? And if the righteous are barely saved, where will the ungodly and sinners appear? So then let those who suffer according to the will of God entrust their souls to a faithful Creator in doing good.

Comment

The good news now comes to Antioch, a city in modern-day Syria. If we can believe the ancient historian, Josephus, Antioch was the third-largest city in the Roman Empire (behind Rome and Alexandria) and had a population of close to six-hundred-thousand people in the first century.[75] Antioch is important for our story because it becomes the sending city for the coming missionary activity throughout Asia Minor.

One of the things to remember about early Christianity was that it was primarily an urban phenomenon. If fact, the word "pagan" comes from the Latin word *"pagus,"* which means a "country district or community."[76] Originally, the pagans were country bumpkins who had never heard about Jesus. As Wayne Meeks, an expert on the social origins of Christianity has written, "Within a decade of the crucifixion of Jesus, the village culture of Palestine had been left behind, and the Greco-Roman city became the dominant environment of the Christian movement."[77]

As usual, Barnabas is the character providing the essential link between Jerusalem and Saul. Having sought out Saul in Tarsus, (where we left him at the end of Chapter 9), Saul and Barnabas ministered together for a year among the Christian community in Antioch. The community was likely made up of those from both Jewish and Gentile backgrounds, united in their confession that Jesus was the Messiah.

Notice that as soon as Jerusalem heard that the good news had spread to another place, they sent an authority figure who had ties back to the mother ship. The spread of the gospel was not some enthusiast-driven free-for-all.[78] Rather, the apostles, or their representatives, always confirmed the genuineness of the movement of the Spirit. The validity of the spread of the gospel was always tested against the eyewitness testimony of the apostles.

Since legitimate succession was a clear focus in the early days of the church, this is one reason why the Episcopal Church's claim of apostolic succession is important. Our tradition can legitimately tie itself all the way back to the early church through our bishops. It's not enough to claim validity as a tradition by simply having the Bible. The apostolic teaching on how to understand the Bible needs to go along with it.

The second thing to notice is that for the first time the term "Christian" shows up in the Bible. It's notable that the early church in Antioch becomes known as those who follow "Christ." We should remember that "Christ," comes from the Greek word "*christos*," which in turn is a translation of a Hebrew word which means "Messiah" or "Anointed One." Although "Christ" was originally a title for the Messiah, it became unavoidably attached to Jesus, so much so that it developed to be part of his name.

The moniker, Christian, however, was probably a derisive term coined by those opposed to the movement. Christians themselves probably knew themselves as the "Way," (cf. Acts 9.2).

This happens over and over again in the history of the church. A term originally used to criticize a movement becomes its name. For example, the first recorded use of the term "Anglican" was in a disapproving sneer uttered by King James VI of Scotland when he was trying to convince the Church of Scotland how much he disliked the English church.[79] The sneer became the accepted term.

The last thing to notice is Agabus. Even though Luke has taken pains to depict Peter and others like prophets, this is actually the first time in Acts he uses the word "prophet" to refer to a contemporary who's not Jesus. This is good evidence that there were legitimate prophets who could successfully predict the future. Yet, because Luke finds such great continuity between the story of the OT and NT, he doesn't seem to be working from a rigid prophecy-fulfillment model.[80] It's just one long continuous story of God's being at work in the world.

To the early church, the presence of legitimate prophets would have confirmed that they were living in the last days. If you can remember all the way back to Peter's first sermon after Pentecost, he quotes the prophet Joel to say, "Your young men will see prophetic visions" (Joel 2.28; Cf. Acts 2.17). To them, the presence of prophets, visions, signs, and wonders were all confirming signs that the consummation of all things was upon them.

Two thousand years later, we're still waiting, still claiming we're in the Last Days. Yet the name Christian has once again become derided in some parts. Being a Christian, or even an Episcopalian, doesn't carry automatic respect anymore. Maybe we have more in common with the early church than we realize.

Questions for Reflection

1. Does it bother you that our tradition isn't highly regarded by many in the culture or in the broader church? Why do you think that is? What are some positive and negative aspects of our tradition?

2. The apostles seemed to care deeply that apostolic eyewitness testimony was being taught well. This required an authority structure. To what extent does your bishop play a role in your Christian life both as one who guards Christian teaching and who guides us?

3. Agabus apparently is able to predict the future, as there is external evidence that his predicted famine actually came to pass. How does Agabus contrast with modern-day prophets who try to explain what God is up to in various natural disasters?

CHAPTER 24

GUARDIAN ANGELS
Acts 12.1-25

Acts 12.1-25

The disciples encounter persecution from King Herod Agrippa I, ruler of Judea. James, the apostle and author of the Epistle of James in the Bible, becomes the first of the apostles to be martyred. Peter looks to be next when he is arrested, but an angel breaks him out of prison, to the great surprise of the church. In the end, however, King Herod dies a grisly death, which the church interprets as God's vengeance upon him.

Now around that time, Herod the King arrested some from the church. He beheaded James, the brother of John, with the sword. And when he saw that it pleased the Jews, he went ahead and also apprehended Peter (this happened during the Feast of Unleavened Bread). Having seized him, Herod put Peter into prison, handing him over to four squads of soldiers to guard him, desiring after the Passover to bring him out for trial before the people. So, while Peter was being kept in prison, the church kept offering fervent prayer to God for him.

Then, on the very night that Herod was going to bring him out for trial, Peter was sleeping in between two soldiers, having been bound with two chains to the guards keeping watch before the door of the prison. And just then, an angel of the Lord appeared and a light shone in the prison cell. Tapping Peter on the side, the angel woke him up, saying, "Get up quickly." And the chains fell off his hands. Then the angel said to him, "Get dressed and put on your sandals." This he did. Then the angel said, "Put on your cloak and follow me." Then, going out, Peter followed — not realizing that what was happening with the angel was real (he thought he was seeing a vision). And passing by the first and second sets of guards, Peter and the angel were at the iron gate that led into the city, which opened by itself for them. And going out, they proceeded down a narrow street. At that point the angel departed from him.

Then Peter came to himself and said, "Now I truly know that the Lord sent forth his angel to rescue me from the hand of Herod and from all the malevolent intentions of the Jewish people." When Peter realized this, he went to the house of Mary, the mother of John, who was called Mark, where many had gathered together and were praying. Peter knocked on the door of the gate, and a servant girl named Rhoda came out. Recognizing the voice of Peter, she was so overjoyed that she didn't open the gate, but ran in and exclaimed that Peter was standing outside the gate. And they said to her, "You're nuts!" But she kept insisting it was Peter. But others were saying, "It's his guardian angel." But Peter remained outside knocking. So when they opened the gate and saw him, they were astounded. Motioning to them with his hand to be quiet, he related to them how the Lord had brought him out from the prison. And he said, "Tell James and the brothers these things." Then going out, they went to another place.

Now, when daybreak came, there was a great commotion among the soldiers about what had happened to Peter. And Herod searched for Peter but couldn't find him. After cross examining the guards, he ordered them to be executed and went down from Judea to Caesarea and remained there.

Now Herod was having a furious squabble with the people of Tyre and Sidon. So with one accord they presented themselves to him and convinced Blastus, the king's chamberlain, to help them. They asked for peace because the country's food supply came from the king. And on the appointed day, Herod put on his royal robes and sat on the judgment seat to deliver a public address to them. But the populace began to shout, "The voice of a god and not of man!" And immediately, an angel of the Lord afflicted him for not giving glory to God. And Herod died and was eaten by worms. But the word of God kept growing and multiplying. And Barnabas and Saul, having completed their service in Jerusalem, returned. They also took along John who is called Mark.

Psalm 91.9-16

Psalm 91 is famous because the devil quotes it to Jesus during his time of trial in the wilderness after his baptism. Satan tells Jesus to throw himself off the portico of the temple since God had promised in the Psalm to send his angels to "bear you up on their hands." Jesus refuses the temptation, recognizing that his ministry will be defined by humility, rather than by a desire to wow big crowds. Later readers would see it as evidence that God has given each person a Guardian Angel to encourage progress in the faith, a view that today's Acts passage might support.

For you, Lord, are my hope, the Most High is your refuge. No evil will come upon you, and no scourge will come near your dwelling since he will command his angels concerning you to protect you in all your ways; they will bear you on their hands lest you dash your foot against a stone. You will tread upon the asp and the serpent and you will tread down the lion and the snake. Because he has hoped in me, I will rescue him; I will shelter him because he knows my name. He will call on me in trouble and I will rescue and glorify him. I will satisfy him with length of days and show him my salvation.

2 Maccabees 9.1-9

When modern-day Jews celebrate Hanukkah (the Festival of Lights), they are remembering Judas Maccabees' great victory over his enemy, Antiochus Epiphanes, described in 2 Maccabees.

Antiochus, likely the source of the "abomination of desolation" in the book of Daniel, was famous for defiling Jewish holy shrines by sacrificing unclean animals (usually a pig) on the altar. However, when he dies a gruesome and painful death, the Jews see this as divine retribution. The description of his being "eaten by worms" is similar to Herod's death in Acts and seems to be a common literary trope to describe the untimely death of an ungodly person.

Now at that time, Antiochus departed with dishonor from the country of Persia for he had entered into a city called Persepolis and had attempted to commit sacrilege in the temple and to hold the city. So the multitude with their arms rushed to help and put Antiochus to flight. Thus it happened that Antiochus was shamefully forced to flee from the inhabitants and to return home.

But when he came to Ecbatane, news was brought to him about what happened to Nicanor and Timotheus. Then, being stirred up with wrath, Antiochus thought about bringing vengeance on the Jews who made him flee with such disgrace. Therefore he commanded his charioteer to drive without ceasing and to commence the journey (but judgment from heaven was now following him since he had spoken arrogantly that he would come to Jerusalem and make it a common burial place of the Jews).

So the Lord God of Israel struck him with an incurable and invisible disease. As soon as he stopped speaking, the Lord brought an incurably painful malady of the bowels upon him, and he became angry because his innards were tormented. This torture was entirely just since Antiochus had tormented other men's bowels with many awful ordeals.

But nothing at all ceased because of his arrogance and because he was still filled with pride, breathing fiery threats in his rage against the Jews. So he commanded them to hasten the journey, but it happened that he fell from his chariot, being thrown off violently. All the members of his body were horribly tortured. So the one who, not long before, had commanded the waves of the sea (such was his superhuman boastfulness) and had weighed the high mountains in a balance, was brought down to the ground. And, being carried in a chair, he made the power of God visible to all. So the body of the ungodly man was consumed with worms while he was still alive in anguish and pain. His flesh rotted away and because of his stench, the whole army was repulsed by the decay. So the murderer and blasphemer, having suffered terribly, as he did unto others, met a most pitiable end among the mountains in a foreign land.

Comment

Although it may not be readily evident, our text today completes Luke's transition away from a focus on Peter. In fact, this is one of the last times Peter will show up in our story. He'll play an important role in a few chapters at the Jerusalem council (Acts 15), but from here on out, the focus of the story clearly shifts to Paul and his missionary work in Asia Minor. We're also observing a transition in leadership taking place, as James, the half-brother of Jesus, takes over as leader of the church in Jerusalem.

The church's ancient historian, Eusebius, claims that Peter went to Rome after this scene.[81] However, most think this is extremely unlikely because when St. Paul writes the book of Romans, sometime in the 50s AD, he seems to be under the impression that no apostle founded the church (Rom 15.20). This is why Paul is so eager "to preach the gospel to you who are in Rome also" (Rom 1.15). We simply don't know where Peter goes from here or why there's a leadership transition from Peter to James.

Today's story is one of great reversals. In the beginning, the Christians are on the ropes, as James the apostle is beheaded and Peter is put into prison. The authorities look like they're in control. But, by the end, it's the exact opposite situation. Herod is dead, Peter has escaped, and the Jewish leadership once again fails to shut down the church. As ever, Luke is showing how the gospel is an unstoppable force because God is behind it.

But this text is also transitional because we're supposed to find it funny. The servant girl Rhoda provides us with some comedic relief.

It's worth mentioning that the church has had long debates as to what extent humor is appropriate. This is probably because the Bible seems to speak against it. As Paul writes, "Let there be no filthiness, nor silly talk ["*morologia*"] nor levity, which are not fitting (Eph 5.4). Is church supposed to be glum and boring?

I certainly hope not. As the Jesuit, James Martin, points out in his book, *Between Heaven and Mirth*, appropriate joy and laughter are the signs of a healthy spiritual life. Paul is probably cautioning us against crassness, not joy. As Martin puts it, "We need, I would suggest, to recover the notion that joy, humor and laughter do not lie outside the believing life, but are at the heart of it."[82] Rhoda provides good evidence that Martin is right.

One of the key things to notice in this passage is how many subtle allusions there are to Jesus' life and death. For example, the primary reason Luke includes the detail that this was all taking place during the Feast of Unleavened Bread is that he wants us to remember that this was when Jesus' arrest took place (Luke 22.1).[83] Thus Luke is quite consciously recounting this story as one that mirrors Jesus' life.

Finally, Luke's description of the angel that rescues Peter is interesting. When Peter shows up at the door no one believes it's him. This is probably because they had resigned themselves to his death. So when some think that Peter's Guardian Angel might be at the door, this is an interesting detail. Some Jews believed that one's Guardian Angel matched one's physical characteristics.[84] They probably assumed that Peter was already dead and was now at the door in the form of an angel.

Yet this leads some to suggest that all of us have a Guardian Angel. Let me admit that the biblical evidence for this is thin. The best evidence comes from Jesus in Matthew: "See that you do not despise one of these little ones; for I tell you that in heaven *their* angels always behold the Face of my Father who is heaven" (Matt 18.10, RSV, emphasis added).

We know for sure that Christians through the centuries have believed in Guardian Angels. What we can say is that the book of Acts is unthinkable without angels as part of the story. Angels are instrumental in carrying out

God's will. Angels deliver Peter from prison, instruct Philip in his preaching and lead Cornelius in his overtures toward Peter. Thus it's not too much to think that angels are watching over you right now as well.

Questions for Reflection

1. Do you think that you have a Guardian Angel watching over you? Why or why not? To what extent can belief in angels either hinder or enhance our worship of God?

2. Do you think James Martin is right that humor is an important part of a healthy spiritual life? If so, why is the church so somber sometimes? Is this a positive or a negative?

3. Peter just disappears from our story after this episode. Pretend you're Luke and are writing Acts. How might you explain his sudden disappearance in the story?

PART III: PAUL'S MISSIONARY JOURNEYS

PAUL'S MISSIONARY JOURNEYS

In this third part of our story, the good news spreads well beyond the regions of Judea and Samaria to Asia Minor, modern-day Europe and beyond. The main impetus for this spread is the preaching of the apostle Paul across three different missionary journeys.

Although the spread of the gospel will continue to be a primary focus, a second important theme emerges in this section. Wherever Paul travels, he encounters resistance, usually, but not exclusively, from certain Jewish groups. The charge always seems to be the same – Paul is brining civic unrest through his proclamation of Jesus as the risen Messiah. By claiming that Jesus is Lord, Paul appears to his opponents to be undermining existing social structures, particularly the authority of Caesar. As a result, Paul and his traveling companions experience riots, beatings and hostility wherever they go.

But, a funny thing keeps happening. Although Paul is constantly being accused of being a traitor, the authorities uniformly find him "not guilty." Somehow Paul manages to escape every sticky situation.

Clearly, Luke is trying to tell us that God is watching out for Paul and is enabling the spread of the gospel. But Luke, telling this story as he is for Theophilus, shows us another reason for his writing in this section. Luke is trying to demonstrate that the charges of sedition against the Christians are obviously false. It can be very easy to miss this, however, so we're going to have to watch for it. Paul, and his Christian companions, are not guilty of sedition, even though they are proclaiming that Jesus is the true King. This is a very difficult balancing act to pull off, but Luke does it marvelously.

Since Paul is planting churches wherever he goes, this section will provide us with some of our best information about what the early church was really like. Naturally, this comes with some controversy about how to understand the biblical evidence. In this section, we will have to untangle several thorny theological issues that present themselves, like the meaning of justification, predestination, the use of images in worship, Christology, the existence of an oral tradition and the appearance of women as prophetesses and preachers. Our Anglican tradition, while not uniform in its handling of these details, will provide us with some help in unravelling these difficulties.

Because Luke depicts Paul's Jewish opponents as being implacably hostile, it is also important for us to notice that not all Jews react this way. Unfortunately, this nuance has often been lost in the history of interpretation of Acts and has led some to think that God is done with the Jews. Much anti-Semitism has been justified with details from this section. I hope to show that this perspective has been misguided and that the church has not replaced Israel in God's redemptive plan, nor is God done with the Jewish people. However, it will take some unpacking to understand why.

Lastly, this third section employs several literary references that are easy to miss. For example, when Paul stands before the Areopagus in Athens, one of the most famous scenes in Acts, Luke depicts him as a "new Socrates." Further, when Paul and Barnabas try to prevent the men of Lystra from worshipping them as gods, Luke writes this in a way that parallels a famous story from Ovid's *Metamorphoses*. These literary references make the story come alive in important ways.

But, most of all, we will observe a confident Christian movement proclaiming forcefully, but respectfully, that the resurrected and ascended Jesus is King. As a result, the world would never be the same.

PAUL'S FIRST MISSIONARY JOURNEY
(ACTS 13–14)

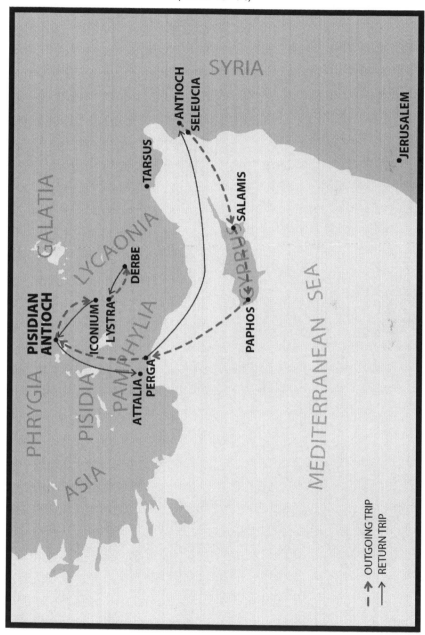

CHAPTER 25

WHAT IS MISSIONS?
Acts 13.1-12

Acts 13.1-12

> *This passage represents another important transition in the book of Acts. Our story now heads directly into Gentile territory as Paul (so-named for the first time) and Barnabas commence their first missionary journey. They head south-west to the Island of Cyprus, where Barnabas is from (Acts 4.36), and wind up on the western end of the Island at Paphos. Luke takes pains to stress that Paul is a prophet just like Jesus and Peter. Paul easily overcomes the resistance of the quack magician, Bar-Jesus (Elymas), to wow the regional Roman magistrate, Sergius Paulus. Of particular importance is the work of the church and the Holy Spirit in sending Paul and Barnabas on this mission.*

Now those in the church at Antioch who were prophets and teachers were Barnabas, Simeon (called Niger), Lucian the Cyrenian, Manean (a childhood friend of Herod the tetrarch), and Saul. While they were worshipping ["leitergeo"] the Lord and fasting, the Holy Spirit said, "Set apart ["aphorizo"] Barnabas and Saul to me for the work to which I have called them." Then having fasted and prayed, they laid hand on them and sent them off.

Therefore, having been sent out by the Holy Spirit, they went down to Seleucia and from there they sailed away to Cyprus. And when they arrived in Salamis, they started proclaiming the word of God in the synagogues of the Jews. They took along John Mark as an assistant.

Then, having traveled around the whole island as far as Paphos, they found a certain magician, a Jewish pseudo-prophet named, "Son of Jesus" ["Bar-Jesus"], who was with the proconsul Sergius Paulus, an intelligent man. The proconsul summoned Barnabas and Saul, desiring to hear the word of God. But Elymas, the magician (for this was how his name was translated), resisted them, seeking to turn the proconsul away from the faith.

But, Saul (also known as Paul), filled with the Holy Spirit, stared right at him and said, "Oh you, who are filled with all treachery and villainy, you son of the devil and enemy of all righteousness, why don't you stop making crooked the straight paths ["euthus"] of the Lord? And now, look, the hand of the Lord is against you and you will be blind, unable to see the sun for a time." And just then mistiness and darkness fell upon him and he went about searching for helpers to lead him by the hand. Then, once the proconsul saw what had happened, he believed, overwhelmed at the teaching of the Lord.

Romans 1.1-5

When Luke says that Paul and Barnabas were set part for the missionary work described above, he describes this using the same word ["aphorizo"] Paul himself will employ to depict his missions work in the book of Romans. Paul is not a lone wolf who goes off to convert the world. Rather, his legitimacy to carry on missions work comes ultimately from Christ and from the church that sends him. Paul, who may have been viewed with some suspicion by the Roman church (since they had never met him), takes pains to stress his apostolic credentials at the start of his greatest letter.

Paul, a bond-servant of Christ Jesus, called an apostle, set apart ["apho-rizo"] for the gospel of God, which he promised beforehand through his prophets in the Holy Scriptures, concerning his son, Jesus Christ our Lord, who was born of the seed of David according to the flesh, declared to be the Son of God with power according to the spirit of holiness by the resurrection from the dead, through whom we also have received grace and apostleship through obedience to the faith, among all nations for his name, among whom you also are called to belong to Jesus Christ. To all who are in Rome, beloved of God, called saints, grace to you and peace from God our Father and the Lord Jesus Christ.

Isaiah 40.1-5

The early church saw John the Baptist as the fulfillment of Isaiah's prophecy since this text plays a prominent role in all the Gospel accounts of the beginning of Jesus' public ministry. In its original context, Isaiah 40 begins the second section of Isaiah's prophecy, look-ing back with excitement at the end of the exile. By contrast, Paul sees Isaiah's text in terms of Jesus, who made "straight the paths of God," when he criticizes Bar-Jesus, the quack prophet, for getting in the way.

Comfort, comfort my people, says God. Speak, O priests, to the heart of Jerusalem. Comfort her since her humiliation is over, and her sins have been put away, since she has received from the hand of the Lord double for her sins.

A voice cries out in the wilderness: "Prepare the way of the Lord, make straight ["euthus"] the paths of our God." Every valley will be filled up and every mountain and hill made low. And all the crooked will be made straight ["euthus"] and the rough places will become a plain. And the glory of the Lord will appear and all flesh will see the salvation of God, since the Lord has spoken it.

Comment

In his book, *Let the Nations be Glad: The Supremacy of God in Missions*, John Piper wrote the following:

> Missions is not the ultimate goal of the church. Worship is. Missions exists because worship doesn't. Worship is ultimate, not missions, because God is ultimate, not man. When this age is over and the countless millions of the redeemed fall on their faces before the throne of God, missions will be no more. It is a temporary necessity. But worship abides forever.[1]

This is very well said. Worship should always be the primary thing we do as a church. Teaching the Christian faith and nurturing discipleship are important. Serving the poor is important. Raising up leaders is important. But worship is foundational to everything we do.

We can observe this idea at work in today's Acts reading. The mission of Paul and Barnabas starts with worship, and attempts to initiate worshipping communities wherever they go. Missions done right fulfills the cry of the Psalmist: "The whole earth bows down to you/sings to you/sings out your name" (Ps 66.4).

But it's also very easy to get the wrong idea from this passage. It might seem that Paul is just hastily going from place to place. But, as we'll see in the coming weeks, this is not really the case. Paul's first missionary journey will take a total of two years. Wherever Paul goes, he is careful to build churches and to teach them the Christian faith. It just might not seem like it from Luke's brief descriptions.

Truth be told, our evidence is mixed. There is very good evidence that prophets and apostles would go from place to place and not stay very long in the early days of the church. In fact, the *Didache*, our earliest Christian source outside the Bible, suggests that if a prophet wanted to stay more than three days, or asks for food, this is how one could tell that he's a false prophet.[2] So, clearly, itinerant ministers were prevalent in the first century.

That said, even a cursory reading of Paul's Epistles will show us that he usually employs a very different missions strategy. Paul's typical pattern is to stay in one place for extended periods of time and not leave until the church is well established.[3] In fact, later in our story, we'll find Paul spending three years in Ephesus (Acts 19.10, 20.31), building up and strengthening the church. This doesn't necessarily make an itinerant ministry wrong. It's simply not the strategy Paul eventually employs.

This is important because Paul's one "convert," Sergius Paulus, the local Roman magistrate, ought to strike us as shaky. There is no evidence that the Spirit falls on him. There is no real confession of faith and no evidence of baptism.[4] He's simply wowed by the spectacle. In the scholarship, there is an on-going debate about whether he is redeemed or not.

In modern times, Roland Allen, one of Anglicanism's greatest overseas missionaries, had similar concerns about short-term missionary strategies. Allen was a life-long missionary in China and East Africa during the early part of the twentieth century. In his book, *Missionary Methods: St. Paul's or Ours?*, Allen wrote the following:

> St. Paul did not gather congregations, he planted churches and did not leave a church until it was fully equipped with orders of ministry, sacraments, and tradition…We desire to impart not only the gospel, but the law and customs. With that spirit, St. Paul's methods do not agree.[5]

Allen's key point is that Paul didn't found missions, but churches.[6] Paul's goal was to raise up local leaders who could administrate the church when he was gone. Only once the work of thoroughly teaching the Christian faith and creating a leadership structure whereby the sacraments could be faithfully administered was complete, did he leave.

Allen was ahead of his time for recognizing that local cultures needed to be respected in foreign missions. Yet Allen also drew upon some timeless principles: the importance of apostolic teaching, a viable authority structure, and an on-going demand for faithfulness.[7] Allen genuinely believed that the Sacraments of Holy Baptism and the Eucharist were central to any missionary strategy.

In fact, the role of the missionary was primarily to imitate Paul in raising up local leaders to be ordained so that they could administer the Sacraments. Thus Allen was key to rethinking overseas missionary strategies in the twentieth century away from older colonialist approaches, emphasizing instead the value of indigenous leadership and cultures. One reason for the vibrancy of the Anglican Church in Africa today is Allen's insistence on respecting local cultures and local leadership.

The descriptions of the church at Antioch in this passage are also interesting. We'll have to read between the lines a bit, but it appears that there's a different church administrative structure in use at Antioch than we've seen before. Luke never uses the words for "bishop," "priest," or "deacon" in this passage. Rather, there are "teachers" (the only time in Acts this word is used as a noun) and "prophets."[8]

This is again a reminder that we must not push the evidence in Acts too hard to argue for a "divinely-mandated" way of structuring the church. Luke is simply not giving us one. Although the model of bishop-priest-deacon became the norm for authority in the church by the second century (and seems also to be the way both Timothy and Titus were functioning in Paul's later Epistles), it takes some time for it to become standard practice.[9]

Finally, we should note that Paul's call to missions work comes after a time of fasting and during what appears to be a formal worship service (Luke employs the word *"leitourgeo"* to describe this, which is where we get the English word "liturgy"). Once again, worship is intimately tied to missions.

This is why the contrast between Paul (a "true" prophet sent by the Holy Spirit) and Bar-Jesus, a false prophet, is so interesting. Luke is depicting Paul in a similar way to both Jesus and Peter. Luke depicts Paul as being in communion with the church leadership in Jerusalem (through Barnabas), as being filled with the Spirit, as having authentic piety, and as being a respected member of the community.[10] Paul then has the power to call down a curse of blindness on his opponent. Just so we don't miss the point, Luke claims that the Holy Spirit himself confirms *Paul's* call and actually does the sending. Let there be no doubt – this is a divinely-ordained commission. Paul is acting like a prophet. Bar-Jesus could not be more different.

Thus, with this passage, we take a fresh turn in our story. Paul and Barnabas start heading to the ends of the earth to spread the message of the good news. As we'll see, this always comes with significant resistance.

Questions for Reflection:

1. How important is regular attendance at worship to you? Do you consider worship one of the most important things that you do? If not, why not?

2. Many report that going on a short-term mission trip has been foundational for their faith. Have you ever considered going on one? What keeps you from doing it? In what ways might it be helpful for your faith?

3. Do you support any missionaries financially or in prayer? How important is God's work in the global church to you? In what ways could this become more central to your Christian life?

CHAPTER 26

JUSTIFICATION AND FORGIVENESS
Acts 13.13-41

Acts 13.13-41

> *Paul and Barnabas head north to Pisidian Antioch. Here, Paul*
> *preaches his first great missionary sermon. Luke sets up this scene*
> *just like Jesus' first sermon after his baptism (Luke 4.21). Like*
> *Peter, Paul makes the same basic claim as Peter's Pentecost sermon:*
> *the promise of Psalm 16 ("you will not see corruption") could not*
> *have been fulfilled in David, but only in Jesus because only Jesus'*
> *body did not see corruption. Yet Paul's sermon heads in a differ-*
> *ent direction as he ties "justification" to the "forgiveness of sins."*
> *Please note that Pisidian Antioch (in modern-day Turkey) from*
> *today's reading is a different city than the Antioch that serves*
> *as Paul and Barnabas' home base (in modern-day Syria).*

Then, having put out to sea from Paphos, Paul and those with him, came to Perga near Pamphylia, but John deserted them and returned to Jerusalem. And crossing over from Perga, they arrived at Antioch in Pisidia. Then, entering into the synagogue on the day of the Sabbath, they sat down. After reading the Law and the Prophets, the leaders of the synagogue sent for them, saying, "Brothers, if you have a word of exhortation for the people, let's hear it."

Then Paul arose, motioned with his hand, and said, "Men of Israel and those who fear God, listen. The God of this people Israel chose our forefathers, and he lifted up the people while they were sojourners in the land of Egypt. With a mighty arm, he led them out from there. Over a period of about forty years, he took care of them in the wilderness. After he conquered seven nations in the land of Canaan, he gave the land to them as their inheritance. This all took about four-hundred-fifty years. Afterwards, he provided judges until the time of Samuel the prophet. And then they asked for a king and God provided Saul, son of Kish, for them, a man from the tribe of Benjamin, for forty years. After God removed him, he raised up David for them to be their king, about whom God testified, 'I have found David, the son of Jesse, a man after my own heart who will do all things according to my desires' (Ps 88.21, 1 Sam 13.14, Isa 44.28).

From David's descendants God brought forth Jesus, a Savior for Israel according to the promise. Ahead of time, before Jesus' arrival, John the Baptist proclaimed a baptism of repentance for all the people of Israel. And while John was finishing his course, he kept saying, 'Who do you suppose that I am? I am not the Messiah. But, look, there is one coming after me whose sandal strap I am not worthy to untie' (Luke 3.16-17).

Fellow Brothers, sons of Abraham's race and those among you who fear God, the message of this salvation has been dispatched to us, since those living in Jerusalem and their rulers did not recognize Jesus, and thus fulfilled the sayings of the prophets read aloud every Sabbath, by condemning him. Although they found no basis for the death penalty, they insisted that Pilate execute him. And once all things were carried out according to what was written, having brought him down from the tree, they placed him in a tomb. But God raised him from the dead and he appeared over the course of many days to those who went up with him from Galilee to Jerusalem, who now are his witnesses to the people. And we proclaim to you the good news promised to our forefathers that has taken place since God has fulfilled this promise for their children, having resurrected Jesus for us as is written in the second Psalm: 'You are my Son, today, I have begotten you' (Ps 2.7).

Now since he raised Jesus from the dead, and he is no longer about to return to corruption, God has spoken this way, 'I will grant you the sure decrees of David' (Isa 55.3). Therefore, he also says in another place, 'You will not hand over your Holy One to see corruption' (Ps 16.10). For David, after he had served the purpose of God in his generation, died and went to his forefathers and saw corruption. But Jesus, the one God resurrected, did not see corruption.

Therefore, let it be known among you, my brethren, that through Jesus, forgiveness of sins is being proclaimed to you. Further, let it be known that through the Law of Moses you are not able to be justified. But everyone who believes in Jesus is to be justified. So be careful that what was written in the Prophets does not happen to you: 'Look you scoffers, marvel and be destroyed since I am performing a work in your days, a work that you will by no means believe, even if someone tells you'" (Hab 1.5).

Habakkuk 1.1-11

> *The Book of Habakkuk is about the justice of God in sending the ungodly Babylonians against Israel as judgment. Habakkuk claims that the Babylonians will fail despite their military might because of their injustice.[11] Thus Israel is to trust in the purposes of God despite confusing circumstances.[12] Paul quotes from this text at the end of his sermon, thus equating what happened to Israel in Habakkuk's time to the threatened judgment of God in his day.[13] To Paul in today's Acts passage, Habakkuk foretold the work that God accomplished in Jesus and the resistance of Israel in rejecting it.[14]*

The pronouncement that the prophet Habakkuk saw: How long, O Lord, shall I cry out and you don't listen? Being mistreated, I cry out to you and you will not save? Why have you shown me troubles and toils, to look upon my wretchedness and ungodliness? Judgment has come out before me and the judge receives a reward. Therefore, the law has been broken and judgment has brought me to an end, since the ungodly oppress the righteous. For this reason, perverted judgment has gone forth. Look you scoffers and see, marvel at the wonders and be destroyed, since I am performing a work in your days, a work that you will by no means believe even if it be told to you.

Look therefore, I will raise up the Chaldean fighters against you, that bitter and swift nation that goes across the breadth of the earth, to seize possession of your dwellings. He is frightful and famous, his judgment shall come from himself, as will his gain. Then his horses will come forth faster than leopards and his horsemen shall ride out. From far away, they will attack and fly like eagles zealous for prey. The end of days will come to the ungodly, having set their faces against them and they will gather them like the sand of the seashore. Then he will change his spirit and will pass through and make atonement, saying "This might is unto my God."

Romans 3.20-28

In one of the central passages of the book of Romans, Paul summarizes his argument from the first section of the Book. Jesus is the place (the Mercy Seat) where sins are forgiven. The Mercy Seat was a piece of furniture placed above the Ark in the Most Holy Place in the temple. Israel understood it to be the very place where God dwelled on the earth. Once a year, the high priest would make atonement for the people by sprinkling blood at its base. But after Jesus' resurrection, this is no longer necessary, since Jesus opened the promise of redemption to all nations, not just Israel. Thus a relationship with God takes place not by keeping a kosher diet, honoring Sabbath regulations, or being circumcised (works of the law),[15] but through God's covenant faithfulness (his righteousness).[16] Paul's reference to justification in the book of Acts similarly links justification to the forgiveness of sins.

By the works of the law no one will be justified, for through the law is the knowledge of sin. But now apart from the law, the righteousness of God has been revealed, being witnessed by the law and the prophets, the righteousness of God through the faithfulness of Jesus Christ to all who believe. For there is no distinction, for all have sinned and fallen short of the glory of God, being justified as a gracious gift through the redemption that is in Christ Jesus whom God set forth as a Mercy Seat ["hilasterion"] in his blood, through faith, in order to demonstrate his righteousness; because in his forbearance God passed over sins previously committed so that he might show his righteousness in the present time, and that he is just and the justifier of those who believe in Jesus. Where is boasting then? It is excluded. By what law, of works? No, but through the law of faith. Therefore, we conclude that one is justified by faith apart from the works of the law.

Comment

Paul's first great missionary sermon is the only place in Acts where his well-known teaching on "justification" appears. What is justification? In its simplest sense, justification is being declared "in the right." Our best understanding today (although admittedly this is controversial to some) is that justification is something that happens in the future, but also has present-day implications.

We should always think about justification in the context of a law-court. Picture yourself standing before God someday giving an account for everything you've done in your life. What justification tries to answer is how someone who "falls short of the grace of God" can ever be declared "in the right" before God. On the surface, since we're all sinners, it would seem that all of us should be declared "guilty."

What Paul is trying to get across is that we'll be declared "in the right" based on our faithfulness to God and his covenant. The covenant is simply the set of promises God made to his people that we appropriate by faith. All the way back to Abraham, God promised that if Abraham was faithful, God himself would be faithful to the promises that he made. Thus to be "declared righteous" (justified) is a term of relationship. We'll be declared "righteous" or "in the right" if we are in a true relationship with God. The implication from this is that our sins will be forgiven through God's faithfulness to the promises of the covenant.

Put more simply, God is asking us to trust him. It was never the expectation in Israel or in the early church that one could somehow be sinless. Yet there was also no provision for quite some time on how to get one's sins forgiven after baptism. The early church certainly thought that sin mattered, but they thought being baptized and living faithfully as Christians within the church was enough. Before Augustine, few thought that sin utterly destroyed our ability to have a relationship with God.

The reason Jesus had to come, and take on human flesh in the Incarnation and stand in our place on the cross, was because Israel — who was supposed to be faithful to the covenant, wasn't. Israel was supposed to be a light to the nations. The law, that was supposed to guide Israel in its relationship with God, ended up simply revealing their sin to them (Gal 3.24), since they were so consistently unfaithful. Thus God sent his Son to set the covenant right and to confirm that it was always God's intention for his promises to apply to all nations, not just Israel.

This is why salvation is ultimately a process, and doesn't just take place at a single point in time. Notice in today's Romans reading that Paul uses the word "justify" in past, present, and future tenses right alongside each other. In a very real sense, we have been saved (starting when we repented and were baptized). We are being saved in the present by living as Christians with the help of God's grace given to us in the Sacraments. And we will ultimately be vindicated in the future based on our faithfulness. What we do (our works) will ultimately vindicate our faithfulness as members in good standing of the covenant (Jas 2.24). This is why works are an essential part of our salvation – they are the visible result of a genuine relationship with God.

I'll let N.T. Wright have the last word here, since he has spent his whole career defending the perspective on Paul's teaching I've sketched above:

'Forgiveness of sins' belongs, in Acts, within a narrative different from the one most people imagine today. The purpose of forgiving sin, then as elsewhere, is to enable people to become fully functioning, fully-image-bearing human beings within God's world, already now, [but] completely in the age to come...The larger reality is that *something has happened within the actual world of space, time and matter, as a result of which everything is different...the long awaited-new age was being ushered in at last.*[17]

The forgiveness of sins is ultimately about having a genuine relationship with God. This is the result of the good news that Jesus came to bring.

Questions for Reflection:

1. **The church has traditionally taught that we formally begin a relationship with God through baptism when we come into the church and make a public confession of faith. When was the last time you read or thought about your baptismal vows (BCP, pp. 302-303)?**

2. **Have you ever felt that God was unfair to you or judging you like in our Habakkuk reading? What happened? Have you been able to resolve such feelings?**

3. **Americans are famously individualistic and independent. We prize self-reliance. So, in the spiritual realm, why can't we save ourselves? Why is God's help (his grace) always necessary for salvation?**

CHAPTER 27

PREDESTINATION AND ETERNAL LIFE
Acts.13.42-52

Acts 13.42-52

> *At the conclusion of Paul's sermon in Pisidian Antioch, everyone is stirred up. Some reject Paul's message, but some believe. But those who disbelieve actively resist Paul, forcing him to leave town. This will become a familiar pattern in the rest of Acts. However, even this resistance does not prevent the continuing spread of the good news throughout the region.*

Now as Paul and Barnabas were leaving, the people kept encouraging them to speak to them on the next Sabbath about these things. And once they left the synagogue, many of the Jews and God-fearing converts followed Paul and Barnabas, who were urging them and persuading them to continue in the grace of God.

Then, on the next Sabbath, nearly the whole city came out together and gathered to hear the word of the Lord. But when the Jews saw the crowds, they were filled with jealousy and started speaking against what Paul was saying and slandering him. Then, speaking out boldly, Paul and Barnabas said, "It was necessary for us to speak the word of God to you first. But since you have rejected it and are judging yourselves unworthy of eternal life, look, we're turning to the Gentiles. For this is what the Lord commanded us: 'I have appointed you to be a light to the Gentiles to bring salvation to the end of the earth'" (Isa 49.6).

Now when the Gentiles heard it, they were overjoyed and began glorifying the name of the Lord. And they believed, as many as had been appointed to eternal life. And the word of the Lord kept spreading throughout the entire region.

But the Jews stirred up the devout upper-class women and the prominent men in the city. They provoked a persecution against Paul and Barnabas and cast them out from their region. And shaking the dust from their feet against them, Paul and Barnabas came to Iconium. And the disciples were filled with joy and the Holy Spirit.

Isaiah 49.1-6

This text is known as Isaiah's second "servant song."[18] In the original context, the servant, a representative term for Israel, is to act as a "light to the nations." Thus Israel's vocation was to live in such proximity to God that all the surrounding nations would be drawn to Yahweh. Yet NT writers (especially Matthew and Luke) thought that Jesus was Isaiah's servant. However, Luke quotes this Isaiah text in Acts in a very surprising way, arguing that Paul and Barnabas, by proclaiming the good news, are actually acting as Isaiah's servant, drawing the Gentiles to Christ. As it turns out, all of these perspectives are right in different ways.

"Listen to me, O islands, and pay attention, O nations, for after a long time it will happen," says the Lord. From the womb of my mother, he called my name and set my mouth as a sharp sword and hid me under the shadow of his hand. He has appointed me as his chosen arrow, and he has covered me with his quiver. And he said to me, "You are my servant, O Israel, and in you I will be glorified." And I said, "I have toiled in vain and with futility; I have spent my strength for nothing. Therefore, my judgment is with the Lord, and my toil has come before God."

And now, thus says the Lord (who formed me from the womb to be his own servant to bring Jacob and Israel to him), "I shall be gathered and shall be glorified before the Lord, and my God will be my strength." Then he said to them, "It is a very great thing for you to be called my servant to establish the tribes of Israel and to return the scattered exiles of Israel. Behold I have appointed you as a covenant of the race, as a light to the nations, to bring salvation to the end of the earth."

Daniel 12.1-3

> *This is one of the clearest texts showing that the resurrection of the dead was not a Christian invention, but was brought into the church from later Judaism. Daniel envisions a general resurrection at the end of time followed by judgment and separation.[19] Of particular interest for our purposes is Daniel's use of "eternal life" which ties together the reality of resurrection with life in God's "new age." Paul's reference to "eternal life" and judgment in Acts seem to find a parallel in this passage from Daniel.*

Now, at that time, Michael, the chief angel who watches over the sons of your people, will pass by. That hour will be a time of distress that has not been from the beginning until that day. And in that day, all the people will be raised up who are found written in the Book. And many who have fallen asleep throughout the breadth of the earth will arise, some to eternal life ["zoe aionios"], some to reproach, and some to dispersion and everlasting shame. And those who understand will appear as the stars of heaven and those who persevere in my words will be like the stars of heaven forever and ever. But you, Daniel, close up these injunctions and seal the Book until the time of the end, until many recover from madness and the earth increases unrighteousness.

Comment

Paul preaches boldly in this episode, and the inevitable result is persecution. This is something very important to remember about the good news— it

215

may be good, but it's not safe. The good news usually threatens those in power (both in the government and in organized religion) which is why insecure leaders throughout history have often tried to suppress it or to alter its intended meaning for their own purposes.

Note that Paul isn't necessarily itching for a fight. Persecution comes quite naturally in response to his message. If we assume that being reasonable and loving will necessarily make us respected by the culture, this passage should make us reconsider.

Of particular interest in today's reading is Paul's use of Isaiah 49. The first thing to note is that Paul changes the text. He drops the phrase "as a covenant of the race" when he quotes it. The original text had a focus on Israel. But now Paul uses the text instead to claim that the message was all about the Gentiles.

In Greek, the word "*ethne*" is usually translated "nation," but can quite legitimately also be translated "Gentile." Although Isaiah almost certainly intended it to be understood originally as "nation," Paul now plays on the multiple possible meanings of "*ethne*" to claim that the good news is supposed to go out to all the Gentiles. Thus Paul claims that Isaiah 49.6, understood in light of Christ, was about a mission to all Gentiles.[20]

What's also interesting is that Luke is reading Isaiah 49 differently here in Acts than he does in his gospel. For example, when Simeon meets the Christ child at the beginning of Luke, he utters these famous words used in our Evening Prayer and Evensong liturgies:

O Lord, now let your servant depart in peace,
According to your word;
For my eyes have seen your salvation,
Which you prepared in the presence of all peoples;
A light to enlighten the Gentiles ["*ethne*"],
And the glory of your people Israel (Luke 2.29-32).

In his gospel, Luke understands Isaiah's servant to be Jesus. Jesus is the promised light to the nations, and thus the fulfillment of Isaiah 49. Now, in Acts, Luke names Paul and Barnabas as the servants, and the focus is on the Gentiles.

This caused a problem for interpreters in the early church who noticed that when Paul quotes Isaiah 49, he renders the pronoun "you" in the singular, a detail simply lost in English unless we say, "y'all." So, in Acts, how could this apply to both Paul and Barnabas, as Luke claims, if the "you" was singular?

This shows us that this text isn't at all about Paul's rejection of Israel (after all, Paul's pattern is always to start in the synagogue and then go out to others), it's about how Paul and Barnabas become instruments of Jesus' on-going work through the Spirit. In other words, the use of the singular pronoun shows that Jesus is still the true fulfillment of Isaiah's prophecy. But Paul and Barnabas, faithfully proclaiming Jesus' name, are acting as Jesus' servants in preaching the gospel.[21] This is a marvelous example of Luke's interpretive creativity.

Next, what does Paul's phrase "as many as had been appointed to eternal life" mean? Some see this as the most unqualified statement on predestination in the Bible.[22] However, this is only really true if we ignore the broader context of the passage. The key question is this: Is it the case that God has simply decided before the creation of the world about who is going to be saved and who is going to hell?

Some teach that God decided before the creation of the world who was going to hell and who was going to heaven. We have nothing to do with it. Thus there is no room for free choices, since sin has so corrupted our wills, we can use them for no good purpose without God's grace. In this understanding, God's grace overwhelms our fallen wills. Some turn to God, but this is simply because God made them do it.

To pick apart this complicated issue would take more space than we have here, but suffice it to say, I don't think this is what Luke means. Moreover, this is not what Paul says elsewhere. Consider what Paul writes in Romans with regard to predestination: "For whom he foreknew, these he also predestined to be conformed to the image of his son" (Rom 8.29). When God "foresees" all that is going to take place, this is another way of describing predestination. This has the advantage of preserving our ability to make free choices while recognizing God's very important role in the whole process.

Further, when Paul says that those who rejected his message "judged themselves unworthy of eternal life," this fits uneasily with predestination as something God determined before time began. After all, the text says nothing about a divine decree. Those who rejected Paul's message were condemning themselves. But how could they condemn themselves if they had no ability to make a free choice? Thus it's very likely that Luke envisions both the grace of God and human free choices as compatible. I think we should as well. We can freely reject the message of the good news, but neither does God force us to accept it. Yet we also need God's help (his grace) to establish and grow in a relationship with him.

This, by the way, is also the view of the early church, both East and West, before Augustine. For example, the second-century theologian Irenaeus puts it as follows:

> We...have received in the times known beforehand the blessings of salvation according to the ministration of the Word who is perfect in all things...by means of persuasion...[God] does not use violent means to obtain what He desires; so that neither should justice be infringed upon, nor the ancient handiwork of God go to destruction.[23]

What Irenaeus is saying is that God woos us, but doesn't force us to believe. Or, as Thomas Aquinas would restate it centuries later, grace "perfects" our nature, but does not destroy it.

One last thing to point out in today's reading is the mention of "eternal life." The literal translation of "*zoe aionios*" (eternal life) is "life of the age." What most translations do (including mine, above) is to claim that "age" means "a really long time." So "*zoe aionios*" must mean "eternal life." That is certainly possible, but there's a bit more to it.

The problem is that "eternal life" makes it sound like we're still living in a time-bound reality after we die. Yet eternal life does not likely depict a "time-bound" existence since God, as Creator, must have existed before the creation of time. If redemption ultimately is about union with God, we won't be living "in time" anymore. Thus the next life may be eternal, but is not necessarily time-bound.

So it might be better to understand this phrase "*zoe aionios*" instead as life in God's "new age." In this rendering, "eternal life" is simply another way of talking about how we're going to live in God's kingdom. Thus "eternal life," properly understood, is really just another way of talking about salvation.[24]

The key thing to understand is that the "new age" or "God's kingdom" has already started as a result of Jesus' resurrection. But its final consummation awaits our own resurrection from the dead.[25] The new age is already here, but it's not yet complete. It is "already," but "not yet." This is all very mysterious, but one thing we can say — we have much to look forward to.

Questions for Reflection

1. What are the problems with a view of predestination that suggests that God decided to send most of humanity to hell before they were created or exercised any choices? What would such an understanding say about the character of God?

2. In what ways has God's kingdom already been inaugurated? What are the visible signs that it's here? How do we know it's not yet complete?

3. If Paul's vocation was to be a light to the Gentiles, how are you acting as a light in our culture that needs to hear some good news?

CHAPTER 28

THE IMPORTANCE OF RECEPTIVITY
Acts 14.1-18

Acts 14.1-18

> *Paul and Barnabas now travel south-east to Iconium and Lystra in modern-day Turkey. Luke once again describes Paul as being similar to Jesus and Peter, both of whom memorably healed men who were lame.*[26] *As usual, they meet resistance after proclaiming the good news. At Lystra, however, the people mistake Paul and Barnabas for the Greek gods Hermes and Zeus and attempt to offer sacrifices to them. Paul aggressively intervenes and stops the practice.*

Now Paul and Barnabas did the same thing at Iconium – they went in together to the synagogue of the Jews and spoke a message that a large number of both Jews and Greeks believed. But the disbelieving Jews rose up and embittered the minds of the Gentiles against their brethren. So Paul and Barnabas remained there for some time, speaking out boldly concerning the Lord, bearing witness to the message of his favor and giving signs and wonders through their hands. But the civic assembly was divided[27] – some were with the Jews and some were with the apostles. However, there arose a desire on the part of both the Gentiles and the Jews, with their rulers, to abuse and to stone them. When Paul and Barnabas became aware of it, they fled to the Lycaonian cities of Lystra and Derbe and the surrounding region. There, they continued proclaiming the good news.

Now there was a certain man in Lystra whose feet were immobile and lame from his mother's womb who had never walked. He was listening to Paul as he was speaking when Paul stared intently at the man. And seeing that he had faith to be restored, Paul said with a loud voice, "Stand up straight on your feet!" And he sprung up and started walking around. And when the crowds saw what Paul had done, they raised up their voices in the Lycaonian dialect, saying, "Gods have come down to us in the form of men!" And they started calling Barnabas "Zeus," and Paul they called "Hermes" because Paul was the lead speaker. Then the priest of the temple of Zeus, which was just outside the city, brought oxen and garlands of flowers to the gates, and, together with the crowds, wanted to offer them a sacrifice.

But when the apostles Barnabas and Paul heard about it, they tore their garments and rushed toward the crowd, crying out and saying, "Friends, why are you doing these things? We are mortals just like you! We are proclaiming the good news so that you might turn from these worthless ["mataios"] things to the living God who made heaven and earth, the sea, and all that is in them. God, in former generations permitted all the nations to go their own ways. And yet God provided a witness to himself by doing good. He gives you rain from the sky and produce in its season; he satisfies you with food and gladdens your hearts." And having said these things, they persuaded the crowds with difficulty not to offer a sacrifice to them.

Exodus 20.1-11

This is the first half of the Ten Commandments. For a long time, there has been disagreement about how to order the commandments. I follow the "traditional ordering," which understands the directive about images to be subordinate to the main commandment against other gods.[28] Luke likely has this text in mind as he frames Paul's sermon in Acts. At a basic level, we know God exists because of his providential actions for us in creation, as God is the Creator of "heaven and earth, the sea, and all that is in them."

Then God spoke all these words to the people: I am the Lord your God, who brought you out from the land of Egypt, from the house of slavery. You shall not have other gods besides me.

You shall make for yourselves neither idol ["eidelon"] nor any likeness ["homoioma"] of anything, whether in heaven above or on the earth below, in the sea or under the earth. You shall not worship them nor serve them, for I, the Lord your God, am a jealous God, repaying the sins of the fathers on the children to the third generation for those who hate me, but showing mercy to thousands, to those who love me and who keep my commandments.

You shall not take the name of the Lord your God in vain ["mataios"], for the Lord will not acquit the one who takes his name in vain. Remember the day of the Sabbath to make it holy. Six days you shall labor and do all your work, but the seventh day is a Sabbath to the Lord your God; you shall not do any work on it, nor shall your son, your daughter, your male or female servants, your ox, your donkey or any of your cattle or the convert sojourning with you. For in six days, the Lord made heaven and earth, the sea and all that is in them, but he rested on the seventh day. Therefore, the Lord blessed the seventh day and declared it holy.

1 Thessalonians 1.2-9

Scholars generally consider 1 Thessalonians to be the earliest extant letter of Paul.[29] Paul gives thanks for the faithful Thessalonians and notes that the good news did not just come to them by a great sermon, but by the power of the Holy Spirit. The power of the Spirit is evident in their works which have become known throughout the whole region. Thus receptivity is critical for the acceptance of the good news. Luke alludes to this text in Acts using very similar language

> *when he has Paul exhort those in Lystra to consider God's provi-*
> *dential actions is caring for them. Those in Lystra and Thessalonica*
> *both turned "from God to idols" to serve "the living God."*

We give thanks to God for you, making mention of you always in our prayers, constantly remembering before God our Father your works of faith, your labor of love, and your steadfast hope in Jesus Christ, knowing brethren, beloved by God, of your election, that our gospel did not come to you in proclamation only, but also in power, in the Holy Spirit and with great conviction (surely you recall what kind of people we were when we were among you!).

And you became imitators of us and of the Lord, having received the message with joy from the Holy Spirit amidst great affliction so that you became a model for all who believe throughout Macedonia and in Achaia. For out of you, the Word of Christ has come forth, not only in Macedonia and Achaia, but in every place that your faith in God has gone out so that we have no need to say anything corrective to you. For people everywhere report what kind of welcome we had with you and how you turned to God from idols ["eidolon"] to serve the living and true God.

Comment

In one of the most touching scenes in Ovid's Epic poem, *Metamorphoses,* Jupiter and Mercury (the Roman equivalent of Zeus and Hermes) change into human form and come to visit a pious elderly married couple named Philemon and Baucis in the Phrygian hills, the same geographic location as today's Acts story. They have a pleasant chat with their guests, but notice in the course of the meal that the wine never runs out (if this ever happens to you, please be sure to invite me over!). This makes the couple realize that they're in the presence of gods, not mortals. Although the gods have come to destroy Phrygia with a flood because of its wickedness, the tender piety of the couple causes the gods to take pity on them. After sparing their lives from the flood, they turn their home into a temple and appoint them as priests. In a ripe old age, Philemon and Baucis are transformed together into trees. The story ends with the following line: "Still to this day the peasants of Phyrgia point to the oak and the linden nearby which once were the *forms* of Philemon and Baucis."[30] Pay attention to the word "form." It matters for today's story.

Almost certainly Luke has this famous story in mind as he's writing. I mention this because this scene is particularly easy to misunderstand if only read at the surface level of the text. Many interpret this story in Acts as a straightforward discussion against idolatry and the need for conversion.

Yet if we don't read this story with Ovid in mind, we're likely missing something. What we're getting with the people of Lystra is a perfectly normal reaction to something supernatural. Remember, this is a culture so steeped in Roman and Greek mythology that they would have assumed that the gods often come down in human form. There is no rigid separation of heaven and earth in this culture.

But it's even more interesting than that. In the story of Philemon and Baucis, this whole region had been wiped out because the people didn't recognize their gods when they were in their midst.[31] In Acts, the people of Lystra weren't going to make that mistake again! So they offered sacrifices to Paul and Barnabas as a sign of devotion. In context, this was a perfectly normal reaction.

But Paul's response shows that this is not just a simple story against idolatry. Paul is out to destroy the entire pagan religious system.[32] There is only one God and they can know that from creation itself. The true God is the one who gives them food by providing rain. This spells the doom of religious pluralism in this region, which is why Paul gets such a strong reaction.

Yet there's an even deeper reading of this text. What Luke really wants us to see is how close the people are to an orthodox Christian confession. The people cry out: "Gods have come down to us in the form of men" (Acts 14.11). If we change just a few of the letters in this sentence, it represents the essence of the Christian confession. Consider this sentence instead: "God has come down to us in the form of *a man*." It's really subtle, but Luke wants you to see how close they are to a genuinely Christian understanding of the Incarnation.

For Luke, these people have faith. As Paul puts it when he sees the man who was lame, "He had faith to be restored." The people in Lystra are receptive just as the Thessalonians were. They're simply missing an important piece of the puzzle. Thus, far from being primitive or stupid, they're inches away from Christian belief. [33] I like how Yale's Jaroslav Pelikan puts it,

> With a grammatically trivial, but metaphysically overwhelming change from the plural to the singular, from the 'gods have come down to us in the likeness of men!' to 'God has come down to us in the likeness of a man!' their Lycaonian shout, so reminiscent and representative of the Greek practice of making human beings into gods, sounds remarkably like the orthodox Christian rule of faith at Nicaea and Chalcedon. [34]

All of our stories today – from Lystra to Thessalonica to Phyrgia – suggest that faith really matters. Of course, we should move on from faith to greater understanding (*fides quaerens intellectum*). But let's never forget that what God wants from us most of all is our trust. [35] That's what faith is really all about.

All of us (perhaps especially me!) will get many things wrong along the way. The real question is whether we'll be receptive and faithful enough to recognize God when he's in our midst. That is the point of religious devotion and prayer. It is also the easily-missed point that Luke is trying to make here.

Questions for Reflection:

1. **What is faith to you? Does it change your understanding to realize that what God really wants from us is to trust him no matter what happens?**

2. Throughout history, there has been a lot of controversy about the appropriateness of images in Christian devotion. Given our penchant for stained glass windows, you probably can see what side Anglicans are usually on. Are religious images such as icons a regular part of your spiritual practice? *no*   *crosses*

3. Can we know God that exists from nature? Have you ever had a *yes* transcendent experience outdoors where you experienced God *no* in some sort of hard-to-explain way? How is the worship of God different than the worship of God's creation? *thankful*

CHAPTER 29

SUFFERING AND SALVATION
Acts 14.19-28

Acts 14.19-28

> *The crowd turns on Paul after opponents show up from the previous places he's preached. After being stoned and left for dead, Paul departs for Derbe (the easternmost stretch of his journey) where he meets no opposition.[36] There Paul makes disciples and appoints leaders. He then goes well out of his way to retrace his steps, revisiting the churches he founded during this journey on his way back to Antioch in Syria. Upon his arrival in Antioch, Paul recounts what God did "with them" during the first missionary journey. It is likely that Paul has been gone for as much as two years when he returns.[37]*

But when the Jews arrived from Antioch and Iconium, they convinced the crowds and stoned Paul, throwing him outside the city and leaving him for dead. But after his disciples encircled him, he rose up and entered into the city.

The next day, Paul went out with Barnabas to Derbe. After he proclaimed the good news to that city and made many disciples, he returned to Lystra, to Iconium and to Antioch. Paul strengthened the souls of the disciples, encouraging them to remain steadfast in the faith because "One must enter the kingdom of God through many sufferings" ["thlipsis"]. Then they appointed ["keirotoneo"] presbyters in every church. With prayer and fasting, Paul and Barnabas entrusted the disciples to the care of the Lord in whom they believed.

Then going through Pisidia, they came to Pamphylia. And speaking the word in Perga, they came down to Attalia. From there, they sailed away to Antioch (in Syria) where they had been entrusted with the work that they had completed by the grace of God. Having arrived, they gathered the church together and recounted everything that God had done with them and how he had opened the door of faith to the Gentiles. And they remained for quite some time with the disciples.

Job 7.1-11

In the Bible, Job is the model of a righteous sufferer. Having done nothing wrong, he nevertheless endures the loss of his children, his wealth, his reputation and, for all intents and purposes, his wife. His friends who come to comfort him, drawing on the popular theology of the day, accuse him of doing something terrible that has caused God to afflict him. We come face to face with the inscrutability of God's ways, especially his oft-heard silence in the midst of our suffering. Paul's admonition that we enter the kingdom of God through suffering and tribulation finds an echo here.

Isn't the life of a person on the earth a trial? Isn't his life like the day laborer? Isn't he like a servant who is anxious over his master or one who meets his shadow or like the wage-earner waiting for his pay? So, too, have I endured empty months and nights of distress that have been appointed to me. If I fall asleep, I say, "When will it be day?" And when I wake up again, I say, "When will it be night?" For I am full of distresses from evening till morning. My body is soaked with decaying worms. I am undone, scraping off lumps of dirt from my pus. And my life is lighter than a spoken word, having perished in vain hope. So remember that my life is a breath and my eye will not again see anything good. The eye of him who sees me will look on me again; your eyes are upon me, but I am nothing. I am like a cloud cleared away from the sky, for if a person goes down to Hades, he won't come up again, nor will he return anymore to his own house, nor will his place acknowledge him anymore. Therefore, I won't restrain my mouth; I will speak of being in distress, I will disclose the bitterness of my soul.

2 Timothy 3.10-17

Paul recalls the sufferings of his first missionary journey and exhorts his protégé, Timothy, to imitate him. Note Paul's insistence that reliable teaching about the scriptures is that which has been handed down from reliable sources. Timothy can trust the scriptures because those who handed them down to him are reliable. While there will always be opponents of the gospel, Paul claims that Timothy's task is to be faithful to what has been given. Paul's reference to "all Scripture" at the end refers to the OT, since these were the only "inspired" writings recognized at the time. It is very likely that the "sufferings" Paul cites in this passage refer to the stoning in today's Acts reading.

You, however, have followed my teaching, my conduct, my plan, my faith, my patience, my love and my perseverance — not to mention the persecutions and sufferings which happened to me in Antioch, in Iconium and in Lystra. I endured these sufferings and through everything the Lord delivered me. Now everyone who desires a godly life in Christ Jesus will be harassed. But evil men and swindlers will progress from bad to worse, deceiving others and being deceived. But you, however, persevere in what you have learned and are convinced of, knowing those from whom you learned it. From infancy you have known the scriptures, which are able to make one wise for salvation through faith which is in in Jesus Christ. All Scripture is inspired by God and is profitable for teaching, for reproof, for correction and for training in righteousness that the person of God may be proficient, equipped for every good work.

Comment

One of the keys to reading today's Acts passage well is to avoid the understandable temptation to see Paul as a kind of "superhero." For example, Heinrich Bullinger, a sixteenth-century Swiss Theologian, seems to fall into this trap when he writes the following:

> It is abundantly clear from this passage that, by the power of God, Paul was raised up as if from the dead; he was not cured by the remedies of the brothers. For who has ever heard of someone who was stoned walking the next day? Especially someone whom they assumed to be dead![38]

Few agree with Bullinger's reading today and for good reason. It misses the central point Luke is trying to make – Paul has unflappable faith. You can stone him, spit on him, insult him, leave for dead, but as long as he draws breath, Paul will continue to pursue his mission. In everything he does, Paul consciously imitates the mission and sufferings of Jesus.

What's behind Bullinger's understanding of Paul's recovery is the laudable motivation to see God's providence at work in everything. Bullinger is undoubtedly right about that, but his reading sits uncomfortably next to what Paul says when he recounted to the church at Antioch "everything that God had done *with* them" (Acts 14.27). To Luke, everything is unfolding according to God's plan, but this does not at all negate human cooperation. Paul is a model of what it looks like to cooperate with the grace of God through the Holy Spirit.

A second issue in this passage is Paul's decision to appoint "presbyters" in each church where he went. Throughout Acts, we've seen an on-going concern for authority and leadership. Paul takes care to appoint leaders wherever he goes.

The verb Paul uses for "appoint" is "*keirotoneo,*" which is relatively rare. This word originally meant to "raise a hand" as in an election.[39] But Paul in his writings never envisions leaders being elected.[40] This is a modern invention. Luke almost always has an apostle (usually Peter or Paul) appoint leaders.

In other words, Paul seems to be envisioning some kind of ordination process here. Like we've seen before (Acts 13.2-3), there is a time of fasting and prayer before these leaders are appointed. So we observe Paul acting as an apostle, appointing leaders wherever he finds disciples. This is not incompatible with what we do today when a bishop ordains leaders (priests and deacons) in a diocese. But, once again, we should exercise caution before we read too much into it because Luke is rarely precise in his language on this front.[41]

Finally, what does Paul mean when he says that we enter the kingdom of God "through many sufferings"? The word translated as "suffering" is "*thlipsis*," which can mean either suffering or tribulation. As we observe from our 2 Timothy reading today, Paul is sure that some suffering will come to everyone. Moreover, Job is the great example of someone who suffered, despite doing nothing to deserve it. If God loves us so much why is suffering so necessary?

To answer this, we have to first understand what the "kingdom of God" is. We've discussed the kingdom before as the in-breaking of God's new age, the time when the Messiah begins to rule as King.[42] This is something that has already started with Jesus and his sending of the Spirit, but is not yet complete. But here, Luke seems to be using it with a slightly different nuance because he gives a future sense to it. Luke is probably not using "kingdom" as a technical term, but simply as a synonym for salvation, which is completed in the future.[43]

Let me simply admit that I'm not sure why God allows so much suffering in our lives. Yet we mustn't lose sight of the centrality of faith in this passage. Our sufferings, which come to all of us, often serve to test our faith. God might be using suffering to teach us humility, to get us to trust him, or to help us have empathy for others. Therefore suffering is sometimes what God uses to shape us.

While great good can come from suffering, I also want to admit that suffering is perhaps the most mysterious part of the human condition, and I am quite sure that God's ways "are past finding out" (Rom 11.33). For some, suffering enhances faith; for some it weakens faith. Everyone, however, experiences some suffering. This can't be avoided.

As some of you know, I suffer from a chronic disease of the central nervous system called Multiple Sclerosis. While my disease progression has been slow over the last few years, it has taken quite a toll. I often experience great fatigue (especially in the heat of summer). I have to work constantly on balance and motor function. I have developed the smallest bladder ever (kind of annoying during a long church service). I am on extremely powerful medication that, for some, has led to a rare brain virus that has killed hundreds of patients and seriously debilitated hundreds more.[44] When I was diagnosed in 2009, my doctors told me I might not be able to walk in five years because of the extensive disease progression. Yet, by God's grace, I'm still ambulatory.

So I've experienced some suffering, but still don't really understand it. All I know is that I would never be writing this book had this disease not happened. While I resented for a while getting sick, since it resulted in the loss of my career and the loss of many relationships, it turned out to be one of the best things that's ever happened to me — despite the very real difficulties it brings.

By no means do I mean to speak for everyone. I know how much it hurts to suffer and never want to suggest how great it is. I would much rather not have MS. My message is simply this: keep going, no matter what. We all hurt. We all suffer. But one of the ways we experience God is by imitating him, even in the parts of life we don't like.

More than anything, MS has taught me to be less certain about most things and more dependent on God with everything (which, as I well know, is easier to write than to do). Yet God is at work in some mysterious way. I just may never understand it all this side of resurrection.

Questions for Reflection:

1. **Why do you think God allows suffering in our lives? How can God be good if he does that?**
2. **Do you ever find yourself falling into Bullinger's trap of seeing the apostles as superheroes and not flesh and blood human beings like yourself? What prevents you from seeing God's power at work like the apostles did?**
3. **What physical or emotional sufferings are bedeviling you? Can you see God at work in them? If not, can you at least look to God for comfort? What keeps you going?**

CHAPTER 30

THE IMPORTANCE OF COUNCILS
Acts 15.1-21

Acts 15.1-21

> *In one of the seminal passages of the book of Acts, the church con-*
> *ducts its first general council. There is no question about the inclu-*
> *sion of the Gentiles. Everyone agrees that the Spirit has fallen on*
> *them. The debate is over how they're to be included. Do they need*
> *to become Jewish in identity through circumcision and by keep-*
> *ing a kosher diet? The monumental decision is "no." Of particular*
> *interest is Luke's re-reading of Amos 9, where the promised restora-*
> *tion of the temple and the Davidic monarchy are interpreted as*
> *the broader Christian community that includes the Gentiles.[45]*
> *To Luke, the Davidic kingdom has been restored in Jesus, thus*
> *allowing the Gentiles to become part of the people of God.[46]*

Then some came down from Judea teaching the brethren that, "Unless you are circumcised according to the custom of Moses, you cannot be saved." Now when Paul and Barnabas had discord and no small dispute with them, they appointed Paul and Barnabas with some others from Antioch to go up to the apostles and the presbyters in Jerusalem concerning this debate.

And after they were sent on their way by the church, they passed through both Phoenicia and Samaria, detailing the conversion of the Gentiles and bringing great joy to all the brethren. And when they came to Jerusalem, they were received by the church, the apostles and the presbyters, and they recounted all that God had done with them. But some believers from the party of the Pharisees stood up, saying, "It is necessary to circumcise the Gentiles and to command them to keep the Law of Moses."

Then both the apostles and the presbyters gathered together to look into this matter. And when a great debate came, Peter rose up and said to them, "Brothers, you know that from the early days among you, God chose me to make the Gentiles hear the message of the good news and to believe. And God, who knows the heart, testified to them, giving them the Holy Spirit just as he did to us. He made no distinction between us and them, cleansing their hearts by faith. Now, therefore, why are you testing God by placing a yoke upon the neck of the disciples that neither our forefathers nor we were able to bear? Rather, we believe that we shall be saved through the gift of the Lord Jesus, just as they are."

The whole crowd kept quiet and heard Barnabas and Paul describing all the signs and wonders God had done among the Gentiles through them. After they stopped speaking, James spoke up, saying, "Brothers, listen to me. Simeon described how God appeared and chose from the Gentiles a people for his name. And the words of the prophets agree with this, just as it stands written:

> After these things I will return and I will rebuild the house of David that has fallen down and I will rebuild and restore what has been torn down so that the rest of humankind might seek the Lord, in particular, all the Gentiles upon whom my name has been invoked, says the Lord, who makes these things known from ages ago (Amos 9.11-12).

Therefore, I conclude that we should stop harassing those from the Gentiles who turn to God, but should write a letter to them that they should abstain from the pollutions of idols, from sexual immorality, from anything strangled and from blood. For Moses has had those who proclaim him from ancient times in every city since he is read aloud in the synagogues every Sabbath.

Leviticus 17.10-11, 14

This passage has importance for the sacrificial system in general, and for Jesus' fulfillment of it on the cross. The blood is sacred, not only because it gives life, but also because it atones for sin.[47] Thus when James urges the Gentiles to refrain from blood, he clearly has these Levitical regulations in mind. The Gentiles are to respect the OT law and make necessary accommodations so that they might not offend their Jewish brethren. The main motivation for this is so that Jews and Gentiles can have table fellowship together.

No man, whether from the sons of Israel or from those sojourning with you may eat any blood. I will set my face against the one who eats blood, and I will remove that one from the people. For the life of all flesh is the blood, and I have given it to you on the altar to make atonement for your lives. For its blood shall make atonement for one's life. And I have said to the sons of Israel, you may not eat the blood of any flesh since the life of all flesh is blood. Anyone who eats it will be utterly destroyed.

Amos 9.8-12

God declares the downfall of the northern kingdom because of its sin in separating from the religious and political structures of Judea, the southern kingdom.[48] The oracle also looks forward to the restoration of Israel under a righteous Davidic king.[49] The restoration of the northern kingdom and reestablishment of the Davidic monarchy will cause other nations (the Gentiles) to be welcomed.[50] James sees this promise fulfilled in the outpouring of the Spirit on the Gentiles in his day.

Behold, the eyes of the Lord God are upon the kingdom of sinners, and I will remove it from the face of the earth. Nevertheless, I will not remove the house of Jacob, says the Lord. Therefore, look, I am giving orders

and am winnowing the house of Israel among all the nations in the same way chaff is scattered so that no piece of it might fall to the earth. All the sinners of my people will die by the sword, especially those who say, "It will not come near to us nor will any calamities happen to us."

In that day, I will raise up the house of David that has fallen down, and I will rebuild what has fallen and I will raise up what has been razed to the ground, just as in the days of old, so that the rest of humankind, in particular all the Gentiles, upon whom my name has been invoked, will search for me says the Lord God who does all these things.

Behold, the days are coming, says the Lord, when the threshing season will overtake the harvest and the grapes will ripen at seedtime, and the mountains will drip sweet wine and all the hills will be thickly wooded. And I will turn back the captivity from my people Israel and they shall rebuild the destroyed cities. They will live there and plant vineyards and drink the wine from them. And I will plant them on their land and they will by no means be removed from their land that I gave them anymore, says the Lord God Almighty.

Comment

A few chapters ago, we saw James beginning to exercise leadership in the church (Acts 12.17). Although Luke took pains to depict Peter as thoroughly in charge in the first part of our story, Peter suddenly exits the story to make room for Paul. Now, once again, as we return to Jerusalem, we see Peter playing an important role (he comes up with all the big ideas at the council), but now it falls to James to pronounce the final decision of the council, speaking for the whole church. A bishop (James) is in charge, but only speaks for the consensus of the leaders of the church.

In fact, this marks Peter's last appearance in our story. We never hear from him again. This causes some consternation for those who see Peter as the first Pope. Luke seriously muddies the evidence for this claim since, at least at this point in the story, James is the de-facto head of the church.

As Anglicans, we agree that one person should be in charge, but have always argued that this is best exercised in the person of a local bishop. All the bishops should periodically get together and be in communion with each other, but authority is ultimately exercised locally, not centrally. For good order at a council, one bishop (in the Anglican system, the Archbishop of Canterbury, or a presiding bishop) might be appointed to speak for the consensus it has reached, but the locus of power is in the diocesan bishop in our system, not in a single head of the church.

The big conclusion of the council is that the Gentiles in Antioch must at least respect the so-called holiness code of the OT law (Lev 17-18) by avoiding the pollutions of idols, sexual immorality, things strangled, and blood.[51] The restrictions on "things strangled" and "blood" are likely speaking of the same thing since if something is eaten after being strangled, the blood is still in it.[52] Admittedly, the restrictions on the "pollution of idols" could just be a blanket prohibition against idolatry, but is more than likely referring to meat "offered to idols," something that will be clarified in the next chapter.[53]

Yet the most important implication of all this is that Gentiles do not have to be circumcised. Jewish identity is not essential to Christianity, faith is.

We also observe that monarchy is not the order of the day, collegiality is. James is in charge, but he speaks to a consensus that has developed from the group. The council is not making its own decision, but simply discerning through the Holy Spirit what God wants.

As a result, today's passage is rightly seen as one of the watershed events in the early church. We've certainly seen hints of what's at stake in previous chapters, but now the issues break out into the open. How exactly are the Gentiles going to get along with Jews if they do things that make them unclean (like eating non-kosher foods and not being circumcised)?

What we get in this passage is a model for how the church discerns the will of God.[54] Notice the key thing: the church always discerns the will of God together. Councils thus become essential in the early centuries of the church to work through theological and administrative difficulties and to discern God's will together.

One of the implications of this is that dissent and fierce argument are not always bad things. This is one reason I suggested earlier in this study that reading the early chapters of Acts as Luke's "idealized" picture of the early church was probably best. Everything was about harmony in the early chapters. Now it's not. Yet the disagreements here ultimately lead to a breakthrough in discerning what God wants.

While disagreements can be healthy, a divided church is not. In fact, it's a disaster. The church has effectively not had a true ecumenical council since the eastern churches broke away in the eleventh century. After the Reformation, this division only became worse, as Protestants and Roman Catholics went their separate ways. This is tragic. Not only has this division harmed the witness of the church in the broader culture, it harms the church's ability to discern what God wants us to do.

If we do nothing else, let's stop endlessly splitting the church. Rather, we should accept that disagreement is inevitable, and that the hard work of figuring out in a spirit of humility how we might forge a consensus with each other is essential. Dividers of the church often get all the attention, but those who work for unity, even when it seems impossible, might just have a more lasting impact.

Questions for Discussion

1. Table fellowship is key to the decisions of the Jerusalem council. To what extent do you see yourself as having the gift of hospitality? Do you ever try to invite someone different than you to break bread?

2. How much effort do you make to understand both sides of the political, social, and economic issues of our day? For example, do you consciously make an attempt to be conversant on both liberal and conservative viewpoints? How could you forge greater understanding?

3. What are the fiercely debated issues in the church where you've lost the ability to see things from your opponent's perspective? What would it take to gain greater perspective?

CHAPTER 31

AN INFALLIBLE CHURCH?
Acts 15.22-35

Acts 15.22-35

> *The church sends Paul and Barnabas back with two representa-*
> *tives from Jerusalem, Judas and Silas. They read out loud the letter*
> *from James that makes clear that Jerusalem is not trying to place*
> *undue burdens on them. Great joy comes to the Gentiles because*
> *it becomes clear that they have been accepted as full members of*
> *the community. The stipulations in the letter are to promote har-*
> *mony in the community so that Jews and Gentiles can fellowship*
> *together. The three key provisions: (1) refraining from meat offered*
> *to idols, (2) from blood and anything strangled and (3) from*
> *sexual immorality are all issues with the potential to cause discord*
> *in the community and are to be avoided for the sake of unity.*

Then the apostles and the presbyters, with the whole church, resolved to select men from among them to send to Antioch with Paul and Barnabas. They sent Judas (who is called Barsabbas) and Silas, leaders among the brethren, having written the following in a letter:

The apostles and presbyters, to the brethren throughout Antioch, Syria and Cilicia, and to the brethren from the Gentiles, greetings. Since we heard that some from among us unsettled you, distressing your souls with messages that were we did not authorize, we have unanimously resolved to select men to send to you with our beloved Barnabas and Paul who devoted their lives for the name of our Lord Jesus Christ. Therefore we have sent Judas and Silas who will explain these same things in person. For it seemed best to the Holy Spirit and to us not to place any greater burden on you more than what is necessary, that you should abstain from meat sacrificed to idols and from blood and from anything strangled and from sexual immorality. If you stay away from these things, you will do well. Farewell.

Then, having sent them off, they went down to Antioch, called together the whole congregation and delivered the letter. And, having read it out loud, the people rejoiced at the exhortation. Both Judas and Silas, themselves prophets, were encouraging and strengthening the brethren with a great message. And after spending time with them, they departed from the brethren with peace back to those who had sent them. Both Paul and Barnabas were going through Antioch teaching and proclaiming the good news (with many others) of the word of the Lord.

Leviticus 18.6-10, 17-24

All these regulations cover sexual relations and can be summed up with three general prohibitions: (1) no sexual relations within the immediate family, (2) no homosexuality and (3) no bestiality. The motivation behind these prohibitions is peace in the community and the clear transmission of the family line that will inherit the Promised Land.[55] *James likely has this section of Leviticus in mind when he tells the Gentiles to abstain from "sexual immorality."*

A man must not come near any of his near kin to have sex with her. It is a disgrace. I am the Lord. You must not have sex with your father or mother, for she is your mother and you must not have sex with her. You must not have sex with your father's wife, for it is a disgrace for your father. You must not have sex with your sister who comes from your father or your mother, whether born in your household or outside. It is a disgrace for her. You must not have sex with the daughter of your son or daughter, you must not have sex with them since it is shameful for you...You must not have sex with your daughter-in-law or your grand-daughter. They're your kin. It's impious! You must not take a wife in addition to her sister as a rival to have sex with her. It is a disgrace while your sister is alive.

You must not have sex with a woman during her period. You must not have sex with your neighbor's wife to copulate with her. You must not give your seed to serve Molech and you must not profane my Holy Name. I am the Lord. You must not lie with a man as with a woman for it is an abomination. You must not have sex with a quadruped to defile yourself with it. A woman shall not stand before any quadruped for copulation for it is loathsome. Do not defile yourselves with any of these things, for with all these things the nations I am driving out from before you have defiled themselves.

1 Corinthians 10.23-33

Paul's basic idea is that Christians should always exercise their liberty by being willing to subordinate their own desires for the sake of others and their consciences.[56] This includes meat offered to idols. In first-century markets, meat left over from pagan sacrifices to idols was usually of the highest quality and thus quite desirable for Gentiles.[57] But Jews believed that eating food offered to idols was a terrible, defiling practice.[58] Paul's suggestion that eating meat offered to idols is a matter of conscience might appear very different than in Acts where James tells Gentiles to avoid it. Yet their concerns are the same — trying to promote harmony between Jews and Gentiles.

All things are lawful, but not all things are profitable. All things are lawful but not all things edify. Let no one seek his own good, but the good of each other. Eat whatever is sold in the meat market without worrying about it because of conscience since "the earth is the Lord's and all that is in it" (Ps 24.1). If an unbeliever invites you for a meal and you want to go, eat everything set in front of you without worrying about it because of conscience. But if anyone says to you, "this is meat offered to an idol," do not eat because of the one who informed you and because of conscience. I don't mean your conscience, but the other's conscience. Why should my freedom be judged by another's conscience? If I partake with gracefulness, why am I blamed for food for which I am giving thanks? Therefore whether you eat or drink, whatever you do, do everything for the glory of God. Do be offensive either to Jews or to Greeks or to the church of God; just as I also please everyone in all things, do not live for your own benefit, but for the benefit of others so that they might be saved.

Comment

In this passage, Paul and Barnabas return to Antioch to deliver the good news. The Gentiles are to be included as full members of the church and without the requirement of circumcision. The Gentile men understandably rejoice!

The stipulations that the church provides for the Gentiles are mainly to ensure that Jews and Gentiles can have table fellowship together in harmony. Gentiles, although not strictly required to follow the ceremonial laws of the OT, are to respect it, nevertheless, out of deference for their Jewish brethren. Those from a Jewish background, on the other hand, are to make reasonable accommodations for their Gentile brethren by accepting them as brothers and sisters even though they're uncircumcised.

But, it's also a bit confusing since just a few years later when Paul writes 1 Corinthians, he apparently doesn't see meat offered to idols as inherently defiling. Idolatry is always bad, but meat offered to idols isn't. So we probably shouldn't see these decrees as necessarily binding for all time. What is binding is the need to make accommodations for the scruples of others. This is about table fellowship, not a new law. Or, as Jaroslav Pelikan puts it, "These 'decisions' or 'decrees' of the apostles and elders at Jerusalem belonged more to Christian observance than to Christian doctrine."[59]

Let me admit that there are some who would take serious issue with this last point (and with good reason). After all, the decrees of a properly constituted church council are usually thought to be binding. Yet food regulations quickly come to be seen as temporary in Scripture, while sexual immorality is understood as being universally binding. If this seems arbitrary, this is one reason why the debates on sexuality in our day are so fierce. How can we ever tell if something is binding for all time or not?

Gilbert Burnet, writing in the eighteenth-century, describes the typical Anglican response:

> [General councils] are received only because we are persuaded from the scriptures that their decisions were made according to them... we reverence those councils for the sake of their doctrine, but we do not believe the doctrine for the authority of the councils.[60]

According to Burnet, the decrees of a council only have validity to the extent that they teach faithfully what the scriptures teach. The food regulations in Scripture quickly come to be seen as temporary. But Scripture shows no such development with regard to sexuality. Of course, this does not end our modern debates around sexuality, but Burnet is nevertheless right that a council must "speak for the whole" and "agree with Scripture" to be valid.

I'll admit that I would ascribe more independent weight to the authority of councils than Burnet does. But notice what is at the heart of all this – love. For example, the sexual prohibitions in our Leviticus reading today aren't arbitrary regulations, they're about the potential for discord in the community and the potential for confusion in the family line. Similarly, refraining from things strangled and from blood is about respecting the conscience of others. The timeless principle to be found here is that we ought to be humble enough to accommodate others if we can.

The second thing this passage brings up is the problem of the infallibility of the church. James claims that what he's sending in the letter to the Gentiles at Antioch was given by the Holy Spirit. This implies that it has divine sanction and is therefore true. So can the church claim that its decisions are infallible like James does?

On the surface, this seems absurd. Maybe James could claim it in biblical times, but not today. The church obviously has erred and continues to err. How could anyone claim with a straight face that the church is infallible in any sense?

This becomes a particular problem when we consider the Roman Catholic claim of infallibility for the bishop of Rome when he speaks for the whole church (*ex cathedra*) on an issue of faith or morals, something the Pope has only done twice in the last one-hundred and fifty years. Do we have to agree with Papal infallibility? For example, do we really have to believe that Mary, the mother of Jesus, was assumed bodily into heaven or conceived without original sin in order to be a good Christian?

I would suspect that some of us might have some issues with that (even if there are good arguments for it – but that's a topic for a different book). Yet all that Papal infallibility is really claiming is that the bishop of Rome is the spokesman for the church which is itself infallible. But how can the church be infallible when it has changed its mind, erred, and done some pretty horrible things through the years? Are we just supposed to ignore the history?

One problem with infallibility is that the bishop of Rome is claiming to be able to speak for the whole church when defining a dogma that must be believed. Yet the church is divided and has been for centuries. As a result, the claim of infallibility is still difficult for most Anglicans to swallow.

But we still ought to believe that God is (1) somehow able to lead the church to correct understandings of his revelation, (2) that the church will prevail and that (3) its teachings are true. Thus, while some might be uncomfortable with infallibility, sometimes theologians will use a different term, "indefectibility," to say something more positive. Forgive the wordsmithing here, but I'm trying to be precise about what I mean. "Indefectibility" is how we describe the idea that while the church might not be infallible, God will nevertheless preserve its existence, its essential characteristics, and its teaching.[61]

We might have the Bible, the Creeds, and the writings of the church fathers, but we ultimately have to trust that we're standing on the shoulders of faithful recipients and interpreters of divine revelation who have handed down a correct understanding to us. Theoretically, revelation might be infallible because its source is God, but our understandings of that revelation are certainly fallible on our own.

This is why tradition is important when reading the Bible. If our understandings match what the Bible and the Tradition say, this should give us some confidence that what we're teaching has at least stood the test of time. This is important because if what we're teaching isn't true, aren't there better things to do on the weekend or more interesting books to read during the week (gulp)?

The church can and has erred grievously throughout its history. What we ought to believe, however, is that God cares about the church enough to keep the core of its teaching pristine.

Questions for Reflection

1. **Can you think of examples of when you had to make a reasonable accommodation for someone else's scruples or belief system? How did it make you feel? How might you become more adept at this skill?**
2. **What do you think about the question of an infallible or indefectible church? How can the church claim that its teaching is true if it has to be communicated by fallible human beings?**
3. **How useful do you find the Bible as a guide for life? Is it realistic to be able to incorporate an ancient set of texts into our modern lives?**

PAUL'S SECOND MISSIONARY JOURNEY
(ACTS 16–17)

CHAPTER 32

REPLACEMENT THEOLOGY
Acts 15.36-16.15

Acts 15.36-16.15

> *Paul begins his second missionary journey by separating from*
> *Barnabas after a fierce fight. Paul first heads north to Cilicia*
> *(where his hometown of Tarsus was located) and then heads west,*
> *at first retracing his steps through Derbe, Lystra, and Iconium,*
> *all towns where he had planted churches on his previous journey.*
> *Along the way, Paul finds Timothy, who becomes an important*
> *ministry partner. Paul eventually makes it across the Aegean Sea*
> *to Macedonia, thus crossing over into what we would know today*
> *as Europe. In Philippi, he encounters Lydia who becomes Paul's*
> *first convert there.¹ At each step of the way, the Holy Spirit guides*
> *Paul on his mission through dreams and visions. For the first*
> *time in Acts, Luke starts writing in first-person plural, indicating*
> *that he might have been an eye-witness to some of these events.*

Sometime later, Paul said to Barnabas, "Come, let's return and visit the brethren in every town where we proclaimed the word of the Lord to see how they're getting on." But Barnabas wanted to bring along John Mark. Yet Paul kept insisting that they shouldn't take along someone who had abandoned them at Pamphylia and had not gone along with them in the work. And so they had a sharp disagreement that resulted in their separating from one another. Barnabas took along John Mark and sailed away for Cyprus while Paul selected Silas, having been entrusted to the gift of God by the brethren. And they were going throughout Syria and Cilicia, strengthening the churches.

Then Paul arrived at Derbe and Lystra. There was a certain disciple there named Timothy, the son of a believing Jewish woman and a Greek father. He was well spoken of by the brethren in Lystra and Iconium and Paul wanted to take Timothy along with him, but first he took him and circumcised him because of the Jews who were in those places since they all knew that Timothy's father was a non-Jew. Then, going through the cities, they handed down to them the decrees decided by the apostles and the presbyters who were in Jerusalem in order that they might observe them. So the churches were being strengthened in faith and were growing in number day by day.

Then they went through the regions of Phyrgia and Galatia, having been prevented by the Holy Spirit from proclaiming the message in the province of Asia. After they came to Mysia, they attempted to go to Bithynia, but the Spirit of Jesus did not let them. So they went down to Troas. A vision appeared at night to Paul, in which a certain Macedonian man was standing and urging him, and saying, "Come over to Macedonia to help us!" After Paul saw the vision, immediately we desired to go to Macedonia, concluding that God was summoning us to proclaim the good news to the Macedonians.

Then putting out to sea from Troas, we set a straight course to Samothrace and the next day to Neapolis. From there we went on to Philippi, which is the leading city in the region of Macedonia, a Roman colony. And we remained in this city for several days. And, on the day of the Sabbath, we went outside the gate to the river where we figured we would find a place of prayer. Sitting down, Paul started speaking to the assembled women. And there was a certain God-fearing woman named Lydia, a purveyor of purple cloth from the city of Thyatira, who listened. The Lord opened her heart to give heed to what was said by Paul. After she and her household were baptized, she encouraged us, saying, "If you have deemed me to be a believer in the Lord, come to my house and stay." And thus did she prevail upon us.

Nehemiah 13.23-27

At the end of the exile, Nehemiah returns to start rebuilding Jerusalem, but finds not only lax security but also lax moral practices among the people. He excoriates the Israelites for their mixed marriages. The people had pledged not to marry foreigners just three chapters previously (Neh 10.30).[2] This presents a problem for Timothy in Acts. Since Timothy himself comes from a mixed marriage, why is Paul so eager to make him a trusted ministry partner? This passage provides an excellent example of how our understanding of God's will develops, even within the pages of Scripture itself.

Now in those days, I saw the Jews who had married women of Ashdod, Ammon, and Moab. Their children spoke in the Ashdodi tongue, and they did not know how to speak Hebrew. So I disputed with them, cursed them and beat some of the men. I plucked out their hair and made them swear by God, "You must not give your daughters to their sons, and you must not receive their sons from your daughters. You must not take their daughters to be with your sons." Did not Solomon, king of Israel, sin in this way? Now there was no king like him among many nations and he was beloved of God, and God made him king over all Israel. Yet his foreign wives turned him away. So we must not hear of your doing this evil in being faithless toward our God by marrying foreign wives.

2 Timothy 1.3-8, 13-14

Paul references Timothy, introduced for the first time in today's Acts passage, as a key ministry partner. The language of this passage becomes central for understanding what occurs at an ordination. By the laying on of hands, Paul passes down a specific charism to his young protégé for ministry. In turn, Timothy is to guard "the good deposit," usually understood as the body of apostolic teaching, passed down from generation to generation in the church.

I give thanks to God whom I serve with a clean conscience as my forbearers did, as I make mention of you without ceasing in my prayers night and day. As I remember your tears, I long to see you so that I might be filled with joy, remembering the genuine faith within you, which dwelt first in your grandmother Lois and your mother Eunice. I am also convinced that the faith is in you. For this reason, I remind you to rekindle the gift of God that is in you through the laying on my hands. For God did not give us a spirit of cowardice, but of power, love, and prudence. Therefore, do not be ashamed of the testimony of our Lord, nor of me, his prisoner, but join with me in suffering for the gospel by the power of God. Hold to the model of sound words that you heard from me in faith and love, which is in Christ Jesus. Guard the good deposit through the Holy Spirit who dwells within you.

Comment

We open up a new phase in our story as Paul commences his second missionary journey which will take him as far west as modern-day Europe. But the story begins inauspiciously as Barnabas and Paul have a big fight. In Greek, the language shows that this might have been an emotionally-wounding, friendship-ending argument.[3] We have to read between the lines a bit to piece together what happened.

The key to understanding this passage comes from an oblique mention of John Mark in Paul's later letter to the Colossians. Paul writes the following: "Mark, the cousin of Barnabas…if he comes to you, receive him" (Col 4.10). First, it seems that Paul and John Mark resolved their differences at some point, since Paul instructs the church to receive him. But the bad news is that at the time of today's Acts reading, Paul resolves to separate from them because of John Mark's disloyalty (John Mark had abandoned them at the start of their last missionary journey).

If John Mark really was related to Barnabas (as his cousin), this might have meant that Barnabas was putting family loyalty over the ministry. Paul sees this as a matter of principle and decides to separate from him. Given that Barnabas never shows up again in Acts, perhaps we can also infer that Luke agreed with Paul and saw Barnabas' misplaced loyalties as fundamentally flawed.[4] Yet the more important conclusion is that even despite the incompatible egos of the missionaries, this does not prevent the spread of the good news. It's still an unstoppable force because God is behind it.

We should never use this passage to justify ugly arguments between Christians.[5] As long as people are involved, however, there are going to be disagreements, but the Bible always urges us toward greater peace, humility, and deference toward others. Sadly, this scene has been repeated again and again in the history of the church. It is a reality of our humanity that we separate from each other.

In this passage, we also meet Timothy for the first time who becomes an important part of our story. Yet his call to be a ministry partner comes with some confusing details. The most confusing thing is why Paul feels compelled to circumcise Timothy. It is exceedingly ironic that Paul is going around proclaiming the decision of the Jerusalem council that denies the need for Gentile circumcision, yet Paul feels compelled to circumcise Timothy. Even worse, note what Paul writes in 1 Corinthians: "Was anyone at the time of his call uncircumcised? Let him not seek circumcision" (1 Cor 7.18).[6] What was Paul thinking?

Let's review some of the details we're given. We know that Timothy's mother is Jewish and that his father was non-Jewish (I say "was" because it's a pretty good bet that his father had already died). In the *Mishnah* (a collection of authoritative rabbinic pronouncements), it is clear that in a mixed marriage, the lineage passes down through the mother. Consider this passage: "But any situation in which a woman has no right to enter into betrothal with this man or with any other man – the offspring is in her status."[7]

Admittedly, there are some problems with dating the *Mishnah*. The above regulation could be something that comes in force in the years after today's Acts reading, but let's just assume it is in force now. That would mean that Timothy was officially Jewish.

If so, why hadn't he been circumcised? It's likely (but not certain) that he hadn't been circumcised because his father had prevented it while he was alive. Thus, since his father had died and since Timothy was officially Jewish, Paul might have had him circumcised in order to round out his Jewish credentials so that there would be no question of his mixed background when he ran into Jews on the journey. Once again we find Paul making reasonable accommodations for cultural sensitives for the purposes of the gospel.

Paul does not believe that circumcision is a source of redemption. Only faith working through God's grace is. Circumcision is simply a source of cultural identity. Nevertheless it is an important source of cultural identity because it marks one off as being a member of the covenant. Just being circumcised doesn't save, but faith in God's promises does.

Why is any of this important? Too many through the centuries have tried to rid Paul of his Jewishness. After Acts 9 when Paul sees the risen Christ in a vision, some have assumed that Paul leaves his Jewishness behind. But this has led to many mis-readings of Paul's writings and much anti-Semitism. We must not think that the Christian church somehow replaces Israel in God's redemptive plan.

Yet our story so far may have made it seem that God is done with Israel. If the glory of God had left the temple and now the Spirit had come to indwell the church, and, by extension, its members, it might seem logical to think that the church has taken over for Israel. But this passage shows us rather forcefully that this is not the case. God is not done with Israel and Paul has not stopped being Jewish.

The other problem with this so-called "replacement theology" is that it is theologically incoherent. As the theologian Robert Jenson has pointed out, if the Messiah has come, the church exists *within* the single messianic advent. Both Jews and Christians are waiting for the Messiah's return. As Jenson puts it, "The church is a *detour* from the expected straight path of the Lord's intentions, a detour to accommodate the mission to Jews and gentiles."[8] Ultimately, Jesus comes to inaugurate a kingdom that includes both Jews and Gentiles, not to forget about Israel.

Paul wants everyone to turn and follow Jesus but he seems to have no problem with circumcision once we remove it from the context of salvation. This is why in the same passage from 1 Corinthians that I cited above, Paul writes, "Was anyone at the time of his call already circumcised? Let him not seek to remove the marks of circumcision" (1 Cor 7.18).

Paul never stops being Jewish, and he welcomes both Jews and Greeks to hear the message of the good news. Cultural identities are fine and ought to be respected. But spreading faith in the risen Christ is what this missionary movement is all about.

Questions for Reflection:

1. Have you ever had to disassociate from someone who was disloyal in your family, at work or in the church? What was that like? How did you handle it?

2. Even after the experience of World War II, anti-Semitism is still alive and well in our world. Have you ever seen this at work in our society or community? How should we express solidarity with our Jewish brethren?

3. What factional fights are going on in your world? Do you have any influence to bring greater harmony to warring parties at work or in your family? Are you the cause of factionalism?

CHAPTER 33

UNJUST PUNISHMENT
Acts 16.16-40

Acts 16.16-40

While in Philippi, Paul and Silas deal with an angry, anti-Semitic mob. Philippi was an important Roman colony originally occupied by former army officers as a means of bringing peace to the region.[9] After casting out a spirit from a servant girl that brought "much profit" to her masters, the owners react violently. Eventually, Paul and Silas are beaten and then thrown into prison by the authorities, but are freed the next day. After revealing their status as Roman citizens, there is a great reversal. The magistrates, having violated Roman law, are shamed while Paul and Silas are honored.[10] This whole scene parallels Peter's actions in Jerusalem at the beginning of our story. Both Paul and Peter make converts, confront demonic spirits, and are imprisoned.[11] But, as always, the good news continues its advance.

Now, as we were going to the place of prayer, a certain servant girl, having a spirit of divination, opposed us. The girl's divination activity brought great profit to her masters. She kept following Paul and us around, crying out, "These men are servants of the most-high God, who will proclaim to you the way of salvation." Now she kept doing this for many days. And Paul became annoyed. Turning, he said to her spirit, "I command you in the name of Jesus Christ to come out from her." And instantly the spirit came out from her.

But when her masters saw that their hope of profit had vanished, they grabbed Paul and Silas, hauling them into the marketplace before the authorities. Leading them to the magistrates, they said, "These men, being Jews, are agitating our city and are proclaiming that our customs are not lawful for us to receive or practice as Romans." And the crowd joined in the attack against them. So the magistrates tore the garments off Paul and Silas and ordered a beating. After striking them with many blows, they cast them into prison, giving orders to the jailor to hold them securely. After receiving the command, they cast them into the inner prison and secured their feet in stocks.

Now at about midnight, Paul and Silas were praying ["proseuxomai"] and singing hymns ["hymneo"] to God and the other prisoners were listening to them. Then, suddenly, a great earthquake came that shook the foundations of the prison. And immediately all the doors were opened and all the stocks came off. And when the jailer awoke and saw that the doors of the prison were opened, he drew his sword and was about to kill himself, assuming that the prisoners had escaped. But Paul cried out with a loud voice, "Don't harm yourself! We're all still here!"

Requesting torches, he rushed in and fell down trembling before Paul and Silas. Bringing them outside, he said, "Sirs, what must I do to be saved?" And they said, "Believe in the Lord Jesus and you will be saved – you and your household." And they explained to him the word of the Lord with all who were in his household. And at that hour of the night, he took Paul and Silas and washed their wounds. And the jailer, together with all his whole household were baptized right away. Then the jailer brought them into the house and set food on the table before them. Having believed in God, the whole household rejoiced greatly.

Now, when it was day, the magistrates sent officers, saying, "Release those men." And the jailor told these words to Paul: "The magistrates have given orders to release you. So now depart and go in peace." And Paul said to the officers, "They beat us in public without a trial. We are Roman citizens thrown into prison and now they want to send us away secretly? No way! They should come and escorted us out!" So the officers went out and told the magistrates these words. And they were afraid when they heard that they were Roman citizens. So they went out, apologized to them and brought them out, asking them repeatedly to leave the city. So they went out from the prison and came to Lydia's house. Seeing the brethren, Paul and Silas encouraged them and then left.

Daniel 3.19-24

> *The story of Shadrach, Meshach, and Abednego is one of the most famous in the OT. For space reasons, I offer just a short excerpt from it here. After refusing to bow down to an image of the Babylonian king, Shadrach, Meshach, and Abednego are cast into a fiery furnace. Not only do they survive this ordeal, but there also appears a mysterious "fourth man" in the furnace, which, while unnamed, Christian readers have usually taken to be Jesus. Their miraculous deliverance leads to the conversion of the king. Luke could have had this story in mind as he was writing because both narratives contain prayer and hymn-singing in the midst of great adversity, before experiencing God's deliverance.*

Then Nebuchadnezzar was filled with fury and the form of his countenance was altered, with the result that he commanded the furnace to be fired 7x hotter than normal. And he commanded the mighty men to bind Shadrach, Meshach, and Abednego and to throw them into the burning fiery furnace. Since the edict of the king prevailed and the furnace was heated seven times more than normal, the men were bound feet first, brought to the furnace and cast inside. Then the shackled three men, Shadrach, Meshach and Abednego, fell into the midst of the burning fiery furnace. Meanwhile the three were praying ["proseuxomai"] and singing hymns ["hymneo"] to the Lord.

1 Thessalonians 2.1-8

Thessalonica is about one-hundred miles south-west of Philippi and is the location of our next episode (Acts 17).[12] Paul writes a tender letter to the church he planted there, recalling his mistreatment in Philippi, which is likely a reference to the events in today's reading. Paul links unjust suffering with his empowerment to proclaim the good news.[13]

For you yourselves know, brethren, that our coming to you was not in vain. Although we suffered previously and were mistreated in Philippi, as you well know, we had courage in our God to speak the good news of God to you in the face of opposition. For our exhortation did not stem from unclean motives or from deceit. But just as we have been approved by God to be entrusted with the good news, thus do we speak, not as people pleasers but it is God who searches our hearts.

For we never came with flattering speech, as you well know, nor with greedy motives, God is our witness. We sought no glory from men, or from you or from anyone, even if we are able to claim importance as apostles of Christ. But we became like little children among you. Like a nursing mother cherishing her own children, with such longing for you, we were well pleased to share not only God's good news but also our own lives with you, so dear have you become to us.

Comment

We should first notice a grammatical detail in this passage. All of a sudden Luke starts writing in the first person (the first unambiguous "we" reference was in yesterday's reading, Acts 16.10-12). Notice the first sentence: "Now as *we* were going to the place of prayer." (Acts 16.16).

The reason this is worth pointing out is that it might provide some evidence that Luke really was the author of Acts. Given that Luke is nowhere named in Acts as the author, this is a significant detail. Luke perhaps employs the first person because he's taking part in the story at this point.

We know from 2 Timothy that Luke was Paul's frequent traveling companion, and was with Paul before his death (2 Tim 4.11). Moreover, we also know that Luke was a physician (Col 4.14). In fact, there was a famous medical college in Philippi during this period.[14] Could it be that Luke joined the missionary endeavor himself at this point and thus is writing eyewitness testimony? We can't really be sure, but it is at least plausible.

The second thing to notice (it's so obvious, that it's easy to miss) is that Paul and Silas are let go the day after the riot. This is important because we're going to start seeing this pattern repeat over and over again. Opponents will consistently accuse Paul during his missionary journeys of various treasonous acts. But it will become clear that Paul is not guilty of sedition. This is a very important point that Luke is trying to make.

Luke is writing Acts, in part, to demonstrate that Christians are good citizens and are no real threat to the Roman government. But this pacific attitude almost always stands in tension with the good news that proclaims Jesus as the Resurrected and Ascended Lord. If Jesus is Lord of all (as we learned from Acts 10.36), then, almost by definition, Caesar is not. Duke's Kavin Rowe, who first noticed this linkage, writes the following:

> Luke narrates the movement of the Christian mission into the gentile world as a collision with culture-constructing aspects of that world…Christianity and pagan culture are competing realities… On the other hand, Luke narrates the threat of the Christian mission in such a way as to eliminate the possibility of conceiving it as in direct competition with the Roman government. Of all forms of sedition and treason, Luke tells, Christianity is innocent.[15]

This important tension will be with us throughout the book of Acts and will govern the rest of our story.

Notice as well that Luke presents this tension in economic terms in today's passage. The owners of the servant girl were angry because their profits were gone once Paul cast out the spirit of divination from her. We ought to realize that this is a very common line of thought for Luke.[16] To Luke, money and spirituality are necessarily entwined.

We see that the owners of the servant girl are greedy. They don't care at all about the girl, only their profits. By contrast, the jailor is more receptive. After he finds Paul and Silas still in the prison, he invites them into his home, offers them table fellowship and washes their wounds. One shares his possessions, receives the good news, and is baptized. Another is greedy and cannot hear the message.

Further, when the jailor finds Paul and Silas, he utters one of the more famous statements in the Bible, a phrase that has been repeated in countless evangelistic sermons: "What must I do to be saved?" Paul's response is the typical shorthand reply for early Christianity: "Believe in the Lord Jesus Christ." Paul links salvation to faith.

We must not forget what happened right before this famous statement, however. There was a huge earthquake, something fairly typical for this seismically-unstable region. It's very likely that the jailor is really asking how he can be delivered from the divine judgment that he thinks is about to come, announced by the earthquake.[17]

Even if he initially misunderstands what the good news entails, the jailor's generosity has made him receptive to God's grace. Right after he hears Paul's teaching, the jailor is baptized together with his whole family. This is receptivity in action.

Finally, although it is impossible to settle this issue from this particular passage or even the book of Acts as a whole, this episode offers important affirmative evidence for the practice of baptizing children, something that continues to be controversial in some traditions. The controversy stems from the claim that there is no place in the Bible where infants or children are baptized.

Yet we observe from today's story how this claim, while understandable, is not particularly well-founded. Notice that the jailor was baptized along with "his own whole household." Although there is no specific mention of babies or children in this text, it strains credulity to think there were no children around in a first-century household.[18]

By contrast, the businesspeople are simply lost in their greed. Once again, we see that God's grace and human activity are not opposed to each other, but instead cooperate together in a profoundly mysterious way. The jailor was generous and welcoming, but the businesspeople were not. Generosity prepares the way for the good news and for baptism in a profound way.

Questions for Reflection:

1. Paul's Roman citizenship helps him in today's episode. In what ways do you take being a citizen seriously? To what extent is the public square an important place for Christians to exercise their influence and witness?
2. Recall a time when you suffered mistreatment at the hands of someone in authority? How did you handle it? Did this impact your faith in any important way?
3. Notice the honor-shame motif at work in this passage. The jailor was about to commit suicide because he had failed at his job. We all carry around shame in one form or another. Are the scars of past shameful events still with you?

CHAPTER 34

HOW TO READ THE BIBLE
Acts 17.1-15

Acts 17.1-15

> *Today's episode is a study in contrasts. Paul and Silas receive resistance in Thessalonica, but broad acceptance in Berea. This passage serves as a kind of summary for the resistance that Paul will encounter wherever he goes. Essentially, the charge is treason. But the political makeup of Thessalonica makes this an especially interesting case because of Thessalonica's status as a "free city" without a Roman administrative structure.[19] Once again, the authorities do not take the charge of treason very seriously since they let Jason, Paul, and Silas' host, go with the payment of a security bond.*

After passing through Amphipolis and Apollonia, Paul, Silas, and Timothy came to Thessalonica where there was a Jewish synagogue. According to his custom, Paul came to the Jews on the Sabbath, and for three weeks, he reasoned from the scriptures, explaining that it was necessary for the Messiah to suffer and to rise from the dead, exclaiming, "This Jesus, who I am proclaiming to you, is the Messiah."

Now some of them were won over and joined with Paul and Silas along with a large group of God-fearing Greeks and quite a number of prominent women. But the Jews turned zealous and taking along some low-life rabble-rousing men, they formed a mob that threw the city into disorder. They attacked Jason's house, seeking Paul and Silas to haul them off to the citizens' council. But when they didn't find Paul or Silas, they dragged Jason out with some associates before the city officials, crying out, "These men, who turned the world upside down, have come to this place too. Jason has served as their host! They are all acting against the decrees of Caesar, claiming that this Jesus is another King. And they whipped up the crowd and the city officials who heard these things. So after receiving bail from Jason and the others, the officials released them.

But the brethren that very night sent away both Paul and Silas to Berea. When they arrived at the Jewish synagogue, they went inside. Now, those in Berea were more open-minded than in Thessalonica. They received the message with all eagerness, day after day investigating the scriptures to see if these things might be so. As a result, many of them believed along with quite a number of prominent Greek women and men.

But when the Jews from Thessalonica became aware that Paul and Silas were in Berea, where Paul was proclaiming the word of God, they came there to incite and whip up the crowds. So right away the brethren sent Paul away to go to the coast, while Silas and Timothy remained in Berea. And those who accompanied Paul brought him all the way to Athens. After taking down instructions for Silas and Timothy to come as soon as possible to Paul, they departed.

1 Thessalonians 2.9-16

This passage continues the reading from 1 Thessalonians from the previous chapter. There is great complementarity between Paul's visit to Thessalonica in Acts and his later reflections on that visit here. The two texts ought to be read together. Paul has not rejected his Jewish brethren, rather he is expressing his sharp frustration over their resistance to the good news. To Paul (and Luke), their charge of treason is baseless. If anything, because of Jewish complicity in handing Jesus over to the Romans, they are closer to treason than Paul is. Yet such resistance never stops Paul from seeking out the Jews in the synagogues.

For you remember, brethren, our labor and our toil, how day and night we worked in order not to be a burden to any of you while we proclaimed to you the good news of God. You are witnesses, as is God, how piously, innocently, and devoutly we acted toward those who believe. As you well know, we treated each of you as a father treats his own child — encouraging, consoling, and imploring you to walk in a manner worthy of God who called you to his own kingdom and glory.

For this reason, we give thanks to God without ceasing since when you received God's message that you heard from us, you received it not as a message from men, but as what it is really is, the word of God, which is at work in those who believe. For you became imitators, brethren, of the churches of God that are in Judea in Christ Jesus since you yourselves also suffered at the hands of your own compatriots just as they did from the Jews who killed both the Lord Jesus and the prophets, having persecuted us severely. They are displeasing to God and opposed to all people, having prevented us from speaking to the Gentiles that they might be saved. Thus they always fill up their sins, and wrath has completely overtaken them.

Luke 24.13-27

This is one of the most important texts in the Bible dealing with hermeneutics, the art and science of biblical interpretation. On the third day after his crucifixion, Jesus appeared to two disciples on the road to Emmaus. They didn't recognize him. After recounting what had happened, Jesus explained that the whole of the OT was to be read in light of himself, making Jesus the interpretive key to the Bible. When Christians read the OT in light of Christ, they are doing so according to the explicit instructions of Jesus given here. Luke might be referencing this text when Paul argues in Thessalonica that "it was necessary for the Messiah to suffer."

Now, on that very day, two of them were going to a village called Emmaus, about seven miles from Jerusalem. And they were conversing with one another about everything that had taken place. And while they were conversing and debating these things, Jesus himself appeared and started walking with them (their eyes were kept from recognizing him). And he said to them, "What are these things that you're discussing with one another while you walk?" And they stopped, looking gloomy.

Then one, named Cleopas, said to him, "Are you the only one living in Jerusalem who does not know what happened there over these days?" Jesus said to them, "What things?" And they said to him, "The things concerning Jesus the Nazarene who was a Prophet, mighty in word and deed before God and before the people. The high priests handed him over and our leaders gave him the death penalty and crucified him. Now we were hoping that he was the one who was going to redeem Israel. But now three days have gone by since these things took place.

Moreover, some women from our group astonished us. They were at his tomb early this morning and didn't find his body. They came and told us that they had seen a vision of some angels, who claimed that he's alive. So some of us went out to the tomb and found it just as they women had said, but they didn't actually see him."

Then Jesus said to them, "O foolish and slow of heart to believe all that the prophets have said! Was it not necessary for the Messiah to suffer and to enter into his glory?" Starting from Moses and all the Prophets, Jesus explained to them all the things written about himself in all the scriptures.

Comment

This episode is very easy to misunderstand without an important piece of background information. Thessalonica, because of its favorable attitude toward the Roman Emperor Octavian (who later became Caesar Augustus), had been freed in 42 BC.[20]

The reason this is important is that it helps us understand the strategy of Paul's opponents. Unlike other places (like Philippi), there was no Roman administrative structure in Thessalonica. Thus the Jews' strategy for ridding the place of Christians by inciting a mob makes sense, since severe punishments could be handed out without the possibility of appeal to higher Roman authorities.[21] Paul and Silas' Roman citizenship doesn't count for much here.

The other reason this is important is that it demonstrates that the local reaction of the Jews to Paul's preaching is not primarily about his interpretation of the Bible. The main problem is political.[22] The Jews incite a mob to show that Paul's exhortations are subversive to the society as a whole.[23] In so doing, they hope to get Paul and Silas thrown out of town and perhaps locked up for good.

As noted in the previous chapter, Luke's burden in Acts is to show that Christians really aren't traitors. He shows this through the reaction of the political authorities. Surprisingly, they let Jason off with the payment of a security bond. Luke once again takes pains to show that although the Jews keep claiming that Christians are treasonous, they're really not. The subdued reaction of the authorities bears this out.

Luke also goes out of his way to paint a contrast between Paul and his Jewish opponents. Paul is depicted as a calm, reasoned philosopher. When he spends his three weeks explaining the scriptures in the synagogue, Luke describes this with distinctly philosophical words. Paul "reasons," "explains," and "points out" the ties between Jesus' life, death, resurrection, and ascension with the Hebrew Bible.

By contrast, Paul's opponents incite a mob of "low-life rabble rousers." Once again, politics, not theology, is the center of the conflict. The tension between declaring Jesus as Lord and maintaining loyalty to Caesar is central to this part of Acts.[24]

Paul then goes to Berea and receives a very different welcome (at least at first). Rightly, I think, the Bereans come to be seen as a model for how to study the Bible well. They do several things: they read (1) "daily," (2) "eagerly," and (3) with an "open mind." They also "investigate" the scriptures, suggesting that they read the Bible as a whole, not as disconnected passages, and ask hard questions of the text. Finally, they read together within the church.

This is quite a bit different than how many Christians in our culture approach Bible study. It's relatively rare to find Bible studies anymore that want to explore the connections between the OT and NT. It's also rare to find studies whose focus is on the church and its teachings. In short, we need each other and the tradition of the church to read the Bible well. Divorcing the Bible from theology, from tradition, and from each other is a lousy way to read.

The way I've tried to organize this book has the "Berean" example in mind. Every day I'm trying to emphasize the connections throughout the scriptures much like Paul did. I'm also very eager to demonstrate how our Anglican tradition has uniquely understood these passages. It would be a very odd thing to study the growth of the early church in Acts while at the same time thinking the church is somehow irrelevant for understanding the scriptures. As modern readers of the Bible, we must not ignore those who have come before us, but instead must embrace them as the strong shoulders on which we stand as we read.

The Bible is God's gift of revelation to us. But we must not think that private Bible study, disconnected from the church, is the key to spiritual growth. After all, few in the first fifteen-hundred years of the church had a private copy of the scriptures. Put simply, we need each other, the church, scholarship, and the tradition of interpretation that has been handed down through the centuries to read the Bible well. The Bereans were a community of learners. We should be too.

Questions for Reflection:

1. **The Daily Office in the BCP is an important way that way Anglicans through the centuries have individually approached the scriptures. Do you find this resource helpful? Why or why not?**

2. **How much time do you allot in your week to meet with other Christians to study the Bible? Would it help you to have a greater commitment to this?**

3. **How helpful has the Berean approach that "searches the scriptures daily" been to you? How might you continue "searching the scriptures" even after completing this study?**

CHAPTER 35

PAUL AS SOCRATES
Acts 17.16-34

Acts 17.16-34

> *For centuries, readers have been enthralled with the episode of*
> *Paul in Athens, a wandering preacher confronting the intelligen-*
> *tsia of his day. Luke shows a mastery not only of Greek philosophi-*
> *cal schools, but also of Athenian practices.[25] The key to this episode*
> *is recognizing that Paul is not having a nice, friendly debate with*
> *some Epicurean and Stoic philosophers. Rather, the Areopagus was*
> *a judicial tribunal and Paul is under arrest. Like Plato's Socrates*
> *(with whom this scene finds multiple parallels), Paul is arguing*
> *for his life here, since the penalty for introducing an unauthor-*
> *ized religious cult was death.[26] But, as we've come to expect, the*
> *authorities find little to charge Paul with, and let him go.*

While Paul was waiting for Silas and Timothy in Athens, his spirit was vexed when he saw that the city was full of idols. So he was debating in the synagogue with the Jews and God-fearers, as well as in the marketplace day after day with whomever happened to be present. Some of the Epicurean and Stoic philosophers were conversing with him and some were asking, "What does this ignorant babbler want to say?" Others were saying, "He thinks of himself as a proclaimer of foreign gods." They said this because Paul was proclaiming the good news about Jesus and the resurrection.

So they arrested him and brought him before the Areopagus council, saying, "We have a right to know what new teaching is being proclaimed by you. For you are bringing some astonishing things into our hearing. Therefore, we want to know what these things are." All the Athenians, as well as the resident aliens, did practically nothing except spend time telling or listening to whatever was new.

But Paul stood up in the midst of the Areopagus council and said, "Men of Athens, I see that you are very religious (and superstitious) in every respect. For when I went about and carefully observed your sanctuaries, I also found an altar inscribed, 'To an unknown god.'

Therefore, what you worship unknowingly, this I proclaim to you: "The God who made the universe and all things in it, he is Lord of heaven and earth and does not dwell in shrines made with human hands ["keiropoietos"], nor is he served by human hands ["keiron"], as if he needed anything. He gave life and breath to all things and to everyone. From one man, he made every human nation to dwell over the whole face of the earth, setting fixed seasons and setting the boundaries of their dwelling places so that they would seek God; so that, perhaps, if they groped around for him, they might find him. For indeed he is not far from each one of us. 'For in him, we live and move and have our being,' as even some of your own Poets have said, 'For we too are his offspring.'

Therefore, being offspring of God, we should not think that the Divine is like gold, silver, or precious stone, an image fashioned by human ingenuity or imagination. Although God has overlooked the times of ignorance, now he is commanding people everywhere to repent. In fact, he has fixed a day on which he is going to judge the world, in righteousness, by a man whom he has appointed, providing proof to all by raising him from the dead."

When they heard about the resurrection from the dead, some began to scoff. But others said, "Let's hear from you about this again." So Paul departed from their midst. And some of the men joined with Paul and believed. Among them were Dionysius, a member of the Areopagus council, and a woman named Damaris, as well as others with them.

Genesis 1.1-3, 26-28, 31

Notice the slight variations in the Septuagint's rendering of the creation story. At creation (according to the Greek translation of the Bible, the Septuagint), the earth was "invisible and form- less." This is why several early Christian authors (in particular, Origen, Augustine, Basil, and Gregory of Nyssa) thought that the first several days of creation were not about physical creation, but about the creation of divine archetypes or even immaterial angels. Luke clearly has the creation story in mind as he records Paul's speech in Athens. Not only does Paul refute the charge of teach- ing "something new" with his speech, his argument flows from the creation of the universe to humankind, thus mirroring Genesis.

In the beginning, God made heaven and earth. And the earth was invisi- ble and unformed and darkness was over the abyss and the Spirit of God was rushing over the waters. And God said, "Let there be light," and there was light. And God saw that the light was good. So God divided the light and the darkness. God called the light 'Day' and the darkness he called 'Night.' And it was evening and morning, one day.

And God said, "Let us make man according to our image and accord- ing to our likeness and let them rule over the fish of the sea and over the birds of the sky and over the all the creatures of the earth and all the creeping things that creep upon the earth." So God made man. According to the image of God he made him, male and female he created them. And God blessed them and said, "Multiply, increase and fill the earth and exercise dominion over it. Rule over the fish of the sea and over the birds of the sky and over all the creatures over the whole earth and over all the creeping things that creep upon the earth"...And God saw all things that he had made and, indeed, it was very good.

Isaiah 31.1-9

> *Isaiah threatens judgment for those who do not look to Yahweh for their help. This includes the Egyptians, Assyrians, and even Israel itself. God has sworn to protect Israel, but they must repent and rid themselves of their idols that God detests.[27] This text is parallel to Paul's speech in Athens because of its polemic against idolatry. In both, "things made with human hands," a common Semitic way of describing idolatry, is invoked. The result is that they must turn away from idols, which cannot save them, to the one true God who will save them on judgment day.*

Woe to those who go down to Egypt for help, who trust in chariots because they are many, or in horses because of their multitude, but have not trusted in the Holy One of Israel and have not sought God. Therefore he has wisely brought calamities upon them and his Word will by no means be foiled. He will rise up against the houses of wicked men and against their futile hopes, who hope in the men of Egypt and not in God, and in the flesh of horses when there is no helper in them.

But the Lord will bring down his hand upon them and the helpers will grow weary and every one of them will perish. Thus says the Lord, "In the same way as a lion might roar when its cub is taken as prey, or cry out over its cub until the mountains reverberate with the lion's voice, or the animals succumb and are terrified at the fierceness of the lion's wrath, so the Lord of Hosts will march against Mt. Zion, Israel's own mountain. As the birds fly, so will the Lord protect, save and deliver Jerusalem."

Repent, O children of Israel who have offered profoundly sinful counsel. For on that day, men will renounce their silver and gold idols ["keiropoietos"], made by human hands ["keires"]. The Assyrians will fall. Neither human sword nor dagger will devour him. He won't flee from the sword but the young men will be overthrown for they will be surrounded by rocks like a trench and will be defeated. But those who flee will perish. Thus says the Lord, "Blessed is he who has offspring in Zion and household friends in Jerusalem."

Comment

In Plato's account of the last days of Socrates, Socrates stands before a jury of Athenian citizens and makes a defense (an "apology") against charges of impiety and corruption of the youth of Athens. For years, Socrates had roamed around Athens, engaging in dialogues with powerful people on various topics. He always presented himself as a student just trying to learn from others.

But, in the course of most of Plato's dialogues, it turns out that the learned and powerful men of Athens have no idea what they're talking about. Great law-makers and judges don't know what justice is (*Republic*, *Euthyphro*); great lovers don't know what love is (*Symposium*); and great teachers don't know how learning takes place (*Meno*). Since Socrates' logic usually shames the powerful, many grow to dislike him, while the youth of Athens thoroughly enjoy watching their elders come undone. Eventually, this leads to Socrates' arrest and trial.

Plato recounts the charges against Socrates as follows:

> Let this suffice as a defense against the charges of my earlier accusers… [Their charge] goes something like this: Socrates is guilty of corrupting the young and of not believing in the gods in whom the city believes, but in other new deities.[28]

This is eerily similar to the charges against Paul, so close that Luke has obviously modeled this scene on Socrates' life. Paul is charged with proclaiming the good news about Jesus and the resurrection (Acts 17.18). Although this is very easy to miss, the reference to the "resurrection" here represents a misunderstanding on the Athenians' part. Given their polytheistic mindset, they think the "resurrection" is the name of another god.[29] So, just like Socrates, Paul is on trial for introducing "new deities" into Athens without authorization.

This is quite a bit different than the way this story is "normally" read. The typical reading is to understand Paul as having a nice, calm, intellectual discussion with some pagan philosophers. But this turns out not to be right. Paul is on trial for his life.

When Paul calls his judges "very religious," he employs the Greek word ["deisidaimon"] which can mean either "religious" or "superstitious."[30] Note that I have kept both of these senses in my translation above. He is deliberately playing on the two possible senses of the word. On the one hand, Paul's listeners would have heard this as a polite opening to his speech (they're very devout). But, we, as readers, are supposed to hear it for what it really is — they are superstitious idolaters.[31]

Paul then makes a reference to the creation account, alluding to today's Genesis and Isaiah readings. In so doing, Paul is refuting the charge of introducing something new by playing his trump card. He is talking about the oldest thing of all, the God who created the heavens and the earth![32] They're the ones introducing something new. After all, the Athenians have an altar to "an unknown God."[33]

Thus, similar to what we observed yesterday, there is an inherently hostile political component to this story. But, following the pattern we keep observing, somehow Paul manages to escape death. This is most unlike Socrates, who was famously forced to drink hemlock and die. This underlines Luke's main point that Christians are not a threat to governmental authorities and can hold their own in any forum.[34]

What should we take away from this story? Paul provides us with a very effective model for speaking about our faith in the public square. Notice that Paul is polite and learned, but never surrenders his faith. He knows enough about pagan ideas and poetry to invoke them approvingly. He certainly respects them. But he offers a distinctly Christian perspective informed by Christ and the resurrection.

Perhaps we will never have to stand before a judicial tribunal, arguing for our lives like Paul does in this scene. But we do need to be good citizens and neighbors. This means respecting others enough to take the time to understand their ideas. Paul has obviously done that.

This doesn't stop Paul from getting upset at what he sees. But he understands what is going on well enough to use the Athenians' own language and popular poets to frame his response. Our task is similar. Our job is not to hide from the culture, but to interact with it using its own language and its sources. The power of a truly transformed life and a genuinely loving attitude is strong enough to meet the superstitions of our age.

Questions for Reflection:

1. **Our culture is all about seeking out "what is new." What are the disadvantages to that mindset? What happens when we are constantly trying to uproot authorities and traditions?**
2. **The church, of course, is very old. But what things within the church should change? What are the risks of being so beholden to tradition that we miss out on legitimate developments?**
3. **What things upset you in our modern culture? What do you do with those who hold to something that you despise? How does that affect your spiritual life?**

CHAPTER 36

THE VALUE OF WORK
Acts 18.1-11

Acts 18.1-11

Paul now moves southwest and comes to Corinth, about sixty-five miles away from Athens. The church at Corinth is the recipient of two letters from Paul that are included in the NT (1ˢᵗ and 2ⁿᵈ Corinthians). As the location of the famous Isthmian Games, as well as the provincial capital of the region of Achaia, Corinth was a bustling commercial and cultural center.³⁵ It was also known for its unbridled sexual license at a level shocking for its day.³⁶ At Corinth, Paul meets Priscilla and Aquila, fellow tent-makers, who become important ministry partners. Luke follows a similar pattern in describing this scene: Paul preaches, meets resistance, threatens to turn from the Jews, but finds some who believe, including the head of the Jewish synagogue. Once again, resistance does not prevent the spread of the good news.

After these things, Paul departed from Athens and came to Corinth. There he found a certain Jewish man named Aquila, who was from Pontus, who had recently come from Italy with his wife, Priscilla, because Claudius had ordered all Jews to depart from Rome. Paul came to them. Because he was practicing the same trade, Paul stayed with them and was working. They were tentmakers by trade. Now Paul engaged in debate in the synagogue every Sabbath, trying to convince both Jews and Greeks.

But, when both Silas and Timothy came down from Macedonia, Paul started occupying himself with the word, bearing witness to the Jews that Jesus was the Messiah. But when the Jews resisted and insulted him, he shook off his garments and said to them, "Your blood be on your heads! I am guiltless. From now on, I am going to the Gentiles."

After Paul left from there, he came to the house of a certain man named Titius Justus, a God-fearing Gentile, whose house was next door to the synagogue. Then Crispus, the head of the synagogue, believed in the Lord together with his whole household. When many of the Corinthians heard the good news, they believed and were baptized.

And the Lord spoke at night through a vision to Paul, saying, "Do not be afraid ["meh phobou"], but speak and do not be silent, since I am with you ["ego meta sou"], and no one will lay a hand on you to harm you because I have many people in this city." So he stayed there for a year and six months, teaching the word of God among them.

Genesis 28.10-20

Jacob, having underhandedly stolen the birthright from his brother Esau, flees, retracing in reverse order Abraham's journey into the Promised Land.[37] God reiterates the promise of the covenant he made with Abraham (blessings will go to all nations) and promises to be with him. When Paul encounters the risen Christ in a night vision in today's Acts passage, he hears an echo of the same promise, "I will be with you." Similarly, God encourages Paul to keep going on the mission to which God has called him, since God will protect him.

Then Jacob departed from the Well of the Oath and went into Canaan. And he came to a certain place and slept there, for the sun had set. And he took a stone from the place and put it under his head and fell asleep in that place. And in a dream there was a ladder ["klimax"] on the ground whose top reached to heaven, and the angels of God were going up and coming down on it.

And the Lord leaned on it and said, "I am the Lord God of Abraham your forefather and the God of Isaac, do not be afraid ["meh phobou"]. I will give the ground on which you are sleeping to you and to your offspring. And your offspring will be like the sand of the earth and they shall spread out to the sea, to the south, to the north, and to the east. And through you and your offspring will all the families of the earth be blessed.

For behold, I am with you ["ego meta sou"], protecting you in all your ways that you might go. And I will return you to this land since I will by no means leave you until you have all the things I have told you." Then Jacob woke up from his sleep and he said, "The Lord is in this place and I didn't know it." And he was afraid and said, "This is place is awesome. This is none other than the house of God and the gate of heaven"...So Jacob took an oath, saying, "If the Lord God will be with me ["met' emou"] , and will protect me on this journey I'm going on and will return me safely to the house of my father, then the Lord shall be God for me."

1 Corinthians 1.10-18

Paul writes harshly to the church at Corinth for falling back into their former patterns of sin. Paul charges them to end their divisions. Although it is clear that Luke did not have 1 Corinthians to use as a source for today's Acts reading, nevertheless the large number of details which match give us confidence about the historicity of Luke's account.[38] In this particular passage, Paul references the baptism of Crispus, the head of the synagogue, who converted after hearing Paul's teaching.

Now I urge you, brethren, by the name of our Lord Jesus Christ, to be in agreement and to end the divisions among you, being united in him in both mind and purpose. For it is reported to me about you, my brethren, by Chloe's people, that there are disputes among you. Some say, "I follow Paul;" others, "I follow Apollos;" others, "I follow Peter;" still others, "I follow Christ." Has Christ been divided? Paul wasn't crucified on your behalf, was he? Or, were you baptized into the name of Paul? I thank God that I baptized none of you except Crispus and Gaius...For Christ did not send me to baptized, but to proclaim the good news, not with wise speech with the result that the cross of Christ might be emptied of its power. For the message of the cross is foolishness to those who are perishing, but to us who are being saved, it is the power of God. For it stands written, "I will destroy the wisdom of the wise and the shrewdness of the intelligent, I will thwart" (Isa 29.14).

Comment

Corinth became one of Paul's most important (and most difficult to manage) church plants. He stayed with them for eighteen months before departing for Ephesus. It is likely that Paul wrote his first letter to the Thessalonians, portions of which we examined in two recent chapters, from Corinth.[39]

The congruency between Paul's first letter to the Corinthians and the details of this episode are remarkable. Both Acts and 1 Corinthians mention Paul's work with Priscilla and Aquila (1 Cor 16.9), Paul's work as a tentmaker (1 Cor 9.12-18), Paul's baptism of Crispus (1 Cor 1.14), Paul's experience of "fear and trembling" (1 Cor 2.3) and the participation of Timothy in the mission (1 Cor 4.17).[40] Once again, even if Luke is shaping the details as he chronicles what happened, he is not just making up these stories. There is a real history here.

We also see the historicity of the story underlined by the detail Luke gives us that Priscilla and Aquila were forced to leave Rome. We know from the Roman historian Suetonius that the Emperor Claudius removed all the Jews from Rome in about 49 AD, which is just a few years before this episode takes place. Suetonius describes it as follows: "Since the Jews constantly made disturbances at the instigation of [Christ], [Claudius] expelled them from Rome."[41] Again, the details match up nicely.

Before the arrival of Silas and Timothy in Corinth, Paul spends much of his time at a trade: tent-making. This would have seemed perfectly normal in a Jewish subculture where almost all rabbis were bi-vocational. Since rabbis were prohibited from charging a fee for performing religious duties, this required them to have an outside vocation.[42]

At the same time, however, Roman culture would have seen manual labor as demeaning and only something only the lower classes did. As Plutarch, a well-known ancient Roman biographer, puts it: "Labor with one's own hands on lowly tasks gives witness, in the toil thus expended on useless things, to one's own indifference to higher things."[43]

Thus the re-appearance of Silas and Timothy is an important detail. They apparently show up with funds raised from Philippi, Thessalonica, and Berea, which enables Paul to stop his work as a tentmaker and concentrate on ministry activities alone (Phil 4.14-16, 2 Cor 8-9).[44]

Paul was always willing to do manual labor so as not to be a burden to the church, but he also insisted that he had a right to be supported by the churches he founded so that he could give his full attention to the proclamation of the good news (1 Cor 9.12). This is also what Peter and the early disciples did earlier in our story (Acts 6.2). Ever since, local parishes have been supporting their clergy with financial gifts. It's a distinctly biblical model.

Over the centuries, however, this division between clergy and laity became distorted in the church. In the Late Middle Ages, for example, the clergy became ever-more separated from the laity in every imaginable way. In fact, the requirement for clerical celibacy, not imposed uniformly until the thirteenth century, was originally introduced as a reform measure by Leo IX in the eleventh century, but had the effect of further separating the laity from their clergy.[45]

I want to be clear that celibacy can be a very beautiful thing when there is a genuine vocation in someone for it. Among celibates, there is a commitment to friendship that the ancients usually saw as a higher form of love. Celibacy is undoubtedly necessary in monasteries, but not so among so-called secular clergy who minister in parishes. Paul confirms this when he writes, "Do we [fellow ministers] not have the right to be accompanied by a wife, as the other apostles and the brothers of the Lord and Cephas" (1 Cor 9.5)?

This is one of the things the Reformation very much got right, in my opinion. The Reformers de-mystified the clerical offices, arguing that it was primarily for good order that certain members of the congregation were set apart for the work of ministry. All Christians — both clergy and laity — were to be seen as ministers, not just "professional" clergy. Undoubtedly, the church has been better off for this. Since the church had married clergy for the first thousand years of its existence, the Reformation returned the church to its more primitive practice.

Although it is a good thing for some to be set-apart for full-time ministry, we must never adopt the ancient Roman attitude toward work and find it demeaning. Christians have learned through the centuries that hard work is an integral part of our spiritual lives. We may not physically all be able to do the same work, but idleness is never held in high regard either in the Bible or in the Christian tradition.

Perhaps the best example of this comes from the Rule of St. Benedict, the sixth-century monastic rule that, because of its wisdom and moderation, became the standard for most subsequent monastic communities. Benedict writes the following:

> Idleness is the enemy of the soul. Therefore the brothers should have specified periods for manual labor as well as for prayerful reading...When they live by the labor of their hands, as our fathers and the apostles did, then they are really monks. Yet, all things are to be done with moderation on account of the fainthearted.[46]

All things in moderation. This is really good advice for the spiritual life.

We live in a culture that finds work annoying. Many dream of having enough money so they can sit around and do nothing. But this is not good for your soul. No doubt, the focus of our work can change. But work, especially laborious work, is good for developing humility for learning to listen for God's voice in the every-day activities of our lives. Or, as Paul puts it (in a verse that would become foundational for the Jesuits), "Whatever you do, do all to the glory of God" (1 Cor 10.31).

Questions for Reflection

1. Do you see your work as a spiritual pursuit? How can you learn to find God in the everyday tasks that you perform?
2. What do you think of St. Benedict's admonition that we should do "all things in moderation?" He was serious about this. How can you apply that to your spiritual life?
3. How do you view ministry? Is this just something that paid clergy are supposed to do, or is this for you as well? Consider the places and people you might be able to reach that someone ordained would never have access to.

CHAPTER 37

HAIR-SPLITTING THEOLOGY
Acts 18.12-28

Acts 18.12-28

> *Paul completes his second missionary journey after overcoming more false charges from his Jewish opponents. The proconsul Gallio, the brother of the stoic philosopher Seneca,[47] made an important judgment that the dispute between Paul and the Jews (who were likely from Corinth) was merely an internal religious conflict and thus not worthy of Roman attention.[48] This decision proved critical, since the Romans initially saw Christianity as a sect within Judaism and thus as being legal.[49] At the end of today's reading, we encounter Apollos, a powerful teacher, who requires gentle correction because of his ignorance of Christian baptism.*

Now, while Gallio was proconsul of Achaia, the Jews, being of one mind, rose up against Paul and brought him before the judicial bench saying, "This man is seducing the people into worshiping God contrary to the law." Just as Paul was about to open his mouth, Gallio said to the Jews, "If this were about some wicked fraud, I might have routinely accepted your complaint, O Jews. But since these are disputes about language, names and your own law, you take care of it yourselves. I don't want to be judge of these things." So he dismissed the case from the court. But they all seized Sosthenes, the leader of the synagogue, and began to beat him in front of the tribunal. Yet none of these things was of concern to Gallio.

After Paul stayed many days with the brethren in Corinth, he bade them farewell and sailed for Syria. Priscilla and Aquila went with him. At the Corinthian port of Cenchreae, Paul cut his hair, since he was making a vow. When they reached Ephesus, Paul left Priscilla and Aquila behind and he entered into the synagogue to reason with the Jews. And when they asked him to stay for a longer period of time, he did not agree. But bidding farewell he said, "I will return to you again, God willing," and he set sail from Ephesus. Arriving at Caesarea, he went up and greeted the Jerusalem church and then went down to Antioch. After spending time there, Paul departed and went through the region of Galatia and Phrygia, strengthening all the disciples.

Now, there was a certain Jew named Apollos, an Alexandrian by birth, a learned man and powerful in the scriptures, who came down to Ephesus. He had been taught the way of the Lord, and being fervent in spirit, he started speaking and teaching the things about Jesus accurately. However, he was only aware of the baptism of John. And he began to speak out boldly in the synagogue.

But when Priscilla and Aquila heard him, they took him aside and more accurately explained to him the way of God. When Apollos wanted to go through Achaia, the brethren encouraged him and wrote to the disciples that they should receive him. When he arrived, Apollos helped many who had believed through grace, for he was vigorously disputing with the Jews in public, demonstrating through the scriptures that Jesus was the Messiah.

Numbers 6.1-5

In the OT, one who had great zeal for God could take an extraordinary vow of separation, generally called a Nazarite vow, which could be for a finite time or for life.[50] This would usually involve abstaining from wine or other products derived from grapes. These vows were somewhat similar to the regulations governing the priesthood, since priests were forbidden from consuming wine while serving at the altar (Lev 10.9).[51] One would typically shave one's head to mark the end of the vow. However, evidence from the Mishnah suggests that there was some development on how this vow was understood in biblical times.[52] Thus Paul likely cut his hair to signify the start to his vow in today's story, not the completion of it.[53] Luke likely includes the description of Paul's vow to signify his on-going Jewishness in identity.

Then the Lord spoke to Moses, saying, "Speak to the sons of Israel and tell them, 'If someone – either man or woman — should make an extraordinary vow ["euxe"] to separate himself with purity to the Lord, he must cleanse himself from wine or strong drink, and may drink no vinegar coming from wine or strong drink. Whatever is made of grapes he must not drink nor may he eat fresh or dried grapes. He may consume none of the things coming from the vine, including wine from grapes. All the days of his vow, he may not eat any grape-related product. All the days of his vow of separation, no razor may come upon his head until the days of the vow are over. Whoever makes a vow to the Lord, he must be holy, growing out the hairs of his head.'"

1 Corinthians 3.1-9

Although Apollos has some deficiencies in his understanding in today's Acts passage, he becomes a powerful Christian teacher in Corinth. Note that for Paul, being a person of the flesh, is primarily about disunity and dissension.[54] An important sign of spiritual maturity is working for unity, not division, in the church.

So, brethren, I was not able to speak to you as spiritual people, but as people of the flesh, as infants in Christ. I fed you with milk, not solid food, since you weren't ready. And you still aren't ready since you're still people of the flesh! For where there is jealousy and dissension, does it not demonstrate your fleshly character and show that you act like everyone else? For when someone says, "I follow Paul," or another says, "I follow Apollos." Are you not human beings? Who is Apollos? Who is Paul? Are they not servants through whom you believed as the Lord gave it? I planted, Apollos watered but God gave the increase so that he who plants is nothing nor is he who waters, but God gives the increase. He who plants and he who waters are one, and each will receive his own reward according to his own labor. For we are fellow-workers of God, cultivators of God, but you are God's building.

Comment

Today's Acts reading is essential for dating not only this section in Acts, but also much of the NT. The reason for this is that we learn in this passage that Gallio is proconsul of the province of Achaia, a term that only lasted a single year. A Greek inscription in Delphi that mentions Gallio as a friend of the Emperor Claudius makes it possible to date this episode rather precisely to about 51-52 AD.[55] As a result, almost without exception, NT scholars accept this passage as genuine since the external evidence lines up so nicely in its favor.

In our story, Gallio refuses to take sides between Paul and the Jews, and he dismisses the charges. He basically claims that since this is a debate between factions within Judaism, Roman jurisprudence has no competency to judge whether Paul's interpretation of the OT is correct or not. As one scholar succinctly put it, Roman law can't tell "whether or not Torah testifies to Jesus' resurrection."[56]

When Gallio dismisses the opponents' charges as mere bickering about "language and names," this might sound very familiar. This is the charge often made against Christian theology: that it is only interested in hair-splitting, irrelevant debates about words.

For example, we might look back to the fifth century when the church was trying to define dogmatically who Jesus was. All kinds of different theories had arisen, each of which exaggerated certain aspects of Jesus' person or nature. Some (the Arians), in a bid to protect Jesus' full humanity, weren't quite sure he was always God. Others (the Apollinarians), in an effort to protect Jesus' divinity, did the opposite and questioned whether Jesus had a human soul, thus denying his full humanity. Still others (the Nestorians) wanted to separate Jesus' divine nature from his human nature. Others (the Eutychians) wanted to smash the two natures together, or more precisely, to posit a united third nature. None of these views was quite right, and this led the church to try to clarify its language.

This might sound like a bunch of hair-splitting distinctions. Can't we just all confess that we love Jesus and not worry about it? Well, no, it's not that simple. There is value in being precise about what language we use when we speak theologically about Jesus.

After all, isn't this how Apollos is described in today's passage? He was teaching powerfully and "accurately" the things of God. But it was only when he got together with Priscilla and Aquila that his teaching became "more accurate." Apollos needed the church's teaching on the sacraments and was deficient without it. In particular, Apollos misunderstood Christian baptism.

This suggests that to get the sacraments wrong is to have the whole message be deficient. Notice that with Apollos, there are no signs and wonders and no real evidence of a great movement of the Spirit at this point. As Erasmus, the great 16th-century biblical scholar put it,

> This Apollos was half a Christian. He had learned from Christians the rudiments of evangelical doctrine, communicated to others with fervent zeal what he had learned, and diligently taught what he knew about Jesus. But he had not yet been baptized with the baptism of Christ, which conferred a richer grace. He knew only the baptism of John, which taught repentance.[57]

In its definition of Jesus, hammered out in the fifth century at Chalcedon, the church steered a middle course between extremes. Jesus was one single person, but had two natures, divine and human, "without comingling, without change, without separation and without division."

But the story doesn't end there. For a whole bunch of complicated reasons, certain regions, particularly those around Egypt, refused to accept the agreed-upon language, thinking that the confession of "two natures" meant that "the divine logos" and the "man Christ" were two separate persons.[58] The result was that the Coptic-speaking churches around Egypt split away. Once again, some might see this as just a silly debate over "language and names," but something more fundamental was at stake.

What is so interesting is that it is only in our day that these ancient wounds are starting to be healed. We live in the first generation in centuries to see some separated factions in the church inching back together. Given how adamant Jesus was that he wanted unity (John 17.21), one might have hoped that this would have happened sooner. Sadly, it hasn't.

Yet what has been essential to this greater unity has been taking seriously the language each side was employing. Consider what happened in our Anglican tradition in 2014. The Anglican Communion reached an agreement with the Oriental Orthodox (made up primarily of the Coptic, Armenian, and Syrian Orthodox Churches) that admitted that we've been talking past each other on the issue of Christology for centuries. Consider the language of the agreement:

> Considering the four adverbs used to qualify the mystery of the hypostatic union [the union of the divine and human natures in the single person of Christ]: 'without commingling' (or confusion), 'without change,' 'without separation' and 'without division,' those among us who speak of two natures in Christ are justified in doing so since they do not thereby deny their in-separate indivisible union; similarly, those among us who speak of one incarnate nature of the word of God are justified in doing so since they do not thereby deny the continuing dynamic presence in Christ of the divine and the human, without change, without confusion.

Only by being more precise in our language and more charitable in our dealings with each other were we able to overcome centuries of suspicion about another tradition. This is undoubtedly a sign of progress. As Paul taught us in our 1 Corinthians reading today, working towards unity is always hard, but is an excellent sign of spiritual maturity.

We should be sure to pray for our Coptic Christian brothers and sisters in Egypt. They are under constant threat of attack from ISIS, who have called the Copts "our favorite prey" and have killed hundreds of Christians in recent times.[59] Their presence in Egypt, while always a minority, has diminished significantly in recent years because of the unrelenting pressure on them. There is a very real risk of the Christian presence in Egypt disappearing altogether. Let's make sure we support them with our prayers.

Questions for Reflection:

1. **Have you ever tried to memorize the language of the Nicene Creed (BCP, P. 326)? If you repeat it weekly in church, you might find that it's easier than you think.**

2. **How seriously do you take the Eucharist? Do you see it as a central part of your Christian life, or is it just "something you do" every now and again?**

3. **How regularly do you take time to pray for Christians who are suffering in other parts of the world? How much do you see yourself as part of a global church rather than just a local parish?**

PAUL'S THIRD MISSIONARY JOURNEY
(ACTS 18–21)

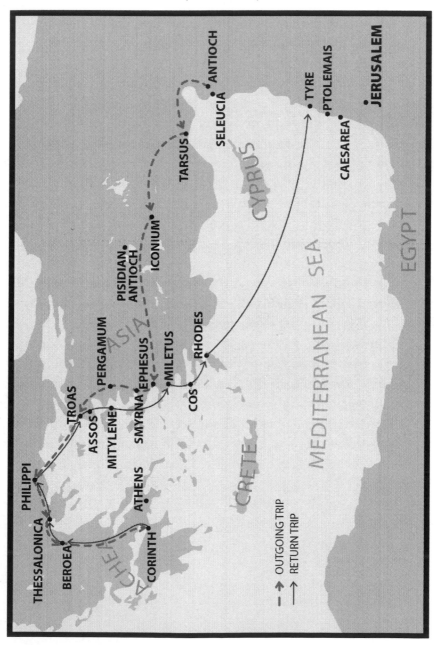

CHAPTER 38

PAUL THE ANABAPTIST?

Acts 19.1-17

Acts 19.1-17

Paul now embarks on his third missionary journey. He begins by spending several years in Ephesus. There are two short vignettes in this passage, as Paul (1) properly baptizes certain disciples and (2) separates from the synagogue after encountering resistance.[1] Similar to yesterday's Acts reading, we encounter "disciples" who have a significant deficiency because they have not been properly baptized. The Spirit has not come upon them, once again underscoring the link between Christian baptism and the coming of the Spirit. This also demonstrates the "messiness" of early Christianity. Luke's intention is to show how Paul works tirelessly to incorporate even fringe elements into the church.[2]

While Apollos was in Corinth, Paul, having gone through the interior regions of Galatia and Phrygia, came down to Ephesus. There he found some disciples. And he said to them, "When you became believers, did you receive the Holy Spirit?" And they said to him, "We haven't even heard that there is a Holy Spirit." And Paul said, "How then were you baptized?" And they responded, "Into John's baptism." And Paul said, "John baptized with a baptism of repentance, telling the people to believe in the one who was to come after him, that is, in Jesus." After they heard him, they were baptized into the name of the Lord Jesus. And when Paul placed his hands on them, the Holy Spirit came upon them, and they began speaking in tongues and prophesying. Now there were about twelve men in total.

Then Paul entered the synagogue and was speaking boldly for three months, reasoning and convincing them in the things concerning the kingdom of God. But when some became hardened and disobedient, insulting The Way before the multitudes, Paul departed from them and took his disciples with him, addressing them every day in the lecture hall at Tyrannus. This went on for two years until all the inhabitants of the province of Asia had heard the word of the Lord, both Jews and Greeks.

God kept doing extraordinary miracles through the hands of Paul, so that even when Paul's face-cloths or aprons that had touched his skin were taken to the sick, they were released from their sicknesses and evil spirits came out from them.

But there were some Jewish exorcists traveling around, naming the name of the Lord Jesus and saying, "I adjure you by Jesus whom Paul proclaims." (There were seven sons of Skeva, a Jewish high priest, who were doing this.) The wicked spirit answered and said to them, "Jesus I know, and Paul I am acquainted with, but who are you?" Then the man possessed by the evil spirit leapt upon them, gaining mastery over all of them. The spirit treated them with such violence that they fled away from that house naked and wounded. This became known to all the Jews and Greeks living in Ephesus and great fear fell upon all of them and the name of the Lord Jesus was continuously being magnified.

Ephesians 4.1-5

This is a central text for understanding Christian baptism and its relationship to the church. We repeat it at every baptismal service. Notice the emphasis on unity. We are to "bear with one another" and to "keep the unity of the spirit" in a conscientious way. This leaves

little room for splitting the church over petty differences, whether
personal or doctrinal. With the focus on unity and the insistence that
there is only "one" baptism, the practice of "re-baptizing" is called into
serious question. This proves important for today's Acts reading since
it is the only place in the Bible in which someone is re-baptized.[3]

Therefore, I, a prisoner for the Lord, urge you to live worthily of your calling with which you were called, with all humility and gentleness, with patience, bearing with one another in love, being conscientious to keep the unity of the Spirit in the bond of peace.

There is one body and one Spirit, just as you were called with one hope of your calling: one Lord, one faith, one baptism, one God and Father of all, who is over all things and through all things and in all things.

Luke 3.1-9

All the gospel writers ascribe great importance to Isaiah 40 since
it anticipates the ministry of John the Baptist who comes before
Jesus and heralds a "baptism of repentance." Emblematic of his
whole ministry, John's baptism points the way to the greater spiri-
tual baptism that Jesus will introduce. Paul references John in
today's Acts reading when he encounters (20 years after John's
death) disciples who had only experienced John's baptism, and
thus have not been properly incorporated into the church.

Now in the fifteenth year of the reign of Tiberius Caesar, when Pontius Pilate was governor of Judea and Herod was tetrarch of Galilee and his brother Philip was tetrarch of the regions of Iturea and Trachonitis, and Lysanias was tetrarch of Abilene, during the high priesthood of Annas and Caiaphas, the word of God came to John, son of Zechariah, in the wilderness. And he went throughout the whole area of the Jordan, proclaiming a baptism of repentance for the forgiveness of sins, as it was written in the scroll of the words of the prophet Isaiah:

> The voice of one crying in the wilderness, 'Prepare the way of the Lord. Make straight his paths. Every valley will be filled and every hill and mountain will be brought low, and the crooked will be made straight and the rough places will be made smooth. And all flesh will see the salvation of God' (Isa 40.3-5).

So John was saying to the crowds that had come out to be baptized by him: "You brood of vipers, who warned you to flee from the wrath about to come? Therefore, bear fruit worthy of repentance and do not begin to say to yourselves, 'We have Abraham as our father.' For I say to you, 'God is able to raise up children of Abraham from these stones.' Even now the axe is laid at the root of the trees. Therefore, every tree that does not bear good fruit will be cut down and thrown into the fire."

Comment

In 1522, significant changes were afoot in the church in Zürich, Switzerland. Ulrich Zwingli, a gifted preacher, had come to be the priest at the Grossmünster, one of the four main parishes in Zürich. An ardent follower of Erasmus, Zwingli was deeply influenced by the humanist reforming ideas of his day.

Although Zwingli always claimed that his reforming ideas were his own, he conveniently managed to come to very similar conclusions as Martin Luther at almost exactly the same time. Recent historical work into the annotations he made in his books has led many historians to think that Zwingli was deeply influenced by Luther's big idea of *Sola Scriptura* – the Bible, and the Bible alone, should be the source for the faith and practice of Christians.[4]

This idea of *Sola Scriptura* was deeply subversive because it undermined the role that tradition played in the church. For at least a thousand years, the church had insisted that the tradition of interpretation handed down from the church fathers was essential for understanding the Bible. Zwingli, while not discarding the church fathers, strongly rejected certain aspects of the tradition that he found faulty, thinking instead that his humanist interpretive tools could tell him what the Bible meant.

The start of the Reformation in Switzerland began with the so-called "Affair of the Sausages." During Lent in 1522, some members of Zwingli's parish (with his tacit approval) decided to defy the city's ban on meat during Lent, pointing out that there was no such ban recorded in the Bible. Having just completed a major publishing effort by putting out an edition of Paul's letters, the proto-Protestants sat down to a giant meal of sausages in a public place. Only Switzerland could turn eating sausage into a subversive act!

This met with immediate outrage. But Zwingli defended his petitioners in a famous sermon, arguing that Lenten fasts should be voluntary, not mandatory. Thus, unlike Luther, Zwingli was more interested in reforming piety and worship than doctrinal understandings.[5] In particular, Zwingli set out to reform teachings on (1) prayers to the Saints, (2) purgatory, (3) fasting, and (4) the use of images in the church.[6] He stopped preaching from the lectionary and started offering expository sermons, going verse by verse through a single biblical book.

But, in his reforming activities, Zwingli was always careful to work within the system, not outside it. He never went against the city council, even if he worked tirelessly to undermine the existing structures of authority. But, for some, his accommodating approach smelled like capitulation.

In particular, Conrad Grebel, one of Zwingli's inner circle, started to criticize Zwingli over the pace of reform. Grebel noted that there was no positive command to baptize infants in the Bible, yet the church did this regularly. Grebel argued that the book of Acts usually required "repentance" and "conversion" before baptism and thus Zwingli was tolerating apostasy by baptizing babies.[7] Zwingli strongly disagreed.

Fed up with the measured pace of reform, Grebel and his followers decided to split from the Zürich church and form their own sect. The way that they read many passages in Acts was that the church is supposed to be made up only of believing adults who had made a confession of faith.[8] After baptizing themselves, they declared themselves to be the true church and separated from what they deemed to be apostasy and compromise.

This new sect came to be called the "Anabaptists," an insulting term, which means "re-baptizers." It is important to note that Grebel and his followers didn't think of themselves as re-baptizers, arguing instead that by following the pattern that they found in the Bible, they were baptizing correctly. There was no re-baptism because without a valid confession of faith, the first baptism never really happened. Zwingli and the Zürich authorities disagreed and did their best to hunt them down and kill them off, a sadly typical sixteenth-century reaction to disagreement. Yet the Anabaptists survived and were always known for their deep piety and unshakable faith in the face of great persecution.

The reason this story is relevant is because today's Acts reading is the only passage in the Bible that ever depicts a re-baptism. However, in appropriating it, Grebel and his followers conveniently ignored the repeated calls in the Bible for unity in the church. They set an unfortunate precedent and, unfortunately, Protestants have been repeating this mistake over and over again for centuries. This, of course, includes our own Anglican tradition which is itself the product of a split from Rome during the Reformation.

When Paul "re-baptizes" the disciples in Ephesus, he is doing this because they were never baptized into Christ (something the sixteenth-century Anabaptists had much more difficulty claiming). He is taking care to teach and to incorporate believers wherever he finds them. Paul is promoting unity in the church, not destroying it with his actions.

The real problem with "re-baptizing" is that it claims that whatever tradition baptized that person in the first place did not know what they were doing and thus were not a true church. Those who reject others' baptisms have rejected the idea of catholicity, and thus the teaching of the Nicene Creed, that that there is one universal church. This is deeply problematic.

But what do we do if someone comes to us and asks to join our tradition who has not been "properly" baptized? In this case, we follow Paul's example from today's reading, employing something called "Conditional Baptism." As the BCP puts it,

If there is reasonable doubt that a person has been baptized with water, "in the name of the Father, and of the Son, and of the Holy Spirit" (which are the essential parts of baptism), the person is baptized in the usual manner, but this form of words is used:

If you are not already baptized, I baptize you in the name of the Father, and of the Son, and of the Holy Spirit.

Notice the very narrow scope given for this. The only time that Conditional Baptism is used is if there is doubt over whether someone has been baptized with water or with the proper baptismal formula. This follows from Paul's example. He encounters "disciples" who have clearly never received the Spirit and were not baptized properly. After Paul lays hands on them, they receive the Spirit and the usual confirming signs come.

The big point today is similar to yesterday's lesson: getting the sacraments right is essential. They really matter. These disciples believed in Jesus, but something was missing – namely, the presence of the Spirit. Believing in Jesus without being properly incorporated into the church through baptism is a significant deficiency.

Questions for Reflection:

1. We live in a very "consumerist" church culture where various parishes "compete" for parishioners. What are the benefits and drawbacks of such a system? What would Paul and the apostles have thought about it?
2. How would you describe the difference between John's baptism for repentance and Paul's baptism into Christ that comes with the Spirit? What is the problem with being a follower of John the Baptist instead of Jesus?
3. Why is the use of tradition so important for understanding the Bible well? What are the problems that ensue from coming to our own private conclusions about what the Bible means?

CHAPTER 39

IDOLATRY IN EPHESUS
Acts 19.18-41

Acts 19.18-41

This is one of Luke's most vivid scenes in Acts, full of color and local detail. In it, we observe how Paul's teaching clashes with the existing culture and threatens certain economic interests. There are contrasting reactions. As always with Luke, those who defend their acquisitiveness are resisting the work of God, while those who surrender their economic interests in a spirit of humility have genuine faith.[9] On the one hand, the magicians, seeing the incompatibility of their practice with the true worship of God, burn their books at a huge economic cost, while the artisans of the goddess Artemis start rioting illegally. Luke is trying to point out that Christianity necessarily entails turning away from pagan practices.[10]

Now many, having believed, were confessing and publicly proclaiming their former deeds. And large numbers of those who practiced magic brought together their books and were burning them before everyone. And the value of them was tallied up and found to be fifty-thousand silver drachmas. In this way the word of the Lord was growing in power and strength.

And after these things happened, Paul made up his mind to go through Macedonia and Achaia on the way to Jerusalem, saying, "After I have gone there, it is necessary for me to visit Rome as well." After he sent two of his assistants, Timothy and Erastus, to Macedonia, he stayed in the province of Asia for a time.

Now, at that time, a big disturbance arose over The Way for someone named Demetrius. He was a dealer in silver, a maker of silver shrines of Artemis that used to bring quite a bit of business to the craftsmen. The craftsmen gathered together with the workers of similar trades, and said, "Gentlemen, you well know that prosperity has come to us from this trade. So pay attention and be aware that not only at Ephesus, but nearly throughout the whole of the province of Asia, this Paul has convinced and misled a large multitude, claiming that man-made gods ["theoi hoi dia keiron"] are not Gods at all. And not only this, but we are in danger of our line of work coming into disrepute, not to mention that the temple of the great goddess Artemis will also be regarded as nothing. This is about to pull down her divine majesty throughout the province of Asia and her worship throughout the whole known world."

When they heard it, they were filled with wrath and cried out, saying, "Great is Artemis of the Ephesians!" The city was filled with confusion. They all rushed together into the theater, seized Gaius and Aristarchus, the Macedonians who were Paul's traveling companions. Now Paul wanted to enter into the assembly, but his disciples would not let him. Even some of the high-ranking Asian officials, who were his friends, sent a warning to him not to venture into the theater. One group was shouting one thing, and others something else, for the assembly was stirred up and most of them did not even know why they had come together.

Then the Jews (convinced that Alexander was the source of the trouble) pushed him forward. Alexander raised his hand and wanted to make a defense to the assembly. But, when he was recognized as a Jew, they all cried out for two hours with one voice, "Great is Artemis of the Ephesians."

After the town clerk quieted the crowd, he said, "Fellow Ephesians, who could possibly not know the city of Ephesus is the guardian of the great Artemis whose sacred stone has fallen from the sky? Because these things are undeniable, you must be quiet and not act rashly since you have brought these men here who are neither temple robbers nor blasphemers of our goddess. Therefore if Demetrius or the craftsmen with him have any complaint against someone, the courts are open and the proconsuls are available. Let them accuse one another there. For we are in danger of being accused of rioting today, since there is no legal defense we can provide against the charge of this seditious gathering. Having said this, he dismissed the assembly.

Psalm 115.3-11

> To the Jews, idolatry was a terrible sin, since idols reduce their makers to nothingness.[11] To worship something lifeless is to render its adherents lifeless as well.[12] In today's Acts reading, it becomes clear that both the Christians and Jews are seen by the Gentiles in Ephesus as opposing the cult of Artemis, thus demonstrating that Christian resistance to idolatry derives directly from its Jewish roots.

Our God is in heaven above, he does whatever he pleases in the heavens and on earth. The idols of the nations are silver and gold, the work of human hands ["keiron anthropon"]. They have mouths but do not speak; they have eyes but do not see; they have ears but do not hear; they have noses but do not smell; they have hands but do not feel; they have feet but do not walk around, and there is no voice in their throats. They are like those who made them, all who trust in them. The house of Israel trusts in the Lord, he is their helper and their defender. The house of Aaron trusts in the Lord, he is their helper and their defender. Those who fear the Lord, trust in the Lord, he is their helper and their defender.

1 Corinthians 16.1-7

> At the end of Paul's first letter to the Corinthians, he announces his intention to come and take up a collection for the church in Jerusalem.

This speaks to the unity of the early church. The Gentile Christians
supported their Jewish brethren. Although Luke doesn't mention it
specifically, the practical reason Paul is intending to travel to Jerusalem
and then to Rome in today's Acts reading is to distribute the funds
he has been collecting from the churches in the region of Asia.

Now, regarding the collection for the saints, just as I have given instructions to the churches of Galatia, do the following as well. On the first day of the week, let each of you set aside what he has stored up, to the extent that God has blessed you, so that when I come, a collection will not have to be taken. Then, when I arrive, I will send those whom you approve to bring your gift to Jerusalem. And if it seems appropriate that I should go, I will take them with me. But I will come to you after I have gone through Macedonia – for I will be coming through Macedonia – then maybe I will stay with you or even spend the winter so that you might send me off, wherever I'm going. I don't want to see you in passing, but I hope to spend some time with you, if the Lord allows.

Comment

During the Tudor Reformations in England, mobs started wandering the country destroying religious objects in churches, trying to rid England of idolatry. Although most images were not destroyed by mobs and were instead taken down by lawful authorities, there was a concerted effort to rid English churches of all stained glass windows, statues, pictures and even organs, sincerely believing that a prime cause of God's wrath on the nation was because of the misplaced worship such images represented.[13] I have referred to this elsewhere as "the war on beauty."

Although it's very important not to draw an unwarranted equivalence between them, we might observe how strangely similar these actions are to what ISIS has done in our day. From 2014-2016, ISIS destroyed and defaced many historic churches, monasteries, Shiite mosques, Buddhist shrines and historical artifacts, believing that they were defending monotheism. A view of God as distant, wrathful, unpredictable, and demanding absolute submission drove both groups to an iconoclastic fury.

Why was there such a strong reaction against religious images? For sixteenth-century Christians, it started with the Ten Commandments, written by Moses, the original lawgiver. The second commandment reads as follows: "You shall not make for yourself a graven image or any likeness of anything that is in heaven above or that is in the earth beneath" (Ex 20.4, RSV). This foundational text seems to provide a solid biblical case against the use of religious images in worship.

However, in the Middle Ages, the church had dealt with the question of images and come to a very different conclusion. It was wrong to apply injunctions against *pagan* idolatry to Christian worship.[14] If Jesus was made fully human in the Incarnation and thus was seen visibly on earth, this must mean that he could be depicted and adored in art. The Saints, Mary, and other biblical actors could also be depicted and venerated. At the Second Council of Nicaea (in 787), the church specifically decided that images of Christ could be used in worship because Jesus' divine nature dwelt fully in his human nature.[15] Or, as Paul put it in Colossians, "For in [Jesus] the whole fullness of deity dwells bodily" (Col 2.9, RSV).

Yet the central mistake of most iconoclasts comes in their understanding of God. God is not some distant demiurge who strikes whimsically whenever he feels like it.[16] Moreover, God is not just a name we apply to something incomprehensible, an object floating around in heaven somewhere or a cause of the universe. God is the ground of being itself and the on-going sustainer of all that exists. Thus God is both transcendent and immanent. I like how Notre Dame's Brad Gregory describes it:

> God is not a highest, noblest, or most powerful entity within the universe, "divine" by virtue of being comparatively greatest. Rather, God is radically distinct from the universe as a whole, which he did not fashion by ordering anything already existent, but rather created entirely ex nihilo [out of nothing]. God's creative action

proceeded neither by necessity nor by chance but from his deliberate love, and *as* love God constantly sustains the world through his intimate, providential care. Although God is transcendent and altogether other than his creation, he is sovereignly present to and acts in and through it.[17]

This is very important for understanding our Acts reading today. There is a clash of cultures going on here which leads to great unrest. Although Luke couches this in economic terms, the Ephesian merchants understand just how much Paul's teaching has the potential to undermine the existing social order. Paul's indictment that "man-made gods are not gods at all," could put them out of business.

Paul in Ephesus shows us the right way to apply the prohibition against images in the Ten Commandments. The Ephesians were worshipping Artemis, a pagan goddess, and using idolatrous shrines. As usual, someone was getting rich providing the religious artifacts. But, to Paul, both the practice of magic and the worship of a pagan goddess are incompatible with the Christian life.[18] Paul doesn't tear down Ephesus' pagan shrines, but his arguments do a fine job of undermining the whole pagan system.

Once again, we see a great tension at work. Paul's message is destabilizing for the society, which leads to civic unrest. Yet Luke's burden in Acts is to show how Christians are no threat to existing governing authorities.[19] This is a very difficult balancing act to pull off. Once again, however, the Christians manage to escape from a very volatile situation.

But what Luke is doing here is foreshadowing where our story is headed. When Paul says, "After I have gone [to Jerusalem], it is necessary for me to visit Rome as well," this is setting up the itinerary for the rest of Acts. All roads lead to Rome at this point. As Jesus said in the last instructions he gave to the disciples before his ascension (Acts 1.8), the gospel must go "to the ends of the earth." For Paul and Luke, that means Rome. Jerusalem may be the center of the church in our story, but Rome is Paul's ultimate destiny. How he gets there will be the focus of our story from here on out.

Questions for Reflection

1. Is it appropriate that we have stained glass windows, icons, and portraiture in our Anglican tradition? What are the advantages and disadvantages of a New-England style whitewashed worship environment devoid of such images?

2. How important is aesthetical and musical beauty for you in worship? Is it possible for these things to become idols? In what ways are they aids to worship?

3. What do you idolize that you don't have (wealth, status, "perfect" children, vacations, cars)? Why do you think having these things will make you happy?

CHAPTER 40

WORSHIP IN THE EARLY CHURCH
Acts 20.1-16

Acts 20.1-16

> *Paul continues his third missionary journey on his way to Jerusalem.*
> *At first glance, this episode might seem like a series of unconnected*
> *(and underdeveloped) travel details with a charming story in the*
> *middle. But the key to reading this passage well is to recognize the*
> *points of similarity between Luke's telling of it and the story of Jesus.*
> *It is no coincidence that Paul sends his disciples "on ahead" two by*
> *two on his way to Jerusalem.[20] Moreover, the details in Eutychus'*
> *story that they are gathered on the first day of the week, in an upper*
> *room after "breaking bread" should remind us of the Last Supper.[21]*

Then, after the uproar had quieted down, Paul summoned his disciples, encouraged them and bid them farewell. He left to go to Macedonia. And while he was passing through those regions and encouraging them with many speeches, he came to Greece and spent three months there. Since the Jews were plotting against him as he was getting ready to set sail for Syria, he decided to return through Macedonia. Now Sopater, son of Pyrrhus from Berea, and Aristarchus and Secundus from Thessalonica, as well as Gaius from Derbe, and Timothy, as well as Tychicus and Trophimus from the province of Asia were all accompanying Paul. These disciples had gone on ahead and were waiting for us in Troas. Then we sailed away from Philippi after the Days of Unleavened

Bread, and within five days we met up with them in Troas, where we remained for seven days.

Then, on the first day of the week, as we gathered together to break bread, Paul preached to the people. Because he was getting ready to depart the next day, Paul extended his talk until midnight. (There were quite a few lamps in the upper room where we were gathered together). A certain young man named Eutychus, sitting at the window, was drifting off into deep sleep since Paul was going on at length. Being fast asleep, he fell from the second story to the ground and was picked up dead.²² Paul went down, threw himself on Eutychus and embraced him, saying, "Do not be afraid, there is life in him." Then Paul went back upstairs and having broken bread and eaten, he chatted with them for an extended time, until dawn, and left. Then they took the boy home alive, being greatly consoled.

Then we came to the boat and set sail for Assos, intending to take Paul aboard there, since he had been making arrangements to travel on foot. We met up with him at Assos, took him on board and went to Mitylene. From there, we set sail. On the next day, we arrived offshore from Chios, on the next, we came near Samos, and on the next, we came to Miletus. Paul had decided to sail past Ephesus, not wanting to spend time in the province of Asia, since he was hurrying, if possible, to get to Jerusalem by the day of Pentecost.

2 Kings 4.18-22, 25-27, 32-37

In the preceding verses, the prophet Elisha had promised that the Shulamite woman would bear a son despite being barren. She did. However, years later, the lad died suddenly after a terrible headache. After the woman sought out Elisha, he came and raised the child from the dead after praying to God. The tradition has usually read Elisha as a forerunner of Jesus, whose commitment to prayer and close walk with God lead to resurrection and new life. Although there are no specific textual links between this story and the raising of Eutychus in Acts, the stories are nevertheless very similar. Paul, like Elisha, is so united with Christ that he can raise the dead.

When the child had grown, he went out to his father among the harvesters. And he said to his father, "O my head, my head." The father said to his servant, "Carry him to his mother." Lifting him up, the servant took him to his mother, and he fell asleep on her lap until noon and then died. She brought him and laid him on the bed of the man of God, shut the door behind her and went away. And she called her husband and said, "Please send me one of the servants and one of the donkeys that I might hurry to the man of God and return"...So she left and came to the man of God at Mt. Carmel.

When the man of God saw her coming, he said to Ghazi, his servant, "Look, there's that Shulamite woman. Now run over to her and ask, 'Is it well with you? Is it well with your husband? Is it well with your servant?'" And she said, "Everything is fine."

And she came to Elisha at the mountain and took hold of his feet. Ghazi came near to push her away, but Elisha said, "Let her alone since her soul is in great affliction and the Lord has hidden it from me and did not tell me."

Then Elisha entered into the house where the child had been lying lifeless on his bed. So Elisha went in to the house, shut the door behind the two of them and prayed to the Lord. Then he arose and laid down upon the child. He put his mouth upon the child's mouth and his eyes on the child's eyes and his hands on the child's hands and he stretched himself out upon him. Then the flesh of the child became warm. Then Elisha got up again and went to and fro in the house and then went up and stretched himself out upon the child. He did this seven times before the child opened his eyes.

Then Elisha cried out to Ghazi and said, "Call the Shulamite woman." So he called her. She came to him and Elisha said, "Take your son." And the woman went in, fell down at his feet, and bowed to the ground, took her son, and left.

Luke 10.1-7

Jesus sends out a larger group of disciples to preach and to prepare the way for the Lord's eventual arrival.[23] The parallels to today's Acts reading are plain, as both texts envision a group of disciples sent on ahead two by two to prepare the way.

Now, after these things, the Lord appointed seventy others and sent them ahead of him two by two into every city and town where Jesus was about to come. And he said to them, "The harvest is plentiful, but the workers are few. Therefore pray to the Lord of the harvest to send out workers for his harvest. Go! Look, I am sending you as sheep in the midst of wolves. Do not take along a money bag, nor a beggar's bag, nor sandals and do not greet anyone on the road. Whatever house you enter, first say, 'Peace be upon this house.' And if a son of peace is there, your peace will rest upon him. But if not, it will return to you. Remain in that same house eating and drinking, whatever they give you, since a worker is worthy of his wages."

Comment

Paul and his traveling companions start making their way towards Jerusalem, stopping in several places along the way. They are likely headed to Jerusalem with the offering that Paul has been taking up for the church there.

The most vivid part of this episode is the raising of Eutychus from the dead. To read this story well, we first need to realize that Eutychus means "lucky" in Greek.[24] Lucky didn't seem so lucky when he drifted off to sleep and fell out the window, but he was certainly lucky that Paul was there to revive him. We shouldn't miss the irony that luck had little to do with it. God's providence was at work.

Unfortunately, some have seen the moral to this story as being that we should be careful not to fall asleep during a sermon. For example, this was the conclusion of Johannes Brenz, an important figure in Wittenberg, Germany during the sixteenth century, who preached the following in a homily: "Because this young man so carelessly and so lazily paid attention to Paul's sermon that he fell asleep, by God's just judgment he collapsed and died."[25]

I think this misses the point rather badly. I agree with John Calvin who wrote the following:

> I see no reason why certain commentators condemn the young man's sleepiness so strongly and sharply by saying that he was punished for his lethargy with death. For what is strange about his struggling with sleep at the dead of night and finally succumbing?...The Lord meant not only by the sleep, but also by the death of this young man to awake and stir up the faith of his, that they might more joyfully receive Paul's doctrine.[26]

This scene is particularly important because it is the first text in the Bible that shows us what an early church service was like. Moreover, it provides our earliest and best evidence that the church from the beginning gathered on the "first day of the week" to remember the resurrection of Jesus and to receive the Eucharist. The language of "breaking bread" is usually connected with the Eucharist in Luke's writings. Given the overt parallels to the Last Supper noted above, it is likely that Luke is telling us that the Eucharist took place within the context of a meal, similar to the Last Supper.[27]

This scene also matches up nicely with some of our extra-biblical sources. Consider what Pliny the Younger, a senior administrator in the Roman government,[28] had to say in a letter to the Emperor Trajan, likely from early in the second century:

> The [Christians] affirmed that they were in the habit of meeting on a certain fixed day before it was light, when they sang in alternate verses a hymn to Christ, as to a god, and bound themselves by a solemn oath not to do any wicked deeds, but never to commit any

fraud, theft or adultery, never to falsify their word, nor deny a trust when they should be called upon to deliver it up; after which it was their custom to separate, and then reassemble to partake of food, but food of an ordinary and innocent kind.[29]

Pliny tell us that Christians were meeting on a fixed day of the week at night. They sang hymns and had a moral code. They also ate together.

This is pretty much what happens in this episode. Although there is some ambiguity in the text, Paul and his disciples likely met Saturday night after sundown into the wee hours of Sunday. The reason for getting together at night is that most of them would have worked all day (another reason why Eutychus' falling asleep is understandable). They got together for some teaching, for the Eucharist, and then later for a meal and some fellowship. Thus Word and Sacrament go together here even if Luke is not yet thinking in those terms.[30]

When we gather on Sunday for worship, we are basically doing what Christians have done from the beginning. Every Sunday is a celebration of Jesus' resurrection and a chance to come together to receive his body and blood in the Eucharist. Our habit today might be to meet on Sunday morning or evening instead of Saturday night, but the effect is the same. The weekly celebration of the resurrection has always been central to Christian practice.

Questions for Reflection:

1. **Do you have a hard time accepting that Paul (or Elisha in the OT) was able to raise someone from the dead? Are you able to read this with the eyes of faith?**
2. **Eutychus dozes off because of the late hour and (probably) because he had been working all day. Are you able to get some rest on Sundays or does work (or some other activity that is not restful) encroach into that time as well?**
3. **How regularly do you share a meal with other Christians? How important is fellowship with other Christians to your spiritual life?**

CHAPTER 41

A POIGNANT FAREWELL
Acts 20.17-38

Acts 20.17-38

This is Paul's poignant farewell address to the leaders of the Ephesian church, and is the only speech in Acts addressed solely to Christians.[31] Not only is it authentically Pauline, cohering with the language from his later Epistles, but it continues the theme of the imitation of Christ.

Just as Jesus exhorted his disciples to humility and service, warned them of impending suffering, and taught them thoroughly on his way to his Passion in Jerusalem, Paul has done similarly.[32] Paul's summary statement, "It is more blessed to give than receive," which he attributes to Jesus, is found nowhere else in the scriptures, a key piece of evidence for the existence of an oral tradition alongside the written scriptures.

From Miletus, Paul summoned the presbyters of the church. When they came to him, he said to them, "You know the way I have been with you, the whole time, from the first day I set foot in the province of Asia; I served the Lord with all humility, with tears and with trials that have come to me because of the plots of the Jews. I have never held back from proclaiming to you whatever was profitable, teaching you in public from house to house. I have born witness both to Jews and Greeks about repentance toward God and faith in our Lord Jesus. And now, look, I have been obligated by the Spirit to go to Jerusalem, not knowing what is going to happen to me there, except that the Holy Spirit is warning me in city after city that handcuffs and persecutions await me. But I do not consider my life worth anything to myself so that I might complete my mission and service, which I have received from the Lord Jesus, to bear witness to the good news of the grace of God.

And now, look, I know that none of you, who went around proclaiming the kingdom with me, will ever see my face again, and I bear witness to you this day that I am innocent of the blood of all of you for I have not shrunk from proclaiming the whole counsel of God to you. Watch yourselves and all your flock over whom the Holy Spirit has appointed you as overseers ["episcopoi"] to shepherd the church of God, which he purchased through his own blood. I know that with my departure fierce wolves will come in among you, not sparing the flock. Even from among you men will arise, speaking perverted things and drawing disciples after them. Therefore be watchful, remembering that for three years, night and day, I have not ceased instructing each one of you with tears. And now I entrust you to God and to the message of his grace. This message is able to build you up and to provide the inheritance to all who are consecrated ["hagiazo"]. I have never longed for someone else's silver, gold, or fine clothing. You yourselves know that my own hands provided for my needs and the needs of those who were with me. By all these things, I have shown you through hard work that it is necessary to assist the weak, remembering the words of the Lord Jesus that he himself said, 'It is more blessed to give than to receive.'"

Then having said these things, Paul knelt down and prayed with all of them. And they all began to weep profusely, hugging Paul and kissing him, being especially distressed at the message he had said that they were about to see his face no more. Then they accompanied him to the boat.

Romans 15.14-19

Using very similar language to his farewell speech in Acts, Paul claims that he has fulfilled his ministry by fully proclaiming the good news

*of Christ. This ministry activity stretches all the way to Illyricum, a
Roman province that covered the Balkan Peninsula and reached all
the way to Italy. Illyricum likely represents the easternmost boundary
of Paul's ministry travels.[33] Paul further maintains that everything he
has done in his ministry results from the outpouring of God's grace.[34]*

I myself am persuaded concerning you, my brethren, and that you are
full of goodness, filled with all knowledge, and are able to instruct one
another. Now, I have written to you boldly in some parts to remind you
through the grace given to me by God, to be ministers of Christ Jesus
to the Gentiles, in the priestly service of the gospel of God so that the
offering of the Gentiles might be acceptable, consecrated ["hagiazo"]
by the Holy Spirit. Therefore I will boast in Christ Jesus in the things
of God. For I will not dare to speak of anything except what Christ has
done through me that resulted in the obedience of the Gentiles in both
word and deed, in powerful signs and wonders in the power of the Spirit
of God. So from Jerusalem and round about as far as Illyricum, I have
fully proclaimed the good news of Christ.

1 Peter 5.1-10

*Paul's farewell address in Acts is also similar to the language of
Peter's later exhortation to the Christian leaders throughout Asia
Minor. They are to have humility, endure suffering and be good
watchmen over the flock of God. They are also to eschew financial gain in ministry. The metaphor of watchmen that represent ministers and flocks is widespread throughout the Bible.*

Therefore, I exhort the presbyters among you as a fellow-presbyter and
witness of the sufferings of Christ, as well as a sharer in the glory that
is about to be revealed, to shepherd the flock of God among you as
Overseers, not by compulsion but willingly by God's direction, not for

dishonest gain but freely. Don't lord it over those entrusted to you, but be models for the flock. Then, when the chief shepherd appears, you will get for yourself an unfading crown of glory. Likewise, young men, be subject to those who are older. For all of you, clothe yourselves with humility since "God resists the proud, but gives grace to the humble" (Prov 3.34).

Therefore you should humble yourselves under his strong hand so that you might be exalted in due time, casting all your cares on him since he cares about you. Be sober. Be watchful ["gregoreo"]. Your adversary the devil prowls about like a roaring lion seeking someone to devour. Resist him, steadfast in your faith, knowing that the fellowship of believers throughout the world is enduring the same sufferings. And after you have suffered for a little while, the God of all grace who called you to his eternal glory in Christ Jesus will restore, support, strengthen and establish you. To God belongs sovereignty forever, Amen.

Comment

Ancient interpreters spent a long time trying to figure out this passage in Acts. Not only did it provide some of Paul's most clear teaching on what effective Christian leadership looks like, but it also anticipated many of his later theological themes.

One of those key themes is Jesus' vicarious suffering on the cross. In some mysterious way, Jesus took our place when he died on the cross. To be clear, this is not the only way to understand what happened on the cross. For example, we could (and probably should) also understand Jesus' work on the cross in terms of his love or his moral example. But the sacrificial death of Jesus for our sins is an early and important way of describing what Jesus did for us.

In today's Acts reading, Paul expresses this idea when he says, "The Holy Spirit has appointed you as overseers ["*episkopoi*"] to shepherd the church of God, which he *purchased* through his own blood" (Acts 20.28). This is the only time in Acts where such "purchase" language appears in this sense.[35]

Although it is rare for Luke to describe the work of Christ in these terms, this passage is clearly employing Paul's distinctive language (cf. Eph 1.7, 14), demonstrating just how uniquely Pauline this speech really is.

The idea of "purchasing" or "ransoming" the people of God is something we have discussed previously in the context of the victory that Jesus won on the cross (Chapter 21 of this guide). But here Paul expresses these ideas less in terms of "victory" and more in terms of "vicarious suffering."

We should note that Paul's formulation probably has its roots in the OT. In the Psalms, for example, it says, "Remember your congregation which you have *purchased* of old, which you have redeemed to be the tribe of your heritage" (Ps 74.2). God "purchased" Israel to be his elect nation in the OT.[36] In Acts, Paul simply expands the metaphor to explain Jesus' work on the cross, thus enabling the redemption of his people from all nations, both Jews and Gentiles. Jesus gave his own life to establish the church.[37]

The other thing of note in this passage is Paul's summary statement, "It is more blessed to give than to receive." Even though we find this statement of Jesus nowhere else in the Bible, Christians immediately recognized its importance and started using it. For example, Clement of Rome, writing at the end of the first century to the church in Corinth, expressed it this way:

> Moreover, you were all humble and free from arrogance, submitting rather than demanding submission, *more glad to give than to receive*, and content with the provisions that God supplies. And giving heed to his words, you stored them up diligently in your hearts, and kept his suffering before your eyes.[38]

This is concrete evidence for the development of an oral tradition in the early days of the church. This may not seem like a very important fact, but the recognition of an oral tradition outside of the scriptures is critical for the development of early Christianity. If we accept the presence of an oral tradition that passed down Jesus' teachings, this means there is more revelation out there than just the Bible. To accept the presence of an oral source alongside the scriptures is controversial in some circles because it necessitates the use of tradition alongside the text of the Bible.

Why is there more revelation out there than just what made it into the Bible? It should be obvious that if Jesus was God, which has been the church's claim from the beginning, everything he said was revelatory. But it should also be obvious that not everything Jesus said was written down. In fact, to the best of our knowledge, Jesus wrote nothing down. All we know of his life and teachings has been handed down to us from others. An important part of the Christian faith is trusting that those who handed down Jesus' teachings were reliable witnesses.

Moreover, most of the NT Epistles are applications of Jesus' teaching to specific situations. So, for example, Paul writes two letters to the church he founded at Corinth to correct some of their practices based on what he knew Jesus' teachings to be. Peter, James, Titus, John, and others did likewise. Thus, in a certain sense, much of the NT is really a witness to the revelatory statements of Jesus applied to particular problems and situations.

Thus much of our task when we're reading the Bible is to tease out what the original teaching was that lies behind the applications. Sometimes this is evident and on the surface, but more often it lies between the lines. We're trying to understand from these writings what Jesus might have taught. This, by the way, is why the church fathers are so important. They offer an authoritative witness to the oral tradition, as it was being passed down in the early centuries of the church.

This is also why tradition is so essential for understanding the Bible well. Reading the Bible on our own, independent of the church's interpretive tradition, has the potential to produce many misunderstandings. Of course, this statements needs to be qualified. Anglicanism has always maintained that simply reading (or hearing) the Bible is a good way to meet Christ. This is no doubt true. But we should always seek to deepen our relationship with Jesus by moving to greater understanding. Faithfully receiving the interpretive tradition of the church helps us do just that.

Questions for Reflection:

1. Have you ever spent any time meditating on Jesus' suffering on the cross on your behalf? If not, mentally picturing Jesus on the cross can be a powerful way of building a relationship with him.
2. Clergy are fallible human beings, but are also held to very high standards. What are the key traits of an effective minister in this passage? Should we expect these things out of our ministers?
3. Paul's farewell address must have been a very emotional scene. Who have you had to say goodbye to that has evoked similar emotions?

CHAPTER 42

HOW TO MAKE DECISIONS
Acts 21.1-14

Acts 21.1-14

> *This marks the end of Paul's missionary work in Acts.*[39] *Paul continues to head to Jerusalem, trying to make it there by Pentecost.*[40] *Once again, Luke consciously depicts Paul as following in the footsteps of Jesus who "set his face to go to Jerusalem" (Luke 9.51, 53).*[41] *At Ptolemais, Paul encounters Philip, the evangelist who led the Ethiopian Eunuch to Christ (Acts 8.30-38), but now twenty years later has four virgin daughters who are prophetesses.*[42] *They warn Paul not to proceed. Paul then encounters Agabus, a prophet we met earlier (Acts 11.28), who dramatically predicts his impending arrest in Jerusalem. Paul ignores all these warnings, and resolutely keeps heading in the same direction.*

After tearing ourselves away from them, we put out to sea, ran a straight course and came to Cos. Then, on the next day, we came to Rhoads and from there to Patara. Then, after we found a ship crossing over to Phoenicia, we embarked and put out to sea. After sighting Cyprus, we left it behind, sailing past it to the left. Then, sailing on to Syria, we arrived at Tyre. There the boat unloaded its cargo. After we found some disciples, we stayed there for seven days. They kept telling Paul through the Spirit not to set foot in Jerusalem, but when our time there was finished, we proceeded to go our way. Everyone, with their wives and children, accompanied us until we were outside the city. After kneeling down on the shore to pray, we said farewell to one another and went up into the boat while they returned to their own homes.

We continued our voyage from Tyre and arrived at Ptolemais. Having greeted the brethren, we remained for a day with them. On the next day, we left and came to Caesarea, entering into the house of Philip the Evangelist, who was one of the seven deacons, and we stayed with him. He also had four virgin daughters who were prophesying.

While we stayed there for many days, a certain prophet named Agabus came down from Judea. Coming to us, he took Paul's belt, bound his own hands and feet, and said, "Thus says the Holy Spirit, the man whose belt this is, in like manner, the Jews in Jerusalem will tie him up and deliver him into the hands of the Gentiles."

And when we heard these things, we together with the locals urged Paul not to go up to Jerusalem. Then Paul answered, "Why are you weeping and breaking my heart in pieces? For I am not only ready to be tied up, but to suffer death in Jerusalem for the name of the Lord Jesus." Not being able to persuade him, we remained silent, saying only, "Let the will of the Lord be done."

Jeremiah 19.1-5, 10-13

It was common for prophets in the OT to make dramatic gestures at the behest of God. In this scene, God commands Jeremiah to procure a jar and smash it before his onlookers, thus symbolizing what God was going to do to the city. He was going to smash it beyond repair because of their long-lasting idolatry. Luke deliberately paints Agabus in today's Acts reading as performing a similar function.

Then the Lord said to me, "Go and procure a jar made of earthen clay and bring some of the Elders of the people and the priests and go out to the burial place of the sons of their children, which is at the entrance gate Charsith, and there you will read all the words that I will speak to you. You will say to them, 'Hear the word of the Lord, O kings of Judah, men of Judah, inhabitants of Jerusalem, and all who have entered into these gates. Thus says the Lord God of Israel, Behold I am bringing calamity to this place so that the ears of everyone who hears will ring because they forsook me and defiled this place, and burned incense to foreign gods in whom they did not know and neither did their fathers. The kings of Judah have filled this place with innocent blood and they have built high places for Baal to sacrifice their children with fire, which I did not authorize, nor did I command, nor did I purpose them with my heart.'

You will crush the bottle before the eyes of the men who went out with you. And you will say, 'Thus says the Lord, in the same way, I will break this people and this city just as an earthen vessel is broken in pieces that cannot be put back together again.' This I will do, says the Lord, to this place and to the inhabitants in it that this city may be given up as something broken down. The houses of Jerusalem and the houses of the kings of Judah will be ruined just as this place has crumbled from the uncleanness in all its houses."

Luke 22.39-42, 45-46

Having just finished the Last Supper with the disciples, Jesus leads them to the Mount of Olives where he will be betrayed. Jesus, in anguish over his impending Passion, asks his Father to "take this cup away" from him. The cup is a metaphor for Jesus' impending suffering.[43] But then he adds, "Let not my will, but yours be done." Luke likely had this scene in mind when he wrote today's Acts passage because Paul's disciples, having failed to dissuade him from going to Jerusalem, respond with very similar language. Once again, Paul is imitating Christ in his journey to Jerusalem.

Then Jesus came out, and according to his custom, he went to the Mount of Olives and his disciples followed him. And when he came to the place, he said to them, "Pray that you do not enter into temptation." He withdrew from them, about a stone's throw away, and he got on his knees and started praying, saying, "Father, if you are willing, take this cup away from me. Nevertheless, let not my will, but your will ["thelema"] be done" ["ginestho"]…And rising up from prayer, he came to the disciples and found them sleeping from grief. And Jesus said to them, "Why are you sleeping? Arise and pray so that you might not come into temptation."

Comment

As we come to the end of Paul's third missionary journey, he encounters several groups of people on his way to Jerusalem. Many of them understandably try to halt his advance. But Paul resists all of them, even at the expense of his own safety.

One group includes Philip the Evangelist with his four daughters, who apparently are prophetesses. The presence of female prophets should not be a big surprise. Not only do we find female prophets in the OT (Isa 8.3, 2 Chron 34.22, 2 Ki 22.14), but Luke specifically singles out Anna as a prophetess during Jesus' infancy narratives (Luke 2.36). Paul also mentions that females were prophesying in Corinth (1 Cor 11.5). Further, when Peter quoted from Joel in his Pentecost sermon, he noted that "your sons *and* daughters shall prophesy" (Acts 2.17). Clearly, female prophets existed. The way Luke expresses this in Greek makes it seem like this was an on-going activity rather than something that just took place occasionally.[44]

What is more controversial is whether this prophetic activity made Philip's daughters itinerant preachers.[45] If so, this would be some of the earliest evidence suggesting that women had a preaching role in the early church. Some might counter this evidence by pointing out that Paul specifically denies the preaching role to women (1 Cor 14.34), but not a few scholars believe this is a later addition to the text.[46]

The prophet Agabus is also a central focus. We've already met him once in Acts 11 when he prophesied a world-wide famine that apparently did take place.

The problem occurs with the details of his prophecy. Agabus claims that the Jews are going to hand Paul over to the "Gentiles" (the Romans) when he gets to Jerusalem. Agabus even claims the authority of the Holy Spirit when he's making the prediction.

The problem is that this is not what happens. As we will see in subsequent passages, the Romans do take Paul into custody, but this seems to be for his own safety to avoid a mob (as we'll see, it's more complicated than that). The Jews are trying to kill Paul, not hand him over to the authorities. In fact, in Paul's own recollection of the event at the end of our story, he claims that it was the Romans who arrested him (Acts 28.17). How can we consider Agabus a legitimate prophet (as Luke clearly does) if he seems to be wrong about the details?

Dan Wallace, a leading expert on the Greek NT, is helpful when he writes the following:

> Paul was not, strictly speaking, *bound* by the Jews, but by the Romans because a riot was breaking out in the temple over Paul. And he was not, strictly speaking, *handed over* by the Jews to the Romans, but was in fact arrested and later protected by the Romans because of a Jewish plot to kill him. What are we to say of this prophecy? Only that because of the Jews' *actions* Paul was bound and handed over to the Gentiles. They were the unwitting cause, but the cause nevertheless.[47]

We should always keep in mind with Luke that he is not rigid when it comes to the fulfillment of prophecy.[48] The spirit of the prophecy is what matters.

The last thing to point out is that Paul gets all kinds of conflicting advice in this episode. Almost everyone encourages him not to go to Jerusalem. Further, if Agabus really was speaking for the Holy Spirit, it might even appear that Agabus was contradicting the instructions Paul had received earlier from the Holy Spirit to head towards Jerusalem (Acts 20.22). How should we react when we get conflicting advice, when we are trying to make a decision about what to do?

The discernment of God's will can be confusing for Christians, often because we think God only has one possible path in mind for us. This leads too many Christians to think that if they somehow miss God's specific instructions to them about what they're supposed to do, they'll wander around aimlessly or worse be found to be disobeying the will of God. I suspect this is not at all how God works.

It was Ignatius of Loyola, the founder of the Jesuits, who came up with a powerful set of tools for the discernment of spirits. Ignatius was probably the greatest spiritual director who ever lived, so he is well worth listening to.

When we are trying to make a decision about what to do, there are a few givens. We should make use of godly counsel wherever we can get it (Prov 15.22). We should certainly do everything to the greater glory of God, and we should never go against God's revealed will in the scriptures. But, admittedly, this only takes us so far. There are an awful lot of things the scriptures never address. Human counselors can be wrong. We always need to apply wisdom to whatever decision we are trying to make.

To Ignatius, however, everything is given to us so that we might draw closer to God. As Ignatius puts it in his *Spiritual Exercises*,

> Man is created to praise, reverence, and serve God our Lord and by this means to save his soul. The other things on the face of the earth are created for man to help him in attaining the end for which he is created. Hence, man is to make use of them in as far as they help him in the attainment of his end, and he must rid himself of them in as far as they prove a hindrance to him…Our one desire and choice should be what is more conducive to the end for which we are created.[49]

What Ignatius realized is that we should pay attention to our desires. Of course, desires can be deformed or wrong, but if they are leading to a place of greater faith, hope, and love, we should realize that those desires might have been given to us by the Holy Spirit, and we should at least pay attention to them.

Further, Ignatius taught that we all experience a constant ebb and flow of consolation and desolation. Consolation leads us to greater openness, harmony and joy, while desolation leads us to secrecy, disharmony, and anger. While desolation is not always a sign that something is wrong, the basic rule is that we should never make a decision while in desolation and should realize that sometimes God allows a sense of desolation in our lives to show us that we're not in control. We might find ourselves in desolation because we have been neglecting our spiritual lives, but, if not, God might just be reminding us that spiritual consolations we receive are a gift from God.

By contrast, we should always follow our sense of joy, consolation, and peace when making decisions. This is often a sign we're are headed in the right direction. However, we should also realize that states of consolation never last forever. "Spiritual highs" should lead us to greater humility, not a sense of invincibility. A sense of peace is a confirming sign that we're on the right track, but it shouldn't be the only one.

Paul was so united with Christ that when well-wishers tried to divert him from his path, he didn't follow, even at the risk of his own life. Even if we are never called to the extreme suffering Paul would endure, this is a pretty good decision-making model for us to follow as well.

Questions for Reflection:

1. Isn't there a problem with just "going with how you feel" when making decisions? Have you ever just felt "peace" about something, but still made the wrong decision?
2. There is great emotion in this scene. Many realize they will never see Paul again. Have you ever had a group of people give you advice that conflicted with what, in your gut, you just knew you were supposed to do? What was that like?
3. What do you make of the existence of female prophets in Paul's day? What does this suggest about the role of women in the church today?

PART IV: PAUL'S TRIALS AND JOURNEY TO ROME

PAUL'S TRIALS AND JOURNEY TO ROME

This final section begins in Jerusalem, but ends up in Rome. Paul, who returns to Jerusalem with the news of the work that the Spirit had done among the Gentile churches during his third missionary journey, is greeted warmly by the church. However, reports of unrest from Paul's Jewish opponents from the province of Asia have reached Jerusalem and present ominous storm clouds.

During the Feast of Pentecost, a crowd of Jews, some of whom had resisted Paul on his missionary travels, come to town. When they see Paul undergoing a purification ritual, they accuse him of defiling the temple. A mob ensues and Paul's opponents try to put him to death. The Roman authorities quickly take Paul into custody, where he will remain through the end of our story.

This section centers around five so-called "defense speeches" in which Paul defends himself against charges of being an insurrectionist and fomenter of unrest. As we've come to expect, neither the Jews nor the authorities can find any charge that sticks, yet Paul still languishes in prison. As we observed throughout the last section, one of Luke's main purposes in writing is to demonstrate that Christians are not insurrectionists. Luke's apologetic task is plain in this section, as he makes it abundantly clear that Paul is non-guilty of anything subversive against the Roman government or the society at large.

Another major theme that emerges in this section is the imitation of Christ. Luke consistently depicts Paul in light of Jesus. As a result, in almost half of the chapters of this section, we will examine a text from Luke's gospel, showing how Luke depicts the ministries of Jesus and Paul as being intertwined.

This final section also witnesses a change in perspective. Whereas in the first three sections of Acts, the main characters made passionate speeches, often to large crowds, as they worked to spread the good news, the targeted hearers of Paul's defense speeches are typically elites in Roman society. As a result, there is an unmistakable political element to this last part of our story. This fulfills Jesus' prophecy that his disciples would proclaim the good news before "kings and governors" (Luke 21.12).

Yet, as we first learned when Paul was leaving Ephesus on his way to Macedonia (Acts 19.21), Paul's ultimate mission is to travel to Rome, presumably to stand trial before Caesar. The final part of this section unpacks how Paul gets there. The journey is far from smooth, as Paul survives a major shipwreck, a dangerous snake attack, and some hostile crew members who want to leave him for dead. But, as usual, Paul manages to survive. God's providence is at work in a remarkable way.

This section will also provide us with ample opportunities to reflect on freedom and our obligations as citizens. We will be reminded how much our own constitution and judicial system are indebted to principles of Roman law. Yet we will also observe how easily corruption and injustice can creep into even the best systems. Although the Romans often appear to be sensible and efficient, we will do well to remember that they are still holding an innocent man in custody on charges everyone knows are false. We will have to ask ourselves how successful we have been as Americans in rooting out similar injustices from our own system.

As usual, however, Paul is faithful even though he is in handcuffs. Even prison can't stop Paul from proclaiming the good news to the "ends of the earth." The good news continues to spread because God is behind its advance.

CHAPTER 43

FINDING FREEDOM (PART I)
Acts 21.15-26

Acts 21.15-26

Paul arrives in Jerusalem and is greeted warmly by James, and the rest of the church, who are overjoyed to hear of the success of his third missionary journey. However, there are indications that the veneer of harmony is not as placid as it seems, since rumors are swirling around Jerusalem that Paul has been encouraging Jews on his travels to abandon Jewish customs and the Mosaic Law. This, of course, is patently false. Yet Paul's eager willingness to make a dramatic and public end to his Nazarite vow (which Paul originally took in Chapter 36) is further evidence that Paul never ceased being culturally Jewish.

Now after these days, we prepared to go up to Jerusalem. And some of the disciples from Caesarea came along with us, bringing us to the house of Mnason of Cyprus, a founding disciple. When we came to Jerusalem, the brethren gladly welcomed us.

On the next day, Paul went in with us to visit James, and all the presbyters were there. After Paul greeted them, he began to report in detail what God had done among the Gentiles through his ministry. Those who heard the report started glorifying God and they said to him, "You see, brother, all the thousands among the Jews who have believed, all being zealous observers of the law. They have been informed about you that you are teaching all the Jews scattered throughout Gentile lands to abandon Moses, instructing them not to circumcise their children nor to live in the customary way. What then should we do, since everyone will hear that you have arrived?

So then do what we tell you: There are four men who have taken a vow for themselves. Take them, be purified together with them, and supply the funds for them to have their heads shaven. Then all will know that what has been reported about you is nothing, but that you yourself follow and keep the law. But concerning the Gentiles who have believed, we have written them, having decided that they should 'keep themselves from meat offered to idols, from blood, from anything strangled and from sexual immorality.'"

Then Paul went with the men the next day, and after purifying himself, he entered into the temple to announce the end of the days of his purification when the sacrifice would be offered for each of the men.

Numbers 6.6-20

These are the regulations in the OT law for dealing with defilement after taking a Nazarite vow and for ending the vow. Both involve a rather elaborate set of sacrifices to be made, which would probably have been quite costly. In today's Acts reading, it appears that Paul ends his Nazarite vow (along with four others) in order to make an elaborate statement to the skeptical Jews in Jerusalem about his continued respect for Jewish practice. Paul also pays for his companions' offerings to end their Nazarite vow, perhaps out of the collection of alms that he has brought from the Gentile churches to Jerusalem.

All the days of his vow ["euxe"] to the Lord he must not come near anyone who has died; whether father or mother or brother or sister, he must not defile himself by them when they have died, since the vow of God is upon his head. All the days of his vow he shall be holy to the Lord. Now, if anyone should die suddenly next to him, the head of his vow will be defiled. He must shave his head on whatever day he is purified and on the seventh day he shall be shaved. And on the eighth day, he shall bring two turtle doves or two young pigeons to the priest at the doors of the tabernacle. And the priest shall offer up one for a sin offering and one for a whole burnt offering, and the priest will make atonement for him concerning the impurity of the dead body, and he will sanctify his head on that day in which he was consecrated to the Lord, all the days of his vow. He shall offer a lamb without blemish for a trespass offering and the former days will not be counted since the head of his vow was defiled.

Now this is the law of the vow. On whatever day he has finished the days of his vow, he will bring his gift to the doors of the tabernacle, and he will offer up his gift to the Lord, a lamb one-year old without blemish for a sin offering, one lamb for a whole burnt offering, and one ram, without blemish, for a peace offering…Then the one who has vowed will shave his vowed head next to the doors of the tabernacle and he will throw the hair on the fire, which is under the sacrifice of the peace-offering…This is the law of the one who has prayed, who has presented to the Lord his gift with respect to the vow, according to whatever he can afford, regarding the value of the vow, which he vowed according to the law of purity.

1 Corinthians 9.1-3, 19-23

Paul defends the flexibility he has shown in his ministry to both Jews and Gentiles. Has Paul been too "wishy-washy" in his pursuit of disciples, as some apparently were charging?[1] Having removed "the works of the law" (circumcision, food regulations, Sabbath requirements, etc.), Paul feels free to work within various cultural norms while proclaiming the good news. This is undoubtedly how Paul would have answered the charge in today's Acts reading that he seems to be contradicting himself by willingly engaging in an

*elaborate purification and sacrificial ritual in the temple. If it will
promote harmony and win him a hearing, Paul finds it harmless.*

**Am I not free? Am I not an apostle? Have I not seen our Lord Jesus? Are
you not my work in the Lord? If I am not an apostle to others, at least
I am to you, since you are the mark of my apostleship in Christ. This is
my defense to those who judge me.**

**For since I am free from all, I have enslaved myself to all so that
I might gain even more. Now, to the Jews, I became like a Jew so that
I might gain Jews. To those under the law, I became as one under the
law (though I'm not myself under the law) so that I might gain those
under the law. To those outside the law, I became as one outside the
law (although I'm not outside the law of God, but am subject to the
law of Christ) so that I might gain those who are outside the law. I
have become weak to the weak so that I might gain the weak. I have
become all things to all people so that I might save some. I do all
things for the sake of the good news so that I might be a participant
in it.**

Comment

After several years of traveling, Paul finally makes it to Jerusalem. This marks
an important transition in our story. Although Luke never mentions it, Paul
has probably arrived with the offering he has been collecting throughout his
missionary travels. We have to read between the lines here, but it appears that
the offering, which was supposed to highlight that the unity of the church
between Jews and Gentiles, did not have its desired effect.[2] Suspicions still
abounded about Paul and his ministry, especially toward the Jews. No doubt
news of Paul's oft-heated conflicts with various Jewish groups in his travels
had made its way back to Jerusalem.

One thing we should have been noticing throughout the book of Acts
is that Paul never stops being Jewish. As I've noted along the way, this claim
is not without controversy. Some want to see Paul, after his conversion, as

leaving behind his old Jewish ways in favor of a new Christian path. Yet if we turn Paul into a Christian convert completely devoid of his Jewish cultural heritage, we leave ourselves incapable of understanding today's passage.

The big problem is how to harmonize Paul's actions in today's Acts passage with what Paul says elsewhere in his letters. James advises (compels?) Paul to undergo purification in the temple so that the skeptical Jews in Jerusalem will know that Paul follows "and keeps the law." But hadn't Paul just traveled for years saying the exact opposite?

Consider the following texts:

- "But now that you have come to know God, or rather to be known by God, how can you turn back again to the weak and beggarly elemental spirits, whose slaves you want to be once more?" (Gal 4.9, RSV)
- "Now it is evident that no man is justified before God by the law… Christ redeemed us from the curse of the law" (Gal 3.11, 13, RSV).
- "For he is not a real Jew who is one outwardly, nor is true circumcision something external and physical. He is a Jew who is one inwardly, and real circumcision is a matter of the heart, spiritual and not literal. His praise is not from men but from God" (Rom 2.28-29, RSV).

In these texts, Paul seems to be saying that observance of the law does nothing for salvation. Yet Paul is not at all saying that the Jews have to leave behind their customs or that Torah observance is useless. Rather, Paul consistently removes circumcision from salvation, continuing to believe that Jewish practice is an effective way to nurture a relationship with God.

After all, consider the things Paul has done in Acts that show how he is still culturally Jewish: Paul consistently proclaims the good news first in the synagogues; he submits to Jewish authority figures; he circumcises Timothy (16.3); he takes a Nazarite vow (18.18); he willingly undergoes a purification ritual (21.16); he brings alms to the Jews in Jerusalem (24.17), and stresses that he is still a Pharisee (23.6).[3]

The key thing we should notice is how free this flexibility makes Paul, not just as an evangelist, but as a Christian as well. He can build relationships with everyone because his allegiance is to Christ, not to a sub-culture or an ideology. He can freely enter the synagogue and complete a Nazarite vow without hypocrisy. But he can also spend time among the Gentiles and reason with them. As Paul puts it in our 1 Corinthians reading from today, he became "all things to all people to gain some of them." Paul is free because he has committed himself to Christ and detached himself from various ideologies that are unhelpful.

Some today would define freedom in terms of politics (if only my party would regain power!) or in terms of money (if only I had a little bit more!). Others would define freedom as the "absence of restraint or coercion." Emory's Mark Bauerlein summarizes our modern views of freedom as follows:

[Modernity] maintains that behavior must originate from within; freedom consists in the capacity to satisfy individual needs and desires. But the damaging results of that definition of liberty are everywhere around us, forcing any open-minded person to acknowledge the value of social constraints, especially those derived from religious doctrine.[4]

But it's not just religious believers who have a problem with these definitions of freedom. Many ancient writers, most notably Plato, railed against such notions of freedom because they are so short-lived. Political movements come and go with alarming regularity. Stock markets go up and down. Not only can these things not bring us lasting happiness, they cannot ultimately make us free.

Only God can really make us free because only God is unchanging and eternal. All of us were made to be in a relationship with God. But we will only find true freedom when we surrender to the restraints God offers for our own good, recognizing that his ways are more perfect than ours. Or, as Jesus put it, "If the Son makes you free, you will be free indeed" (John 8.36). Thus freedom is not the absence of restraint (as our culture suggests); it is willingly surrendering to the path God has laid out for each of us. We find our life by losing it (Matt 10.39).

This is probably why, in 1517, right at the start of the Reformation, Martin Luther took a different name. In the sixteenth century, it was fashionable to take a pseudonym because of the influence of humanism and its attempts to re-capture the grandeur of Greek and Roman culture.

What name did Luther take? He became known as *Martinus Eleutherius* – "Martin the Free."[5] Luther found freedom in Christ that no human magistrate or earthly wealth could provide. He was free, indeed, because, having received it as a gift, no one could take it away. To genuinely live by faith is to experience true and lasting freedom.

Questions for Reflection:

1. **What upsets you when it gets taken away (food, alcohol, drugs, power, notoriety, approval, etc.)? How could you work toward a greater degree of detachment with whatever you think you need?**

2. **Politicians are always promising greater prosperity and freedom, yet the results are often disappointing. To what extent are you relying on something completely outside of your control to make you happy or free?**

3. **Imagine what it was like for Paul to finally come back to Jerusalem and have all kinds of false rumors floating about. Has this ever happened to you? Has anyone, with a lack of evidence, spread falsehoods about you? How did you handle it?**

CHAPTER 44

FINDING FREEDOM (PART II)
Acts 21.27-40

Acts 21.27-40

> *Paul is in Jerusalem, presumably at the time of Pentecost (the
> late-spring harvest festival), which is why a throng of hostile Jews
> from the province of Asia are in Jerusalem. Once again, their charges
> against Paul prove to be false, but the danger to Paul's life is very
> real. This marks another transition in our story. When Paul is taken
> into custody by Roman authorities he will never be released again.
> Although Luke will take pains to show that Paul has done nothing
> wrong and is not trying to start an insurrection ["stasis"], neverthe-
> less he will be subject to the Roman military for the rest of the story.*

N ow, when the seven days of Paul's purification were almost finished,
the Jews from the province of Asia saw him in the temple and started
stirring up the whole crowd. And they laid their hands on him, crying
out, "O dear Israelites, help! This is the man who is teaching everywhere
against the people, the law and this temple. Furthermore, he has brought
uncircumcised Greeks into the temple and has profaned this holy place."
(They had previously seen Trophimus the Ephesian with Paul in the city
and they assumed that Paul had brought him into the temple.) Then
the whole city was stirred up and the people formed a mob, seized Paul,
dragged him out of the temple courts and locked the gates at once.

As they were trying to kill him, a report went up to the tribune of
the Cohort that all of Jerusalem was in an uproar. At once, taking some

soldiers and centurions, he ran down to them. And when they saw the tribune with the soldiers, they stopped beating Paul. Then the tribune drew near and arrested Paul and commanded him to be bound to two soldiers on either side.

Then the tribune inquired who Paul was and what he had done. But one group started shouting one thing, and a different group another thing, so that the tribune was not able to ascertain the truth because of the commotion. So he commanded Paul to be brought into the barracks. While Paul was going up a flight of stairs, he had to be carried by the soldiers because of the crowd's violence, since a crowd of people were following them, screaming, "Away with him!" ["aire auton"].

And when he was about to be brought into the barracks, Paul said to the tribune, "Can I ask you something?" And the tribune replied, "You know Greek? Are you not the Egyptian who rose up and led four-thousand men who belonged to the 'Assassins' into the desert some time ago"? And Paul answered, "I am a Jewish man, from Tarsus in Cilicia, no shabby city. Please, I ask you, let me speak to the people." Having been granted permission, Paul stood on the flight of stairs and motioned with his hand to the people. After they became silent, he addressed them in Aramaic.

Ezekiel 44.1-2, 6-10

Ezekiel's final vision in his prophecy is of a restored temple in which absolute purity is once again found. No uncircumcised foreigners (who desecrated the sanctuary when they destroyed Jerusalem) will be allowed inside. Although moderns might find such a strong polemic against inclusivity disturbing, God's injunction for holiness in sacred space is something we ought to take seriously.[6] Note the textual links between today's Acts reading and this vision – Paul is accused of allowing "uncircumcised Greeks" into the sanctuary whose gates are then locked behind them. The mistake of the Jews in today's Acts reading is that they used the injunction for holiness as a means of excluding others from the presence of God.

Then he brought me back by the way of the outer gate of the sanctuary, which faces the east. It was shut. And the Lord said to me, "This gate has been shut and will not be opened. No one will pass through it since the Lord, the God of Israel will enter by it, though it has been shut."

And you shall say to the rebellious house, to the house of Israel, "Thus says the Lord God, let all your transgressions be finished, O house of Israel, which you have brought sons of foreigners, uncircumcised in heart and uncircumcised in flesh to be in my sanctuary when you offered up bread, fat and blood. You have broken my covenant with all your transgressions. And you have appointed other guards to watch over my sanctuaries." Therefore, thus says the Lord God, "No foreigner, uncircumcised in heart or uncircumcised in flesh, shall enter into my sanctuary among all the sons of the foreigners who are in the midst of the house of Israel."

Luke 23.13-21

In one of the climactic scenes in the Passion narratives, Luke describes how Pilate finds no wrongdoing in Jesus. Yet the crowds yell all together, "Away with him!" Under pressure from the crowds, Pilate decides to have Jesus flogged and crucified. Luke has written today's episode in Acts with this scene in mind. He continues to describe Paul as imitating Christ, employing the same phrase, "Away with him," to describe the reaction of the crowds.

Then Pilate called together the high priests, the rulers and the people and said to them, "You have brought this man to me as one who mislead the people, but I have examined him before you and found nothing in this man as a basis for accusation against him and neither did Herod, since he sent him back to us. So, look, he has done nothing deserving of death. Therefore, I will flog him and release him."

But they all started yelling in unison, "Away with him ["aire touton"] and release Barabbas for us." (Barabbas had been thrown into prison for insurrection ["stasis"] in the city and murder.) So again Pilate addressed them, saying, "Do you want me to release Jesus?" And they cried out, "Crucify, crucify him!" And a third time he said to them, "Why? What evil has he done? I have found nothing deserving of death in him. I will flog him and release him." But they were insistent, demanding with a loud voice for him to be crucified and their voices prevailed.

Comment

At first blush, this episode seems pretty straight-forward. The crowds of Jews, many of whom recognize Paul from the province of Asia, make up some charges against him and stir up the people. Since most are in Jerusalem for the Jewish Feast of Pentecost, any hint of desecration in the temple is met with anger and violence. Just like Jesus, Paul is innocent, but that does not mean he's safe. The Jews start beating Paul in an attempt to kill him. The Romans step in and whisk Paul away.

Although this scene does not seem complicated, we have a real problem as modern readers of this text. Our issue is that we live on this side of the Enlightenment. As children of the Enlightenment, we typically bring certain unexamined assumptions to the text when we read.

The first big assumption is that every human being has inherent dignity. The Romans would have found such an idea laughable and easily disproved from experience. We also assume that authorities should treat prisoners as "innocent until proven guilty," but the Romans had no such understanding (even if Jewish jurisprudence did, cf. Acts 23.3).[7] Moreover, as we will observe more clearly in the next Chapter, it was standard practice to employ torture to determine what had happened. Finally, we might also assume that the Roman soldiers, by taking Paul into custody, were doing so to protect him. Yet a closer reading of the text undermines this understanding. Thus the key to reading this episode well is to suspend our modern assumptions and to step into the Romans' shoes as we read.

To the Romans, religiously-motivated unrest was the biggest threat they faced. The Romans had no trouble facing down other armies. They voluntarily offered at least the appearance of freedom to those they conquered. But the unwritten assumption was that the "right" to practice one's religion was always tied to the requirement for public order. This is one reason why Pilate acquiesced to the crowds' demands to put Jesus to death in today's Luke reading. He was looking for a way to avoid a riot, which his higher-ups in Rome would have frowned upon. Pilate's basic job was to maintain order.

Thus the motivation of the Romans in taking Paul into custody is not to protect him (as this scene is usually read as accomplishing), but to avoid unrest.[8] In so doing, the tribune manages to quell what could have been a serious riot.[9]

When Paul is interrogated, the Romans think he might be an Egyptian insurrectionist who had come back to town. Although some of the details are different, we know something about this Egyptian from the writings of Josephus, who described him as follows:

> There was an Egyptian false prophet that did the Jews more mischief than the former; for he was a cheat and pretended to be a prophet and also got together thirty-thousand men that were deluded by him; these he led roundabout from the wilderness to the mount which was called the Mount of Olives and was ready to break into Jerusalem by force from that place; and if he could but once conquer the Roman garrison and the people, he intended to domineer them by the assistance of those guards of his that were to break into the city with him, but Felix prevented his attempt and met him with his Roman soldiers...the Egyptian ran away, with a few others, while the greatest part of those that were with him were either destroyed or taken alive; but the rest of the multitude were dispersed everyone to their own homes and there they concealed themselves.[10]

This Egyptian insurrectionist was a serious threat to public order and had not been captured. No wonder the Romans jumped to the conclusion that he had returned to Jerusalem to lead an insurrection.

But, when the tribune heard Paul speaking Greek, he immediately recognized that his assumptions were wrong. Paul couldn't be the Egyptian insurrectionist because he could speak both Greek and Aramaic.

Luke continues to hammer home the same point. The Christian movement is not an insurrection.[11] Christians are not trying to topple Caesar and his government. The unrest that keeps happening is not their fault, at least according to how Luke tells the story.

But why does Paul not just say at this point that he's a Roman citizen? We, as readers, know that Paul is a Roman citizen (Acts 16.37-38) and thus is entitled to gentler treatment than he's getting. Yet, at this point in the story, Paul never informs the tribune of this fact (although he will in short order). At first blush, this might seem odd.

Moreover, we know from Paul's other writings that "three times" he was "beaten with rods." The Greek word Paul uses here is "*rabdizo*," which carries a specific legal connotation (2 Cor 11.25). As Paul was probably flogged three times by the Roman government, his status as a Roman citizen did not prevent it.[12] How can we explain this?

We assume (largely because of Acts) that Roman citizenship was the ultimate trump card. In Acts, his status as a citizen often gets Paul out of trouble. Yet, as Kavin Rowe points out, "The privileges of Roman citizenship were far less by the letter of the law than by the spirit of status…the primary distinction operative in the avoidance of physical brutality was not that of citizenship but of class or rank."[13] Thus Paul does not let on (at this point) about being a Roman citizen, but employs his extensive education (by speaking several languages) to position himself as an educated person in stark contrast to the riffraff trying to put him to death.[14] It was a clever strategy on Paul's part.

Yesterday, we learned that true freedom is ultimately found in Christ. Yet today's reading reminds us not to dismiss the very real freedoms our constitution affords us: freedom of speech, freedom of religion, freedom of the press, freedom of assembly, the right to bear arms, the right to a speedy jury trial, the right not to be burdened by unlawful searches or by cruel and unusual punishment, among others. These rights are fundamental to our lives, even if we too often take them largely for granted. Of course, all of these rights can be misused. Free speech can turn into hate speech. The right to bear arms can be used for killing innocent people. The prohibition against unlawful searches can make crime spread. Yet we should never forget that these fundamental freedoms were only won over centuries of struggle.

There is a big reason that this tradition of "rights" developed in the West and nowhere else. That reason is Christianity. To be clear, Christianity is hardly the only reason for the development of civil liberties, but it is an important one nevertheless. The notion that all human beings have dignity, and thus have rights, comes, in part, from our status as bearers of the Image of God. If each human being has inherent dignity because each person bears the image of God, then each life has value and attendant rights attached to it. It is exceedingly difficult to maintain a tradition of uniform human dignity without God.

Let's never forget that our Christian faith has civic implications and has been instrumental to the shaping of our "national experiment." The notion of "Rights" may be a distinctly modern concept, but it is almost inconceivable without the distinctively Christian emphasis on the inherent dignity of every human person. Our society looks very different than the Roman one in today's reading. We have Christian teaching, in part, to thank for that.

Questions for Reflection:

1. **There are many pressures on Christians to "privatize" our faith. How do you live out your Christian life among people who may not share your beliefs?**
2. **Should Christians withdraw into the safety of enclosed communities rather than being "sullied" by the world? What are the advantages and disadvantages to doing this?**
3. **When was the last time you read the Bill of Rights and gave thanks for the freedoms you enjoy? How does being a Christian help you appreciate these rights that (in our system) are thought to be intrinsic to each human being and not granted by the state?**

CHAPTER 45

GOD'S UNCREATED LIGHT
Acts 21.39b-22.29

Acts 21.39b-22.29

> *This is the second time Luke has recounted Paul's experience of the*
> *risen Christ on the road to Damascus, a sign of its central impor-*
> *tance.[15] Paul is defending himself before the unruly crowd that has just*
> *tried to kill him. He appeals to his pedigree as a zealous persecutor of*
> *the Christian church and as a Pharisee whose credentials cannot be*
> *doubted. However, when Paul starts speaking of how God sent him*
> *to proclaim the good news to the Gentiles, the crowd erupts again.*
> *Before the Romans start torturing Paul to extract information, Paul*
> *finally invokes his Roman citizenship to the tribune who arrested him.*

Please, I ask you, let me speak to the people. The tribune granted
permission, and Paul stood on the flight of stairs and motioned with
his hand to the people. After they became silent, he addressed them in
Aramaic.

Brethren and Fathers, hear me as I now make my defense to you.
When they heard that he was addressing them in Aramaic, they became
even quieter. And Paul said, "I am a Jewish man, born in Tarsus of
Cilicia, but brought up in this city at the feet of Gamaliel, having been
trained in the exactness of our ancestors' law, being zealous ["zelotes"]
for God just as all of you are this day. I persecuted ["dioko"] this Way
unto death, arresting and hauling off to prison both men and women
as also the high priests and all the elders will testify about me, having

obtained letters to the brethren in Damascus. I was on my way to make arrests there and especially to bring them back to Jerusalem so that they might be punished.

While I was on my way, drawing near to Damascus at around midday, a very bright light appeared out of heaven that was flashing around me. I fell to the ground and heard a voice saying to me, "Saul, Saul why are you persecuting me?" And I responded, "Who are you, Sir?" And he said to me, "I am Jesus the Nazarene whom you are persecuting." Now those with me saw the light but did not hear the one speaking to me. So I said, "What am I to do, Sir?" And the Lord said to me, "Rise up, go into Damascus. There you will be told everything that has been designated for you to do." Since I could not see because of the intensity of that light, I came into Damascus, those with me leading me by the hand.

And a certain God-fearing man according to the law, Ananias, spoken well of by all the Jews living there, came to me, stood near and said to me, "Brother Saul, receive your sight." And in that moment I regained my sight and looked at him. And he said, "The God of our forefathers has chosen you to know his will, to see the Righteous One and to hear a solemn declaration from his mouth, since you will be his witness to all the people about what you have seen and heard. So now why are you delaying? Rise up, get yourself baptized and have your sins washed away, calling upon his name."

Then, when I returned to Jerusalem and was praying in the temple, I fell into a trance and saw the Lord saying to me, "Hurry, leave quickly from Jerusalem, since they are not going to accept your testimony about me." So I said, "Lord they well understand that from one synagogue to another I used to imprison and beat those who believed in you. When the blood of Stephen, your witness, was poured out, I approvingly stood near, and watched over their garments while they did away with him." And the Lord said to me, "Go, since I will send you far away to the Gentiles."

The crowd was listening to him as he spoke these things and they raised up their voices, saying, "Away with this man from the earth, for he doesn't deserve to go on living." And they were crying out, throwing off their outer garments and heaping dust into the air. The tribune commanded Paul to be brought into the barracks, ordering him to be interrogated by lashing so that he might ascertain why the Jews were shouting at Paul.

But, as they were stretching Paul out for the lashing, Paul said to the centurion standing by, "Is it legal for you to flog an un-condemned man who is a Roman citizen?" And when the centurion heard it, he went to the tribune and told him about it saying, "Why are you about to do this, since this man is a Roman citizen?" Then the tribune came to Paul and said to him, "Are you a Roman citizen?" Paul responded, "Yes." Then the tribune said to Paul, "I procured this citizenship with a tidy sum." And Paul replied, "But, look, I was born a citizen." Then those who were about to examine him withdrew from Paul and the tribune became afraid when he realized that Paul was a Roman citizen and that he had bound him.

Luke 9.28-36

The story of the transfiguration is one of the key episodes in Jesus' life — Moses and Elijah appear to talk about Jesus' departure (literally, his "exodus") from the earth. Notice that the descriptions of the transformation of Jesus' face and garments are tied to prayer in Luke's account.[16] These transformations provide a glimpse of what Jesus looks like in his glorified state and how the kingdom of God appears in its fullness. Luke seems to be tying the "light" of Paul's Damascus Road experience to the "uncreated light" seen on the Mount of transfiguration in the revelation of God's glory.

Now about eight days after these sayings, Jesus took with him Peter, James and John and went up to the mountain to pray. And while he was praying, the appearance of his face was transformed and his garment became as brilliant as light. Then two men, Moses and Elijah, started speaking with him. They appeared in glorious splendor and were speaking about his departure, which was about to take place in Jerusalem.

Now Peter and those with him, having been weighed down with sleep, woke up and saw Jesus' glory as well as the two men standing with him. Then, as the men were starting to depart from Jesus, Peter said to Jesus, "Master, it is good for us to be here. So let's make three huts: one for you, one for Moses and one for Elijah." (Peter did not know what he was saying.) After he said these things, a cloud appeared and overshadowed them. And they were afraid as they entered the cloud. And a voice came from the cloud, saying, "This is my Son, the Chosen One, listen to him." After the voice came, Jesus was found alone. So they kept silent and no one spoke of anything that they had seen in those days.

Galatians 1.11-14

The Book of Galatians is tough. Paul excoriates the church he founded for wandering away from the gospel he had received "by revelation." In the early part of the letter, Paul emphasizes how zealous he was to persecute the Christian church before his conversion. Paul's descriptions of his "former behavior" match up very well to Paul's defense speech in today's Acts reading.

Now I want you to know, brethren, the good news that was proclaimed by me was not of human origin, since I did not receive it from a human source nor was I taught it, but I received it through a revelation of Jesus Christ. For you heard of my former conduct in Judaism, how I used to persecute ["dioko"] the church of God to an extraordinary degree and tried to destroy it. As a result, I was advancing in Judaism beyond many of my peers in my race, so extremely zealous ["zelotes"] was I for the traditions of my forefathers. But God, who set me apart from my mother's womb and called me through his grace, was well pleased to reveal his son to me so that I might proclaim the good news among the Gentiles.

Comment

This speech is the first of five so-called defense speeches that Paul will give between here and the end of our story.[17] This is important because the tenor of our story is changing. From here on out, Paul will be in the custody of the Roman government. Paul will continue to proclaim the good news, but now will do so before senior authorities. Apparently, God has engineered Paul's arrest to fulfill his prophecy that Paul would carry Jesus' name "before the Gentiles, kings and sons of Israel" (Acts 9.15). Paul may not have realized that his access to senior leaders would come from imprisonment, but this is how God's plan was unfolding.

Paul's speech is a bit strange in that it never really addresses the core reason that the Jewish crowds were rioting.[18] Remember from the previous chapter that they had accused Paul of "defiling the temple" by bringing uncircumcised Gentiles into it, something that was clearly false. Yet Paul spends his time describing his impressive Jewish pedigree. Clearly, Luke has some other purposes in mind as he recounts the speech.

There are three interesting differences between the two accounts of Paul's calling in Acts 9 and in today's reading. The first is an addition. This is the only place we learn that Paul returned to Jerusalem and was praying in the temple when he received another vision of Jesus. Paul is probably trying to show his hearers that even though he had an encounter with the risen Christ, he is still authentically Jewish, prays to the same God, and is tied to the temple.[19]

The second notable addition is the detail Paul offers about his baptism. Paul was baptized by Ananias, whom we now learn was "well-spoken of by all the Jews" in Damascus. But Luke adds that Paul was to be baptized to have his sins "washed away." The Greek word Luke uses here is *"apolouo,"* which carries with it the sense of "purification."[20]

On the one hand, this would have been familiar terminology for Paul's Jewish audience, which would have connected so-called "Proselyte Baptism" with the "washing" language Paul employs. Jewish Proselyte Baptism was a purification ritual one undertook in the process of converting to Judaism. However, by biblical times, this purification rite had developed to become a "symbol of new life" as well.[21]

Thus Luke employs the language of "washing" in a sense that a Jewish audience would have understood, but pushes it even further. Now, in a Christian sense, baptism has the effect of "washing away" sins. This is one of the clearest statements we have in the Bible that baptism is able to forgive sins when there is genuine faith. This is also a reason why we call the sacraments "Means of Grace." As Michael Fahey helpfully puts it, "The human beings' role in the sacrament is not the cause but the condition for the effective application of divine grace offered in the sacrament."[22] Baptism really can wash away sins where there is authentic faith.

The final thing to notice is the centrality of "light" in Paul's Damascus Road experience. As Paul puts it, "A very bright light appeared out of heaven" (Acts 22.6). Luke adds the detail (not given in Acts 9) that this all takes place at "midday." How could one see a bright light in the middle of the desert at noon?

Further, Paul seems to contradict his previous description of what happened when he tells us that his traveling companions "saw the light, but did not hear the voice" (Acts 22.9). This seems to be the exact opposite of what Paul said previously, that his traveling companions "heard the voice," but could not see "anyone" (Acts 9.7). How do we make sense of this apparent contradiction?

The trouble many modern readers encounter here is that they assume "light" in this passage is a physical, rather than a metaphysical force. This is why I included Luke's description of the transfiguration from his gospel. When Peter and the others saw the glorified Jesus on Mt. Tabor, they were not seeing a naturally created light, they were seeing what eastern theologians would later call God's "uncreated energies." What does that mean?

On the one hand, the Bible clearly tells us that "no one has ever seen God," meaning God in his divine essence (1 John 4.12). But on the other hand, humans clearly have seen God in the person of Jesus who appeared on the earth in the flesh.

It took until the seventh century to figure all this out, but the church decided at the sixth ecumenical council (680-681) that there had to be two "natural principles of action" in Jesus — one for each nature, divine, and human.[23] The uncreated light seen by the Peter at the transfiguration and Paul on the Damascus Road was the "energy" flowing from the divine Persons: Father, Son, and Holy Spirit. When Paul sees "the light" from heaven, he is experiencing the uncreated energies of God, which are mighty to save. This is not a description of a natural force.

This is how we explain, in Acts 9, how Paul's companions see "no one," but in today's Acts reading see "the light." No one can see God in his essence, but we can experience the grace of God through his uncreated energies. This is what Paul experiences on the road to Damascus.

It's a puzzling thing, but the word "energy" ["*energeia*" in Greek] appears almost twenty times in the NT and yet, in English translations, it is almost never translated "energy." Frankly, this is a giant blind spot for westerners. Western theology, until recently, has been uncomfortable with the idea that God could be known through his energies. But as Paul writes, "God is at work ["*energon*"] in you, both to will and to work ["*energein*"] for his good pleasure" (Phil 2.13).

The experience of God is not just for the spiritual elite. It is for us all Christians. Perhaps it will come with none of the bells and whistles like Paul and Peter describe, but, make no mistake, God wants to be known. The question for all of us is whether we will be receptive and quiet enough to see the invisible God through his uncreated energies.

Questions for Reflection:

1. Have you had a "Damascus Road experience" where you turned toward God? What was it like to start following in Jesus' footsteps? Can you recount your "conversion" experience?
2. Paul speaks after he has almost been killed by the crowd and tortured by the Romans. Picture this scene in your mind and the pain Paul was probably in as he spoke. Could you have had the emotional and spiritual strength to witness to the risen Christ after being beaten?
3. So-called New Age mysticism also fairly frequently talks about "energies." Is there a difference between the "uncreated" (i.e. eternal) energies of the eastern theology and the "energy" language of New Agers?

CHAPTER 46

PAUL AND THE CONSCIENCE
Acts 22.30-23.10

Acts 22.30-23.10

> *The tribune summons the Jewish council to try to discern why*
> *they are in such an uproar over Paul. This gives rise to Paul's sec-*
> *ond defense speech. In it, Luke pointedly describes Paul as being*
> *similar to Jesus, who was also hauled before the high priest, falsely*
> *accused and struck (John 18.22-23). However, interpreters have*
> *long noted that Paul's sharp reply to the high priest is quite unlike*
> *Jesus, as is the result. Paul is not handed over to be killed, but lives*
> *to argue another day. This brings up the difficult interpretive ques-*
> *tion about just how genuine Paul's apology is. Paul cleverly man-*
> *ages to divide the council over the Doctrine of the Resurrection*
> *of the Dead, a teaching the Sadducees denied, primarily because*
> *of their sole adherence to the Pentateuch — the five Books of*
> *Moses — where the promise of resurrection is difficult to find.*

Then, the next day, wishing to learn the truth about what Paul was being charged with by the Jews, the tribune released Paul and summoned the high priests and the whole council. Bringing Paul down, the tribune made him stand before the council.

Then Paul stared right at the council and said, "Brothers, I have conducted myself with a completely good conscience ["suneidesis agathos"] before God to this day." The High priest, Ananias, then ordered those standing by Paul to strike him on the mouth. Then Paul said to him, "It's you that God is going to strike, you whitewashed wall. How can you sit there judging me according to the law when you give orders to have me struck contrary to the law?" Those standing by him said, "Do you dare insult the high priest of God?" Then Paul responded, "Brothers, I didn't know that he was the high priest. For it stands written, 'You shall not speak evil against a ruler of your people'" (Ex 22.28).

Then, when Paul became aware that one part of the council was made up of Sadducees and the other of Pharisees, he exclaimed in the council, "Brothers, I myself am a Pharisee, a son of Pharisees. I am being accused for hoping in the Resurrection of the Dead!" After saying this, a fight ["stasis"] ensued between the Pharisees and the Sadducees. The assembly was divided. On the one hand, the Sadducees say that there is no resurrection, nor angel nor spirit, but on the other hand the Pharisees confess all these things. Then a great clamor arose and some of the scribes from the faction of Pharisees took up the battle, saying, "We find no guilt in this man. Perhaps a spirit or angel spoke to him." Such a huge argument ["stasis"] developed that the tribune was afraid they were going to tear Paul apart, so he ordered the soldiers to go down and carry Paul away from their midst and bring him into the barracks.

Hosea 6.1-3

Hosea was an eighth-century BC prophet who wrote primarily to the northern kingdom in Israel to get them to turn back from their idolatrous ways.[24] The following text is part of an abrupt change of tone in Hosea's prophecy, wherein the northern kingdom is called to repentance.[25] Later Christians read this text as a promise of resurrection for all God's people. When Paul refers to the Resurrection of the Dead in today's Acts reading, it becomes clear that the Doctrine of Resurrection is also a widespread belief in pharisaic Judaism because of their recognition of the authenticity of the later prophets such as Hosea.

In their affliction, they will arise early and come to me, saying, "Let us go and return to the Lord our God since he has snatched us away, and he will heal us. He will strike us and then bind us up. After two days he will heal us, and on the third day we will be raised and will come to life in his presence. And we will know him. So let us seek to know the Lord, as we will find him ready early in the morning. He will come like an early-morning and late-season rain.

1 Timothy 1.3-7, 18-19

> *Paul writes to his young protégé, Timothy, to keep the faith through orthodox teaching, which will result in a good conscience. To Paul, the goal of all Christian instruction was love, something Augustine would later echo when he claimed that the only valid interpretation of the Bible is that which results in love.[26] The centrality of conscience is one of Paul's most distinctive themes in his letters, and is picked up in today's Acts reading when he claims to have had a good conscience his whole life.*

As I urged you while I was going to Macedonia, stay in Ephesus so that you might instruct certain persons not to teach anything heterodox, nor to occupy themselves with various myths or endless genealogies that promote useless speculation more than the redemptive plan of God, which is faith. Now the goal of our instruction is love from a pure heart, a good conscience ["suneidesis agathos"] and an un-hypocritical faith. Some have deviated from these things and turned away to fruitless talk, wanting to be teachers of the law, but understanding neither what they're saying nor what they're talking about so confidently.

I set this charge before you, my child Timothy, in accord with the prophecies that preceded you, that with the prophecies you might fight the good fight, having faith and a good conscience ["suneidesis agathos"]. Some, by rejecting conscience, have made a shipwreck of their faith.

Comment

This is a very important speech in Acts because Paul manages to get the Pharisees to agree with him, at least on the surface. By claiming that he is being accused simply for teaching something that any good pharisaic Jew would have believed, Paul manages to divide the council who again show themselves to be unreasonable.

Of course, what Paul means by the Resurrection of the Dead is probably different from what the Pharisees had in mind. Paul is likely speaking not only of the general resurrection of the dead, but also of the specific Resurrection of Jesus. Underneath it all, Paul is claiming that he's on trial because his Jewish opponents will not recognize Jesus as the Messiah. Yet Luke has Paul state this ambiguously enough not only to advance Paul's apologetic claims about Jesus, but also to drive a wedge between the two factions on the council. It's a clever rhetorical strategy, and it works.

The Resurrection of the Dead is a teaching that developed in later Judaism. The *Mishnah*, the collected authoritative sayings of the rabbis, is abundantly clear on the subject: "He that says the resurrection of the dead is a teaching which does not derive from the Torah and the Torah does not come from heaven [is] an Epicurean."[27] Since Epicureans taught that "man was mortal and that the cosmos was the result of an accident," they denied an afterlife.[28] Thus the *Mishnah* is saying that anyone who denies the general resurrection is repudiating any share in the life to come. Those are strong words. Resurrection was a mainstream teaching for the Pharisees.

The Sadducees, on the other hand, were the upper-crust Jewish leaders responsible for the temple. They explicitly denied the general resurrection because they recognized only the written law found in the Books of Moses.[29] They also rejected that Jesus was the Messiah since they refused to accept even the promise of a messiah because it was found in the OT prophets (and not in the books of Moses).

We have to be careful when reading this episode because we might conclude that the Pharisees are siding with Paul against the Sadducees. It is especially important to remember what Luke's strategy is as he writes, both here and in his gospel.[30] Luke usually depicts the Pharisees as being "not far from the kingdom of God" (Mark 12.34), but this does not mean that he thinks they're right. The Pharisees have the right theology about the general resurrection, but have missed the point entirely because they reject Jesus. This makes them blameworthy to Luke, not praiseworthy.[31]

Notice as well that Paul gets in trouble before the council because he claimed that he had a "good conscience." Why did this annoy the high priest so much?

The high priest is probably annoyed because Paul is implicitly claiming that despite his conversion and teachings about Jesus, he is still a good Jew, perhaps even a better Jew than the leaders.[32] Of course, the high priest does not share this view at all, suggesting that Paul's repeated attempts to paint himself as a good Pharisee have not worked.

Paul's response is then to swear at the high priest using a curse formula found in Deuteronomy. What Paul is saying by invoking this curse is that the Jewish leadership, charged with keeping the law, are violating it themselves by falsely accusing Paul and denying him due process. Paul had not been charged with anything formally, yet the Jewish leadership looked on while the mobs tried to beat Paul to death.[33] They were not very impressive keepers of the law.

When someone pointed out that Paul's retort was itself improper, Paul then seems to back off. But, once again, we need to be careful readers here. Even if Paul had been away from Jerusalem for a long time, it's hard to believe that he would have failed to recognize the high priest (he was the one who ran council meetings after all).[34] So what was Paul doing?

I think it's best to read this as an ironic statement. Because the one charged with upholding the law is breaking it by mistreating Paul, Paul can't even recognize him as the high priest.[35]

One of Paul's favorite tropes in his writings is his appeal to conscience. With Paul, conscience acquires a moral connotation that would prove to be very influential for Christians through the centuries.[36] Paul's basic point is that, even if we're wrong, it is never right to ignore our consciences.

John Henry Newman, the nineteenth-century leader of the so-called Oxford Movement, that was instrumental in recovering the ancient sacramental sensibility of the Anglican Church, wrote the following about conscience in a famous letter to the Duke of Norfolk:

Conscience is the voice of God…[It is] a principle planted within us, before we have had any training, although training and experience are necessary for its strength, growth and due formation. [It is] a constituent element of the mind, as our perception of other ideas may be, as our powers of reasoning, as our sense of order and the beautiful, and our other intellectual endowments…[it is] the internal witness of both the existence and the law of God.[37]

Following Newman, Christians have taught in more recent times that when we listen to our consciences, we are hearing the voice of God. This is why Christians generally believe that one should never disobey one's conscience, even if it's mistaken. Our consciences are not infallible guides to right action, since sin can deaden the conscience, but listening to the conscience is a central way for us to hear what God wants from us.

However, it is also entirely possible to take this idea too far. The teaching of the inviolability of the conscience developed during a time when there was a general consensus on right and wrong. The assumption is that the conscience, when it has been properly formed and is functioning well, is a generally reliable guide to what is true according to natural law. As one church leader has written,

Conscience is a hard, objective thing – a challenge to self, a call to conversion, and a sign of humility. And this sits uncomfortably with those who see conscience as a sign of freedom, and freedom as the right to reject what is unpalatable. When we imagine that conscience is primarily a mark of individual autonomy, we have to pay certain costs; among these is the decay of the idea of moral truth – even when that truth is something we agree with.[38]

We might also note that the centrality of the conscience also forms the backdrop for why religious freedom is a basic human right. The state should be careful not to coerce someone to violate their conscience because the conscience is sacred ground. The Second Vatican Council's "Declaration of Religious Freedom" (*Dignitatis Humanae*) says it well:

Every human person has a right to religious freedom…No one should be forced to act against his conscience in religious matters, nor prevented from acting according to his conscience whether in private or in public…The right to religious freedom is firmly based on the dignity of the human person as this is known from the revealed Word of God and from reason itself.[39]

When Paul claims that he has a clear conscience, this is a remarkable statement given that he had persecuted the church and was present at the martyrdom of Stephen, a stance he would show great remorse for in his later writings (1 Cor 15.9). Paul has a clean conscience not because he has never erred, but because all his actions, whether misguided or not, have always been about the zealous pursuit of God.

Our society has become so noisy and distracted that many can no longer listen to their consciences. Still worse, many is our culture form their consciences from the dictates of popular culture. Therefore, part of the urgent educational work of the church is forming consciences to help Christians make better choices. Correct choices should lead us to greater love, faith, and humility in the long run. Thus a clean conscience is one of the important aspects of a flourishing human life.

Questions for Reflection:

1. **Paul seems to think that the general resurrection is important. How does the teaching that we all will be resurrected from the dead at Christ's return make any difference in your life?**
2. **How much quiet time do you give yourself? Do you follow the practice of regularly examining your conscience?**
3. **Is anything bothering your conscience right now? How might you resolve that burden?**

CHAPTER 47

HOW TO THRIVE IN ADVERSITY
Acts 23.11-35

Acts 23.11-35

> *The Jewish zealots (in town from the province of Asia) cook up a*
> *plot to kill Paul. But somehow Paul's young nephew gets word of*
> *it and passes this information on to him. This is the first and only*
> *time we hear about Paul's relatives who are apparently living in*
> *Jerusalem. The Roman tribune springs into action and sends a huge*
> *military force (half of the garrison in Jerusalem) to accompany Paul*
> *to his boss, Felix.[40] The key to this scene is the tribune's claim, in his*
> *otherwise self-serving letter, that Paul has done nothing deserving*
> *of "death or imprisonment." Luke very much wants us to under-*
> *stand that Paul is innocent of the charges brought against him.*

The following night the Lord stood near Paul and said, "Take courage, since, just as you bore witness to me in Jerusalem, so it is necessary for you to bear witness in Rome also."

Now, when day came, the Jews hatched a plot and bound themselves
with an oath not to eat or drink until they had killed Paul. There were
forty of them who formed the conspiracy who went to the high priest
and to the elders and said, "We have put ourselves under an oath not to
eat until we have killed Paul. Now, therefore, tell the tribune with the
council that he should bring Paul down to you as if you are about to

examine the matters concerning him more thoroughly. But we are prepared to kill him as he approaches this place."

When Paul's nephew heard about the ambush, he came, entered into the barracks and told it to Paul. Then Paul summoned one of the centurions and said, "Bring this young man to the tribune, since he has something to tell him about me." So the centurion took him and brought him to the tribune and said, "The prisoner, Paul, summoned me and requested me to bring this young man to you, as he has something to tell you."

Then the tribune took his hand, went to a private place, and inquired what it was that he had to tell him. And Paul's nephew said, "The Jews are about to request you to bring Paul down tomorrow to the council as if they are going to examine him more thoroughly. Don't be fooled by them, since forty of their men are planning to ambush Paul. In fact, they have bound themselves with an oath not to eat or drink anything until they have killed him. Even now they are making preparations, waiting on an agreement from you." Then the tribune dismissed the young man, directing him to tell no one that, "you have made these things known to me."

Then the tribune summoned two of his centurions and said, "Prepare two-hundred soldiers to travel to Caesarea along with seventy horses and two-hundred bowmen at 9:00 tonight. Prepare, as well, a mount for Paul to ride to bring him safely to Felix, the governor. Then he wrote a letter and the gist of it was like this:

> Claudius Lysias to his Excellency governor Felix, greetings. This man was apprehended by the Jews and was about to be killed by them, when I came upon him with my soldiers and rescued him after I learned that he was a Roman citizen. Desiring to ascertain the reason for their accusation against him, I brought him down to their council where I discovered that he was being accused with reference to controversial questions of their law, but no

accusation against him deserved death or imprisonment. Later, a plot was revealed to me that the Jews were just about to send men against this man so I immediately sent him off to you, instructing his accusers to state their accusations against him to you.

The soldiers then acted according to their orders and went up to Paul and brought him by night to the city of Antipatris. The next day, they let the horsemen go on with him while they returned to the barracks. Then the horsemen came to Caesarea, delivered the letter to the governor, and handed Paul over to him. After the governor read the letter, he inquired what province Paul was from. When he learned that Paul was from Cilicia, he said, I will give you a hearing when your accusers arrive. Then the governor ordered that Paul be guarded in the praetorium of Herod.

1 Samuel 14.24-32, 35

This passage comes in the midst of Saul's demise as king of Israel. Saul has proved to be an ineffective leader and starts making bad decisions, including ordering his people to fast even though they are at war. Saul not only endangers his troops by doing so, but also endangers his son Jonathan's life, who unknowingly eats in violation of the vow.[41] This leads to further problems when the famished army violates the OT regulations against eating blood, and satisfies their hunger with the spoils of battle. Luke may have had this scene in mind when he referenced the vow "not to eat" that the Jewish zealots take in today's Acts reading, an action that reflects badly on the Jewish leadership in Jerusalem.

Then Saul committed a great misdeed of ignorance on that day when he bound the people with an oath, saying, "Cursed is the man who eats bread before evening. Until I avenge my enemy, no man shall eat bread (even though the whole rest of the land had eaten)."

Now, there was a thicket that had a bee hive on the ground and the people went up to the hive and continued speaking, but no one put his hand to his mouth since the people were afraid of the oath of the Lord. But Jonathan had not heard about the oath that his father had given to the people, and he stretched out the tip of his walking staff that was in his hand and dipped it in the comb of honey and returned his hand to his mouth. Then his eyes were brightened.

Then, one of the people said, "Your father solemnly made the people swear an oath, saying, 'Cursed is the man who eats bread today.'" However, the people were faint. Then Jonathan understood and said, "My father has destroyed the land, and look now at my eyes so soon after I have tasted this honey. Surely if the people had eaten today from the spoils of their enemies that they procured, the slaughter of the Philistines would have been even greater."

And on that day Jonathan struck the Philistines at Michmash, but the people were exceedingly weary. Then the people took some of the flocks, herds and the cattle, and slew them on the ground and the people ate it with the blood. This was reported to Saul, saying, "The people have sinned against the Lord by eating meat with the blood"...Then Saul built an altar to the Lord. This was the first altar he had built to the Lord.

Luke 23.6-12

Under Roman law, a prisoner was often tried by the authorities in his province of origin. Herod Antipas, tetrarch of Galilee, who just happened to be in Jerusalem for the Festival of Passover, technically had jurisdiction over Jesus. Thus Pilate ships him off to Herod. In today's Acts reading, Luke depicts Paul similarly to Jesus. Like Jesus, Paul has been falsely accused by the Jewish leadership and is sent to another Roman leader for his case to be heard. The big difference is that Felix decides not to send Paul to his district of origin (Cilicia), but decides to hear the case himself.

After Pilate heard the charges of the Jews, he asked Jesus if he was Galilean. Recognizing that Jesus belonged under the jurisdiction of Herod Antipas, Pilate sent Jesus away to Herod, since he was in Jerusalem in those days.

When Herod saw Jesus, he was very glad, since, for a long time, Pilate had wanted to see him because he had heard about Jesus and had hoped to see some miracle performed by him. So Herod examined Jesus for a long time, but Jesus gave no answer to him. And the high priests and the scribes were standing by and kept vigorously accusing Jesus. Even Herod and his soldiers treated Jesus with contempt. They dressed Jesus up in splendid finery and sent him back to Pilate. Now Herod and Pilate became friends with one another from that very day, since before they had been at enmity with one another.

Comment

Our Acts reading today begins with another vision from Jesus to Paul who tells him to "take courage" because Paul is about to bear witness in Rome. Truth be told, it would take several years for Paul to get to Rome, but the vision serves to give Paul some confidence that everything is unfolding according to plan, even if it all seems a bit haphazard on the surface. As we've observed from the very first chapter of Acts, the gospel has to go to the "ends of the earth," in this case, Rome.

Many attribute Paul's outwardly calm demeanor in the next several chapters to this vision. After all, if this vision really came from Jesus, Paul has little to worry about when he stands before Felix in Caesarea. Somehow he is going to get to Rome and along the way he is going to preach the gospel "before kings" (Acts 9.15). This vision also serves as confirmation to Paul of his earlier prediction that, after Jerusalem, he "must also see Rome" (Acts 19.21).

I suspect that all of us, when we face difficulties of various kinds, wish that God would show up in a vision, and tell us that everything is going to be ok. I further suspect that this would provide great comfort, but only for a brief period of time. After the excitement of the vision died down, we would still have to go on trusting God. In other words, our wish for visions or signs is really a wish for certainty, but this is usually not what God offers us. One of the key things all of us need to learn is how to trust God in the face of difficulties and uncertainty. This is a big part of learning to live the Christian life.

Unfortunately, many theological systems seem to have certainty as the primary purpose of their existence. If you just do "x, y, and z," you can be certain that everything will be ok in the end. Yet, with Paul, this vision provided the broad scope of what would unfold in our story, but none of the details. Paul would languish in prison for years waiting to get to Rome.

Put simply, God does not offer us certainty. He offers us faith. This is probably why James says the following:

> Count it all joy, my brethren, when you meet various trials, for you know that the testing of your faith produces steadfastness. And let steadfastness have its full effect, that you may be perfect and complete, lacking in nothing (James 1.2-3, RSV).

Count it all joy when we encounter suffering? This sounds simply masochistic. But what James understands is that it is only by learning to walk through trials with Jesus at our side that we learn how to trust him. And it is only by learning to trust Jesus that we really start living the Christian life.

I'm reminded of the biblical scholar, Pete Enns. After graduating from Harvard with a PhD in Near Eastern Languages and Civilizations, Enns went back to his alma mater, Westminster Theological Seminary, as an OT Professor. Westminster is a conservative reformed seminary outside of Philadelphia that was once a part of Princeton, but broke away in the early part of the twentieth century out of fear that Princeton was embracing too many "modernist" ideas. In other words, Princeton was starting to employ the tools of modern biblical scholarship, which went against some of the tenants of their doctrinal statement, the Westminster Confession of Faith.

Enns got in trouble when some new blood joined the faculty and wanted to drive out "heresy" from their midst. Enns had just published a book called *Inspiration and Incarnation* that pointed out some of the obvious absurdities that exist in a strictly literalist reading of the Bible. As a result, Enns got in their cross hairs and was eventually removed from the faculty after a wrenching multi-year fight.

Enns went through years of looking for work and was forced to re-examine his core spiritual assumptions. He eventually became an Episcopalian and describes his transition this way:

> It was huge for me to discover, in the midst of all this, an entire Christian tradition that confirmed my experience, which is when I began reading about the dark night of the soul – a cleaning acid bath to my preoccupation with correct thinking. My familiar pattern of needing to know, now felt wholly out of place, even sacrilegious. I was being led to a much bigger God – and a much more interesting and caring one…And a crucial part of all this was finding a flesh-and-blood community of faith that already modeled this expression of faith – and for me that wound up being a welcoming, Christ-centered Episcopal community. I needed to be in a place where the pulpit was off to the side and the table was central, symbols for me of letting go of old patterns, where lengthy sermons were the center of worship…I need Sunday morning centered on what is trans-rational, the fundamental Christian mysteries of incarnation and resurrection, the very heartbeat of Christian faith…I need a God bigger than my arguments. I like a prayer book and liturgy to guide me in my faith rather than falling back into my comfort zone of controlling reality with my learned and carefully chosen words, and without leaving it up to me to come up with what to say here and now when I just may not feel like it.[42]

Enns needed to learn how to trust God and embrace mystery. But I suspect this is true for all of us.

Despite all his intelligence and training, and despite the amazing "signs and wonders" that keep happening, Paul had to learn the same thing. As Paul would put it later,

> I have learned, in whatever state I am, to be content. I know how to be abased, and I know how to abound; in any and all circumstances I have learned the secret of facing plenty and hunger, abundance, and want. I can do all things in him who strengthens me (Phil 4.11-13, RSV).

In the midst of suffering and difficulty, which life invariably brings, pious bromides only go so far. What matters for the Christian life is learning to trust God no matter what the outward circumstances. This is rarely easy, but, as Paul points out, it is one of the keys to finding true contentment in life.

Questions for Reflection:

1. **In what areas of your life do you find it difficult to trust God (finances, health, kids, grandkids, etc.)?**
2. **Many (but not all) come into our Anglican tradition from elsewhere. What brought you to the Episcopal Church? What do you miss about where you came from?**
3. **Can you live like Paul does and find contentment in both "abundance and want?" To what extent is your happiness and contentment tied to material resources?**

CHAPTER 48

PAUL ON TRIAL
Acts 24.1-23

Acts 24.1-23

*This is Paul's third defense speech in Acts, and is likely a sum-
mary of what took place.[43] Paul is on trial before the regional
governor Felix in Caesarea. Although it seems like both Tertullus,
the Jews' lawyer, and Paul resort to flattery in their respec-
tive speeches, this is not the case. Luke has depicted this scene
in a very authentic way from a rhetorical and legal perspective. Because Felix is essentially being asked to find Paul guilty
for matters beyond Roman law, both sides appeal to Felix'
goodwill to do so in a rhetorically-appropriate way.[44] When
it comes down to it, however, the most serious charge is sedition, which Paul handles with great deft, questioning both the
standing of the accusers and the quality of the evidence. Paul
proves himself to be quite a defense lawyer in this passage.*

Now, after five days, the high priest, Ananias, with certain elders and
an attorney ["rhetor"] named Tertullus, came down and laid out the
charges to the governor against Paul. When Felix called upon Tertullus,
he began to accuse Paul, saying, "We have experienced a great deal of
peace through your administration and reforms that have come to this
nation through your foresight. In fact, everyone everywhere acknowledges it, most excellent Felix, with all thankfulness.

In order to not take up too much of your time, I urge you to hear us briefly with your customary graciousness. For we found this man to be a public plague who brought about an insurrection ["stasis"] among the all the Jews through the whole world. He's a ringleader of the sect of the Nazoreans, who attempted to profane the temple, so we apprehended him. When you are able to examine him yourself, you will find out all these things about which we are accusing him." Then the Jews also joined the attack, asserting that Paul had done these things.

Then, when the governor gestured to Paul to speak, Paul responded, "Knowing that you have been a judge over the nation for many years, I now cheerfully offer my defense of myself. As you can well understand for yourself, it was not more than twelve days ago when I went up to worship in Jerusalem. They didn't find me disputing with anyone or riling up a crowd, either in the synagogues or in the city, and thus they're not able to prove anything about which they're accusing me. But I admit this to you that concerning The Way, which they call a sect ["heresis"], I worship the ancestral God of our forefathers, believing everything according to the Law of Moses and all that is written in the Prophets. I have hope in the God whom they themselves also look forward to, that there is going to be a resurrection of both the just and the unjust. This is why I do my best always to have a clear conscience before God and before the people.

After many years, I came to give alms for my nation and to present offerings, which I was doing when they found me ritually purifying myself in the temple with no crowd or trouble. But some Jews from the province of Asia — who ought to have come before you to present their accusations if they would have anything to say against me. Barring that, these men here ought to explain what crime they found — when they made me stand before the council, there is only one declaration that I shouted out while standing among them: 'I am on trial before you today for the Resurrection of the Dead!'"

When Felix understood the facts about The Way more accurately, he adjourned the hearing, saying, "When Lysias the tribune comes down, I will decide your case." Felix then directed the centurion to guard Paul, but to let him have some liberty and not to forbid his own companions from visiting him.

Psalm 74.1-11, 22-23

Psalm 74 is a lament over the destruction of the temple by God's enemies that includes an implicit accusation against God for allowing this to happen.[45] When the temple is destroyed all stability goes with it.[46] The Psalm concludes with a plea for God's intervention against Israel's enemies.[47] This Psalm shows how serious the charge of desecrating the temple was to the Jews. Not only would the Jewish leadership have been appalled by an act of defilement, but also the Roman government would have been concerned over this as well, since such an action would invariably lead to civic unrest.[48] Thus the charge against Paul of "profaning the temple" is very serious, and could have carried the death penalty if he were found guilty.

A Psalm of Asaph for Understanding

O God, have you rejected us forever? Why is your wrath kindled against the sheep of your pasture? Remember your synagogue that you purchased from the beginning. You redeemed the rod of your inheritance, this Mount Zion where you dwell. Lift up your hands against their arrogance until the end because your enemy has done wrong in your holy places.

All who hate you declare their pride in the midst of your feast; they have ignorantly set up their signs for signs in the entrance above. They cut down its doors with axes like wood in a forest. They have broken it in pieces with hatchets and hammers. They have set your sanctuary on fire; they have profaned the tabernacle of your name. Their generation says the same thing in their heart: "Come, let us wipe out all the feasts of God from the earth." There are no signs for us to see; there is no prophet left; God will not know us anymore. How long, O God, will the enemy scoff? Will the opposition be hostile to your name forever? Why do you draw back your hand? Will your right hand be withdrawn into your chest forever?

Arise, O God, plead my case; remember how fools reproached you all day long. Don't forget the voice of your supplicants; let the arrogance of those who hate you continuously rise up before you.

Revelation 20.11-15

According to the final section of the Bible, at the end of time, both the "living" and the "dead" will be resurrected for judgment. Each is judged according to his deeds done in his life. Although, in his letters, Paul usually focuses on the "resurrection of the just," our Acts passage today makes clear that Paul believed both the "just" and the "unjust" would be resurrected in the end, a teaching that seems to be congruent with this passage in Revelation.

And I saw a great white throne and one sitting upon it, from whose presence the earth and the sky fled away and no place was found for them. And I saw the dead, both the great and the small, standing before the throne. And books were opened, then another was opened, which is the Book of Life. And the dead were judged by what was written in the books according to their deeds. And the sea gave up the dead who were in it and Death and Hades gave up the dead in them. And each was judged according to his deeds. Then Death and Hades were thrown into the lake of fire. This is the second death, the lake of fire. And if anyone was not found written in the Book of Life, he was cast into the lake of fire.

Comment

It might help to have some background information on Felix, the Roman governor of Judea who is Paul's judge in this episode, since Luke could have assumed most of his original readers would have known something about him. Felix was generally known in his day as an incompetent and corrupt administrator. For example, the Roman historian Tacitus says that Felix, "practiced every kind of cruelty and lust, wielding the power of a king with all the instincts of a slave."[49]

Tacitus' point is that Felix, who had been born a slave but gained his freedom, was anti-Semitic, brutal, and distrusted.[50] In fact, in just a few years after this scene, Felix would lose his position because of the unrest that occurred between the Jews and Gentiles.[51]

Although Paul's accusers show up in this scene with a great entourage, a good lawyer and seemingly the upper hand, their case is pretty weak. They essentially accuse Paul of three things: (1) being a public "plague," (2) fomenting an insurrection ["*stasis*"], and (3) profaning the temple. All three of these accusations point in one direction – sedition – a very serious charge that could result in Paul's execution if convicted.[52]

Notice that the Jews do their best to play down the theological part of the dispute, since Felix has no expertise to hear it. They do not want the case dismissed and are also understandably eager to ignore their role in the unrest in Jerusalem.

Paul's response is clever. Like a good trial lawyer, he reframes the issue and shows how the Jews' case falls apart on technical and evidentiary grounds. Paul couldn't possibly be a public "plague." He had simply come to Jerusalem after years of being away to worship. In fact, when he was seized by the Jews, he was undergoing a purification ritual. He's a pious Jew, not an insurrectionist.

Secondly, the charges of insurrection and profaning the temple can't be proved because the Jewish leaders didn't bother to bring along any eyewitnesses. It was the Jews from the province of Asia who witnessed the event. Thus all the evidence being presented against Paul is mere hearsay.

Finally, Paul questions the standing of Felix to hear these charges since they really boil down to questions about Jewish law and, in particular, the Resurrection of the Dead. The Roman government had no particular expertise to decide such matters. Thus Felix should release Paul.

Notice that in arguing this way, Paul is essentially saying that the Christian movement is broadly in line with historical Judaism. He claims to be teaching nothing different than is found in the Prophets and the Books of Moses. Thus Paul reframes his entire defense in terms of Jewish theology.

I have been trying to show all through this guide that Christianity, at least in the beginning, was closely related to Judaism. The followers of The Way were simply claiming that the Resurrection of Jesus provided further evidence that what the Pharisees had been teaching all along is true.

Of course, it's more complicated than that. The Christians are also implicitly arguing that Jesus was the long-awaited Messiah promised by the prophets. This is a claim that the Jewish leadership could not accept because it seemed to deviate from the literal sense of the scriptures. Thus those who today argue for a consistently "literal" reading of the Bible are arguing against the way of reading that made Christianity possible in the first place. Paul's reading of the OT is consistently non-literal. Our problem is that we are so used to the Christian appropriation of the OT that we have forgotten that the interpretations we take for granted were thought to be downright subversive in the first century.

This provides an instructive lesson for all of us. Although we can look back today at the OT and see many passages that point to Christ, there is little chance that anyone could have ever guessed that these passages were meant to be understood that way before Jesus came along. In fact, very little of what we consider to be "Messianic prophecy" today would have been understood that way in rabbinic interpretation. In other words, it would have been practically impossible to figure out the deeper meaning imbedded in those passages ahead of time.

Thus the unfolding of God's redemptive plan is simply a mystery and those who try to concoct elaborate schemes to explain it all are bound to be mistaken. We may be sure that Jesus will return someday and that we will all be raised from the dead. But beyond this we ought not to speculate too much. Although teaching about how the world is going to end has proved to be very popular over the centuries, it has, to date, consistently been wrong — not to mention needlessly inflammatory.

Although Paul makes an effective defense, in the end, his case is not dismissed. This is, of course, in keeping with God's plan. We'll have to wait until the next Chapter to see the real reason why.

Questions for Reflection

1. Have you ever had to defend yourself in a formal setting, in a deposition or trial? What was that like for you?
2. Why do you think speculation about the end of the world has proved to be so consistently popular over time? What does that say about us? Where should our hope reside?
3. Christians today are not infrequently charged with being a public menace, since at times we stand against some things the society desperately wants to do. In what ways have you encountered this? How do you answer this charge?

CHAPTER 49

SPEAKING TRUTH TO POWER
Acts 24.24-25.12

Acts 24.24-25.12

Most of this episode takes place about two years after the events in the last chapter which ended with Paul's being sent from Jerusalem to the governor Felix in Caesarea.[53] Paul has apparently been languishing in prison the entire time. However, a leadership change takes place as the governorship passes from Felix to Porcius Festus. In an effort to placate the Jews, both Felix and Festus, neither of whom apparently see any legal merit to the case against Paul, nevertheless keep him in custody. After the handover of leadership, the Jews in Jerusalem press Festus, the new governor, to have Paul brought back to Jerusalem with the familiar motive of wanting to kill him along the way. Paul is backed into a corner when Festus asks if he is willing to be tried in Jerusalem. So Paul exercises his right as a Roman citizen to be tried in Rome.

After some time, Felix came with his wife Drusilla, who was Jewish. He summoned Paul and heard him speak about faith in the Messiah Jesus. After conversing with Felix about righteousness ["diaisune"], self-control and the coming judgment, Felix became frightened and responded, "That's enough for now. When I have time, I will summon you." At the same time, he was also hoping that money ["krehma"] would be given to him by Paul. So, Felix frequently summoned Paul to converse with him. After two years had gone by, Porcius Festus succeeded Felix. Wanting to do a favor for the Jews, Felix left Paul locked up.

Then, three days after Festus arrived in the province, he went up to Jerusalem from Caesarea. And the chief priests and the leaders among the Jews brought formal charges against Paul, imploring Festus and asking for a favor against Paul to recall Paul to Jerusalem. (They were planning to ambush Paul on the way.)

But Festus replied that Paul was being kept in Caesarea and that he himself was planning to travel there shortly. "Therefore," said Festus, "Let those who are powerful people among you come down to Caesarea together with me. If anything is improper with this man, accuse ["kategoreo"] him there."

After Festus stayed no more than eight or ten days with them, he went down to Caesarea. The next day, he sat on the judgment bench and commanded Paul to be led in. When Paul came, the Jews from Jerusalem who had come down stood around him and brought many weighty charges that they were not able to prove. Paul defended himself, saying, "I committed no offense: either against the law of the Jews, against the temple or against Caesar."

But, Festus, wanting to grant a favor to the Jews, answered Paul and said, "Are you willing to go up to Jerusalem to stand trial before me regarding these charges against you?" Paul responded, "I am standing before the judicial bench ["bema"] of Caesar where I ought to be tried. I have done no wrong to the Jews as you well know. But if I am in the wrong and have done anything deserving death, I am not trying to be excused from dying. Yet, if there is nothing to their charges against me, no one can hand me over to them. I appeal to Caesar!"

Then Festus talked it over with his council and answered, "You have appealed to Caesar. Therefore, to Caesar you will go."

Psalm 15.1-5

Psalm 15 is a wisdom Psalm that lays out the moral qualities necessary for authentic Jewish worship.[54] *In particular, taking bribes, although commonplace in Roman jurisprudence, was strictly forbidden in Judaism.[55] Since bribery corrupts justice and usually harms the poor, there was no place for paying or accepting a bribe in the practice of a pious Jew.[56] Thus Paul's refusal to pay a bribe either to Felix or to Festus is an important piece of evidence not only of his innocence, but also of his superior moral character.*

A Psalm of David

O Lord, who can sojourn in your tent and who can dwell in your Holy Place? He who walks blamelessly and acts righteously ["dikaisune"], who speaks truthfully in his heart and who does not falsify with his tongue. He does not act wickedly against his neighbor, nor does he take up a reproach against those close to him. In his sight, one who acts wickedly is treated with contempt and he honors those who fear the Lord. He keep his promise to his neighbor and does not disappoint him. He does not lend his money at interest and does not receive bribes ["doron"] against the innocent. He who does these things shall never be moved.

Matthew 27.11-20

Yet again, Luke depicts the trials of Paul in light of Jesus. In this scene, Jesus stands before Pilate who is seated on the judicial bench judging him. Pilate's wife plays a background role in the proceedings. Similarly, in today's Acts reading, Paul stands before the governor Felix and his Jewish wife Drusilla while Felix sits on the judicial bench, judging Paul.[57]

Of course, the immediate outcomes are quite different, as Paul uses his Roman citizenship to fight another day, while Jesus is executed. However, the use of similar language suggests at least a tenuous connection between the two scenes.

Then Jesus stood before the governor who asked him, saying, "Are you the King of the Jews?" And Jesus said, "If you say so." Jesus was being accused ["kategoreo"] by the high priests and the elders, but did not respond. Then Pilate said to him, "Are you not hearing all the things they're accusing you of?" And Jesus did not answer him a single word, which amazed the governor greatly.

Now, it was the custom of the governor at the feast to release one prisoner to the crowd, whomever they wanted. At that time, they had a notorious prisoner named Barabbas. Pilate said to those assembled, "Whom do you want me to release to you: Barabbas or Jesus, who is called the Messiah?" (Pilate knew that they had handed Jesus over out of envy.)

Then, while Pilate was sitting on the judicial bench ["bema"], his wife sent a message to him, saying, "Have nothing to do with that righteous ["dikaios"] man, since I have suffered much today from a vision concerning him." But the high priests and the elders stirred up the crowds to request the release of Barabbas and the execution of Jesus. The governor answered and said to them, "Which of the two do you want me to release to you?" And they said, "Barabbas." Pilate said to them, "What then should I do with Jesus who is called Messiah?" They all said, "Let him be crucified." And he said, "Why, what has he done wrong?" And they cried out all the more, saying, "Let him be crucified!"

Comment

We might have wondered somewhere along the way if Luke really has all of this right. After all, Luke keeps describing these trials as if Paul is obviously innocent of the charges of sedition and of violating the Jewish law. Yet, two years have gone by and no one has bothered to release Paul. Shouldn't this at least make us wonder about whether Luke is telling us the whole truth? Why not just release Paul if he is so obviously innocent?

In this Acts passage, we learn why the wheels of justice are turning so slowly for Paul. Felix, who, in the last chapter, had promised to consult with the tribune, Lysias, (Acts 24.22) but apparently hadn't, has been expecting Paul to pay a bribe. Paul mentioned at the end of his defense speech in the previous episode that he had come to Jerusalem with some money, likely the collection of alms he had taken up from the Gentiles in the province of Asia (Acts 24.17). This must have peaked the interest of the Roman governor. He decided to keep Paul in custody until he paid a bribe. Paul steadfastly refused to do so, and thus he stayed in prison.

This might seem very strange (and corrupt) to us. No doubt the corruption charge is at least partially true. As the historian Suetonius wrote (describing the Emperor Vespasian),

> [Vespasian] made no bones of selling…acquittals to men under prosecution, whether innocent or guilty. He is even believed to have had the habit of designedly advancing the most rapacious of his procurators to higher posts, that they might be the richer when he later condemned them; in fact, it was common talk that he used these men as sponges, because he, so to speak, soaked them when they were dry and squeezed them when they were wet.[58]

Although it was illegal, bribery was evidently a widespread practice in Roman jurisprudence.[59] Paul would remain in jail until he paid up. Of course, Luke makes a much bigger deal out of the government's on-going desire to "show favor" to the Jews, but the expectation of a bribe was a key reason why Paul languishes in jail despite having apparently done nothing wrong.

Luke tells us that Felix "frequently" went to meet with Paul (probably dropping hints along the way that this would go better for him if he paid a bribe), but all Felix got in return was Paul's moral exhortation about "righteousness, self-control, and the coming judgment."[60] We have little evidence that Paul's admonishments had much of an effect.

Yet, if that's true, then why does Felix react with "fear"? Some further background information might help. We learn in this passage is that Felix was married to Drusilla, who was Jewish. There's quite an interesting back story about how their marriage took place.

Drusilla, who was reported to be very beautiful, was the granddaughter of Mark Antony and Cleopatra.[61] According to Josephus, Drusilla was originally married to a Syrian king.[62] Apparently, Felix fell in love with Drusilla's beauty and sent one of his friends, Simon, to persuade her to leave her husband and marry him instead. She did, thus flagrantly violating Jewish law.[63]

This is apparently what causes Felix's fear. He's in an adulterous marriage that he secured by dubious means. Thus, when Paul starts preaching to him about "righteousness, self-control, and the coming judgment," this apparently got to poor old Felix. It hit a nerve, since what he was doing was wrong. In fact, the Greek word Paul uses for self-control, "*egkrateia*," comes with the sense of "impulse control."[64] This is precisely what Felix had failed to do.

Isn't it interesting that Paul doesn't flinch from moral preaching even at the cost of his freedom? He is perfectly willing to tell a provincial governor that he has sinned grievously and that he should repent. Let's not forget how Peter, at the very start of our story, began his proclamation: "Repent and be baptized…for the forgiveness of your sins" (Acts 2.38). Paul and Peter are very similar here in their approaches.

It's a popular saying in our day that we should speak "truth to power." But what Paul shows is that the ability to do so effectively starts with having integrity and character. Paul, in imitation of Jesus, is willing to suffer for the mission set before him. Paul might very well have had the money to pay a bribe to gain his freedom. But he refuses to do so. Why? Because he knew that giving into something that was wrong would harm his own soul.

Right before his death, Socrates famously argued that no evil can ever really happen to a good man.[65] On the surface, this seems absurd. But what Socrates meant is that your true self, your soul, exemplified by your character, cannot be affected by mere extrinsic evils. We harm our own souls by choosing wrong instead of good. No one can do this for us.

If we really believed that we should *always* choose what is good because choosing what is evil harms our souls, I suspect that we would be happier. But Paul recognizes, as moral philosophers have taught from ancient times that choosing the good is *always* the right decision, even if it costs us our freedom or our lives, as it did for Socrates. Had Paul paid a bribe, not only would this have gone against his religious beliefs, but it would have hindered the task God that had set before him. The ends simply do not justify the means.

Questions for Reflection

1. How would you define "good character?" Do you just know it when you see it? Or, is character something more concrete for you?

2. What does it take to instill character in children or grandchildren? Is this a priority for you? How are you doing with this task?

3. What socially-accepted (but shady) practices tempt you? Are you ever persuaded to do something because "everyone is doing it"?

CHAPTER 50

INJUSTICE
Acts 25.13-27

Acts 25.13-27

When King Agrippa II comes to Caesarea with his sister, Bernice, Festus, the governor, asks for some counsel on how to describe the charges against Paul. Although Paul has exercised his right as a Roman citizen to appeal his case to Caesar, this must go along with a detailed report from the governor. The problem is that Festus has no idea how to describe a case that boils down to Paul's belief that a dead man, Jesus, is really alive.[66] This simply sounds like non-sense. Yet the Jews almost rioted over it. Since Agrippa and Bernice are both Jewish, but were also very well-regarded in Roman circles, Festus is hoping to win Agrippa over to his view of the case, so that he will not be embarrassed when Paul reaches Caesar.[67]

After several days had gone by, King ["Basileus"] Agrippa and Bernice arrived at Caesarea to pay their respects to Festus. They stayed there many days. Festus laid out the case against Paul, saying, "There is a certain man in Jerusalem left behind as a prisoner by Felix. While I was in Jerusalem, the high priests and the elders of the Jews brought charges, requesting a guilty verdict against him. I answered that it is not the custom of the Romans to hand over any man before the one accused ["kategoros"] meets his accusers ["kategoros"] in person, that he might receive the opportunity to offer a defense against the indictment.

So when Paul's accusers ["kategoros"] came back together with me to this place, I did not delay, but the very next day, I sat on the judicial bench and gave orders for the man to be brought in. Then, when the accusers ["kategoros"] stood around him, they did not bring charges of wrongdoing as I expected, but they had various disputes with him about their own superstition and about a certain Jesus who was dead, but whom Paul asserted was alive. I was at a complete loss about how I might investigate such things, so I asked Paul if he might be willing to go to Jerusalem to be tried concerning these things. But Paul appealed to be kept in custody for the decision of his majesty, the emperor. So I commanded him to be held until I could send him up to Caesar." Then Agrippa said to Festus, "I want to hear this man's case." Then Festus replied, "Very well, tomorrow you will hear it."

Then, the next day, Agrippa and Bernice arrived with great pomp ["phantasia"] and entered into the audience hall with the military tribunes and the city's prominent men. Festus then commanded Paul be to be brought in. Then Festus said, "King ["Basileus"] Agrippa and all the men present with us, you see this man about whom the whole legal assembly of Jews petitioned me, both in Jerusalem and here, crying out loudly that he no longer deserved to live. But I found that he had done nothing deserving of death ["axios thanatos"]. When Paul appealed to his majesty, the emperor, I decided to send him.

But I have nothing certain to write to my lord. Therefore I brought him before you all, but especially you, King Agrippa, so that after a preliminary hearing, I might have something to write. For it seems contrary to reason to me to refer a prisoner without first laying out the charges against him."

Matthew 10.5-8, 16-20

*When Jesus sends out his disciples to preach, he predicts
that they will meet resistance from both the religious and*

governmental authorities. This will provide them an opportunity to proclaim the good news before both governors and kings. This prediction finds fulfillment in today's Acts reading. Luke is shaping this narrative to demonstrate how Paul's imprisonment, although unjust, nevertheless is used for God's purposes.

Jesus sent out these twelve, instructing them and saying, "Do not go to the Gentile regions or to enter into any Samaritan town. Rather, go to the lost sheep of Israel. While you are going, preach, saying, "The kingdom of heaven is near!" Heal the sick, raise the dead, cleanse lepers, cast out demons. You have received freely, give freely.

Behold, I am sending you out as sheep in the midst of wolves. Therefore be wise as serpents and as innocent as doves. But beware of people, since they will hand you over to the council and they will flog you in the synagogues. You will be led ["ago"] before governors ["hegemon"] and kings ["basileus"] for my sake, as a testimony to them and to the Gentiles. And when they hand you over for trial do not worry about what you should say, since it will be given to you in that you hour what you should say. For you are not the one who speaks, but the Spirit of your Father is speaking through you.

Luke 23.22-25

All throughout this last section of Acts, we have seen how Luke shapes the story to demonstrate how Paul is following in the footsteps of Jesus. This was especially apparent on the way to Jerusalem, but it also continues here. Just as Pilate found "nothing worthy of death" in Jesus, Festus reiterates a very similar sentiment about Paul. Paul may be innocent, but nevertheless cannot be released.

And a third time Pilate said to them, "Why? What evil has Jesus done? I have found nothing deserving of death ["aitios thanatos"] in him.

I will flog him and release him." But they were insistent, demanding with a loud voice for Jesus to be crucified and their voices prevailed. So Pilate decided to grant their demand. Pilate freed Barabbas, the one cast into prison for insurrection ["stasis"] and murder ["phonos"], and he handed over Jesus to their will.

Comment

It might be helpful at the start to understand a bit about who King Agrippa and Bernice were. We met King Agrippa's father (Agrippa I) in Chapter 25 when he had James, the apostle of Jesus, executed (Acts 12.1-2).

Agrippa II was a favorite of the Emperor Claudius, who kept giving him more territory to run as he got older. Thus Agrippa was someone who was well-liked by all the right people, which is probably why Festus was so eager to discuss Paul's case with him.

Bernice is Agrippa's sister.[68] After she lost her husband, she had moved in with her brother. As a result, there was all kinds of malicious gossip about an incestuous relationship going on between Bernice and Agrippa during this period.[69] But, as best as we can tell, this was just gossip, since Bernice was also known as being quite serious about practicing Judaism.

Their arrival must have been a godsend to Festus. This case simply seemed bizarre to him. How could he possibly explain to Caesar that Jesus, who was dead, was now actually alive (Acts 25.19)? He rightly sees that this case boils down to the resurrection of Jesus. Yet, from a Roman perspective, this was just rank superstition.[70] How could anyone possibly take seriously a dead man who comes to life? Could Agrippa and Bernice, both of whom were Jewish, explain this to Festus?

Paul had already appealed his case to Rome, so we might wonder why another judicial proceeding was necessary. To be clear, there was nothing binding about this particular hearing. On the surface, Festus was simply trying to gather enough information to write up his transfer report to Caesar.

We should realize that, although Paul had a right as a Roman citizen to appeal his case, this was not an absolute right. The provincial governor, in this case, Festus, still had wide discretion about how to handle things in his territory. Festus still could have simply refused Paul's request.[71]

Yet Festus does refer the case to Rome, which must be significant.[72] Luke is setting up a contrast between the unreasonableness of the Jews (who are falsely accusing Paul and trying to kill him at every turn) and the reasonableness of the Romans who, at least in Festus' narrative, are following proper criminal procedure.

But Festus still seems bewildered over the facts of the case. What appears to be happening behind the scenes is that Festus is also trying to get King Agrippa to agree with his perspective on the facts. While Paul may not be guilty of sedition, he is nevertheless a threat to good order. Thus Festus should not just release Paul. Given how odd the facts of the case sound to a Roman ear, Festus probably wanted to have some political backup for why he was still holding Paul.

Thus, when Festus speaks before the gathered dignitaries, he is putting on a show. Paul may be on trial, but this is entertainment for Festus' visiting guests. We must not miss the very self-serving shape Festus gives to the events that have transpired. For example, Festus never bothers to mention that he was seeking to "do a favor for the Jews" (Acts 24.27, 25.9), which is actually why he won't release Paul. But, on the other hand, he cannot just execute a Roman citizen on charges that are obviously false. This might make him look like an incompetent administrator to the higher-ups in Rome. Given that Festus had just replaced Felix for incompetence, this must have figured somewhere into his calculations.

Although Festus seems like an ideal administrator and jurist in this scene, we simply should not take what he tells us about the Roman legal system at face value. Luke does not actually want us to think that the Roman elites are reasonable. After all, Paul is locked up for a crime he didn't commit. And, most importantly, Jesus was crucified by Roman authorities simply to placate a mob. This is an inherently unjust legal system, not a just one, even if on the surface its principles sound pretty good.

For example, as Festus speaks to Agrippa, he first blames his predecessor, Felix, for leaving him this mess, noting that Paul was "left behind as a prisoner" (25.14). Then, as he recounts what took place in Jerusalem, Festus makes himself out to be a great impartial jurist as he invokes the Roman legal principle that every defendant had a right to face his accuser (25.15-16). He sounds so reasonable!

Festus then emphasized how he adjudicated Paul's case "the next day" after he got back from Jerusalem (25.17). Paul gets a speedy trial, exactly what we would hope for from an effective and impartial judiciary. But Paul's Jewish accusers were so incompetent that they only had religious complaints against him (25.18).[73]

In Festus' telling, this messy case is everyone else's fault. The Jews are unreasonable. His predecessor left Paul in jail for two years for no good reason. And Paul has appealed to Rome. What was he supposed to do to placate the Jews now that Paul had appealed to Caesar? On the other hand, how could Festus possibly describe this to Caesar without sounding kooky?

To be sure, we get many of our own legal principles from Roman law. Due process, the right to face an accuser, the right to a speedy trial of one's peers, rules of evidence, restraint on government power, and impartiality all came down to us in one form or another from the Romans, through English common law. We should be grateful for every one of these principles.

Yet, our legal system, at its best, brings something else to the table. All these "rights" do little good unless they are adjudicated within a system that assumes the dignity of every human being. As we have discussed in prior chapters, Christianity played a significant role in the development of this key idea.

Yet, today, our legal system can seem unjust in some important ways. It has the appearance of respectability — even goodness — but the reality is often uglier. Is it just that thousands of poor people sit in jail, sometimes for lengthy periods, for accusations of petty crimes because they cannot make bail or afford an attorney?[74] Is it just that prisons are increasingly being used to manage the mentally ill instead of treatment facilities?[75] It is just that drug laws are so inequitably enforced against white and African American communities? Just one statistic here. Despite studies that show that drug consumption is similar between whites and people of color, the US black incarceration rate rose from 6.5 to 26.3 per 1,000 people from 1980 to 2015, while the white drug arrest rate increased from 3.5 to 4.6.[76]

We may be rightly dismayed at the shoddy treatment Paul is receiving at the hands of the Roman legal system. Yet injustice for the poor and downtrodden never seems to disappear. We may have an enviable judicial system in the US, but there are aspects of it that still need improvement.

In the great hymn "America the Beautiful" we sing, "thy liberty in law." This is certainly true. The collective restraint of law provides the essential framework for freedom. Yet the law most successfully upholds liberty when it also promotes fairness and equity. As Christians, we should care about injustice in our society wherever we might find it, standing up for those who cannot defend themselves. We might admire Paul for enduring his unjust incarceration, but this should also spur a desire in us to help others avoid Paul's fate.

Questions for Reflection

1. **Our parents probably told us that life isn't fair. What injustices have you encountered in your life? What have you been able to do about them?**
2. **What role does the church have in advocating for the poor when they are being mistreated? How much of the church's focus should this occupy? How are you involved in this effort?**
3. **Why does injustice never seem to go away? Do we attribute this simply to the human condition or is something else to blame?**

CHAPTER 51

KICKING AGAINST THE GOADS
Acts 26.1-32

Acts 26.1-32

This is Paul's fifth (and final) defense speech in Acts. This is also the third time in Acts that Luke has had Paul recount his conversion, an indication of how central it is to the story. Similar to the first description of Saul's calling in Acts 9, Luke presents Paul in Acts 26 as a great philosopher and prophet. But, here, Luke goes beyond what he has done in the past, as he has Paul lay out a powerful case for why everyone hearing him should repent and turn towards Christ. Paul is offering his hearers light, a whole new way of seeing the world, through the lens of resurrection.[77] The scene concludes with the clearest indication yet that the powers-that-be know full well that Paul is not guilty.

Then Agrippa said to Paul, "Permission is granted to you to speak for yourself." Then Paul motioned with his hand and started making his defense.

"Concerning everything I have been accused of by the Jews, O King Agrippa, I consider myself fortunate that I am about to offer my defense before you today, especially because of your deep knowledge of all the customs and controversial claims of the Jews. Therefore I beg you to listen to me with patience.

The Jews have been well acquainted with my way of life from my youth, which, from the start, has been carried out both in Jerusalem and among my own people. They have known me from long ago — if they wanted, they could testify to it — that I lived as a Pharisee within the strictest sect of our religion. But now, I am on trial for hope in the promise that has come from God to our forefathers. Our twelve tribes hope to attain the promise by worshipping rightly night and day, for which hope, I have been accused by the Jews, O king.

Why is it considered unbelievable by any of you that God raises the dead? Of course, I myself was formerly convinced that I had to do many things opposed to the name of Jesus the Nazarene. This I did in Jerusalem. I incarcerated many of the saints in prisons under the authority I received from the high priests, also voicing my approval when they were being condemned. I often punished them harshly across many synagogues, continuously forcing them to blaspheme. I was so furiously enraged, that I pursued them even to foreign cities.

While doing this, I was on my way to Damascus with the authority and authorization of the high priests. On the road, in the middle of the day, I saw, O king, a light from heaven, greater than the splendor of the sun, shining around me and those traveling with me. All of us fell down to the ground. I heard a voice saying to me in Aramaic, 'Saul, Saul, why are you persecuting me? It is hard for you to kick against the goads.' And I responded, 'Who are you, Sir?' And the Lord said, 'I am Jesus whom you are persecuting. But get up and stand on your feet ["stethi epi tous podas sou"]. This is why I have appeared to you: I have appointed you as a minister and witness to the things that you have seen and that I will make visible to you, rescuing you from the people and from the nations to which I am sending ["apostello"] you. I have appointed you to open their eyes ["anoixai ophthalmous"], to turn them from darkness to light ["apo skotous eis phos"], and from the authority of Satan to God, that they might receive forgiveness of sins and might be set apart for a share among those made holy by the faith that is in me.'

Wherefore, O King Agrippa, I was not disobedient to this heavenly vision, but first in Damascus and also in Jerusalem and then throughout all the territory of Judea and then to the Gentiles, I have announced that they should repent and turn to God, doing deeds worthy of repentance.

This is why the Jews apprehended me in the temple and attempted to murder me. No doubt, I have experienced assistance from God to this day, as I have stood and testified to both small and great, speaking nothing but what the prophets and Moses have said was going to happen: that the Messiah might very well suffer, might very well be the first to rise from the dead with the result that light ["phos"] would be proclaimed to the people and to the Gentiles."

As Paul was making his defense, Festus interrupted him with a loud voice, "You are out of your mind! Paul, your great learning is making you go insane ["mania"]!" But Paul replied, "I am not mad, most excellent Festus, but I am speaking out with sound words of truth, since the king is well acquainted with these things about which I am speaking so boldly. For I am convinced that none of these things has escaped his attention, for nothing has been done in secret. Do you believe in the prophets, O King Agrippa? I know that you believe." But Agrippa said to Paul, "You are persuading me in such a short time to act like a Christian!" And Paul responded, "I would pray to God that, over both short and long times, that everyone who hears me today would become like I am — apart, of course, from these handcuffs."

Then, the king, the governor, Bernice, and those sitting with them, arose. As they were leaving, they were saying to one another, "This man has done nothing deserving of death." And Agrippa said to Festus, "This man could have been set free, had he not appealed to Caesar."

Ezekiel 2.1-7

This text describes Ezekiel's call to be a prophet. It was not enough
for a prophet to see great visions, to perform great wonders or to
predict the future, the prophet had to be specifically commissioned

and sent by God.[78] In fact, it was God's act of sending that cre-
ated the authorization for the prophet to proclaim the word of the
Lord.[79] Luke has Paul describe his own commissioning by employ-
ing the language of this text in Ezekiel. In Acts, the Lord com-
mands Paul to "rise and stand upon your feet" before he "sends"
Paul to the Gentiles (who are also an embittered people).

Then the Lord said to me, "Son of man, stand on your feet ["stethi epi tous podas sou"] and I will speak to you." Then his Spirit came upon me, raised me and lifted me up. Then the Lord stood me on my feet and I heard him speaking to me and he said to me, "Son of man, I am sending ["exapostello"] you to the house of Israel who are provoking me, who embittered me, both they and their forefathers until this very day. And you will say to them, 'Thus says the Lord, whether or not then they might hear or fear – since it is an embittered house – they will know that you are a prophet in the midst of them. And you, son of man, do not be afraid of them nor be dismayed at their presence, since they will be enraged and will gather together against you on all sides. You will dwell in the midst of scorpions. Do not be afraid of their words nor be dismayed at their countenance, since they are an embittered house. And you will speak my words to them – whether or not they should hear or fear – for it is an embittered house."

Isaiah 42.5-9, 16-17

This is Isaiah's first "servant song." God has commissioned his ser-
vant (Israel) to be a light to the nations.[80] This is also the first
great prophecy of the salvation of the Gentiles and the ultimate
vindication of Israel.[81] This salvation motif manifests itself in the
moving of the people from "darkness into light." Paul alludes to
this text in today's speech in Acts when he recounts what the risen
Jesus had told him on the road to Damascus. Paul was being sent

*to the Gentiles "to open their eyes," and "to turn them from dark-
ness to light," both of which are allusions to this passage.*

**Thus says the Lord God, who made heaven and established it, the one
who made the earth firm and the things in it, who gave breath to his
people living on it and spirit to those who walk upon it. I am the Lord
God, I have called you in righteousness and I will hold your hand and
will strengthen you. I have given you as a covenant to the tribes, as a
light ["phos"] to the Gentiles to open the eyes of the blind ["anoixai
ophthalmous"], to lead out the captives from prison — even those sitting in darkness ["skotos"], out of the prison-house. I am the Lord God,
this is my name, my glory I will not give to another nor my powers to
idols. Indeed, the things of old have come to pass and I will announce
new things. Before it springs up, it is made manifest to you.**

**I will lead the blind by a way that is not known, and I will cause
them to tread on unknown paths. I will make darkness into light ["skotos eis phos"] and crooked things into what is straight. I will do these
things and I will not abandon them. Those who are turned back will be
utterly put to shame. Likewise, those who trust in idols and those who
say to the molten images, 'You are our gods.'**

Comment

This is Paul's longest and most comprehensive defense speech in Acts.
However, Paul lays out the same basic story about what happened on the
Damascus road that we've heard before: (1) Paul was zealously persecuting
the church, but he (2) encountered the risen Jesus on his way to Damascus,
(3) converted, and (4) started proclaiming the good news that Jesus was
risen from the dead.

Yet, as always, it is fascinating to look at the small differences between
the accounts. One of the strangest additions is the phrase "kick against the
goads," found only here in Acts 26. The basic point is clear enough – Paul
was resisting the invitation of the Spirit while he was persecuting the church.

Yet the phrase itself does not come from the Bible or from any extant Jewish literature, but is a Greek proverb found in Euripides, Aeschylus, and Pindar.[82] The proverb expresses the basic idea that it is foolhardy to try to counter the influence of the gods in one's life. Perhaps colloquially paraphrased, it would go something like this: "Try as we may, the gods will always get their way."

But the use of this proverb, supposedly from the mouth of God, provides an excellent example of how Luke has Paul tell the story differently to diverse audiences. He is in front of a sophisticated, learned audience, steeped in Greek literature. Thus Paul includes a Greek proverb in this version of the speech because it will help his listeners (and also us) understand and identify with what he experienced.

But, are we to believe that the risen Jesus appeared to a pious Pharisee on the road to Damascus and actually employed a pagan Greek proverb to convince Paul that he should convert? Anything is possible, of course, but this would be something like Jesus appearing to the Ayatollah Khomeini on his way to Damascus and quoting Nietzsche to aid his conversion. This is possible, but not particularly likely. It's far easier to see this as Luke's shaping of the story in a way that will make sense to his audience.

A second issue this recounting of Paul's Damascus road experience raises is the evidence from the Bible that Paul employs to show how the OT prophets anticipated the resurrection of Jesus. Paul offers two key pieces of evidence. Paul claims that the OT predicted (1) that the Messiah would suffer and (2) that the Messiah would rise from the dead (Acts 26.23). There's just one problem: one is hard-pressed to locate either of these predictions anywhere in the OT.

The OT prophets did envision a coming Messiah that would set the world aright (Isa 61.1). The prophets also talked about resurrection, but as something that would happen at the end of time, after the "time of trouble." (Dan 12.2). The prophets also envisioned a "new heaven and new earth" where the worship of Yahweh would go on ceaselessly (Isa 66.17-24). But nowhere does it say that the Messiah would suffer. How can Paul claim that this is what the OT said?

This was not just a problem in Paul's time, but was central to the dispute between Christians and Jews over what the Bible really meant in the early days of the church. Take, for example, the church father Justin Martyr when he recounts his conversation with his Jewish dialogue partner, Trypho, sometime in the second century:

> You know very well, said Trypho, that we Jews all look forward to the coming of the Christ, and we admit that all your Scriptural quotations refer to Him....But we doubt whether the Christ should be so shamefully crucified, for the law declares that he who is crucified is to be accursed (Deut 21.23)...[Justin] replied...all who have grasped the meaning of the prophets' words, as soon as they hear that He was crucified, will affirm that [Jesus] is the Christ and no other.[83]

We observe here how Paul recounts something of central importance to our story. Because of Jesus, Christians read the OT differently. According to Jesus' own instructions to his disciples (Luke 24), Christians are to read the entire Bible in light of Christ. This leads to a completely different set of insights from the OT than the rabbis had taught.

This is probably why Festus thinks that Paul has gone mad. Paul is basing his whole argument on something that cannot be found in a literal reading of the OT. Yet, when Paul reads Isaiah 42 (which was one of our readings in this chapter), he reads that the movement "out of darkness and into light" is what Jesus accomplished. Isaiah's servant (which is Israel in the actual text of Isaiah) is now re-interpreted in light of Jesus, as the one who has come to open the eyes of the blind and to set people free. Those who read the OT with slavish literalism will never understand it properly, at least according to Paul.

To be sure, the path from darkness into light is not just a metaphor. It is the depiction of a dramatic new way of life, a life that centers on the hope of resurrection — not just for Jesus, but for all people. Yet Paul's interpretive point here is essential – Christians read the OT differently than Jews because their interpretations are based on the assumption that Christ is speaking in the text of the Bible.

This episode ends with Festus, Agrippa, and others coming to the conclusion that Luke has been suggesting to us all along: Paul is not guilty of the charges against him. He (and the Christians he represents) are not seditious. Paul did not start a riot. Paul did not defile the temple. Paul is not unfaithful to the scriptures. In a word, Paul is "righteous," which in a Greek sense means "in the right" or "not-guilty."

Thus, once again, Paul imitates Christ in this episode. Just as Herod concluded three times that Jesus had done nothing deserving of death (Luke 23.2, 14, 22), so, too, Paul has now been declared innocent by three successive rulers: Lysias (23.29), Festus (25.25) and now Agrippa (26.31).[84] Since the dispute boils down to the reality of the resurrection, a theological question, Paul is certainly not guilty of sedition and should be set free. Yet, in the end, Paul is not set free, but now travels on to Rome in fulfillment of his mission.

Questions for Reflection

1. Can you remember a time when you had an argument with someone where you were just talking past each other because you were starting from different assumptions about the subject under discussion? How did you resolve things? How do you see unexamined assumptions tainting our world today?

2. Is it fair that Paul is still a prisoner at this point in the story? How do you square God's intention that Paul would preach the gospel in Rome with his status as a prisoner? How do you explain Paul's apparent willingness to remain a prisoner?

3. Luke keeps making the point that Paul is imitating Christ. What would you have to do to imitate Jesus more intentionally?

PAUL'S VOYAGE TO ROME
(ACTS 22–28)

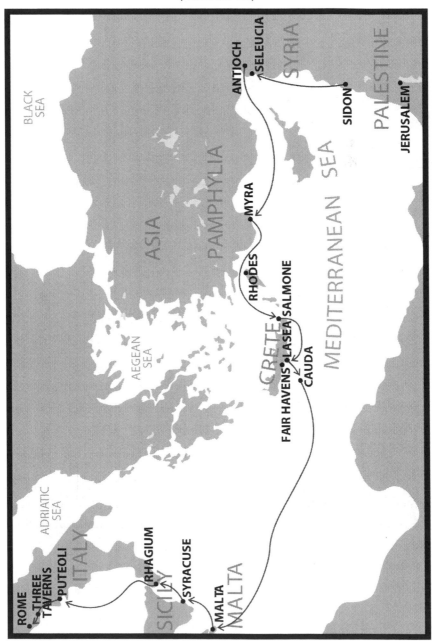

CHAPTER 52

FAITHFULNESS IN A STORM
Acts 27.1-26

Acts 27.1-26

Paul now embarks on a dangerous sea voyage to Rome. After running into some problems with the winds, the centurions, the captain and the boat-owner all ignore Paul's counsel to seek safety near the city of Lasea (on Crete). When their boat gets stuck in a violent nor'easter, almost everyone on board despairs for their lives and assumes that all is lost. But Paul bucks up the crew with a prediction that although the ship is doomed, none of their lives are. They make plans to run aground on a nearby island.

After it had been decided that we would sail to Italy, they were handing over Paul and some other prisoners to a centurion named Julius, who was of the Augustan cohort. We then boarded a ship from Adramyttium, that was about to sail to the ports around the province of Asia. We set sail with Aristarchus, a Macedonian from Thessalonica. On the next day, we put into port at Sidon. Julius acted benevolently toward Paul and he allowed Paul's friends to come aboard and provide him with whatever he needed.

Then setting sail, we skirted by Cyprus because the winds were against us. After we had set sail across the open sea near Cilicia and Pamphylia, we arrived at Myra in Lycia. There, the centurion found a boat from Alexandria sailing for Italy and put us on it. In those days, we started sailing slowly and came near Cnidus with difficulty. Because the wind prevented us from going on, we skirted by Crete near Salmone. With difficulty we hugged the shoreline and came to a place called "Fair Harbors," which is near the city of Lasea.

Since a long time had gone by and the voyage was now unsafe because Yom Kippur had already ended, Paul recommended the following, "Men, I foresee that not only the cargo and the boat, but our own lives are about to suffer calamity and great loss." But the centurion was persuaded more by the captain and the ship-owner than by what Paul said. Since the harbor was unsuitable for wintering, the majority decided to put out to sea from there, hoping to reach Phoenix and spend the winter where there was a Cretan harbor to the southwest and northwest.

When a gentle south wind began to blow, they thought they had overcome the obstacle to their plan. So they raised the anchor and sailed nearer alongside the coast of Crete. Not long afterward, however, a hurricane-force wind called the "Euraquillo" blew down from Crete. It seized the ship and we were not able to sail into the wind. Having given up fighting it, we were carried along by the wind. Sailing under the protection of a certain island called Cauda, we were able (with difficulty) to regain control over the lifeboat. After hoisting it up, the crew made use of helps to undergird the boat. Being careful not to run aground on Sytris, they lowered the anchor, thus letting themselves be driven by the wind. The next day, after being violently beaten by the storm, we started jettisoning cargo overboard. On the third day, they started tossing the rigging of the ship overboard with their own hands. Neither sun nor stars appeared for many days while the violent storm continued to pound us. We were losing all hope of being delivered ["sotzo"].

Since many had lost their appetite, Paul stood in their midst and said, "Gentlemen, you know that you should have listened to me, and not set sail from Crete only to gain this calamity and loss. But now I advise you to cheer up! For there will be no loss of life among you; only the ship will be lost. Last night an angel of God, to whom I belong and whom I worship, appeared to me, saying 'Do not be afraid, Paul. It is necessary for you to appear before Caesar. So, look, God has graciously granted deliverance to you and those sailing with you.' Therefore cheer up, gentlemen, because I trust in God that it will turn out just like it was spoken to me. But first we have to run aground on some island."

Jonah 1.1-5

Christians have traditionally read the story of Jonah as a great allegory of salvation. It is one of the clearest indications in the OT that God's plan for redemption was not limited to the Jews, but was always intended for all nations. In this opening scene, Jonah is called to go preach repentance to the Ninevites, the capital of the Assyrian empire and a traditional enemy of Israel.[1] Apparently horrified at the prospect of preaching to the godless Ninevites, Jonah traveled in the exact opposite direction to Tarsus, which, incidentally, is Paul's hometown. The depictions of sailors desperately throwing cargo and equipment overboard finds an analogue in today's Acts reading. However, Paul represents the reversal of Jonah's story. Instead of being unfaithful like Jonah, Paul faithfully endures hardship in obedience to his mission and to the will of God.[2]

And the word of the Lord came to Jonah, son of Amathi, saying, "Rise up and go to Nineveh, the great city and proclaim the following: 'The outcry of its wickedness has come up to me.'" But Jonah arose and fled to Tarsus away from the presence of the Lord. Then he went down to Joppa and found a boat bound for Tarsus and paid his fare. Jonah came aboard to sail with them to Tarsus, away from the presence of the Lord. But the Lord raised up a wind on the sea and there were huge waves on the sea. The boat was in danger of capsizing. The sailors became afraid and cried out, each to his own god, and started heaving the manufactured equipment on the boat into the sea in order to lighten the load. But Jonah had gone down into the hollow of the boat, had fallen asleep, and was snoring.

Colossians 4.10-11

It seems likely that the Aristarchus mentioned here in Colossians is the same Aristarchus who is traveling with Paul to Rome in our Acts passage. A fellow Jewish Christian, Aristarchus appeared in our story during the riot in Ephesus (Acts 19.29) where he was seized by the angry mob.[3] He was also Paul's traveling companion on his third missionary journey (Acts 20.4-6).[4] By tradition, Aristarchus is known as the first bishop of Thessalonica.[5] Note, as well, that this is the only place in the Bible where Luke, listed as Paul's traveling companion, is called a "physician."

Aristarchus, my fellow prisoner, sends his greetings, as does Mark, the cousin of Barnabas (about whom you received instructions. If he comes to you, receive him). Jesus, also called Justus, sends his greetings as well. Among those from the circumcision party, these men alone are among my fellow workers for the kingdom of God and have become a comfort for me. Greet Epaphras, who is one of you, a bond-servant of Jesus Christ, always striving on your behalf in prayer that you might stand perfect, having been filled in everything with the will of God. For I testify to you that he has toiled much for you, for those in Laodicea and for those in Hierapolis. Luke, the beloved physician, greets you, as does Demas.

Comment

As we come to Paul's ill-fated sea voyage across the Mediterranean, questions abound. Most importantly, why does Luke include this remarkably detailed story about a sea crossing right at the end of the story? As we will see in a few days, there are a whole bunch of things that Luke does not bother to tell us that we would like to know about what happens in Rome. Why, instead, does he give us this seemingly irrelevant, but comparatively exhaustive, travelogue?

For the first time since Acts 21, Luke starts writing again in first person plural.[6] Luke tells us in v. 1, "After it had been decided that *we* would sail to Italy…" Many Christian readers see this as evidence that Luke is again telling us the story as an eyewitness.[7] This is a perfectly plausible position to take. We see from today's Colossians reading that Luke was a physician. It could also be the case that Luke was an accomplished mariner, as well.

In the Ancient Near East, the sea was a foreboding place. In fact, to ancient Israelites, the sea was a source of chaos in the world. We encounter this idea right at the beginning of the Bible: "The earth was without form and void and darkness was upon the face of the deep and the Spirit of God was moving over the face of the waters" (Gen 1.2, RSV). Although one of the points of the first creation account in Genesis 1 was that God brought order to the chaos, the seas were evidence that chaos still existed on the earth, and thus the universe required God's on-going providential care to sustain its order and its very existence.

As a result, there are few references to everyday sea crossings in Jewish literature. The Jews, at least in the Bible, seemed to be more comfortable on land than in the water. The great counter-example to this, of course, is Jonah. However, Jonah went over the sea to escape the presence of God, something that did not turn out particularly well for him.

By contrast, sea voyages were foundational for the Greeks and Romans. Both Homer's *Odyssey* and Virgil's *Aeneid* have significant sections of their stories that include adventures at sea. The great heroes, Odysseus and Aeneas, overcame the obstacles presented by the sea to fulfill their destinies.

As a result, it is not too much of a stretch to see Luke's descriptions of this sea voyage in terms of a clash of cultures. This is certainly what we observed in the preceding chapters when Paul got caught up in Roman legal proceedings. Whether it was with the Jews or the Romans, we saw that the Christian belief system at times grated against Jewish and Roman culture. Thus there is more continuity to this narrative than is generally understood. It is almost as if Luke is symbolically representing Paul, the converted

Christian evangelist, who still holds onto certain Jewish norms, as taking God's people into uncharted waters.

We might even read the unsettled waters in this story as a metaphor for life. Sometimes the greatest witness we can provide comes in the midst of a terrible storm, when God seems distant and the answers to our "why" questions are non-existent. Our job is just to keep going. This is really what faithfulness is all about. No matter what — sickness, calamity, grief, poverty – we keep moving in the same direction.

The power of faith is not just about a belief system. God is not asking us for perfection in belief or practice. He is asking us to be faithful, especially in the midst of storms. The great ancient preacher John Chrysostom said it very well:

> Look at our whole life: it is just such (as was this voyage). For at one time we meet with kindliness, at another with a tempest...For Paul is sailing even now with us, only not bound as he was then: he admonishes us even now and says to those who are (sailing) on the sea, 'take heed unto yourselves'...'In the last times perilous times shall come: and men shall be lovers of their own selves, lovers of money, boasters' (2 Tim 3.2). This is more grievous than all storms. Let us therefore abide where he bids – in faith, in the safe haven: let us hearken unto him rather than to the pilot that is within us, that is, our own reason. Let us not straightway do just what this may suggest; not what the owner of the ship: no, but what Paul suggests: he has passed through many such tempests.[8]

Paul was faithful even when everything was falling apart. This is what God wants from us as well.

Questions for Reflection:

1. **What are the worst storms you have faced in your life? What was it like to walk through the storm? Did God seem distant or near?**

2. Can you remember a time in your life when you were unfaithful? Did you still have a sense of God's grace and loving care while you were in that period or did God seem distant?

3. Our Jonah reading from today is one of the great examples of someone trying to run away from God because he does not like what God is asking. In what areas of your life are you trying to hide from God because you do not like the demands he makes on you? Is it possible to hide from God in this way?

CHAPTER 53

ALLEGORY OF A SHIPWRECK
Acts 27.27-44

Acts 27.27-44

Paul and the ship's crew experience a ruinous shipwreck off the island of Malta. Paul gains ever-more credibility with the authorities on the ship, especially the Roman centurion who, in the end, follows Paul's counsel without question. Luke has Paul employ the Greek word for "salvation" ["sotzo"] in this passage, yet in an overtly non-spiritual context (as physical deliverance). Additionally, Luke describes Paul as sharing a meal with his fellow sailors by taking "some bread," giving "thanks to God," "breaking it," and "eating it." Although clearly not a Eucharistic Meal, Paul once again imitates Jesus, this time in his post-resurrection appearances and meals. These are tantalizing clues that Paul's imitation of Christ has reached a new level.

Then, after the fourteenth night had come, we were adrift across the Sea of Adria. Around midnight, the sailors thought that we were approaching some land. Taking some measurements, they found the water was about one-hundred-twenty feet deep. Then, going a little farther, they measured again and found it was about ninety-feet deep. Then they became afraid that we were about to run aground on the rough coast, so they threw four anchors off the stern and prayed for day to come. Then the sailors were trying to flee from the boat by appearing to let down the anchors from the bow when, in reality, they were letting down the lifeboat.

Paul said to the centurion and the soldiers, "If these men don't stay with the ship, you cannot be saved" ["sotzo"]. Then the soldiers cut away the rigging for the lifeboat and they let it drift off.

Now, when it was almost day, Paul urged everyone to take some food, saying, "Today is the fourteenth day you have been anxious and have remained without food. You have partaken of nothing. Therefore I urge you to take some nourishment, since this is critical for our survival. For not one hair of your head will be lost."

Having said these things, he took some bread, gave thanks to God before everyone, broke it, and began to eat. So all became cheerful and they took food themselves. In total, we were two-hundred-twenty-six souls on the ship. Having eaten their fill, they started lightening the boat by tossing grain into the sea.

Then, when day came, they did not recognize the land, but noticed a certain bay with a beach on which they wanted to run the ship aground, if at all possible. So, they took away the anchors, letting them go into the sea, and at the same time, unfastened the bands of the rudders. They hoisted up the foresail into the wind and were holding a course toward the beach.

But, when they encountered a sandbank, they ran the ship aground and the bow became stuck and unmovable, while the stern was breaking up under the force of the waves. But the soldiers were planning to kill the prisoners, not wanting them to escape by swimming away. But, the centurion, wanting to save Paul's life, forbade them from carrying out their plan. He commanded those who were able to swim to jump first and go onto the land. Then the rest would follow — some on planks, some on pieces of the ship. But, in this way, they all made it safely onto the land.

Luke 21.12-19

Jesus speaks with his disciples about what the in-breaking of the kingdom of God will look like. The prophecy that Jesus' followers would stand "before kings and governors" has been forefront

in our story since the Romans took custody of Paul. Therefore,
it's probably not a coincidence that on his way to Rome to
stand before Caesar, Luke reiterates Jesus' promise from this pas-
sage that "not one hair of your head will perish." But the next
verse is equally important, "By your perseverance, you will gain
your souls," precisely what Paul models in our Acts reading.

But before all these things, they will seize you with their hands and persecute you, handing you over to the synagogues and prisons, hauling you
before kings and governors for my name's sake. This will lead to your testimony. But settle in your hearts not to prepare your defense. For I will give
you such speech and wisdom that your adversaries will not be able to resist
or to contradict anything. But you will be betrayed by parents and brothers and relatives and friends; some of you, they will even put to death. In
fact, you will be hated by everyone because of my name. But not one hair
of your head will perish. By your perseverance, you will gain your souls.

Luke 24.13-31

After Jesus was crucified, he later met two disciples on the road to
Emmaus, a town not far from Jerusalem. Mysteriously, the disciples
did not recognize the risen Jesus. But after explaining that the entire
OT was to be interpreted in light of the Messiah, he dined with the
disciples. However, only "in the breaking of bread" do they recognize
Jesus. The meal Paul shares with his captors and fellow-travelers
seems to allude in a mysterious way to the post-resurrection appear-
ances of Jesus. The combination of how to read the scriptures with
sacramental signs infuses our Acts reading with deeper meaning.

Now, that very day, two of them were going to a village called Emmaus,
about seven miles from Jerusalem. And they were conversing with one
another about all the things that had taken place. And while they were

discussing and debating these things, Jesus himself drew dear and started walking along with them. Now, their eyes were prevented from recognizing him. Then Jesus said to them, "What things are you discussing with one another while you walk along?" They stopped, looking downtrodden. The one named Cleopas answered and said to him, "Are you the only inhabitant of Jerusalem who does not know what has taken place over these days in the city?" And Jesus asked them, "What things?" And they said to him, "Things about Jesus the Nazarene, who was a Prophet, mighty in word and deed before God and all the people. The high priests and our rulers gave him the death penalty and crucified him. But we had hoped that he was about to redeem Israel. Not only this, but now it's been three days since these things took place. Moreover, some women, associated with us, astonished us, when they came to the tomb early in the morning and did not find his body. They came and told us that they had seen angels in a vision who claimed that Jesus was alive. Then some went out with us to the tomb and found it just as the women had said, but did not see him." Then Jesus said to the travelers, "O foolish and slow of heart to believe all that the Prophets have said. Was it not necessary for the Messiah to suffer and to enter into his glory?" And beginning from Moses and continuing through all the Prophets, Jesus interpreted for them throughout all the scriptures the things in light of himself.

Then they drew near to the town where they were going and he acted like he was planning to go on farther. But they strongly prevailed on him, saying, "Stay with us since it is already evening and the sun has set." And after he dined with them, he took bread, blessed it, broke it, and give it to them. And their eyes were opened and they recognized him. But he vanished from their sight.

Comment

It is important once again for us to ask a simple (but, in this case, difficult) question about why Luke chose to include this scene. Luke has to get Paul to Rome somehow, so perhaps this is just an entertaining way to move the plot forward. Or, maybe Luke is showing us how Paul grows as a leader and gains respect. Or, perhaps Luke is demonstrating how God continues to be at work in the world, even in the midst of a shipwreck. All of these theories are certainly plausible.

But almost every modern commentator agrees that we must not read this text allegorically and see anything sacramental in this scene. When the text tells us that Paul encouraged his fellow travelers to eat after fourteen days of fasting (really, fourteen days?), this is obviously not a Eucharistic Meal. After all, Paul is traveling with pagan Roman soldiers and sailors. Outside of Aristarchus and Luke, there do not appear to be many Christians here.

Let me admit that I demur from this consensus and think it is a mistake to not see at least some oblique sacramental significance in this scene. Here, ancient interpreters are more insightful than many moderns. I agree with the eighth-century English monk, Bede, who interprets this episode as an allegory for the spiritual life. Bede writes the following:

> A most beautiful allegorical sense is evident in this passage, when Paul persuaded the men he had promised would be saved from shipwreck to take food...No one escapes the tempests of this world except those who are nourished by the bread of life...one who in the night of present tribulations...will soon, with the shining forth of divine help, reach the port of salvation which he had sought, provided that, unencumbered by things of the world, he seeks only the flame of love with which he may warm his heart.[9]

To be sure, modern interpreters make good points in refusing to consider this story an allegory. They correctly note that when Paul takes bread after giving thanks, this is simply the act of saying grace, something very common in Jewish circles (Luke 9.16). They also rightly note that the reference to "salvation" (using the Greek word "*sotzo*") is in its secular form, meaning physical deliverance, not spiritual salvation. To modern scholars, an allegorical interpretation reads into the text what one would like to see, not what Luke really intended.

I beg to differ. From the start, the book of Acts has been about the spread of the good news that Jesus is King. In Parts III and IV, while Paul has been in focus, we have seen how this good news gets proclaimed to "governors and kings," with the subtext that The Way was not a seditious movement. Thus, to read one of the last scenes in Acts as devoid of its gospel context seems odd to me.

For the past several weeks, Luke has been careful to depict the apostle Paul as following in Jesus' footsteps, first on his way to Jerusalem and then in the trials he endured in Caesarea. Why would that stop now? The breaking of bread is probably supposed to remind us of Jesus with the disciples on the road to Emmaus. While Jesus was with them, he showed the disciples how the scriptures were supposed be read – in light of him. Yet they only recognized Jesus "in the breaking of the bread." Is it a stretch to think that the survivors of the shipwreck similarly come to see Jesus, through Paul, at a meal that carries subtle sacramental overtones?

After all, this is an episode where a group of confused people are "saved" (physically delivered) from a terrible calamity with water. Does this not sound at least a little like what happens at baptism? Of course, it is not an exact match — those baptized are saved through water, while the sailors are saved from water. Nevertheless, baptismal overtones also seem to be present.

Moreover, we have an episode that after fourteen days (this might be an allusion to the Passover that was sacrificed on the fourteenth of Nissan), Paul encouraged his co-travelers to take some food, but describes it in overtly sacramental terms: "He took some bread, gave thanks to God before everyone, broke it, and began to eat" (Acts 26.35). This resulted in great joy among those who were with Paul. Since we understand the Eucharist as the fulfillment of the Jewish Passover, the associations are self-evident (at least to me). Even if there is no actual Eucharistic Meal at the literal sense of the text, the good news that Jesus, the true Passover lamb, died, was raised, and was enthroned as King seems clearly evident here.

With its oblique references to Jesus on the Emmaus road after his resurrection, and with his disciples talking about the coming kingdom before his crucifixion, Luke is making an important point. Jesus seemed to care a great deal that his followers read the OT scriptures well.

Thus Luke presents us with an episode filled with odd details to see if we have learned how to read appropriately by this late point in the story. Jesus is enthroned as King and now the whole world has been turned on its head. The OT Prophets are to be read in light of Jesus. Hence, the shipwreck, understood well, is likely an allegory of salvation, just as it was for Jonah. The good news has even come to the island of Malta.

Questions for Reflection

1. We learned in today's reading that "saying grace" before meals is an ancient practice. How important a practice is this to you? How do you thank God for his provision for your daily needs?

2. Why do you think Luke included all these details about Paul's travels? What is he trying to teach us in this section?

3. Notice that Paul has won the respect of the Roman centurion, which becomes an important reason why he survives the shipwreck. How important is it for Christians to be respected by those outside the church?

CHAPTER 54

THY KINGDOM COME
Acts 28.1-16

Acts 28.1-16

Paul wows the natives and the local Roman government by surviving what should have been a deadly attack from a snake, going from being perceived as a murderer to a god in just two verses.[10] Imitating Jesus and the disciples, Paul then goes throughout the whole island of Malta healing people. As Paul and the crew re-commence their voyage, we shouldn't miss the irony of the ship's name – the "Twin Gods." Named after Castor and Pollux (Gemini and Dioscouri in Greek), the satirist Lucian mentions that they were part of every good shipwreck story, yet Paul is in need of no help from pagan deities.[11] At the end, Paul finally arrives in Rome and is received with joy by certain members of the church who come out to greet him from various towns along the Appian Way.[12]

After we had been brought safely through our ordeal, we learned that the island was called Malta. The natives were showing us uncommon kindness ["philanthropia"], as they lit a fire once it started to rain, and invited us to come on in, on account of the cold. But, when Paul gathered up a pile of brushwood and put it on the fire, a serpent, escaping from the heat, fastened onto his hand. When the natives saw the snake hanging from his hand, they said to one another, "This man must be a murderer! Although he was rescued ["diasotzo"] from the sea, Lady Justice ["dikehy"] must not want him to live."

But Paul shook off the snake into the fire and suffered no injury. They kept waiting for Paul to swell up or suddenly to fall over dead. They waited for some time, but having observed nothing out of place in him, they changed their minds, concluding that Paul was a god.

Now in the region surrounding that place, there were fields belonging to the chief Roman administrator of the island named Publius, who received us and entertained us hospitably for three days. However, the father of Publius was lying down, being afflicted with a chronic fever and dysentery. Paul came in, prayed, laid hands on him, and healed him. After this happened, the rest of the island who had sicknesses also came and were being healed. And with great fanfare, they honored us as we were putting out to sea, having provided us with the supplies we needed.

Then, after three months, we put out to sea in an Alexandrian ship, called "the Twin Gods." We put in at Syracuse and remained there for three days. After casting off, we arrived at Rhegium. Then, after one day, a south wind came up, enabling us, on the second day, to come to Puteoli. There we found some brethren and we were invited to remain with them for seven days.

Thereafter, we arrived at Rome. The brethren from Rome, when they heard about us, came all the way from the Appian Forum and the Three Taverns to meet us. When they saw Paul, they gave thanks to God and took courage. Then, when we entered into Rome, Paul was permitted to live by himself with a soldier who was guarding him.

Mark 16.15-20

This text is from the so-called "longer ending of Mark." It appears in none of the earliest manuscripts we possess, so the modern scholarly consensus is to reject it as a later addition to the text. Yet, the early church accepted it as authentic, almost without question. Whether or not it is a later addition, it still provides a nice window into the theology of the early church; namely, that Christians "worked together" with God in their ministries, that

> *baptism was a central component of salvation, and that the ascension of Jesus was central to the gospel. This text finds an analogue to today's Acts reading because of its reference to snakes.*

And Jesus said to them, "Go into the whole world and preach the good news to the whole creation. He who has believed and is baptized will be saved, but the one who has not believed will be condemned. All these signs will accompany those who believe: in my name they will cast out demons and they will speak in new tongues. They will pick up snakes in their hands and if they drink anything deadly, it will not injure them. They will lay their hands on the sick and they will recover."

Then, after the Lord Jesus had spoken with them, he was taken up into heaven and sat at the right hand of God. And they went forth and preached everywhere. Then God worked together with them, establishing the message through the signs that accompanied it.

Luke 10.1, 8-12, 17-20

> *Jesus sends out seventy "other" disciples and gives them authority to preach the good news and to heal people. Notice the characteristic proclamation in Luke that the "kingdom of God has come near." Not only does this text nicely reflect Paul's ministry of preaching the good news wherever he goes, the reference to treading upon snakes and healing the sick in every city also finds a parallel in today's Acts reading.*

After these things, the Lord appointed seventy others and sent them ahead of him, two by two, to every city and place where he was about to come. And he said to them:

> If you enter into a city and it receives you, eat the things set before you, heal the sick in it and say to them, 'The kingdom of God has come near to you.' But whatever city you enter that

does not receive you, go out into its streets and say, 'Even the dust from your town attached to our feet we wipe off against you.' Nevertheless, know this, that the kingdom of God has come near. I say to you that it will be more bearable for Sodom in that day than for that city.

Then the seventy returned with joy, saying, "Lord, even the demons were subject to us in your name." And he said to them, "I am starting to see Satan falling like a star out of heaven. Look, I have given you authority to tread upon serpents and scorpions and on every power of the enemy, and nothing will injure you. However, rejoice in this because your names are written in the heavens."

Comment

As our story has progressed, we have discovered that the promise that the good news would be proclaimed to "ends of the earth" specifically means Rome for Paul. Yet, the city of Rome is rarely referenced in the NT, outside of Acts and the book of Revelation. In fact, the word "Rome" only appears three times outside of Acts, twice in the introduction to Romans and once in 2 Timothy.

Further, in the first two-thirds of our story, Rome appeared only once (Acts 2.10). Thus we could read much of the book of Acts and not have any concrete idea that Rome would be the geographic goal of the story.

But, after Paul leaves Ephesus, the Spirit starts leading him to Rome. For example, in Acts 19.21, Paul learns that after returning to Jerusalem, he would go to Rome. Jesus himself appeared to Paul with news that he was going to Rome, just before Paul uncovered the Jewish plot to murder him (Acts 23.11). Finally, Paul's decision to appeal to Caesar (Acts 25.11) set in motion the voyage that we have been tracking over the past few chapters.

Although the process of getting to Rome has occupied us for some time now, we still have to figure out why Luke includes the descriptions he does of the events that take place on Malta.

The most logical answer is that Luke is simply pushing the story forward, and that some very interesting things happened there. Naturally, Luke frames these events as Paul's imitation of Christ, especially when he goes around and heals the natives by "laying hands" on them. As is typical for Luke, those who show hospitality and generosity are the ones who are open to the good news.[13]

But, we might also wonder whether there is anything more going on here. Interestingly, Paul and his companions board another Alexandrian ship. Alexandria might have more importance than first meets the eye, since this was a center of allegorical interpretation in the ancient world. Could this be a subtle signal from Luke that we are supposed to be searching for meaning below the surface level of the text?

I suspect this is the case, even if most scholars would find this reading arbitrary. Yet the possibility of reading the snake attack as an allegory is just too delicious to ignore.

Paul's incident with the snake provides for a thrilling scene. Somehow Paul is attacked by a snake, but suffers no ill effects from it. Most modern readers are quick to point out that the text never specifically says that the snake "bit" Paul, but one would have to be a pretty poor reader not to think that a snake hanging off Paul's hand did not constitute some sort of physical attack. What could all this mean?

Of course, a serpent plays a key role in the biblical story, in particular in the early pages of Genesis. We should realize, however, that Jewish readers did not typically understand Genesis 3 in terms of the "Fall," a word that does not actually show up in the text of Genesis, but rather as an explanation of Adam and Eve's loss of immortality.[14]

Christians, by contrast, got the idea of reading Genesis 3 as the story of the "fall of man" and the serpent as Satan, by reading it through the lens of the NT (cf. Rom 5.12, Rev 12.9, 20.2). Is Luke trying to tell us that we are witnessing the mitigation of the effects of the fall through Paul's ministry? This could be, but is nevertheless doubtful, since most first-century Christians might have still been thinking in Jewish terms with regard to Genesis 3. Thus the real task here is to figure out how to read this passage in light of Jesus' ministry.

I think what Luke really wants us to understand with Paul's victory over the snake is that this is what the in-breaking of the kingdom of God looks like. Remember, the kingdom of God is all about the inauguration of God's new age, where Jesus reigns as King.[15]

Luke's point is that the good news is supposed to be having a tangible effect in the world in the here and now. The kingdom of God is not just otherworldly. Thus, when we respond to injury with kindness, to the poor with empathy and to declarations of war with overtures of peace, we are, little by little, starting to usher in Jesus' kingdom rule.

Yet the kingdom is not a political program, a slogan, or an ideology. The kingdom is ultimately about the in-breaking of God's love, mediated by his servants to a world that so desperately needs it. The implication of the good news is that we ought to be living out the example that Jesus and Paul provide for us through generosity and self-sacrificial love to others who would receive it. In this way, the gospel takes root and grows in unexpected places.

Thus the gospel is not about escaping the world, but is about working for the world's gradual transformation, something, of course, that will never be complete until Jesus' return. When we pray "thy kingdom come" and imitate Jesus in humility and generosity, we carry on a project over two-thousand years in the making.

Questions for Reflection:

1. **It is popular today to claim that our "country is falling apart." How is life better or worse today than it was for your parents or grandparents?**
2. **Is there a connection between the "fruits of the Spirit"— love, joy, peace, patience, kindness goodness, faith, gentleness, and self-control (Gal 5.22-23) – and the coming of the kingdom? How have you seen these fruits at work in your own life and in the life of your family? What has changed for the better?**
3. **Do you ever wish God would just take you out of the world and relieve you of all your problems? Why do you think he doesn't?**

CHAPTER 55

AN OPEN ENDING
Acts 28.17-31

Acts 28.17-31

> *In this final episode, we observe that Paul's messianic reading*
> *of the OT scriptures once again causes division among the Jews,*
> *this time in Rome. Luke describes this community as being sus-*
> *pect of Paul's messianic interpretation of the OT, but as being*
> *somewhat positively disposed to Paul himself.*[16] *Once again, the*
> *kingdom of God is in focus. If Jesus has been raised in accor-*
> *dance with OT prophecy, allegiance to Jesus as Lord is required.*
> *Some hear his message, but most (maybe all?) reject him. Yet*
> *the last two words of the book of Acts "without hindrance" dem-*
> *onstrates that although in chains, Paul is really free. Paul "has*
> *finished the course. He has kept the faith" (2 Tim 4.7).*

Now, after three days, Paul called together the Jewish leaders. After they had assembled, he started speaking to them, saying, "Brethren, I have done nothing against our people or the customs of our forefathers. From Jerusalem, I have been handed over as a prisoner into the hands of the Romans who examined me and wanted to release me because they could find no basis for the death penalty for me. But, since the Jews spoke out against me, I was forced to appeal to Caesar – not that I wanted to bring any charge against my own nation. Therefore, for this reason, I have requested to see and to speak with you; because, it is on account of the hope of Israel that I bear these handcuffs."

Then the Jews said to Paul, "We have not received any letters about you from Judea nor have any of the brethren come and reported or spoken anything bad concerning you. We simply want to hear from you what you are thinking, since all that is known to us is that people everywhere are speaking out against this sect."

Having designated a date to meet, the Jews came to Paul at his guest house in greater numbers. Paul was carefully explaining everything, by testifying from early morning until evening about the kingdom of God, and convincing them concerning Jesus, from the Law of Moses and the Prophets.

Now, some were persuaded by what Paul said, but some refused to believe. But, after a disagreement arose with one another, they started leaving after Paul made one last statement, "The Holy Spirit spoke well through Isaiah the prophet to our forefathers, saying:

> Go to this people and say, 'You listen and listen, but will by no means understand;
> You look and look, but will by no means see,
> For the heart of this people has become unresponsive,
> And their ears are hard of hearing;
> And they have closed their eyes,
> Lest they should see with their eyes,
> And hear with their ears,
> They would understand, and turn, and I would heal them' (Isa 6.9-10).

Therefore, let it be known among you that this salvation has been sent to the Gentiles. They will listen."

Then Paul remained there for two whole years at his own expense and he gladly received everyone who came to him, proclaiming the kingdom of God and teaching the things of the Lord Jesus Christ with all boldness and without hindrance.

Isaiah 6.1-13

*In this famous scene, Isaiah receives a commission to be a
prophet through a vision of the heavenly throne room. Yet, as
is often the case for the prophets, the people to whom Isaiah
is being sent are hard of hearing. The point is that God will
bring his judgment on those who obstinately refuse to listen.[17]
Paul thus employs this text to suggest that the Roman Jews have
broadly rejected the good news he was trying to proclaim.*

Now, it came to pass in the year that King Uzziah died, I saw the Lord
sitting on the throne, high and exalted, and the house was filled with his
glory. And the Seraphs stood around him, each having six wings – with
two wings they covered their face and with two they covered their feet
and with two they flew. They were saying, one to another, "Holy, holy,
holy, Lord of Hosts, the whole earth is filled with his glory." And the lin-
tel of the door shook at his voice, which was crying out, and the house
was filled with smoke.

And I said, "Woe is me, since I am pricked to the heart, since I am
a man having unclean lips living in the midst of a people with unclean
lips, and I have seen the King, the Lord of Hosts with my eyes." Then
he sent one of the seraphs to me. He had in his hand a coal that he had
taken from the altar with a tong. And he touched my mouth and said,
"Look, this has touched your lips and taken away your iniquities and
purged away your sins."

Then I heard the voice of the Lord, saying, "Whom shall I send and
who will go to this people?" And I said, "Look, here I am, send me!"
And the Lord said, "Go and tell this people:

'You will listen and listen, but will by no means understand;
You will look and look, but will by no means see,
For the heart of this people has become unresponsive,
And their ears are hard of hearing;

And they have closed their eyes,
Lest seeing with their eyes,
And hearing with their ears,
They should understand and turn and I would heal them'"
(Isa 6.9-10).

And I said, "How long, O Lord?" And He said, "Until the cities are laid waste and are not inhabited and their houses contain no people and the land is left desolate." Then, after these things, God will remove the people from afar off and those remaining on the land will be multiplied. But there will be a tenth upon it and again it will be for plunder like a terebinth tree, or like an acorn tree when it falls from its grave.

Psalm 67.1-8

As we have observed throughout Acts, there is textual ambiguity with the meaning of the Greek word "ethne." It can either have a generic sense ("nations") or a specific sense ("Gentiles"). I have chosen to translate this text with the latter sense in mind. Paul seems to be alluding to this Psalm when he claims that God's salvation has been "sent to the Gentiles." Thus Psalm 67 envisions the fulfillment of the original vocation of Israel to be a "light to the nations" (Gentiles). Jesus came to earth in the Incarnation to set in motion the original promise to Abraham that "all the nations of the earth would be blessed through him" (Gen 12.3). Given the positive, even enthusiastic, response of the Gentiles in the book of Acts, this promise is well on its way to finding fulfillment.

For the End, a Psalm of David among the Hymns
May God be merciful to us and bless us, and let the light of his countenance shine upon us, that we might know your way upon earth, and

your salvation among the Gentiles. Let the peoples give thanks to you, all the peoples. Let the Gentiles rejoice and be glad since you will judge the peoples with uprightness and the Gentiles you will lead on the earth. Let the peoples give thanks to you, O God, let all the peoples give thanks. The earth has given its fruit. May God, our own God, bless us. May God bless us and may all the ends of the earth stand in awe of him.

Comment

Many readers, having intrepidly journeyed through twenty-eight chapters of the book of Acts, have considered this last episode as something of a letdown. Luke certainly knows how to set up and tell us an exciting story. We've seen great courtroom scenes throughout the book of Acts. Why do we now find nothing about Paul's defense before Caesar? In fact, why is there not a "real" ending here at all? Let me admit that as a twenty-first century American, I'd prefer a good Hollywood ending, but that is not what we receive.

We have several choices when envisioning an ending for this story: (1) Paul might have died in Rome after Caesar found him guilty and put him to death; (2) Caesar might have set Paul free, enabling Paul to fulfill his desire to travel on a fourth missionary journey to Spain (Romans 15.28); (3) Paul might have languished in prison until his death; (4) Paul might have died of natural causes, or (5) Paul might have been killed in the unrest that ensued when Nero blamed the Christians for a fire in Rome in 64 AD. One could make a speculative case for any of these outcomes. Tradition tells us that Paul died in Rome, but concrete details of how it happened elude us.

Yet, perhaps the real point of this "non-ending" to the story, is that the book of Acts is not primarily about the stories of Peter and Paul at all. Acts is more about the message that Paul and Peter have been taking to the "ends of the earth." The message of good news lives on in the lives of believers everywhere.

As we have seen, this message is, at its core, a re-reading of the OT in light of the resurrection and ascension of Jesus. The good news that Paul, Peter, and others have proclaimed is that if Jesus has been raised and is now seated at the right hand of the Father as King, the whole world is a different place.

Unfortunately, this episode has also been used for centuries to justify anti-Semitism among Christians. This has to be one of the saddest legacies of Christian history and of the book of Acts. The Christian religion claims that Jesus, himself a Jew, is the Messiah. Paul, also a Jew, and Jesus' greatest early interpreter, who makes it a point everywhere to say that he is doing nothing against the "customs of our forefathers," is later read as somehow meaning that God has rejected the Jewish people. Supposedly taking their lead, some of the church fathers would also claim that the church replaces Israel in God's redemptive plan. Later, some of the Reformers — most notably Martin Luther in his final years — were rabidly anti-Semitic. Figure that one out.

In this perspective, the Jews had their chance. They had the truth of the Messiah proclaimed to them clearly and yet they stubbornly rejected the message. Thus God is done with Israel as a whole and has now moved on to the Gentiles through the church. This scheme has a fancy name ("supercessionism") that simply means that the church "replaces" Israel in God's redemptive plan.

Although the surface level of the text might lead us to believe that Paul ends this story by saying that God has rejected Israel, I demur from this perspective. All we have to do is read the book of Romans when Paul writes that "all Israel will be saved" (Rom 11.26) to conclude that Paul was not turning his back on his own people.

In fact, if we read closely, we find that Acts ends on a very different note. Paul "welcomed all who came to him" (Acts 28.30). I take it that "all" means "all." Jew and Gentile alike, they came to Paul and he, without hesitation, proclaimed that the kingdom of God was in their midst.

Perhaps Luke gives us this strange ending because he is leaving it open for all of us to make our own conclusion to the story. The gospel is going forth, Jesus' Kingship is tangible, and the world has been set on fire. In other words, the world is the stage, the Holy Spirit is the medium and, the good news is the message. How will it all turn out?

In a sense, the ending of Acts is open because it really hasn't been written yet. The shape it takes depends on the on-going cooperation of God's people with God's Spirit who leads them. Or, as Paul would put it, "No eye has seen, nor ear has heard, nor the heart of man conceived, what God has prepared for those who love him" (1 Cor 2.9).

We have our marching orders. We have the Spirit that makes it all possible. The world has been set ablaze. The kingdom of God has been inaugurated. Our task, if we choose to accept it, is to cooperate with God's Spirit in his on-going work. The success of the mission often seems improbable, yet Acts teaches us that the spread of the good news something we should pursue with vigor and confidence.

Questions for Reflection:

1. **If you had to supply an ending for the book of Acts, how would you do it? What happens to Paul in the end?**
2. **Why does God not simply prevent us from making grave errors (like anti-Semitism)? What criteria do you use to examine yourself to make sure your "dislikes" do not turn into open prejudices?**
3. **After reading about Paul for weeks, what characteristics in him would you like to emulate? What would you like to avoid?**

Endnotes

Notes to Preface and Introduction

1. This story is adapted from https://www.americamagazine.org/issue/627/columns/god-forsakenness, accessed 6-14-2017.

2. Joseph A. Fitzmyer, *The Acts of the Apostles*, Anchor Bible Commentary (New Haven: Yale University Press, 1998), 55.

3. N. T. Wright, *Paul and the Faithfulness of God*, Christian Origins and the Question of God (Minneapolis, MN: Fortress Press, 2013), 915–16.

4. Ibid., 915. Italics in the original.

5. Ibid., 916.

6. U. S. Catholic Church, *Catechism of the Catholic Church: Complete and Updated* (New York: USCCB Publishing, 1995), 2548–2550, P. 671.

7. http://scriptoriumdaily.com/boersma-writes-back/, accessed 6-26-2017.

8. N.T. Wright, *Jesus and the Victory of God* (Minneapolis, MN: Fortress Press, 1996), 623.

9. C. Kavin Rowe, *World Upside Down: Reading Acts in the Graeco-Roman Age* (Oxford: Oxford University Press, 2010), 91–92.

10. Darrell L. Bock, *Acts*, Baker Exegetical Commentary (Grand Rapids, MI: Baker Academic, 2007), 25.

11. Fitzmyer, *The Acts of the Apostles*, 52.

12. Ibid., 53.

13. Bock, *Acts*, 26.

14. Ben Witherington, *The Acts of the Apostles : A Socio-Rhetorical Commentary* (Grand Rapids, MI: Eerdmans, 1997), 60.

15. D. A. Carson and Douglas J. Moo, *An Introduction to the New Testament*, 2nd ed. (Grand Rapids, MI: Zondervan, 2005), 181.

16. Fitzmyer, *The Acts of the Apostles*, 54.

17. C. K. Barrett, *Acts 1-14*, vol. 1, International Critical Commentary (London: Bloomsbury T&T Clark, 2004), 15.

18. Irenaeus, "Against Heresies," in *Ante-Nicene Fathers*, ed. Philip Schaff, vol. 1 (Buffalo, NY: Christian Literature Company, 1885), 3.14.1, P. 437.

19. Witherington, *The Acts of the Apostles*, 56.

20. Fitzmyer, *The Acts of the Apostles*, 50.

21. Craig S. Keener, *Acts: An Exegetical Commentary: Introduction and 1:1-2:47* (Grand Rapids, MI: Baker Academic, 2012), 402.

22. http://www.pewforum.org/files/2011/12/Christianity-fullreport-web.pdf, Accessed 6-16-2017.

23. Veli-Matti Kärkkäinen, *Pneumatology: The Holy Spirit in Ecumenical, International, and Contextual Perspective* (Baker Books, 2002), 34–35.

24. Yves Congar, *I Believe in the Holy Spirit* (New York: Crossroad, 1997), 3:81-82.

25. Quoted in Wright, *Jesus and the Victory of God*, 622.

26. Robert W. Jenson, "Toward a Christian Theology of Judaism," in *Jews and Christians: People of God*, ed. Carl E. Braaten (Grand Rapids, MI: Eerdmans, 2003), 13.

27. Witherington, *The Acts of the Apostles*, 65.

28. Fitzmyer, *The Acts of the Apostles*, 66.

29. Bruce Metzger, *A Textual Commentary on the Greek New Testament*, 4th ed. (Stuttgart: Deutsche Bibelgesellschaft, 1994), 222.

30. Luke Timothy Johnson, *The Acts of the Apostles*, Sacra Pagina (Collegeville, MN: Liturgical Press, 2006), 2.

31. Ibid.

32. Witherington, *The Acts of the Apostles*, 66.

33. Barclay Moon Newman and Eugene A. Nida, eds., *A Handbook on the Acts of the Apostles* (New York: United Bible Societies, 1972).

34. Lancelot C. Brenton, *The Septuagint with Apocrypha: Greek and English* (Peabody: Hendrickson, 1986).

Notes to Part I

1. Allen C. Myers and Freedman, David, eds., *The Eerdmans Bible Dictionary* (Grand Rapids, MI: Eerdmans, 2000), 906.

2. Douglas Farrow, *Ascension Theology* (New York: Bloomsbury T&T Clark, 2011), 7.

3. Jaroslav Pelikan, *Acts*, Brazos Theological Commentary on the Bible (Grand Rapids, MI: Brazos, 2006), 42–43.

4. Matthew W. Bates and Scot McKnight, *Salvation by Allegiance Alone* (Grand Rapids, MI: Baker Academic, 2017), 71–72.

5. N. T. Wright, *How God Became King: The Forgotten Story of the Gospels* (San Francisco: HarperOne, 2012), 246.

6. N. T. Wright, *Simply Good News: Why the Gospel Is News and What Makes It Good* (San Francisco: HarperOne, 2017), 12–13.

7. Francis Brown, S. R. Driver, and Charles A. Briggs, "Apokathistemi," *The Brown-Driver-Briggs Hebrew and English Lexicon* (Peabody, MA: Hendrickson, 1994), 111.

8. Wright, *Paul and the Faithfulness of God*, 480–81.

9. Wright, *How God Became King*, 90–95.

10. Gary A. Anderson, *Christian Doctrine and the Old Testament: Theology in the Service of Biblical Exegesis* (Grand Rapids: Baker Academic, 2017), 148.

11. Pelikan, *Acts*, 248.

12. Johnson, *Sacra Pagina*, 2006, 38.

13. Konrad Schaefer, *The Psalms*, Berit Olam (Collegeville, MN: Liturgical, 2001), 165.

14. I. Howard Marshall, "Acts," in *Commentary on the New Testament Use of the Old Testament*, ed. D. A. Carson and G. K. Beale (Grand Rapids, MI: Baker Academic, 2007), 530.

15. Craig S. Keener, *The IVP Bible Background Commentary: New Testament* (Downers Grove, IL: IVP Academic, 1994), v. 1.14.

16. Pelikan, *Acts*, 206.

17. J. Dwight Pentecost, *New Wine: A Study of Transition in the Book of Acts* (Grand Rapids, MI: Kregel, 2010), 42–43.

18. Fitzmyer, *The Acts of the Apostles*, 232.

19. Matthew Levering, *Engaging the Doctrine of the Holy Spirit* (Grand Rapids, MI: Baker Academic, 2016), 242.

20. Ibid., 244–45.

21. Ibid., 242.

22. Bock, *Acts*, v. 2.3.

23. Ibid., 102.

24. Nancy L. deClaisse-Walford, Rolf A. Jacobson, and Beth LaNeel Tanner, *The Book of Psalms*, New International Commentary on the OT (Grand Rapids, MI: Eerdmans, 2014), 838.

25. Johnson, *Sacra Pagina*, 2006, 52.

26. Rowe, *World Upside Down*, 122.

27. F. L. Cross and E. A. Livingstone, eds., "Joel," in *The Oxford Dictionary of the Christian Church*, 3rd Revised edition (Oxford: Oxford University Press, 2005), 884.

28. Hans Walter Wolff, *Joel and Amos: A Commentary on the Books of the Prophets Joel and Amos*, Hermeneia (Philadelphia: Augsburg Fortress Publishers, 1977), 11.

29. Levering, *Engaging the Doctrine of the Holy Spirit*, 311.

30. Joseph Blenkinsopp, *Isaiah 56-66*, Anchor Bible Commentary (New York: Yale University Press, 2003), 169.

31. Robert B. Jr Chisholm, *Handbook on the Prophets* (Grand Rapids, MI: Baker Academic, 2009), 127.

32. Some details of this story of Melchior Hoffman derive from Carlos M. N. Eire, *Reformations: The Early Modern World, 1450-1650* (New Haven, CT: Yale University Press, 2016), 270–76.

33. Keener, *Acts*, 971.

34. Bock, *Acts*, 157.

35. Robert Wall, *Acts*, ed. Leander E. Keck, The New Interpreters Bible Commentary (Nashville, TN: Abingdon Press, 2002), 77.

36. Christopher R. Seitz, *Isaiah 1-39*, Interpretation Commentary (Louisville, KY: Westminster John Knox Press, 1993), 238–39.

37. John N. Oswalt, *The Book of Isaiah, Chapters 1–39*, New International Commentary on the OT (Grand Rapids, MI: Eerdmans, 1986), 620–21.

38. Joseph A. Fitzmyer, *The Gospel According to Luke I-IX: Introduction, Translation, and Notes*, Anchor Bible Commentary (Garden City, N.Y: Doubleday, 1982), 664–65.

39. Luke Timothy Johnson, *The Gospel of Luke*, Sacra Pagina (Collegeville, MN: Liturgical Press, 2006), 125.

40. Wall, *The New Interpreter's® Bible Commentary Volume IX*, 77.

41. Jacob Neusner, *The Mishnah: A New Translation* (New Haven: Yale University Press, 1991), m.Sabb 6.8.

42. Johnson, *Sacra Pagina*, 2006, 71.

43. Anthony Gottlieb, *The Dream of Enlightenment: The Rise of Modern Philosophy* (New York: W. W. Norton, 2016).

44. David Hume, *An Enquiry Concerning Human Understanding*, ed. Eric Steinberg, 2nd ed. (Indianapolis: Hackett Publishing Company, Inc., 1993), chap. 10.

45. Quoted in Eire, *Reformations*, 750.

46. Ibid., 750–51.

47. Wall, *The New Interpreter's® Bible Commentary Volume IX*, 78.

48. John Stott, *The Message of Acts* (Downers Grove, IL: IVP Academic, 1994), 93.

49. William Barclay, *The Acts of the Apostles*, 3rd edition (Louisville: Westminster John Knox Press, 2003), 31–32.

50. Hans Urs von Balthasar, *Dare We Hope That All Men Be Saved?: With a Short Discourse on Hell*, Second edition (San Francisco, CA: Ignatius Press, 2014), 181.

51. Origen, *On First Principles*, ed. John C. Cavadini and Henri de Lubac, trans. G. W. Butterworth (Notre Dame, IN: Christian Classics, 2013), 1.6, pp. 70–75.

52. Balthasar, *Dare We Hope That All Men Be Saved?*, 12–13.

53. Ibid., 176.

54. Ibid. Italics in the original.

55. Quoted in Pelikan, *Acts*, 68.

56. David Brickner, *Christ in the Feast of Tabernacles* (Chicago, IL: Moody Publishers, 2006), 55–56.

57. Neusner, *The Mishnah*, m. Suk, 3.9.

58. Bock, *Acts*, 193.

59. Johnson, *Sacra Pagina*, 2006, 325.

60. http://www.christianitytoday.com/history/issues/issue-28/ad-70-titus-destroys-jerusalem.html, accessed 4-18-2017.

61. Keener, *The IVP Bible Background Commentary*, l. 4.3.

62. Myers and Freedman, David, *The Eerdmans Bible Dictionary*, 537.

63. Ibid., 573.

64. F. L. Cross and E. A. Livingstone, eds., *The Oxford Dictionary of the Christian Church*, 3rd ed. (Oxford: Oxford University Press, 2005), 1136.

65. Francis X. Weiser, *Handbook of Christian Feasts & Customs* (New York: Harcourt, 1958), 138.

66. Barrett, *Acts*, 2004, 1:231.

67. Ibid., 1:231–32.

68. Pelikan, *Acts*, 293–94.

69. Rowe, *World Upside Down*, 154.

70. Schaefer, *Berit Olam*, 8.

71. Frank-Lothar Hossfeld and Erich Zenger, *Psalms 3: A Commentary on Psalms 101-150*, ed. Klaus Baltzer, Hermeneia (Minneapolis, MN: Fortress Press, 2011), 609.

72. Schaefer, *Berit Olam*, 340.

73. Bock, *Acts*, 204.

74. Pelikan, *Acts*, 256.

75. John Barry, David Bomar, and Derek Brown, "Pesher," *Lexham Bible Dictionary* (Bellingham, WA: Lexham Press, 2016).

76. Richard B. Hays, *Echoes of Scripture in the Gospels* (Waco: Baylor University Press, 2016), 270–71.

77. Johnson, *Sacra Pagina*, 2006, 85.

78. John Chrysostom, *Homilies on the Acts of the Apostles*, ed. Philip Schaff, vol. 11, Nicene and Post Nicene Fathers 1 (New York: Christian Literature Company, 1889), 73. Cf. Stott, *The Message of Acts*, 100.

79. F. F. Bruce, *The Book of the Acts*, NICNT (Grand Rapids, MI: Eerdmans, 1988), 345.

80. Saint Augustine, *Teaching Christianity*, ed. John E Rotelle, trans. Edmund Hill, 2nd Edition (Hyde Park, NY: New City Press, 1996), 3.10.14,17, P. 176-177.

81. Fitzmyer, *The Acts of the Apostles*, 319.

82. Telford Work, *Deuteronomy* (Grand Rapids, MI: Brazos Press, 2009), 196.

83. Johnson, *Sacra Pagina*, 2006, 90.

84. Peter Brown, *The Body and Society: Men, Women, and Sexual Renunciation in Early Christianity*, 2nd edition (New York: Columbia University Press, 2008), xlv. Quoted in Rod Dreher, *The Benedict Option: A Strategy for Christians in a Post-Christian Nation* (New York: Penguin, 2017), 199.

85. Ephraim Radner, *A Time to Keep: Theology, Mortality, and the Shape of a Human Life* (Waco, TX: Baylor University Press, 2016), 6–7.

86. This event is recounted in Saint Augustine, *Confessions*, trans. Henry Chadwick, Oxford World's Classics (Oxford: Oxford University Press, 2009), 9.7. Cf. Ambrose's letter to his sister Marcellina, Ambrose, *Letters, 1-91* (The Catholic University of America Press, 1702), 61, P. 376.

87. Robert A. Orsi, *History and Presence* (Cambridge, MA: Harvard Belknap Press, 2016), chap. 3.

88. http://kingencyclopedia.stanford.edu/kingweb/popular_requests/frequentdocs/birmingham.pdf, Accessed 5-2-17.

89. Charles T. Mathewes, *Evil and the Augustinian Tradition* (Cambridge University Press, 2001), 93.

90. Thomas Joseph White, *Exodus*, ed. R. Reno, Brazos Theological Commentary on the Bible (Grand Rapids, MI: Brazos Press, 2016), 284.

91. David L. Stubbs, *Numbers*, ed. R. Reno, Brazos Theological Commentary on the Bible (Grand Rapids, MI: Brazos Press, 2009), 211–12.

92. Irenaeus, "Against Heresies," 4.26.2, P. 497.

93. Barclay, *The Acts of the Apostles*, 49–50.

94. Stott, *The Message of Acts*, 126.

95. Johnson, *Sacra Pagina*, 2006, 143.

96. Fitzmyer, *The Acts of the Apostles*, 367–68.

97. D. A. Carson and G. K. Beale, eds., *Commentary on the New Testament Use of the Old Testament* (Grand Rapids, Mich. : Nottingham, England: Baker Academic, 2007), 565.

98. Stott, *The Message of Acts*, 137.

99. Quoted in Matthew Levering, *Jesus and the Demise of Death* (Waco, TX: Baylor University Press, 2012), 49.

Notes to Part II

1. William H. Propp, *Exodus 1-18*, Anchor Bible Commentary (New Haven, CT: Yale University Press, 2008), 345–46. Propp disagrees with this view.

2. John N. Oswalt, *The Book of Isaiah, Chapters 40–66*, New International Commentary on the OT (Grand Rapids, MI: Eerdmans, 1998), 503.

3. Stott, *The Message of Acts*, 157.

4. Thomas Aquinas, *Summa Theologicae* (New York: Christian Classics, 1981), 1.1.8, pp. 5–6.

5. Irenaeus, "Against Heresies," 4.37.1. Cf. Christopher A. Hall, *Learning Theology with the Church Fathers* (Downers Grove, IL: InterVarsity, 2009), 124.

6. Michael Brown, "Jewish Interpretation of Isaiah 53," in *The Gospel According to Isaiah 53*, ed. Darrell Bock and Mitch Glaser (Grand Rapids, MI: Kregel Academic, 2012), 64.

7. Marshall, "Acts," 2007, 573.

8. Chisholm, *Handbook on the Prophets*, 449.

9. Myers and Freedman, David, *The Eerdmans Bible Dictionary*, 434.

10. Bock, *Acts*, 341.

11. Ibid.

12. Johnson, *Sacra Pagina*, 2006, 154.

13. Barrett, *Acts*, 2004, 1:439.

14. Ibid., 1:443–44.

15. White, *Exodus*, 150–51.

16. Robert Jenson, *Ezekiel*, Brazos Theological Commentary on the Bible (Grand Rapids, MI: Brazos Press, 2009), 46.

17. William James, *The Varieties of Religious Experience* (Courier Corporation, 2013), 14.

18. Keener, *Acts*, 1614–15.

19. Oxford Dictionaries, "Uoco," *Oxford Latin Dictionary* (Oxford: Oxford University Press, April 1, 2012), 2311.

20. Fitzmyer, *The Acts of the Apostles*, 421.

21. Stott, *The Message of Acts*, 168.

22. Ibid., 178.

23. Keener, *Acts*, 1676.

24. L. Daniel Hawk, *Berit Olam: Joshua*, ed. David W. Cotter, Berit Olam (Collegeville, MN: Liturgical Press, 2000), 45.

25. Walter A. Elwell, ed., *Baker Encyclopedia of the Bible*, vol. 2 (Grand Rapids, MI: Baker, 1988), 1516.

26. Myers and Freedman, David, *The Eerdmans Bible Dictionary*, 100.

27. Barclay, *The Acts of the Apostles*, 77.

28. Ibid., 80–81.

29. Barrett, *Acts*, 2004, 1:477.

30. Jerome T. Walsh, *1 Kings*, Berit Olam (Collegeville, MN: Liturgical Press, 1996), 231.

31. I. Howard Marshall, *Acts*, Tyndale New Testament Commentary (Downers Grove, IL: IVP Academic, 2008), 190.

32. Pelikan, *Acts*, 127.

33. Rowe, *World Upside Down*, 104.

34. Tertullian, "An Answer to the Jews," in *Ante-Nicene Fathers*, ed. Philip Schaff, vol. 3 (Buffalo, NY: Christian Literature Company, 1885), 7, P. 158.

35. J. R. H. Moorman, *A History of the Church in England*, 3rd ed. (Harrisburg, PA: Morehouse Publishing, 1980), 4.

36. http://www.newadvent.org/cathen/15733b.htm, Accessed 4-29-2017.

37. Cf. Norman Tanner, ed., "Lumen Gentium," in *Vatican II: The Essential Texts* (New York: Image, 2012), 8, P. 114.

38. Witherington, *The Acts of the Apostles*, 338.

39. Anderson, *Christian Doctrine and the Old Testament*, 194.

40. Ibid., 195.

41. Witherington, *The Acts of the Apostles*, 350.

42. Myers and Freedman, David, *The Eerdmans Bible Dictionary*, 263.

43. Ephraim Radner, *Leviticus*, Brazos Theological Commentary on the Bible (Grand Rapids, MI: Brazos Press, 2008), 107.

44. Greogy of Nyssa, *Homilies on the Song of Songs*, ed. Richard a Jr Norris, Writings from the Greco-Roman World (Atlanta: SBL Press, 2013), 10.

45. Bruce, *The Book of the Acts*, 206.

46. Radner, *Leviticus*, 115.

47. Johnson, *Sacra Pagina*, 2006, 186.

48. Gary M. Burge, *A Week in the Life of a Roman Centurion* (Downers Grove, IL: IVP Academic, 2015), 12.

49. Anderson, *Christian Doctrine and the Old Testament*, 194.

50. Johnson, *Sacra Pagina*, 2006, 190.

51. Witherington, *The Acts of the Apostles*, 353.

52. Stott, *The Message of Acts*, 188–89.

53. Keener, *Acts*, 1783.

54. Rowe, *World Upside Down*, 21.

55. Church Publishing, "39 Articles: Article XIII: Works Before Justification," in *The Book of Common Prayer* (New York: Church Publishing, 1979), 870.

56. John Calvin, *Institutes of the Christian Religion*, ed. Henry Beveridge (Peabody, MA: Hendrickson, 2007), 3.7.3, P. 395-396.

57. John Calvin, *Commentary upon the Acts of the Apostles*, ed. Henry Beveridge (Bellingham, WA: Logos Bible Software, 2010), 432–33.

58. Gary A. Anderson, *Charity: The Place of the Poor in the Biblical Tradition* (Yale University Press, 2014), 28–34.

59. Fitzmyer, *The Acts of the Apostles*, 462.

60. Joseph Blenkinsopp, *Ezekiel*, Interpretation Commentary (Louisville, KY: Westminster John Knox Press, 2012), 160.

61. Jenson, *Ezekiel*, 267.

62. Bock, *Acts*, 397.

63. Rowe, *World Upside Down*, 106.

64. Ibid., 87.

65. Ibid.

66. Ibid., 104.

67. Ibid., 73–74.

68. Pelikan, *Acts*, 135.

69. Levering, *Engaging the Doctrine of the Holy Spirit*, 65.

70. Stephen Tomkins, *William Wilberforce: A Biography* (Grand Rapids, MI: Eerdmans, 2007), 78–79.

71. Daniel K. Finn, *Christian Economic Ethics: History and Implications* (Minneapolis, MN: Fortress Press, 2013), 47.

72. Francesca Aran Murphy, *1 Samuel*, ed. R. Reno, Brazos Theological Commentary on the Bible (Grand Rapids, MI: Brazos Press, 2010), 42.

73. Gwilym Jones, "1 and 2 Samuel," in *The Oxford Bible Commentary*, ed. John Barton and John Muddiman (Oxford: Oxford University Press, 2001), 197.

74. Gerhard Kittel, ed., *Theological Dictionary of the New Testament*, vol. 9 (Grand Rapids, MI: Eerdmans, 1964), 426.

75. Flavius Josephus, "The Wars of the Jews," in *The Works of Josephus: Complete and Unabridged*, ed. William Whiston (Peabody, MA: Hendrickson Publishers, 1987), 3.29, P. 640.

76. P. G. W. Glare, ed., "Pagus," *Oxford Latin Dictionary* (Oxford: Oxford University Press, April 1, 2012), 1413.

77. Wayne A. Meeks, *The First Urban Christians: The Social World of the Apostle Paul* (New Haven, CT: Yale University Press, 2003), 11.

78. Barrett, *Acts*, 2004, 1:545.

79. Diarmaid MacCulloch, *The Reformation: A History* (London: Penguin Books, 2005), xx.

80. Christopher Kavin Rowe, *Early Narrative Christology: The Lord in the Gospel of Luke* (Berlin: Walter de Gruyter, 2006), 33.

81. Eusebius of Caesarea and Joseph Defarrari, *Ecclesiastical History*, vol. 19, The Fathers of the Church (Washington DC: The Catholic University of America Press, 1965), 2.14, P. 109.

82. James Martin, *Between Heaven and Mirth* (San Francisco: Harper Collins, 2011).

83. Johnson, *Sacra Pagina*, 2006, 211.

84. Bock, *Acts*, 429.

Notes to Part III

1. John Piper, *Let the Nations Be Glad!: The Supremacy of God in Missions*, 3 edition (Grand Rapids, MI: Baker Academic, 2010), 15.

2. Gerald G. Walsh S.J, trans., "Didache," in *The Apostolic Fathers*, The Fathers of the Church (Washington DC: Catholic University of America Press, 2008), 11.3, P. 180.

3. Marshall, *Acts*, 2008, 227.

4. Witherington, *The Acts of the Apostles*, 402–3.

5. Roland Allen, *Missionary Methods: St. Paul's or Ours?* (Dallas, TX: Gideon House Books, 2016).

6. Stott, *The Message of Acts*, 235.

7. Ibid., 236–37.

8. Johnson, *Sacra Pagina*, 2006, 220.

9. Stott, *The Message of Acts*, 324.

10. Johnson, *Sacra Pagina*, 2006, 225–26.

11. Marvin A. Sweeney, "Habakkuk," in *The Twelve Prophets*, ed. David W. Cotter, vol. 2, Berit Olam (Collegeville, MN: Michael Glazier, 2000), 453.

12. O. Palmer Robertson, "Habakkuk," in *The Books of Nahum, Habakkuk, and Zephaniah*, 2nd ed., New International Commentary on the OT (Grand Rapids, MI: Eerdmans, 1990), 136.

13. Marshall, "Acts," 2007, 587.

14. Barrett, *Acts*, 2004, 1:652.

15. Wright, *Paul and the Faithfulness of God*, 364.

16. Ibid., 857.

17. N. T. Wright, *The Day the Revolution Began* (San Francisco: HarperOne, 2016), 155–56. Italics in the original.

18. Charles E. Shepherd, *Theological Interpretation and Isaiah 53* (London: Bloomsbury, 2014), 41.

19. John J. Collins, *Daniel*, Hermeneia (Minneapolis, MN: Fortress Press, 1994), 390.

20. Hays, *Echoes of Scripture in the Gospels*, 273.

21. Francis Martin, *Acts*, vol. 5, Ancient Christian Commentary (Downers Grove, IL: IVP Academic, 2006), 170.

22. Barrett, *Acts*, 2004, 1:658.

23. Irenaeus, "Against Heresies," 5.1.1, P. 526-527.

24. Fitzmyer, *The Acts of the Apostles*, 521.

25. Wright, *Paul and the Faithfulness of God*, 1069.

26. Johnson, *Sacra Pagina*, 2006, 251.

27. Ibid., 247.

28. MacCulloch, *The Reformation*, 145–46.

29. F. F. Bruce, *The First and Second Letters Fo the Thessalonians*, New International Commentary on the OT (Grand Rapids, MI: Eerdmans, 2009), 5.

30. Ovid, *Metamorphoses*, ed. Denis Feeney, trans. David Raeburn, Penguin Classics (London: Penguin, 2004), 8.719. Italics added.

31. Marshall, *Acts*, 2008, 251.

32. Rowe, *World Upside Down*, 23.

33. Johnson, *Sacra Pagina*, 2006, 251.

34. Pelikan, *Acts*, 164.

35. Peter Enns, *The Sin of Certainty: Why God Desires Our Trust More Than Our "Correct" Beliefs* (New York, NY: HarperOne, 2016), 5–6.

36. Marshall, *Acts*, 2008, 255.

37. Stott, *The Message of Acts*, 235.

38. Esther Chung-Kim and Todd R. Hains, eds., *Acts*, Reformation Commentary on Scripture (Downers Grove, IL: IVP Academic, 2014), 197.

39. Fitzmyer, *The Acts of the Apostles*, 535.

40. Martin, *Acts*, 5:178.

41. Witherington, *The Acts of the Apostles*, 429.

42. Wright, *Paul and the Faithfulness of God*, 480–81.

43. Fitzmyer, *The Acts of the Apostles*, 535.

44. https://medinfo.biogen.com/secure/download?doc=workspace%3A%2F%2FSpacesSt ore%2Fded9df8f-d785-444a-ae89-888bef72aa7e&type=pmldoc&path=null&dpath= null&mimeType=null, accessed 5-12-2017.

45. Marshall, "Acts," 2007, 592.

46. Johnson, *Sacra Pagina*, 2006, 265.

47. Radner, *Leviticus*, 178.

48. Marvin A. Sweeney, "Amos," in *The Twelve Prophets*, vol. 1, Berit Olam (Collegeville, MN: Michael Glazier, 2000), 269.

49. Shalom M. Paul, *Amos: A Commentary on the Book of Amos*, ed. Frank Moore Cross, Hermeneia (Minneapolis, MN: Fortress, 1991), 289.

50. Hays, *Echoes of Scripture in the Gospels*, 274.

51. Fitzmyer, *The Acts of the Apostles*, 556–57.

52. Johnson, *Sacra Pagina*, 2006, 267.

53. Pelikan, *Acts*, 180.

54. Ibid., 175.

55. Radner, *Leviticus*, 191.

56. Richard B. Hays, *First Corinthians*, Interpretation Commentary (Louisville, KY: Westminster John Knox Press, 2011), 178.

57. Bruce, *The Book of the Acts*, 299.

58. C. K. Barrett, *Acts 15-28*, vol. 2, International Critical Commentary (London: Bloomsbury T&T Clark, 2004), 731.

59. Pelikan, *Acts*, 184.

60. Gilbert Burnet, *An Exposition of the 39 Articles of the Church of England* (Oxford: The University Press, 1831), 239.

61. http://www.catholictradition.org/Tradition/indefectibility.htm, accessed 5-24-2017.

62. Bruce, *The Book of the Acts*, 310.

63. Charles Fensham, *The Books of Ezra and Nehemiah*, New International Commentary on the OT (Grand Rapids, MI: Eerdmans, 1983), 266.

64. Johnson, *Sacra Pagina*, 2006, 282.

65. Ibid., 288.

66. Stott, *The Message of Acts*, 253.

67. Fitzmyer, *The Acts of the Apostles*, 575.

68. Neusner, *The Mishnah*, m. Qid. 3.12, P. 495.

69. Jenson, "Toward a Christian Theology of Judaism," 7.

70. Loveday Alexander, "Acts," in *The Oxford Bible Commentary*, ed. John Barton and John Muddiman (Oxford: Oxford University Press, 2013), 1049.

71. Ibid.

72. Johnson, *Sacra Pagina*, 2006, 297.

73. Stott, *The Message of Acts*, 270.

74. Abraham J. Malherbe, *The Letters to the Thessalonians*, Anchor Bible Commentary (New York: Doubleday, 2000), 136.

75. Witherington, *The Acts of the Apostles*, 490.

76. Rowe, *World Upside Down*, 92.

77. Johnson, *Sacra Pagina*, 2006, 298.

78. Witherington, *The Acts of the Apostles*, 498.

79. Pelikan, *Acts*, 240–41.

80. Witherington, *The Acts of the Apostles*, 503.

81. Marshall, *Acts*, 2008, 293.

82. Rowe, *World Upside Down*, 95.

83. Ibid., 93.

84. Ibid., 95.

85. Ibid., 99.

86. Johnson, *Sacra Pagina*, 2006, 318.

87. Robert Parker, *Athenian Religion: A History* (Oxford: Oxford University Press, 1998), 199–200.

88. Seitz, *Isaiah 1-39*, 225.

89. Plato, "The Apology," in *Plato: Complete Works*, ed. John M. Cooper, trans. G.M.A Grube (Indianapolis, IN: Hackett, 1997), 24B-C, P. 23.

90. Rowe, *World Upside Down*, 32.

91. Walter Bauer, *A Greek-English Lexicon of the New Testament and Other Early Christian Literature, 3rd Edition*, ed. Frederick William Danker, 3rd edition (Chicago: University of Chicago Press, 2001), 1760.

92. Rowe, *World Upside Down*, 33.

93. Ibid., 34.

94. Ibid.

95. Ibid., 54.

96. Stott, *The Message of Acts*, 295.

97. Bruce, *The Book of the Acts*, 436.

98. David W. Cotter, *Genesis*, Berit Olam (Collegeville, MN: Michael Glazier, 2003), 211.

99. Witherington, *The Acts of the Apostles*, 550.

100. Bock, *Acts*, 575.

101. Johnson, *Sacra Pagina*, 2006, 324–25.

102. Suetonius, *Life of Claudius*, trans. J. C. Rolfe, Loeb Classical Library (Cambridge, MA: Harvard University Press, 1914), 25.4.

103. Marshall, *Acts*, 2008, 310.

104. Plutarch, *Plutarch's Cimon and Pericles* (New York: C. Scribner's Sons, 1910), 2.1, P. 104.

105. Stott, *The Message of Acts*, 297.

106. David Bentley Hart, *The Story of Christianity* (New York: Quercus, 2015), 176.

107. Timothy Fry, ed., *RB 1980: The Rule of St. Benedict in English* (Collegeville, MN: Liturgical Press, 1981), 48.1, 8-9, P. 69.

108. Bruce, *The Book of the Acts*, 352.

109. Martin, *Acts*, 5:227.

110. Stott, *The Message of Acts*, 300.

111. Stubbs, *Numbers*, 65.

112. Timothy R. Ashley, *The Book of Numbers*, New International Commentary on the OT (Grand Rapids, MI: Eerdmans, 1993), 141.

113. Neusner, *The Mishnah*, m. Naz 1.4, P. 431; m. Naz 3.2, P. 434.

114. Johnson, *Sacra Pagina*, 2006, 330.

115. Hays, *First Corinthians*, 48.

116. Fitzmyer, *The Acts of the Apostles*, 622.

117. Rowe, *World Upside Down*, 147.

118. Desiderius Erasmus, "Paraphrase on Acts of the Apostles," in *Collected Works of Erasmus* (Toronto: University of Toronto Press, 1991), 115.

119. Robert Louis Wilken, *The First Thousand Years: A Global History of Christianity* (New Haven, CT: Yale University Press, 2013), 206.

120. https://www.nytimes.com/2017/05/26/opinion/coptic-christians-islamic-states-favorite-prey.html?action=click&pgtype=Homepage&clickSource=story-heading

&module=opinion-c-col-left-region&region=opinion-c-col-left-region&WT.
nav=opinion-c-col-left-region&_r=0, accessed 5-26-2017.

121. Johnson, *Sacra Pagina*, 2006, 342.

122. Fitzmyer, *The Acts of the Apostles*, 642.

123. Bruce, *The Book of the Acts*, 364.

124. MacCulloch, *The Reformation*, 138.

125. Eire, *Reformations*, 225.

126. Ibid., 227.

127. William R. Estep, *The Anabaptist Story*, 3rd ed. (Grand Rapids, MI: Eerdmans, 1995),
     12–13.

128. Eire, *Reformations*, 249.

129. Johnson, *Sacra Pagina*, 2006, 347.

130. Rowe, *World Upside Down*, 45.

131. Schaefer, *Berit Olam*, 284.

132. Hossfeld and Zenger, *Psalms 3*, 204.

133. MacCulloch, *The Reformation*, 558–59.

134. Jaroslav Pelikan, *The Spirit of Eastern Christendom*, vol. 2, The Christian Tradition: A
     History of the Development of Doctrine (Chicago, IL: University Of Chicago Press,
     1977), 106.

135. Pelikan, *Acts*, 213.

136. David Bentley Hart, *The Experience of God: Being, Consciousness, Bliss* (New Haven:
     Yale University Press, 2014), 36–37.

137. Brad S. Gregory, *The Unintended Reformation: How a Religious Revolution Secularized
     Society* (Cambridge, MA: Harvard Belknap Press, 2015), 30.

138. Rowe, *World Upside Down*, 49.

139. Ibid.

140. Johnson, *Sacra Pagina*, 2006, 357–58.

141. Ibid., 358.

142. The text says "third story," but this would mean second story in our understanding.
     The ground floor was counted as the first story in biblical times.

143. Johnson, *Sacra Pagina*, 2006, 167.

144. Witherington, *The Acts of the Apostles*, 607.

145. Chung-Kim and Hains, *Acts*, 278.

146. Calvin, *Commentary upon the Acts of the Apostles*, 236–37.

147. Witherington, *The Acts of the Apostles*, 606.

148. Robert Louis Wilken, *The Christians as the Romans Saw Them*, 2nd ed. (New Haven, CT: Yale University Press, 2003), 5.

149. http://www.vroma.org/~hwalker/Pliny/Pliny10-096-E.html, accessed 5-25-2017.

150. Bruce, *The Book of the Acts*, 384–85.

151. Ibid., 387.

152. Fitzmyer, *The Acts of the Apostles*, 676.

153. Myers and Freedman, David, *The Eerdmans Bible Dictionary*, 631.

154. Douglas J. Moo, *The Epistle to the Romans*, New International Commentary on the NT (Grand Rapids, MI: Eerdmans, 1996), 891.

155. Bock, *Acts*, 630.

156. Johnson, *Sacra Pagina*, 2006, 363.

157. Bock, *Acts*, 630.

158. Michael W. Holmes, ed., "1 Clement," in *The Apostolic Fathers: Greek Texts and English Translations*, 3rd ed. (Grand Rapids, MI: Baker Academic, 2007), 2.1, P. 47. Italics added

159. Marshall, *Acts*, 2008, 356.

160. Bruce, *The Book of the Acts*, 398.

161. Martin, *Acts*, 5:259.

162. Stott, *The Message of Acts*, 331.

163. Johnson, *Sacra Pagina*, 2006, 351.

164. Johnson, *Sacra Pagina*, 2006, 370.

165. Barrett, *Acts*, 2004, 2:994.

166. Hays, *First Corinthians*, 247.

167. Daniel B. Wallace, *Greek Grammar Beyond the Basics* (Grand Rapids, MI: Zondervan, 1997), 412.

168. Rowe, *Early Narrative Christology*, 33.

169. Ignatius of Loyola, *The Spiritual Exercises of St. Ignatius*, trans. Louis J. Puhl (Chicago: Loyola Press, 1968), para. 23, P. 12.

Notes to Part IV

1. Bruce, *The Book of the Acts*, 469.

2. Witherington, *The Acts of the Apostles*, 646.

3. Fitzmyer, *The Acts of the Apostles*, 145.

4. https://www.firstthings.com/web-exclusives/2017/06/ossoff-does-the-right-thing, Accessed 6-27-2017.

5. http://www.nybooks.com/articles/2017/06/08/martin-luthers-burning-questions/, Accessed 6-4-2017.

6. Jenson, *Ezekiel*, 317.

7. Bruce, *The Book of the Acts*, 425.

8. Rowe, *World Upside Down*, 64.

9. Ibid., 63.

10. Josephus, "The Wars of the Jews," 261–263, P. 614.

11. Rowe, *World Upside Down*, 66.

12. Bruce, *The Book of the Acts*, 420.

13. Rowe, *World Upside Down*, 68.

14. Alexander, "Acts," 1055.

15. Johnson, *Sacra Pagina*, 2006, 393.

16. David Lyle Jeffrey, *Luke*, Brazos Theological Commentary on the Bible (Grand Rapids, MI: Brazos Press, 2012), 140.

17. Pelikan, *Acts*, 234.

18. Fitzmyer, *The Acts of the Apostles*, 703.

19. Ibid.

20. Bauer, *A Greek-English Lexicon of the New Testament and Other Early Christian Literature, 3rd Edition*, 117.

21. Everett Ferguson, *Baptism in the Early Church* (Grand Rapids, MI: Eerdmans, 2013), 79.

22. Michael J Fahey, "Sacraments," in *The Oxford Handbook of Systematic Theology*, ed. John B. Webster and Iain Torrance (Oxford: Oxford University Press, 2009), 272.

23. Pelikan, *Acts*, 236.

24. Tremper Longman and Raymond B. Dillard, "Hosea," in *An Introduction to the Old Testament*, 2nd ed. (Grand Rapids, MI: Zondervan, 2006), 400.

25. Chisholm, *Handbook on the Prophets*, 353.

26. Augustine, *Teaching Christianity*, 1.36.40, P. 124.

27. Neusner, *The Mishnah*, m. sanhedrin 10.1, P. 604.

28. David John Furley and D. Sedley, "Epicurus," ed. Simon Hornblower, *The Oxford Classical Dictionary* (Oxford: Oxford University Press, May 4, 2012), 513.

29. Cross and Livingstone, *The Oxford Dictionary of the Christian Church*, 1449.

30. Johnson, *Sacra Pagina*, 2006, 401.

31. Ibid., 402.

32. Barrett, *Acts*, 2004, 2:1070.

33. Bruce, *The Book of the Acts*, 425–26.

34. Contra Fitzmyer, *The Acts of the Apostles*, 719.

35. Johnson, *Sacra Pagina*, 2006, 397.

36. Myers and Freedman, David, *The Eerdmans Bible Dictionary*, 275.

37. http://www.newmanreader.org/works/anglicans/volume2/gladstone/section5.html, accessed 6-1-2017

38. https://www.firstthings.com/article/2005/05/the-inconvenient-conscience, accessed 6-19-2017.

39. Norman Tanner, "Dignitatis Humanae," in *Vatican II: The Essential Texts* (New York: Image, 2012), 1.2, pp. 305–306.

40. Fitzmyer, *The Acts of the Apostles*, 699.

41. David Jobling, *1 Samuel*, Berit Olam (Collegeville, MN: Liturgical Press, 1998), 95.

42. Enns, *The Sin of Certainty*, 192–94.

43. Fitzmyer, *The Gospel According to Luke I-IX*, 732.

44. Witherington, *The Acts of the Apostles*, 707.

45. Hossfeld and Zenger, *Psalms 3*, 241.

46. deClaisse-Walford, Jacobson, and Tanner, *The Book of Psalms*, 594.

47. Schaefer, *Berit Olam*, 181.

48. Barrett, *Acts*, 2004, 2:1099.

49. Cornelius Tacitus, *Annals of Tacitus* (New York: Macmillan and Company, 1921), 12.54.

50. Witherington, *The Acts of the Apostles*, 699.

51. Rowe, *World Upside Down*, 71.

52. Ibid., 76.

53. Johnson, *Sacra Pagina*, 2006, 422.

54. Mitchell Dahood, *Psalms I, 1-50*, vol. 16, Anchor Bible Commentary (New Haven: Yale University Press, 2008), 81.

55. Ibid., 16:85.

56. Schaefer, *Berit Olam*, 36.

57. Fitzmyer, *The Acts of the Apostles*, 739.

58. Quoted in Rowe, *World Upside Down*, 79.

59. Fitzmyer, *The Acts of the Apostles*, 740.

60. Rowe, *World Upside Down*, 79.

61. Fitzmyer, *The Acts of the Apostles*, 739.

62. Josephus, *Josephus: The Complete Works*, trans. William Whiston (Peabody, MA: Hendrickson, 1987), Ant., 19.355, P. 524.

63. Johnson, *Sacra Pagina*, 2006, 418.

64. Bauer, *A Greek-English Lexicon of the New Testament and Other Early Christian Literature, 3rd Edition*, 274.

65. Plato, "The Apology," 40d, P. 36.

66. Marshall, *Acts*, 2008, 408.

67. Fitzmyer, *The Acts of the Apostles*, 749–50.

68. Bruce, *The Book of the Acts*, 457.

69. Stott, *The Message of Acts*, 368.

70. Rowe, *World Upside Down*, 84.

71. Peter Garnsey, "The Lex Iulia and Appeal Under the Empire," *Journal of Roman Studies* 56 (1966): 169.

72. Rowe, *World Upside Down*, 82.

73. Witherington, *The Acts of the Apostles*, 729.

74. http://www.cbsnews.com/news/cook-county-jail-sheriff-tom-dart-on-60-minutes/, Accessed 6-12-2017.

75. https://law.stanford.edu/index.php?webauth-document=child-page/632655/doc/slspublic/Report_v12.pdf, Accessed 6-12-2017.

76. http://sentencingproject.org/wp-content/uploads/2016/01/Trends-in-US-Corrections.pdf, accessed 6-12-2017. Cf. http://www.nybooks.com/articles/2017/06/22/truth-about-our-prison-crisis.

77. Rowe, *World Upside Down*, 86.

78. Jenson, *Ezekiel*, 46.

79. Walther Zimmerli, *Ezekiel 1: A Commentary on the Book of the Prophet Ezekiel, Chapters 1-24*, Hermeneia (Philadelphia: Fortress Press, 1979), 132.

80. Hays, *Echoes of Scripture in the Gospels*, 177.

81. Ibid., 178.

82. Johnson, *Sacra Pagina*, 2006, 758.

83. Justin Martyr, *Dialogue with Trypho*, trans. Thomas B. Falls, Fathers of the Church (Washington, DC: The Catholic University of America Press, 2008), 89, P. 290-291.

84. Johnson, *Sacra Pagina*, 2006, 440.

85. Phillip Cary, *Jonah*, Brazos Theological Commentary on the Bible (Grand Rapids, MI: Brazos Press, 2008), 35.

86. Alexander, "Acts," 1059.

87. Elwell, *Baker Encyclopedia of the Bible*, 2:101.

88. Myers and Freedman, David, *The Eerdmans Bible Dictionary*, 101.

89. http://catholicsaints.info/book-of-saints-aristarchus/, accessed 6-8-2017.

90. Ajith Fernando, *Acts*, NIV Application Commentary (Grand Rapids, MI: Zondervan, 1998), 610.

91. Stott, *The Message of Acts*, 385–86.

92. Chrysostom, *Nicene and Post-Nicene Fathers*, 11:53, P. 318.

93. Quoted in Martin, *Acts*, 5:307–8.

94. Pelikan, *Acts*, 290.

95. Alexander, "Acts," 1060.

96. Fitzmyer, *The Acts of the Apostles*, 787.

97. Johnson, *Sacra Pagina*, 2006, 4z67.

98. James L. Kugel, *How to Read the Bible: A Guide to Scripture, Then and Now* (New York: Free Press, 2012), 50–51.

99. Wright, *Paul and the Faithfulness of God*, 480–81.

100. Johnson, *Sacra Pagina*, 2006, 470.

101. Marshall, "Acts," 2007, 601.

Made in the USA
Lexington, KY
05 August 2017